Trans-Reality Television

Trans-Reality Television

The Transgression of Reality, Genre, Politics, and Audience

Edited by Sofie Van Bauwel
and Nico Carpentier

LEXINGTON BOOKS
A division of
ROWMAN & LITTLEFIELD PUBLISHERS, INC.
Lanham • Boulder • New York • Toronto • Plymouth, UK

Published by Lexington Books
A division of Rowman & Littlefield Publishers, Inc.
A wholly owned subsidiary of The Rowman & Littlefield Publishing Group, Inc.
4501 Forbes Boulevard, Suite 200, Lanham, Maryland 20706
http://www.lexingtonbooks.com

Estover Road, Plymouth PL6 7PY, United Kingdom

British Library Cataloguing in Publication Information Available

Library of Congress Cataloging-in-Publication Data
Trans-reality television : the transgression of reality, genre, politics, and audience / edited
by Sofie Van Bauwel and Nico Carpentier.
    p. cm.
  Includes bibliographical references and index.
  ISBN 978-0-7391-3188-6 (cloth : alk. paper) -- ISBN 978-0-7391-3189-3 (pbk. : alk.
paper)
  1. Reality television programs--Social aspects. 2. Reality television programs--Political
aspects. I. Van Bauwel, Sofie. II. Carpentier, Nico.
  PN1992.8.R43T73 2010
  791.45'3--dc22   2010010241

Printed in the United States of America

Contents

v

Introduction

Chapter 1
Trans-Reality TV as a Site of Contingent Reality
Sofie Van Bauwel and Nico Carpentier

Un-fixing Reality

Understanding reality has become a long-term project for humanity, reflecting the difficulty involved in capturing this concept. Although since the age of Enlightenment, the idea that reality is a fixed and unchangeable notion, has frequently been challenged, our desire for immediate access to truth and reality has not withered, while our fantasies have been increasingly frustrated by intellectual projects that emphasize the cultural component in our ways of dealing with reality. The idea that reality is a social construct challenges some of our most basic certainties, and has opened up a range of questions. It has evoked an equally wide range of critiques that accuse constructivist project(s) of radical relativism and nihilism.

Despite attempts at resistance, it has become more and more difficult to ignore the fluidity of the social, since the grand narratives no longer provide socio-discursive stability and are being replaced by the incessant play among competing reality claims.[1] Universalist and essentialist models have emerged as processes of universalization and essentialization, which nevertheless are vulnerable to the counter-hegemonic processes of re-articulation and re-signification. However, acknowledging the social contingent does not imply entry to a world of ultimate instability, where the concept of reality ceases to play any kind of role. On the contrary, contemporary constructivist models show that reality exists, but that it receives its meaning through the processes of signification, which are susceptible to change. These constructions can become stabilized and sedimented; in some cases they become social imaginaries[2] that benefit from the luxury of taken-for-grantedness, and act as horizons beyond which no alternatives seem to exist. But, again, because of the openness of the social—and however rigid the reality seems—the possibility that these sedimentations become contested, and that the hegemonic framework is resisted by counter-hegemonic discourses, can never be excluded.

This dynamic process of rigidity and fixity versus contingency and fluidity alters the realness of reality, and the absolute nature of reality becomes permanently bracketed. The constructivist logics transform reality into a contingent reality, a reality that is real, but which could become another reality at any given point in space and time. Our starting point is that this constructed nature of the social has entered the common sense, and reality has lost its universal and essential capacity, but not its universalizing and essentializing capacity. The increase in societal reflexivity—which is focused not just on self-identity,[3] but also on the self's position toward reality—means the constructed nature of reality receives greater acknowledgment and becomes seen more and more as an intrinsic part of reality. We use the term trans-reality to describe this process of reflexivity and acknowledgement. This is not to indicate that we abandon the concept of reality or recommend that it should be abandoned, rather it implies a stretching of the signifier reality to include the idea that reality is constructed. As a concept, trans-reality expresses integration of the idea that reality is constructed within the concept of reality itself.

Many institutions contribute to these processes of reality construction. They act as discursive machineries that help to produce our realities. Within this multitude of discursive machineries we find one cluster that merits special attention. Media organizations, whether formally or informally organized, have access to our everyday lives and provide an almost continuous flow of discursive constructions of the social, with all its continuities and discontinuities, contradictions and hegemonies, for audiences to accept or to reject. But as their audiences become more media savvy, media organizations become more aware of the media constructions that are almost permanently on display. Moreover, as Olson[4] argued (writing about meta-television at the end of the 1980s), media institutions have played with their conventions and constructions, in some cases offering viewers medium-reflexive and genre-reflexive structures, but also auto-deconstructions (or as Olson calls them, text-reflexive narrative). Media institutions, in turn, respond to the media savvyness of their audiences, consciously adding more layers of signification to their products and becoming, in Collins's[5] formulation, hyperconscious. This complex interplay of showing and reading the constructed nature of media products contributes to strengthening the trans-real configuration. Not only are media organizations functioning as permanent reminders of the construction of the social by exposing their own constructedness, some of their basic categories—for example, the audience, the media professional and the genre—have begun to slide, contributing further to the formation of a trans-reality.

At the same time, the role of (mainstream) media organizations in this process of trans-realization is dubious, as the societal focus on the media as the "ultimate" site of trans-reality acts to protect other social fields from being considered integrated parts of this trans-real configuration. The idea that the media are constructing our reality continues often to be depicted within a soft constructivist framework, where the idea that media construct reality is accompanied by the belief that reality can be accessed directly by having the media function in a better way, or by simply bypassing them. Here, belief in what Jensen[6] calls the Garden of Eden still persists. In other words, the soft constructivist framework tends to focus on the construction of the social through one (set of) institution(s), making the media field the sacral site of construction, thereby protecting the phantasmagoric belief that there are also unconstructed realities. In this book, we take a hard constructivist position, which is based on the idea that the processes of mediation are always required to access reality, through a matrix of discourses, practices and formations, supported by a multiplicity of institutions and other social structures.

Trans-Reality TV

Despite the diversity of discursive machineries, here we want to focus on the subset of media institutions, and analyze in more detail how one specific (trans)genre is signifying this trans-real configuration. From this perspective, Reality TV is a highly relevant format, which has become a stronghold within the media landscape. Moreover, the relatively recent explosion of different (sub)formats of Reality TV has resulted in a similarly large body of academic work. Much effort has been devoted to programs such as *Big Brother*,[7] and also to formats that are reality-based such as crime shows[8] and dating shows.[9] The diversity of Reality TV formats and practices—and their reception[10]—have been discussed extensively, and new definitions and concepts have been proposed, for example, the idea of "first person media"[11] or the genre of "factual entertainment."[12] A variety of approaches is used: Reality TV is analyzed, for instance, as an event[13] or a ritual.[14] Some scholars have tried to generate overarching reflections on the genre and its subgenres.[15] But, despite this highly relevant debate involving academia and society, in the discussions on television formats and visual culture in general, the relationships between Reality TV and trans-reality, and between the media field (and its concepts, identities and values), and the social, the political and the real are too rarely examined. Much of the most interesting work on Reality TV relates to studies of its format and the conceptualization of an umbrella term to encompass several subgenres and formats.

Reality TV is articulated as a television genre that emphasizes the factual elements of everyday life and makes strong claims about authenticity, reality, the ordinary.[16] Notwithstanding debate over the relevance of the term Reality

TV,[17] its conceptualization is based mostly on articulations of the form or the thematic character of the meta-genre, as described by Kilborn:[18]

> Reality programming will involve (a) the recording, "on the wing," and frequently with the help of lightweight equipment, of events in the lives of individuals or groups, (b) the attempt to simulate such real-life events through various forms of dramatized reconstruction and (c) the incorporation of this material, in suitable edited form, into a attractively packaged television programme which can be promoted on the strength of its "reality" credentials.

This post-documentary culture, which has also been described by Corner,[19] refers to cinema vérité and the need to record reality through a fly on the wall camera. Most academic work on this hybrid television genre focuses on the relation between the reality claim and the format of the subgenre.[20] Reality programming is especially "loaded, since by definition, it should occupy a more privileged position in relation to the representation of the 'real' than overtly fictional forms."[21]

This changing culture of production was reinforced by technological innovations, such as the lightweight cine-camera and the possibilities for audiences to create their own content (e.g., the format of the home video). Walter Benjamin[22] in 1930 refers to such technical transformations in discussing how the camera would become smaller and smaller. Dovey points out that lightweight camcorders were available in the market in 1964, but were used only by documentary filmmakers or artists.[23] Later, "go-anywhere cameras" became part of everyday life for a much wider audience. And today, people have access to the knowledge and technology to create their own user-generated content, in which images and reality footage play a large part. New technologies, such as Web 2.0, and social networking software, such as Facebook, are media that provide stimuli to create "own content," but, similar to other "new" media technologies, this knowledge, access, and participation is confined mostly to rich Western countries and media literacy is not global. This political economic dimension is linked to the history of technological development, but also has a meso and micro dimension. The relatively low production costs of Reality programming mean that such formats were (and still are) sold globally and that broadcasters invest in its production. These interwoven technological and economic transformations mean that: "Undoubtedly these programmes represent important elements in the commercial operation of currently popular TV as it 'desperately seeks the audience.'"[24] This third element is of interest to scholars, but less so than production and content.[25] Some large audience studies have been conducted to investigate mainly audiences' perceptions and signifying practices. This recent strand of academic research stems from a longer tradition of audience studies that analyze their reception of talk shows or formats, which, to a greater or lesser extent, elaborate on democratic potential.[26] In the work of Biressi and

Nunn, in particular, these two genres come together and are conceptualized and analyzed as separate, but common Reality genres.[27] And audiences watch these different formats in the ways described by Williams in 1930: "Till the eyes tire, millions of us watch the shadows of shadows and find them substance; watch scenes, situations, actions, exchanges, crises."[28] Academic interest in this phenomenon in relation to the ordinary or the exceptional—for example, celebrities—has increased. Studies have been conducted on the creation and representation of celebrity in and by means of Reality TV formats.[29] In these analyses the concept of celebrity is linked to the possibility of greater social standing, and especially Reality TV participants who start off as "ordinary" people and end up as stars or some other type of celebrity, based mostly on the praxis of social mobility. This tension between the ordinary and the extraordinary, embodied in the idea of social mobility, is a theme frequently represented in Reality programming. The preoccupation with the real capacities of participants seems to be a core element of this genre, described by Ouelette and Hay[30] as:

> The many subgenres of popular reality TV (dating shows, make-overs, job competitions, gamedocs, reality soaps, interventions, lifestyle demonstrations) share a preoccupation with testing, judging, advising, and rewarding the conduct of "real" people in their capacities as contestants, workers, housemates, family members, homeowners, romantic partners, patients, and consumers. In the process, reality TV circulates informal "guidelines for living" that we are all (at times) called upon to learn from and follow.

In another recent development in the study of media in general,[31] and in more specific research on Reality TV, the Foucauldian concept of governmentality[32] is used to look at this format as a form of "governing at a distance."[33] This line of studies stresses the embeddedness of a neo-liberal ideology and a capitalist economy, where the discipline is imposed from above, but includes also a large degree of self-governance, exemplified by "[l]iberalism's schematization of civil society as the field of self-governance is not only about making society civil and making government rational. It is also about making the social and the governmental economic."[34] This new conceptualization within media studies based on the "technologies of the self"[35] provides a way of thinking about media in contemporary society, and is developed in the chapters in this volume.

Several books have been written on Reality TV; the topic has generated much academic and societal interest. However, our aim is to articulate Reality TV as one of the sites of trans-reality. In this book, while it maintains a clear focus, a wide variety of areas (and many different perspectives, themes, empirical paradigms and subjects) are scrutinized. The balance between thematic broadness and focus is managed by our deployment of the three levels of television text, production site and audience, which is quite novel in publications on Reality TV, which generally stress the textual or the audience perspective. And the coherence of the current book is increased because these three levels are analyzed by the use of a specific focus, that is, trans-reality. Among the growing numbers of books on the subject of Reality TV, relatively few academic works deal with this meta-perspective: most focus on a specific program, type of audience, genre, etc. However, there are exceptions: the four key concepts exploited in this book (trans-real, trans-genre, trans-politics and trans-audience) are also referred to in work by Andrejevic, Biressi and Nunn, and Murray and Ouellette.

Meta-Perspectives on Reality TV

To further broaden the Reality TV debate, this book starts from the idea that Reality TV and the diversity of new hybrid television formats claiming reality, are located in a contemporary transformation of reality, which is turning into a trans-reality. As media institutions are not outside of society, they too have not escaped this transformation.

The study of Reality TV is not an end itself: it raises questions about the status of representation and reality in contemporary societies. Reality TV offers a valuable entry point into the trans-reality configuration as it explores authenticity and makes strong claims about reality, which often are connected to a celebration of "real" people, the reality of everyday life and a new participatory relationship between viewer(s) and screen. For instance, Dovey[36] links the genre's strong claims to reality, its focus on a subjective individual experience and on a framed fragmented self, to the rise of new "regimes of truth." In this way, Reality TV becomes a body of formats that articulate the idea of the real, and construct realms of trans-reality through the merging (for instance) of authenticity and production techniques. Combined with the idea of hybridization and the focus on the scopic, this inevitably raises questions about the status of reality and, more specifically, about the real becoming the spectacle. This spectacle of the real can be seen as a simulation[37] in which a so-called "new reality" is hyped and a hyper-real realm of authentic emotions, experiences, and pleasures is constructed. These "newly" conceptualized realities are articulated within a society that is obsessed with the "new." Here, it is important to stress the economic context of this contraction of the new: "Contemporary society is in fact fascinated to the point of obsession by all that is 'new.' It pursues change with maniacal faith in its beneficial side-effects. It disrupts the very social fabric and the modes of exchange and interaction which were established by industrial culture."[38]

This form of reality construction is confronted by potential resistance from and the media-savvyness of an empowered audience, emphasizing the possibilities of participation in the production, interpretation and use of texts. Related to the trans-audience is the idea of transposition, where subjectivity means "nomadic, dispersed, fragmented vision, which is nonetheless functional and accountable, mostly because it is embedded and embodied."[39] It is within this element of entanglement, growing disconnection but also a lingering connection to the "basis" of the transformation, that we need to situate the trans-idea. Braidotti uses the concept of transposition, which can be seen as related to our position, when she says that transposition: "has a double source of inspiration: from music and from genetics. It indicates an intertextual, cross-boundary or transversal transfer, in the sense of a leap from one code, field or axis into another, not merely in the quantitative mode of plural multiplications, but rather in the qualitative sense of complex multiplicities."[40]

Trans-concepts refer to the leaping of codes, and attempts to capture a series of connections that are transfigured in a specific connection between the text, and the social and historical contexts. This is similar to, but not the same as, Bhabha's[41] concept of "translational" which he uses in relation to a transnational space where there are traces of a relation with the "essential" notions or consciousness of the self. This is a more essentialist or even universalist notion of the fluidity of identities in a trans-national context, but has a similar focus on the movement of praxis, discourses, and materiality.

The shift toward trans-reality also puts pressure on a number of other key concepts cherished by the media system (and by media studies), including the concepts of genre and audience. First, the diversity and hybridity of the different formats allows the genre concept to be problematized. Here, Reality TV can be understood as a trans-genre, which questions format/genre boundaries and conventions, and (even) the construction of TV and visual culture. Second, in Reality TV our rather fixed conceptualizations of the viewer, the spectator, the audience and the media professional also become destabilized. The complexity of the textual relations with a diversity of audiences, combined with the crossing of boundaries in the material relations with these audiences, might even work to turn them into trans-audiences.

At the same time, we should avoid too exclusive a focus on media-related concepts and isolating (trans)Reality TV too much from our societies, cultures, politics. Through its embeddedness in neo-liberal discourses, Reality TV can be seen as one of the sites offering individualistic practices and pleasures, where new forms of discipline and power are being practiced and normalized, and where (ordinary) people are fragmented into competing, but still docile bodies. As Reality TV is unavoidably part of our political (trans-)reality, it also distinguishes (and contributes to) the transformation of the political. At the level of politics (and the relationship of Reality TV with the political system) we see, for instance, the increase in celebrity-politics, with its transgressions of "traditional" politics and ideologies and its move toward the "ordinary" and the "celebrity." But the political cannot be reduced to politics; there is a variety of less conventional identities, representations and ideologies that organizes its struggles in the political realm (in its broadest possible meaning), traces of which can also be found in the world of Reality TV.

> If a "politics" exists in reality TV, and we aim to show that it does, it will be differently articulated from the traditional forms of politicised documentary and it often requires different conceptual tools than those employed to unpack the politics of classic documentary genres. The politics of reality TV is a cultural politics.[42]

The chapters in this volume can be used as tools to navigate definitions, theories, academic debates, reception, and conceptualizations of the meta-perspectives on (trans-) reality TV, which, in turn, focuses on and acts as an analytical and conceptual tool for the examination of Reality TV.

Trans-Reality, Trans-Genre, Trans-Politics and Trans-Audience

The contributions in this volume provide an overview of Reality TV, focusing on its societal and mediated transformations and on their complex, but mutually supportive relationship with factual entertainment, stressing the ideas of transformations in the contemporary mediascape. The book discusses a diversity of perspectives and reflections that are related to the Reality TV format, in the form of a transgressive site and practice. They are written from a range of scholarly angles: Several chapters investigate theoretical issues, while others approach these questions through empirical studies of specific Reality TV formats and programs. The book is structured around four approaches: the trans-real; trans-politics; trans-genre; and trans-audience.

In the first approach, which stresses the concept of the trans-real, there are four chapters investigating the construction of reality, and contributing to the debate on the construction of the reality claim in Reality TV. The first of these chapters by Sofie Van Bauwel on the spectacle of the real and other constructions, elaborates the dislocation of "reality" in the realm of Reality TV. Her starting point is the recent surge in different formats that explore authenticity and make strong claims concerning reality. This explicit focus on the real (and its implicit reality claims) has provoked concern in society, fed by the perceived dangers of hyper-reality, that our worlds are being reduced to televisual simulations.[43] These pessimistic discourses (or moral panics) have entered the academic agenda. This chapter revisits these debates by questioning whether, how and to what degree these representations construct a reality claim that is dangerously dislocating the pain, trauma, and horrible experience of tragedies. How can we deal with representations of the real, without accepting these realities (as realities) at face value, or rejecting them as completely unreal. In the chapter by Fernando Andacht, the notion of representation is revisited through the debate on Reality TV's much discussed transgressions (of good taste, of traditional values of entertainment and of civilization), through an analysis of the *Big Brother* formats in Brazil and Argentina. *Big Brother* is conceptualized as a commercially successful hybridization and adaptation of the aristocratic, high mimetic epic, set in a domestic and demotic environment, in which the mundane is inextricably tied to the epiphany of the spiritual (or emotional). Using Peirce's idea about the construction of meaning as a kaleidoscopic, shifting the interplay of three modes of representation of the real: the iconic, the indexical and the symbolic, Andacht analyzes the authentic and the fabricated in this Reality TV format. The fate of the representations generated by the 24/7 observed house, is to be interpreted, to become symbols that reveal fallible aspects of the real. The claim is that in the overtly artificial, uncanny domesticity of the *Big Brother* setting, nothing of the real is represented. Trans-reality denotes those aspects of the real that survive despite the mighty industrial media machinery. This new-fangled Barthes "effet du réel"[44] is reminiscent of early meditations on another show, which was also based on exposure under close scrutiny, and subject to huge skepticism from its audience. In the chapter by Anastasia Deligiaouri and Mirkica Popovic, Foucault's[45] ideas on the construction of the truth are used to look at the dominant discourses in Reality TV. They argue that the difference between Reality TV as a sub-genre and other representations of media reality, is based on the idea that the former ontologically "fulfils" more prerequisites of the approved definition of "reality," such as real time representations, truthful simu-lations of space and the possibility of spontaneous and unsolicited action by the protagonists (who are alleged to be completely unsusceptible to the rules of me-diation). Deligiaouri and Popovic's chapter provides a critical approach to the ongoing discussion on the difference between constructed reality and reality itself. The huge indistinctness among several facets of reality has triggered chain reactions with the lived realities (outside TV). This chapter explores the blurred boundaries between Reality TV, which is articulating hegemonic representations of the social world based on the fact that the "simulacrum is true," and living reality, perceived beyond the boundaries of TV. It pinpoints the ontology of the concept of reality, drawing on several critical approaches. The fourth chapter in this part on trans-reality is by Matthew Hibberd, who examines trans-professionalism through a case study of the British TV scandals of 2007. Hib-berd investigates the numerous responses to accusations of "rigged" phone-in competitions on U.K. television. He argues that there is nothing new about cor-rupt practices in TV and radio programs with audience participation; they have gone on since the 1950s at least, and have been a feature of early popular entertainment TV in many countries. Producers, time and again, have been willing to bend programming rules and stretch ethical mores, which demonstrate that new forms of power are being practiced and TV audiences are being duped or defrauded. This chapter traces the origins of the scandals debacle, relating it to other international examples and examining the extent to which broadcasting professionalism around the world has been undermined.

The second group of chapters develops the idea of trans-politics and the trans-political, also in relation to the concept of post-democracy. The notions conceptualize the diversity of constructions of the political, but also try to capture the explicit or implicit strategies to hegemonize or normalize specific discursive constructions. In "Post-democracy, Hegemony, and Invisible Power: The Media as '*Primum Movens Immobile*'," Nico Carpentier examines the problematic relationship between Reality TV participants and media professionals. Media professionals largely control the production setting of Reality TV: They have developed (*in casu* adapted) the format, they make the rules for participants, they select (*in casu* cast) the participants, they draft the participants' contracts, their cameras (partly visible and partly hidden) surveille the participants, they do the interviewing, and they select and edit the footage into a cohesive narrative which is broadcast on their respective stations. Although participants are not totally powerless, many Reality TV programs that feature "real" participants are alarming discourses of obedience, where participants are prepared to pay heavy prices for the sake of the televized game, and for the entertainment of the many. From this perspective, Reality TV is an example of the normalization of television as an impassive mover, as the "primum movens immobile," which manages to hegemonize its own basic assumptions, principles and methodologies. This chapter argues that the relevance of the concept of media power is situated not so much at the external level (in relation to television audiences), but mainly (and crucially) within the televisional system itself. In his chapter, Jan Pinseler looks at punitive Reality TV as a way to produce law and order. According to Pinseler, these shows reflect a shift in how the political is organized in today's societies by encouraging an idea of politics that goes beyond traditional ideas of policies that are proposed and developed by politicians or interest groups and, therefore, can be identified as trans-political. He argues that punitive Reality TV shows are political in pushing a certain political agenda—seemingly by proving the neo-liberal view that holds every individual solely responsible for his or her destiny: one can change if one only wants to. And, if the individual does not want to change, society must enforce a change. In this way, these shows shape everyday conceptions of normality and, hence, influence political thinking on a deeper, that is, a trans-political, level. The last chapter in the trans-politics section is by Jan Teurlings and focuses on police videos and the neo-liberal order, arguing that the arrival of the police video has to be seen in the light of this neo-liberal hegemony. One of the first expressions of the emerging genre of Reality

TV, the police video, quickly became a genre in its own right, and many countries now produce their own police video shows. This genre is intrinsically linked to the post-political era, since it is explicitly about undesirable behavior and how to reduce it. Teurlings examines two shows, *The World's Wildest Police Videos*, and *Blik Op De Weg*, to establish what kinds of behavior are criminalized, the solutions that are proposed, and why they constitute a self-negation of the neo-liberalism of its own politics. This analysis shows that neo-liberalism is not a unified doctrine, but in each show is enacted as being different, respectively authoritarian and communitarian.

The third group of chapters looks at the concepts of the trans-genre and trans-format in which modern conceptualizations of genre and format are transcended. The concept of trans-genre is seen as related to the strong reality claims of Reality TV, rooted in the transgression of the boundaries between different television formats. It is linked to the broader concept of trans-reality where self-reflexivity can be seen as a core element of the re-articulation of reality. Winnie Salamon's chapter examines the possibilities of resistance and subversion in Reality TV by looking at the Australian version of *Big Brother* and *The Loser*. She examines the positions of Merlin Luck as a participant in *Big Brother* and Chris Garling as the participant who won *The Loser*. They both tried to raise political issues, but in very different ways. By analyzing the discourses that emerge from a set of interviews, Salamon tries to link the idea of the savvy viewer and the possibility of popular mass culture becoming a political text. In the chapter "Genre as a Discursive Practice in Post-Documentary Television Production," Frank Boddin looks at post-documentary genres and revisits the concepts of genre and format by examining recent changes in the production context of television documentary programs. His chapter suggests going beyond the format perspective (toward the trans-format), because it overemphasizes the repressive rather than the productive power mechanisms at work within television production contexts. Also, the concept of "genre" is considered to have become problematic in relation to the diversity and hybridity of post-documentary texts. In contrast, the chapter focuses on genre as a discourse and a discursive practice, using Foucault's governmentality approach.[46] The chapter shows that production practices and processes allow for the continuous negotiation of genre discourses. From this perspective, a program format is one of the material outcomes of trans-generic, discursive struggles. Gunn Sara Enli and Brain McNair examine in their chapter the format *Wife Swap*, in order to look at the trans-national aspects of the Reality TV genre. This initially U.K.-based Reality format was first aired on Channel 4 in 2003, and has since become a global brand. The formula is that two families swap wives for fourteen days, exposing the contrasts between lifestyles and daily routines—how the respective wives run the households, raise their children and relate to their spouses, for example. The producers achieve the desired contrasts by focusing on cultural factors specific to the country in which the program is made; the original U.K. format involved families from different social classes, while the Israeli version involves an Arab family and a Jewish family. The format shows how trans-national Reality formats are adjusted to local cultures and identities, and the social realities in different countries. The chapter compares *Wife Swap* in the United Kingdom and in Norway, two West European countries with significant cultural differences in the areas of gender equality and class structure.

The last group of three chapters elaborates the concept of trans-audience, using case studies of particular audiences or reality celebrities. The concept of the trans-audience here refers to transgression of the boundaries between media professionals and audiences, where audience activity has become a material reality. Mikko Hautakangas analyzes the audience concept through the different positions of *Big Brother* fans, producers and participants. He continues the study of Reality TV audiences by examining the relationship between intensely involved *Big Brother* audience members and other "core actors," that is, participants and the production team. His study is based on material gathered during the first season of the Finnish *Big Brother* (autumn 2005-spring 2006). He analyzes interviews and related material, in addition to material from other ethnographic audience and production studies. He also analyzes *Big Brother* as a text, to depict the different yet intertwined experiences and participations of *Big Brother* audiences, producers, and housemates. Based on this case study he argues that the positions of audiences, producers, and participants (the text or content of *Big Brother*) are increasingly hybrid. Audiences and housemates participate in the show's production in several ways. Active followers can be seen, and see themselves as an essential part of the content production. Housemates and producers function as audiences of the whole *Big Brother* entity. Also, the production team admits to being a function of various *Big Brother* texts. The experience of (watching/participating in/belonging to) *Big Brother* is formed by the dynamics and interrelations among the three core positions (it is not merely the producing and consuming of a text). This analysis suggests that the "audience 2.0," or the trans-audience, does not only translate to a reconfiguration of conventional viewership. Su Holmes's chapter also uses *Big Brother* (U.K. 2002 version) to investigate conceptualizations of "ordinary" people, performance, and authenticity. She revisits the academic debates, reflecting on Reality TV's construction of "ordinariness," its deliberate blurring of the line between contestant and viewer, and its complex mediation of celebrity identity. She uses the term fame to look at the changing celebrity culture. She stresses that it is useful to consider the past in order to ascertain what in the present is "new." For example, although Reality TV has often been linked to the longer heritage of the generic game show (*Big Brother, Survivor* and *The Apprentice* have been described as Reality Game Shows), there has been little focused discussion of the generic relationships—especially with regard to the roles offered to "ordinary" audience members as performers. However, since the American quiz show scandals of the 1950s, the extent to which ordinary people on TV are real has been a cause for anxiety. Reality TV fame often ends in cautionary tales about "knowing one's place," in so far as contestants are often relegated to the "bottom of the celebrity scale," or are returned to cultural obscurity. In the United Kingdom, the most spectacular example of this trajectory was the *Big Brother* contestant, Jade Goody. Working-class Jade Goody from South London achieved fame in the 2002 series of *Big Brother,* and then featured in the celebrity version of the show (*Celebrity Big Brother*) in 2007. Following accusations of racism and bullying (Jade and two fellow female housemates were accused of bullying the Bollywood film star Shilpa Shetty), Jade experienced a spectacular fall from grace. Press analysis reveals how this international media scandal became a privileged site for debate on the status and future of modern fame—with Reality TV positioned center stage. But while the 2007 U.K. version of *Celebrity Big Brother* became an exceptional media event, there is a history on television and in the press of warnings about "knowing one's place," which go back to the formative years of TV as a mass medium. The last chapter in this group on trans-audience is by Tanja Thomas who writes about Lifestyle TV. She argues that Lifestyle TV is a rewarding subject for contemporary critical media studies, which remind us of the political dimensions of popular culture. In her chapter, Lifestyle TV is examined within societal diagnosis of individualization, mediatization, and globalization, and against a Foucauldian and a Gender and Cultural Studies perspective. It discusses Lifestyle TV as a model of acceptable standardized subjectivities, a pattern in which to enact new forms of "subjectivizations" or "technologies of the self" that correspond to new societal challenges. Thomas confronts the analysis of the transformative potential of Lifestyle TV with empirical data from audience research.

To provide a conceptual framework for the reader, Nico Carpentier and Sofie Van Bauwel further conceptualize the idea of trans and its different elements in the concluding chapter to this volume. This last chapter provides a more detailed discussion of the notion of trans, differentiating between the trans and the post prefix. This chapter is based on poststructuralist theory and provides a framework for thinking about and analyzing Reality TV and the media in general, in times of contemporary transformations and the increased importance of trans-reality.

To conclude this introduction, we want to thank all the authors for their contributions, Cynthia Little for her wonderful editing work, an anonymous reviewer(s) for his/her/their valuable feedback, and Lexington for making this book reality.

Notes

1. Lyotard, 1979.
2. Laclau, 1990.
3. Giddens, 1991.
4. Olson, 1987.
5. Collins, 1991.
6. Jensen, 1990.
7. Bignell; Meers and Van Bauwel.
8. Fishman and Cavender.
9. Carpentier.
10. Hill, 2005; 2007.
11. Dovey.
12. Hill, 2000; Kilborn, 2003.
13. Scannell.
14. Couldry.
15. Andrejevic; Biressi and Nunn; Holmes and Jermyn; Izod, Kilborn and Hibberd; Murray and Ouellette.
16. Biltereyst, Van Bauwel and Meers.
17. Hill, 2000. Annette Hill refers to speech of factual entertainment rather than Reality TV.
18. Kilborn, 1994, 423.
19. Corner.
20. See Corner; Nichols; Bondebjerg; Kilborn, 2003; Mast.
21. Biressi and Nunn, 3.
22. Benjamin in Fetveit.
23. Dovey, 57.
24. O'Sullivan, 207.
25. E.g., Hill, 2005; 2007.
26. E.g., Livingstone and Lunt; Shattuc.
27. See Biressi and Nunn.
28. Williams in Gitlin, 24.
29. See Biressi and Nunn; Holmes.
30. Ouellette and Hay, 2.
31. E.g., Palmer; Lewis.
32. See Foucault, 1977; 1978; 1988.
33. Ouellette and Hay, 2.
34. Ouellette and Hay, 11.
35. Foucault, 1988.
36. Dovey.
37. Baudrillard.
38. Braidotti, 2.
39. Braidotti, 4.
40. Braidotti, 5.
41. Bhabha, 1996.
42. Biressi and Nunn, 2-3.

43. Baudrillard, 1984.
44. Barthes, 1968.
45. Foucault, 1971; 1987.
46. Foucault, 1978.

References

Andrejevic, Mark. *Reality TV. The Work of Being Watched.* Oxford: Rowman and Little-field Publishers, 2004.

Barthes, Roland. "L'Effet du Réel." *Communications* 11 (1968): 84-89.

Baudrillard, Jean. *Simulations. Semiotext(e).* New York: Autonomedia, 1984.

Bhabba, Homi. *The Location of Culture?* London: Routledge, 1994.

Bignell, Jonathan. *Big Brother: Reality TV in the Twenty-first Century.* Basingstoke: Palgrave Macmillan, 2005.

Biltereyst, Daniël, Sofie Van Bauwel and Philippe Meers. *Realiteit en Fictie: Tweemaal Hetzelfde?* Brussel: Koning Boudewijnstichting, 2000.

Biressi, Anita and Heather Nunn. *Reality TV: Realism and Revelation.* London: Wall-flower, 2005.

Bondebjerg, Ib. "Public Discourse/Private Fascination: Hybridisation in 'True-life-story Genres.'" *Media, Culture & Society* 18, no. 1 (1996): 27-45.

Braidotti, Rosi. *Transpositions.* Cambridge, U.K.: Polity Press, 2006.

Carpentier, Nico. "Participation and Power in the Television Program Temptation Island." In *Researching Media, Democracy and Participation. The Intellectual Work of the 2006 European Media and Communication Doctoral Summer School,* edited by Nico Carpentier, Pille Pruulmann-Vengerfeldt, Karl Nordenstreng, Maren Hartmann, Peeter Vihalem and Bart Cammaerts, 135-148. Tartu, Estonia: University of Tartu Press, 2006.

Collins, Jim. "Batman: The Movie, Narrative: The Hyperconscious." In *The Many Lives of The Batman,* edited by Roberta E. Pearson and William Uricchio, 164-181. London: Routledge, 1991.

Corner, John. "Performing the Real. Documentary Diversions." *Television & New Media* 3, no. 3 (2002): 255-269.

Couldry, Nick. *Media Rituals: A Critical Approach.* London: Routledge, 2003.

Dovey, John. *Freakshow: First Person Media and Factual Television.* London: Pluto Press, 2000.

Fetveit, Arild. "Reality TV in the Digital Era: a Paradox in Visual Culture?" *Media, Culture & Society* 21 (1999): 787-804.

Fishman, Mark and Gray Cavender (eds.). *Entertaining Crime. Television Reality Programs.* New York: Aldine de Gruyter, 1998.

Foucault, Michel. *The Order of Discourse.* New York: Pantheon, 1971.

———. *Discipline and Punish: The Birth of the Prison,* translated by Alan Sheridan. New York: Pantheon, 1977.

———. *The History of Sexuality Vol. I. The Will to Knowledge,* translated by Robert Hurley. New York: Pantheon, 1978.

———. *The Archaeology of Knowledge.* New York: Pantheon, 1987.

———. "The Ethic of the Care of the Self as a Practice of Freedom." In *The Final Fou-*

cault, edited by James Bernauer and David Rasmussen, 1-20. Cambridge, Mass.: MIT Press, 1988.

Giddens, Anthony. *Modernity and self-identity. Self and Society in the Late Modern Age.* Cambridge: Polity, 1991.

Gitlin, Todd. *Media Unlimited. How the Torrent of Images and Sounds Overwhelms our Lives.* New York: Metropolitan Own Book, 2002.

Hill, Annette. "Fearful and Safe: Audience Response to British Reality Programming." In *From Grierson to the Docu-Soap: Breaking the Boundaries*, edited by John Izod, Richard Kilborn and Matthew Hibberd, 131-144. Luton, U.K.: University of Luton Press, 2000.

―――. *Reality TV: Audiences and Popular Factual Television.* London and New York: Routledge, 2005.

―――. *Restyling Factual TV. Audiences and News, Documentary and Reality Genres.* London and New York: Routledge, 2007.

Holmes, Su. "It's a Jungle out There! Playing the Game of Fame in Celebrity Reality TV." In *Framing Celebrity: New Directions in Celebrity Culture*, edited by Su Holmes and Sean Redmond, 45-65. London and New York: Routledge, 2006.

Holmes, Su and Deborah Jermyn (eds.). *Understanding Reality Television.* London: Routledge, 2004.

Izod, John, Richard Kilborn and Matthew Hibberd (eds.). *From Grierson to the Docu-Soap: Breaking the Boundaries.* Luton, U.K.: University of Luton Press, 2000.

Jensen, Joli. *Redeeming Modernity. Contradictions in Media Criticism.* Newbury Park, U.S.A.: Sage, 1990.

Kilborn, Richard. *Staging the Real: Factual TV Programming in the Age of "Big Brother."* Manchester: Manchester University Press, 2003.

―――. "'How Real Can You Get': Recent Developments in 'Reality' Television." *European Journal of Communication* 9 (1994): 421-439.

Laclau, Ernesto. *New Reflections on the Revolution of our Time.* London: Verso, 1990.

Lewis, Tania. *Smart Living. Lifestyle Media and Popular Expertise.* New York: Peter Lang, 2008.

Livingstone, Sonia and Peter Lunt. *Talk on Television. Audience Participation and the Public Debate.* London and New York: Routledge, 1994.

Lyotard, Jean-François. *La condition postmoderne: Rapport sur le savoir.* Paris: Minuit, 1979.

Mast, Jelle. "Reality-tv in Vlaanderen: Een Controversieel Fenomeen." *Psw-papers* 5 (2003): 9-33.

Meers, Philippe and Sofie Van Bauwel. "Debating Big Brother Belgium. Framing popular media culture." In *Big Brother. Formats, Critics and Publics*, edited by Ernest Mathijs and Janet Jones, 77-92. London: Wallflower Press, 2004.

Murray, Susan and Laurie Ouellette. *Reality TV: Remaking Television Culture.* New York: New York University Press, 2004.

Nichols, Brian. *Blurred Boundaries. Questions and Meaning in Contemporary Culture.* Bloomington: Indiana University Press, 1994.

O'Sullivan, T. "Television Memories and Cultures of Viewing 1950-65." In *Popular Television in Britain: Studies in Cultural Viewing*, edited by John Corner, 159-230. London: BFI, 1991.

Olson, Scott. "Meta-television: Popular Postmodernism." *Critical Studies in Mass Communication* 4, 3 (1987): 284-300.

Ouellette, Laurie and James Hay. *Better Living Through Reality TV. Television and Post-Welfare Citizenship.* Malden, Mass.: Blackwell, 2008.

Palmer, Garreth. *Discipline and Liberty. Television and Governance.* Manchester: Manchester University Press, 2003.

Scannell, Paddy. *Media and Communication.* London: Sage, 2007.

Shattuc, Jeanne M. *The Talking Cure. TV Talk Shows and Women.* New York: Routledge, 1997.

Part 1
TRANS-REALITY

Chapter 2
A Short Introduction to Trans-Reality
Sofie Van Bauwel

Media have always held the promise of immediate access to reality, access that has always been frustrated structurally by the process of mediation. The new hybrid television formats incorporate strong claims of reality, driven by a number of societal and media transformations. At the same time, these recent evolutions are questioning the "traditional" status of mimetic representation and fixed reality in our contemporary societies. According to John Dovey,[1] we see the rise of new "regimes of truth," and media with strong reality claims, focusing on subjective individual experiences and framed fragmented selves. But also the constructed nature of reality becomes more and more visible, partially because media reveal more about their construction activities, and in part because audiences are more savvy about (mainstream) media constructions.

This articulation of reality with its constructions and its contingency does not do away with the strong reality claims of the Reality TV genre (and of other formats, both fictional and factual). These fluid genres (or trans-genres) explore authenticity and celebrate "real" people, the reality of everyday life and a new participatory relationship between viewer(s) and screen. In doing so, they provide particular articulations of the real and construct realms of trans-reality through the merger (for instance) of authenticity and production techniques. The trans-real is borne out of this merger of strong professional intervention in the way that reality is mediated and constructed, and the desire for unmediated access to reality, authenticity and ordinariness. It results in representations of a constructed and contingent reality that combines an explicit process of manufacturing reality with glimpses of authenticity.

This transformation of the reality concept is embedded in the market-driven institution of a global media market and has become part of TV culture of the 1990s and 2000s. Combined with the idea of hybridization and the focus on the scopic, this inevitably raises more questions about the status of reality and, more specifically, about the real becoming a spectacle. This spectacle of the real can be seen as a simulation,[2] in which a so-called "new reality" is hyped. Here, a hyper-real realm of authentic emotions, experiences, and pleasures is constructed.

These "newly" conceptualized realities are articulated within a society that is obsessed with the "new." This form of reality construction is confronted by potential resistance and the media-savvyness of an empowered audience. The practices of this audience indicate the possibilities for participation in the production, interpretation, and use of texts. Exploiting Anthony Giddens's[3] perspective, trans-reality is fed by societal self-reflexivity. Although trans-reality is more and more becoming part of the common sense, it has raised concern in society—fed by the perceived dangers of hyper-reality—that our worlds are being reduced to televisual simulations. As a result, debates are emerging about the degree to which these representations construct reality claims, formulating the problematic of whether these realities should be accepted at face value as realities, or whether they should be considered completely unreal.

The trans-reality concept focuses on a rearticulation of reality as part of the everyday life spectacle and as part of our visual culture. These rearticulations of the real are contextual and temporal, but at the same time are rooted in the transgression of the boundaries between TV formats and the societal transformation of the ontology of reality through visual culture. Embedded in a neo-liberal consumer culture, the mediated and consumed trans-reality can be conceptualized as multi-layered, produced and highly particular representations of reality.

Notes

1. Dovey, 2000.
2. Baudrillard, 1984.
3. Giddens, 1991.

References

Baudrillard, Jean. *Simulations. Semiotext(e)*. New York: Autonomedia, 1984.
Dovey, John. *Freakshow: First Person Media and Factual Television*. London: Pluto Press, 2000.
Giddens, Anthony. *Modernity and Self-identity*. Cambridge, U.K.: Polity, 1991.

Chapter 3
The Spectacle of the Real and Whatever Other Constructions
Sofie Van Bauwel

Claiming the Real

Since the 1990s, the media has been obsessed with the idea of reality. These Western societal preoccupations with reality, the truth, the visual and the real are an integral part of the scopic culture which has been boosted by the omnipresence of advertising and television since the 1980s. These preoccupations do not only affect the content of different media formats, they have triggered considerable academic interest. Fields of scholarly research, such as visual culture[1] and television studies,[2] have become established, and societal and academic concerns about the real formulated. These concerns, pessimistic discourses and "media panics"[3] have been and are being fed by the perceived dangers of hyperreality and the fear that our worlds are being reduced to televisual simulations.[4] This chapter revisits these debates, asking whether, how and to what degree these representations construct the reality claim, and how this claim is dealt with by audiences. The main question then becomes: How can we deal with representations of the real, without either accepting such realities as realities, or rejecting them completely? More specifically, this dislocation of "reality" is investigated in the realm of Reality TV. This umbrella genre of Reality TV seems to be an embodiment of the above-mentioned obsession, which makes it an interesting case through which to look at the claims, constructions and epistemology of reality and authenticity in relation to TV and scopic culture.[5] This deconstruction of the core element of the Reality TV format (i.e., its reality claim), by looking at young audiences' reception, will eventually be captured by the concept of the trans-real, which will be developed as an intellectual strategy to deal with the culture of spectacle in media theory. I focus, therefore, on representations of trauma and tragedy in Reality TV, which seem to be a good case to examine the scopic claim of the real, since these programs provide moments of authenticity and restoration through the reconstruction of "real" events. Moreover, in showing fear, pain and emotion, these Reality TV programs' promise of reality is placed at the center.[6]

Claiming the Format: The Reality Genre

The "new" format(s) of Reality TV entered the TV market in the contemporary multi-media environment of the 1980s. This transformation is described as an explosion of the genre of reality. It is important to stress, however, that Reality TV[7] is not new: Factual TV formats have existed for many years.[8] With its roots in the documentary tradition and direct cinema, the use of "new" technologies such as light hand-cameras has facilitated this seeming explosion. In the 1980s especially, we saw a rise in factual TV formats in the US, which emphasized reality, and used dramatic reconstruction techniques.[9]

As a concept, Reality TV referred and still refers to different program formats at whose core are so-called "real events" and through which "real life" events are dramatically constructed or reconstructed.[10] This explosion began with American programs such as *Rescue 911*, where police or rescue teams were followed by "fly on the wall" cameras, and which often depicted tragedies such as car crashes, or showed victims of tragedies suffering from post-traumatic stress disorders.[11] These formats entered the European broadcasting market in the early 1990s and are being aired by public and commercial broadcasters around Europe. Daniël Biltereyst[12] argues that from a historical point of view, West-European broadcasting companies became dependent on American input (such as Reality TV programs) for a variety of reasons. Hollywood (as a place where both films and TV are produced) represented the first major entertainment industry that offered transnational culture products. And when European countries finally lifted the monopolies on the public broadcasting companies, the new private companies wanted a new approach to TV programming, as pointed out by Jo Bardoel and Kees Brants[13] in the case of the Dutch Public Broadcaster. The purchase of American series and serials was not only a financially wise decision; it was one that served to bind vast audiences to channels based on the serial nature and trans-national appeal of such programming.

Eventually, the American fiction formats were seen as *only* formats, creating high expectations among audiences toward national productions, which resulted in substantial amounts of European productions. From the 1990s onwards the "Europeanization in programming is noticeable only in the success of reality TV formats, as the same formula can be adapted to any national situation."[14] These formats are often based on ordinary people in unusual situations, often in a "group-challenge" context (e.g., *Survival*). This first wave of Reality TV formats was not just copied from the United States,[15] but U.S. examples were incorporated within European, national, cultural, social and historical contexts. European broadcasters and production companies soon found that these formats were low cost and relative easy to reproduce. Richard Kilborn[16] stresses that these traveling, adapted genres were embedded within the different European TV traditions. An example is the French tradition of "télé-réalité" based on the national obsession with psychotherapeutic discourses (e.g., *Perdu de vue*; *Témoin No. 1*).

Not all Reality TV programs are inspired by U.S. productions. Programs grouped within formats such as docu-soaps, real life soaps, home video programs, and so on, were also developed in Europe. Of course, these formats are not exclusively European, but a majority are produced within Europe and sold worldwide (e.g., *Big Brother*). Divina Frau-Meigs argues that the production of Reality TV formats in Europe in the 1990s can be seen as an "answer" to the domination of American imported programs.[17] The Dutch Endemol format *Big Brother* would seem an excellent example of this phenomenon, and initiated the beginning of the mass production of European "home made" Reality TV genres.

Analyzing the Reality Claim

In academia, strong emphasis is placed on Reality TV as part of the medium of TV and the claim to reality of the medium.[18] All these formats, from news to *Temptation Island*,[19] have a claim to reality in common. According to John Dovey[20] we see new "regimes of truth" with strong reality claims and the focus on a subjective individual experience and a framed fragmented self. This market-driven focus[21] became part of the TV culture of the nineties. As John Corner[22] put it: "Certainly, it is right to be wary and skeptical at the moment. A new fluidity of representational boundaries in documentary had appeared . . . in response to the market need to hybridize across genres in the search for competitively attractive new recipes."

The strong reality claims are broader than the Reality TV formats, as they also encompass fictional or factual formats. For instance the OJ Simpson trial and its media coverage (or spectacle) is emblematic.[23] But also with the occurrence of events such as 9/11 and the Asian tsunami, "just normal citizen/people" were covering real, tragic events, using their cameras, putting the images on the net and selling them to news agencies. These representations of dramatic events made by so-called amateurs are also part of the obsession with reality. Moreover, these representations are (considered) even more real than the images produced by news camera crews. On the other side of the fiction-fact continuum we have fictional formats, such as the *CSI* crime investigation series, which depicts the reality of a crime, of a dead body, of a forensic search. Also, body trauma series, such as *ER,* show surgical procedures and physical suffering. The soap genre includes similar constructions and generated representations of drama and emotions, which are shown to us as if they were real.

Despite this broad range of formats that makes some claim to reality, Reality TV is specific. As a format it can be conceptualized as a narrative form in contemporary modernity in which the storytelling is embedded in the truth claims, and the conception of reality is linked to the visual and to the notion of authenticity. It is this specific representation of authenticity which seeks to tell us stories about "real" identities—often represented in everyday life settings. The stereotypical images of hegemonic citizens and identities that are represented are watched mainly by (or targeted to) a female middle class audience.[24] We see national identities,[25] regional identities, gender identities, political identities, ethnic identities and even class identities.

But there are also other discourses circulating in these factual TV formats, in which the dominant hegemonic identities are less clearly delineated. We can find representations and discourses of societal issues. We are shown identities that are seen as deviant but within the margins, sometimes represented in novel ways.[26] Participants articulate discourses that create uncertainty about their identities, putting question marks against hegemonic identities. From this perspective, Reality TV can be seen as a resistance strategy pushing the limits of identities.[27] These sometimes deviant representations are regarded as non-hegemonic or anti-hegemonic, despite their circulation within the context of a dominant mainstream popular culture. This optimistic standpoint suggests that people are able, by means of these TV formats, to criticize hegemony, or that the formats themselves are instruments for contesting hegemony through the specificity of the program content. We find the idea of a Reality TV genre becomes a platform of resistance discourses in several academic texts,[28] which make very positive evaluation of these representations (using reinterpretations of Fiske's work[29]). However, to date, few academic studies have been undertaken to scrutinize the signifying practices of audiences in this context.[30]

On the other hand, authors, such as Nichols, point to the crisis in the media landscape, arguing that radical resistance is impossible within present-day popular culture. Nichols contends that within a flexible market economy, people constantly are preoccupied with the threats of sliding down the social ladder, and being confronted with poverty and uncertainty. His argument is that the flexibility of the market economy is linked to uncertainty, fear of loss, etc. which, in turn, is linked to what Reality TV has to offer to its audiences:

> Reality TV offers another version of the effort to represent anxieties of social stability and mobility at a time when economic solvency, let alone prosperity, hangs in doubt. The fate of the middle class "in-betweeners" is uncertain . . . Beset by dreams of rising and nightmares of falling, plagued by the terror of pillage, plunder, and rape, the "target" audience for reality TV (white, middle-class consumers with "disposable" income) attends to a precarious world of random violence and moment-to-moment contingency.[31]

This emphasis on violence, fear, and uncertainty has an ideological dimension. Nichols sees this as the fundamental perversity of Reality TV, which is situated in the "gleeful abandon with which it mocks, or rejects, civic mindedness and the positivist social engineering behind it."[32] We see representations of chaos, violence, and trauma in a world full of danger and unpredictable events. And the victims of all of them are ordinary, authentic "real" people. But they are not us.

Debating the Real, and the Possibilities of the Real

However these representations are evaluated, Reality TV is a format that elaborates the idea of the real, often with an emphasis on authenticity. This authenticity is often structured on the basis of an "ordinary" or everyday component[33] and stresses the self-reflexivity of the audience. Using Anthony Giddens's[34] perspective: Reality TV can be considered a self-reflexive format in late modernity.[35] One component that supports this claim is the role of visibility. Andrejevic[36] makes this point in his analysis of Reality TV, using Lacanian theory to look at Reality TV formats based on surveillance camera footage. He maintains that "getting real—attaining authenticity—means being seen."[37] Important to the genre, thus, is the focus on the scopic, the moment when the real becomes the spectacle.[38] This spectacle of the real is often related to the work of Jean Baudrillard[39] and the *idées* or concepts of simulacra and hyper-reality. At the same time, the real and the concept of reality are questioned from this perspective. The emphasis on the spectacle argues that a dislocation of the real has taken place. Reality and its representations are rearticulated as part of the reality claim, as part of the everyday life spectacle, as part of the visual culture, as part of TV, as part of the public sphere. This spectacle of the real can be seen as a simulation of the real, where we see "fake" people in soap operas in "real" situations, and real people in "fake" situations, for example, in docusoaps. The reality of everyday life, or the horrible reality of a disaster, is situated again and again, using filmic techniques that stem from the genre of pornography. Certain lighting and close-ups are used to frame the private and to represent the unseen. The conceptualization of the real has to be rearticulated and reframed or, as Baudrillard, has it:

> The eye of TV is no longer the source of an absolute gaze, and the ideal of control is no longer that of transparency. The latter still presupposes an objective space and the omnipotence of a despotic gaze . . . a position of exteriority, playing the distinction between active and passive is abolished. Such is the slope of a hyperrealist sociality, where the real is confused with the model.[40]

Dislocated Tragedies

The closed-reality claim of Reality TV is often linked to the representations of "real" tragedies, such as real time car crashes. The so-called "reality credentials" or claims to reality, are high when they refer to bodily traumas. Representations of emotion, of anger, tears, and so on, are an ingredient in these reality claims and are often witnessed in so-called talk shows (e.g., *The Jerry Springer Show*). As Anita Biressi and Heather Nunn[41] argue, trauma seems to be a popular script in Reality TV formats. Drawing on Kirby Farrell's[42] analysis, Biressi and Nunn describe trauma as a clinical concept and a cultural trope. Media "function as a vehicle for the expression of violent cultural events and their aftermath as well as a 'register of dissonance,' the jolt of cultural recognition of the individual and collective capacity of violence and atrocity."[43]

Although there are many different Reality TV formats representing the ordinary, these claims seem most real in programs that show bodies: human bodies in ruins, fragmented, distorted or destroyed, or being fixed, and so on. This is the "pure gaze":[44] we are provided with footage of accidents or extracted from surveillance camera tapes. This marker of authenticity increases when we can see these images in real time and when we—as audience—witness them as "they happen." In addition to the real time articulation of the reality claim, the material body is also an important focus or spectacle articulated within this claim. So-called scopophilia (based on Freud's psychoanalysis) or voyeurism is very present in claiming the real, especially in representations of the material body.

Discourses on Trauma in Reality TV

In order to establish (empirically) how audiences deal with the reality claims of Reality TV, we analyzed the discourses on representations of tragedies in contemporary factual entertainment and Reality TV genres. In this case study we investigated specifically how tragedies are presented in contemporary Reality TV genres at the level of reception, with an emphasis on the articulation of reality. Following the "audience cum content research" tradition[45] we investigated both the mass media discourse and its reception by a particular audience group, namely young people aged between fourteen and twenty-nine. We used a discourse-theoretical approach, in which the media text is seen as a product of "discourse practices," concentrated particularly on representations of tragedies in Reality TV genres. Through a combination of in-depth interviews and media diaries, seventy-nine participants articulated their thoughts on TV, Reality TV and portrayals of tragedy on Reality TV.[46] In analyzing their discourses, we singled out four items related to the representation of tragedy on Reality TV (e.g., *Het Leven zoals het is: kinderziekenhuis,*[47] *Expeditie Robinson,*[48] *America's Most Wanted, Big Brother* and *Man bijt Hond*[49]).

The first set of articulations emphasizes authenticity. The televised reality is often linked to a real time construction, which is part of the construct itself. Participants considered it an especially authentic and emotional viewing experience when the programs depicted rescue teams, and the audience /spectators "witnessed" bodily trauma, for example, in actual car crashes. As Karina (aged nineteen) put it: "Television is a 'peeping hole of the people.'" Reality is depicted but manipulated. This "peeping" experience is channeled by the gaze of the narrator and is often presented as a fly-on-the-wall view, or from the reporter's/camera's perspective.[50] This point-of-view is articulated as objective, making this an "embedded" authenticity, based on the scopic and visual elements.

A second core of articulations refers to the social acceptability of looking at "forbidden things." This is the scopophilia in which participants refer to looking into people's lives and looking at the tragedies of everyday life. They do not perceive themselves to be voyeurs, looking at deviant practices. But the "watching" is part of the scopic culture and "looking at" is considered to be a part of a sometimes controversial representation of real people and real emotions. These articulations, in turn, are frequently linked to representations of emotion in relation to dramatic events or tragedies, as illustrated in the next quote from Benito (aged twenty-nine) who said that "some programmes are kitsch because they are strange people that we are looking at."

A third group of articulations refers to the possibility of social learning. In this context, the participants referred especially to practices of rescue (or first aid) and claimed to gain (some) situated knowledge about how to save a life, or how to react in specific dangerous situations. They also referred to representations of emotions from experienced participants as an important element in the practice of learning. Such interpretations are quite equal to the analyses of daytime talk shows and their representations of trauma and emotion.[51] Empathy is another element that sneaks in at this point. "Real emotions" displayed by "real experts" create empathy, exemplified in Tine's (aged twenty-one) saying that: "Some programmes can be starting point of thinking about it. For example, recently I saw a cancer patient filmed by her sister. Then I think for a moment: 'Aagh!, this can also happen to me.'" Or as Jelle (aged fifteen) said: "Some programmes really make you think. Also, victims of a disaster make you think. It can equally be me." These outcomes are similar to what Minna Aslama and Mervi Pantti found in their analysis of the confessional culture of Reality TV.[52] They analyzed several Finnish-made Reality TV formats and looked at the disclosure of emotion. Stressing the element of the confessional voice, they show that therapeutic strategies are prominent in Reality TV formats. The "real" claim to intimacy and authenticity, according to them,[53] is an extreme claim that "the audience and the audience 'only,' will get to know their raw emotions and naked feelings."

A last group of articulations is about the centrality of the body, which generates strong claims to reality. As already mentioned, alongside the "real time" articulation, the material body is an important focus (or spectacle) articulated within the reality claim. Here scopophilia is prominent, as in (the reception of) makeover shows.[54] Participants claim to experience uncomfortable feelings when confronted with "real bodies" in Reality TV formats of those who are or were "real people." For example Marc's (aged sixteen) statement that: "They are influencing the soul of state of mind of the people" (in relation to representations of dead bodies). This quote illustrates the unease of Western audiences when looking at human bodies on a TV screen. When these depictions are labelled as non-fiction or Reality TV, the discomfited feelings increase: The corporeality of the corpse is linked to the "real self" of the person who inhabited it. This "visual evidence" seems to feed an ambiguous longing for the authentic and the real. But, as Marc Andrejevic[55] argues, Reality TV can be considered a reflexive machine that shows mediated appearances, which (in his opinion) can act as demonstrations of the artificial character of these mediated realities, but on the other hand can also be representations that highlight the reality of the artificial. Without over-celebrating the active audience and falling into the romanticism trap, this case study points out that the media savvy-ness[56] that defines the real as artificial is present in our young Western audience members. The media-literate respondents in this research project articulate a critical signifying practice of Reality TV, stressing very openly the strategies of the production to control and manipulate "the audience." Nele (a twenty-year-old female) stated that: "Reality is manipulated, and it is hard to make the difference between what is truth and what is not." Not all respondents were able so clearly to express the ambivalence and the uncertainty of the truth claims made on TV and in Reality TV formats. However, some were critical and saw the mediated reality as a constructed perspective. Sally (aged eighteen), for example, said: "One perspective on reality is broadcast, asking me. But through TV you know certain things, but it is only one side of the story," or, as Wim, a young man of twenty-two, put it: "Reality is always represented, although news agencies select the news. Depending on the experience of the journalist important information can be lost. Besides in the process of the montage things are cut and pasted. Television does not represent all aspects of reality—but gives us a 'made reality.'" Some participants referred to the commercial context of the media, pointing to the importance of the market economy and advertisers as agents in the production of Reality TV and in the production of reality.

Despite the market ideologies that create the reality claim[57] and the factual formats that transgress the traditional fact/fiction dichotomy boundaries,[58] questions about the ontology of these formats unavoidably lead to multi-layered answers. As the audience reactions show, we see a twofold position, which we can term trans-real, and which combines reality and management, authenticity and manipulation. This, as Jack Bratich[59] stresses, makes Reality TV much more than a representational vehicle. It relates it to everyday life, to audiences and to their contexts. The point here is that Reality TV (and TV in general) and reality are not one and the same, and that we can "displace the debates over realism, reality, and representation altogether."[60] This means that Reality TV: "does not represent the current conjuncture—it interjects itself into the conjuncture and enhances particular components required by it."[61]

Navigating within the Trans-Real

> Truth is not like a product in which one can no longer find any trace of the tool that made it.[62]

As Georg Wilhelm Friedrich Hegel accurately argued in 1807, truth—or for that matter reality—is a complex concept, which is multilayered and hybrid in its form. It is contextual and temporal, but at the same time is rooted in a conceptual framework that feeds reality and our understanding of reality. Reality and the mediations of reality still refer to something, to a context. This context is important to read the representation and to signify it as authentic and truthful. Baudrillard's simulation[63] seems to be a wonderful tool to think about visual culture, but, in looking at the claims to reality in media, the roots of this visual culture are still present in the conceptualizations of the real. A hyper-real spectacle is not totally and fully present, in part because of the scopic element and its relation to the reality claim. Although audiences are well-aware of the processes of gate-keeping, the production of images, and their framing of (and through) the visual, are part of a transformation of the conceptualization of the real. The old idea that "if we see it, it is real" persists in the real of audiences, but with a twist: Audiences may not be very media illiterate and do know that these representations are managed. At the same time, they are presented with a reality in terms of emotions, or in relation to the body. This allows the transformation of the trans-real, which is embedded in the consumption of representations in a hybrid mediascape, revealing rawness, feelings, and emotions in an authentic matter while simultaneously being mediated and managed in a neo-liberal space. The trans-real is part of contemporary TV culture and has a "parallax error"[64] in its analysis. According to John Hartley[65] the object of analysis is situated on a different level. He suggests that the analysis of TV—within the context of a new economy and consumer-led creativity—should not start from prescriptions and inherited presumptions about what are consumption, reality and truth, and audiences.

In the present case study, it thus becomes important to stress the paradox located in the format and genres of Reality TV in relation to their reality claims, and the representations of trauma and tragedy. As is clear from our reception study, participants watch different Reality TV formats, but do not articulate pessimistic views of these representations. They enjoy being Peeping Toms, and they do experience emotions when looking at emotion. They may be prompted to think about societal issues, they can sometimes learn from these programs and they are shocked by footage of dead bodies or body parts. More importantly in this context, they know that Reality TV is a format that is a hybrid in terms of its relation to reality. They are, after all, often critical viewers, who are knowledgeable about the constructions and reconstructions of trauma in Reality TV. Although we may live in a scopic culture, there is no absolute gaze. And as Baudrillard puts it "the eye of TV is no longer the source of an absolute gaze, and the ideal of control is no longer that of transparency."[66] Or as one participant, aged eighteen, put it: "A perspective on reality is broadcast using real bodies, real emotions and ultimate real people with real tragedies."

Notes

1. See Barnard.
2. See Hartley, 1999.
3. Biltereyst, 2004.
4. Baudrillard.
5. See Andrejevic, 2004; Biressi and Nunn; Hill, 2007.
6. Aslama and Pantti, 2006.
7. Referring to all formats that make a claim to reality.
8. See Kilborn, 1998; 2003.
9. See Willis.
10. See Holmes and Jermyn; Murray and Ouellette.
11. Schlesinger and Tumber; Fishman and Cavender.
12. Biltereyst, 2004.
13. Bardoel and Brants.
14. Mast, 7.
15. See Dauncey; Kilborn, 1994.
16. Kilborn, 1994, 430.
17. Frau-Meigs, 34.
18. Hartley, 1999.
19. See chapter Carpentier.
20. Dovey.
21. Magder.
22. Corner, 183.
23. See Barak.
24. For examples see Aslama and Pantti, 2006; see also partly chapter Gunn and McNair.
25. See Oulette and Hay.
26. See chapter Salamon.
27. Dovey.

28. See Dovey; Meijer and Reesinck.
29. E.g., Fiske.
30. See e.g., Curry; Hill, 2005.
31. Nichols, 58.
32. Nichols, 51.
33. See Biressi and Nunn, 2005.
34. Giddens.
35. See also chapter Holmes in relation to celebrities.
36. Andrejevic, 2004.
37. Andrejevic, 2004, 189.
38. Bondebjerg, 2002.
39. Baudrillard.
40. Baudrillard, 54-55.
41. Biressi and Nunn.
42. Farrell.
43. Biressi and Nunn, 109.
44. Andrejevic, 2004, 189.
45. Jensen.
46. The data were collected in October-December 2002 in Belgium and the interviews were fully transcribed.
47. *Life as it is: children's hospital.*
48. *Survival.*
49. An infotainment program on the local stories behind the "news."
50. For an analysis of Reality TV and the use of technology such as lightweight cameras etc., see Fetveit.
51. See for example Grindstaff; Shattuc; Lunt and Stenner.
52. Aslama and Pantti, 2006.
53. Minna Aslama and Mervi Pantti, 2006, 179.
54. For an analysis see Heller; chapter Thomas.
55. Andrejevic, 2004.
56. See also chapter Salamon.
57. Rapping; McMurria.
58. Bondebjerg, 1996.
59. Bratich, 6-22.
60. Bratich, 7.
61. Bratich, 7.
62. Hegel, 67.
63. Baudrillard.
64. Hartley, 2008, 33.
65. Hartley, 2008.
66. Baudrillard, 54.

References

Andrejevic, Marc. *Reality TV. The Work of Being Watched.* Oxford: Rowman and Littlefield, 2004.

Aslama, Minna and Mervi Pantti. "Talking Alone: Reality TV, Emotions and Authenticity." *European Journal of Cultural Studies* 9, no. 2 (2006): 167-184.

Barak, Gregg (ed.). *Representing O. J. Media Criminal Justice and Mass Culture*. London: Harrow and Heston, 1999.

Bardoel, Jo and Kees Brants. "Public Broadcasters and Social Responsibility in the Netherlands." In *Broadcasting & Convergence: New Articulations of the Public Service Remit*, edited by Gregory Ferrell Lowe and Taisto Hujanen, 167-186. Tampere, Finland: Nordicom, 2003.

Barnard, Malcolm. *Approaches to Understanding Visual Culture*. London: Palgrave, 2001.

Baudrillard, Jean. *Simulations. Semiotext(e)*. New York: Autonomedia, 1984.

Biltereyst, Daniël, Sofie Van Bauwel and Philippe Meers. *Realiteit en Fictie: Tweemaal Hetzelfde?* Brussels: Koning Boudewijnstichting, 2000.

————. "Reality-TV, Troublesome Pictures and Panics; Reappraising the Public Controversy Around Reality-TV in Europe." In *Understanding Reality Television*, edited by Su Holmes and Deborah Jermyn, 91-110. London: Routledge, 2004.

Biressi, Anita and Heather Nunn. *Reality TV. Realism and Revelation*. London: Wallflower, 2005.

Bondebjerg, Ib. "Public Discourse/Private Fascination: Hybridisation in 'True-life-story Genres.'" *Media, Culture & Society* 18, no. 1 (1996): 27-45.

————. "The Mediation of Everyday Life. Genre Discourse and Spectacle in Reality TV." In *Realism and "Reality" in Film and the Media*, edited by Anne Jerslev, 159-192. Copenhagen: Northern Lights, 2002.

Bratich, Jack Z. "Programming Reality. Control Societies, New Subjects and the Powers of Transformation." In *Makeover Television. Realities Remodelled*, edited by Dana Heller, 6-22. London: Tauris, 2007.

Carpentier, Nico and Erik Spinoy (eds.). *Discourse Theory and Cultural Analysis: Media, Arts and Literature*. Creskill, N.J.: Hampton Press, 2008.

Corner, John. *Critical Ideas in Television Studies*. Oxford: Oxford University Press, 1999.

Curry, Kathleen. "Mediating Cops: An Analysis of Viewer Reaction to Reality TV." *Journal of Criminal Justice and Popular Culture* 8, no. 3 (2001): 169-185.

Dauncey, Henri. "French 'Reality Television.'" *European Journal of Communication* 11, no. 1 (1996): 83-106.

Derrida, Jacques. *The Truth in Painting*. Chicago: University of Chicago Press, 1987.

Dovey, John. *Freakshow. First Person Media and Factual Television*. London: Pluto Press, 2000.

Ellis, John. *Visible Fictions: Cinema, Television, Video* (second edition). London: Routledge, 1992.

Fairclough, Norman. *Discourse and Social Change*. Cambridge, U.K.: Polity Press, 1992.

Farrell, Kirby. *Post-traumatic Culture. Injury and Interpretation in the Nineties*. Baltimore, Maryland: Johns Hopkins University Press, 1998.

Fetveit, Arild. "Reality TV in the Digital Era: A Paradox in Visual Culture?" *Media, Culture & Society* 21 (1999): 787-804.

Fishman, Mark and Gray Cavender (eds.). *Entertaining Crime. Television Reality Programs*. New York: Aldine de Gruyter, 1998.

Fiske, John. *Understanding Popular Culture*. London: Unwin Hyman, 1989.

Foucault, Michel. *La Volonté de Savoir*. Paris: Gallimard, 1976a.

———. *Histoire de la Sexualité, vol. 1: La volonté de savoir*. Paris: Gallimard, 1976b.

———. *Power/Knowledge*. New York: Pantheon, 1980.

Frau-Meigs, Divina. "Big Brother and Reality-tv in Europe." *European Journal of Communication* 21, no.1 (2006): 33-56.

Giddens, Anthony. *Modernity and Self-identity*. Cambridge, U.K.: Polity, 1991.

Grindstaff, Laura. "Producing Trash, Class and the Money Shot: A Behind-the-Scenes Account of Daytime TV Talk Shows." In *Media Scandals: Morality and Desire in the Popular Culture Marketplace*, edited by James Lull and Stephen Hinderman, 164-202. Cambridge, U.K.: Polity Press, 1997.

Hall, Stuart. "Media Power and Class Power." In *Bending Reality: The State of the Media*, edited by James Curran, Jakes Ecclestone, Giles Oakley and Alan Richardson, 5-14. London: Pluto Press, 1986.

———. "Who Needs Identity." In *Identity: A Reader*, edited by Paul Du Gay, Jessica Evans and Peter Redman, 15-30. London: Sage, 2000.

Hartley, John. *Uses of Television*. London and New York: Routledge, 1999.

———. *Television Truths*. Maldon, Mass.: Blackwell, 2008.

Hegel, Georg Wilhelm Friedrich. *Phenomenology of the Mind*. London: Mohilal, 1998 (1807).

Heller, Dana. *Makeover Television. Realities Remodelled*. London: I.B. Tauris, 2007.

Hill, Annette. *Restyling Factual TV: The Reception of News, Documentary and Reality Genres*. London: Routledge, 2007.

———. *Reality TV: Audiences and Popular factual television*. London: Routledge, 2005.

Holmes, Su and Deborah Jermyn (eds.). *Understanding Reality TV*. London: Routledge, 2003.

Jensen, Klaus B. "Media Reception: Qualitative Traditions." In *Handbook of Media and Communications Research: Quantitative and Qualitative Research Methodologies*, edited by Klaus B. Jensen, 156-169. London/New York: Routledge, 2002.

Kellner, Douglas. *Media Culture: Cultural Studies, Identity and Politics Between the Modern and the Postmodern*. London: Routledge, 1995.

Kilborn, Richard. "How Real Can You Get?: Recent developments in 'Reality Television.'" *European Journal of Communication* 9 (1994): 421-439.

———. "Shaping the Real; Democratization and Commodification in U.K. Factual Broadcasting." *European Journal of Communication* 13, no. 2 (1998): 201-218.

———. *Staging the Real: Factual TV Programming in the Age of "Big Brother."* Manchester: Manchester University Press, 2003.

Lunt, Peter and Paul Stenner. "The Jerry Springer Show as an Emotional Public Sphere." *Media, Culture & Society* 27, no.1 (2005): 59-82.

Magder, Ted. "End of TV 101: Reality Programs, Formats, and the New Business of Television." In *Reality TV: Remaking Television Culture*, edited by Susan Murray and Laurie Ouellette, 137-156. New York: New York University Press, 2004.

Mast, Jelle. "Reality-TV in Vlaanderen: Een Controversieel Fenomeen." *Psw-papers* 5 (2003): 9-33.

McMurria, John. "Desperate Citizens and Good Samaritans: Neoliberalism and Makeover Reality TV." *Television & New Media* 9, no. 4 (2008): 305-332.

Meers, Philippe and Sofie Van Bauwel. "Debating Big Brother Belgium. Framing Popular Media Culture." In *Big Brother. Formats, Critics and Publics*, edited by Ernest Mathijs and Janet Jones, 77-92. London: Wallflower Press, 2004.

Meijer, Irena and Mark Reesinck (eds.). *Reality Soap! Big Brother en de Opkomst van het Multimediaconcept.* Amsterdam: Boom, 2000.

Mirzoeff, Nicholas (ed.). *The Visual Culture Reader* (second edition). London/New York: Routledge, 2002.

Murray, Susan and Laurie Ouellette. *Reality TV: Remaking Television Culture.* New York: New York University Press, 2004.

Nichols, Brian. *Blurred Boundaries. Questions and Meaning in Contemporary Culture.* Bloomington: Indiana University Press, 1994.

Ouellette, Laurie and James Hay. *Better Living Through Reality TV. Television and Postwelfare Citizenship.* Malden, Mass.: Blackwell, 2008.

Palmer, Gareth. "Big Brother: An Experiment in Governance." *Television and New Media* 3, no. 3 (2002): 295-310.

Pickering, Marc. *Stereotyping. The Politics of Representation.* London: Palgrave, 2001.

Rapping, Elayne. "Aliens, Nomads, Mad Dogs, and Road Warriors: The Changing Face of Criminal Violence on TV." In *Reality TV: Remaking Television Culture,* edited by Susan Murray and Laurie Ouellette, 214-230. New York: New York University Press, 2004.

Schlesinger, Philip and Howard Tumber. *Reporting Crime. The Media Politics of Criminal Justice.* Oxford: Oxford University Press, 1995.

Shattuc, Jeanne M. *The Talking Cure. TV Talk Shows and Women.* New York: Routledge, 1997.

Willis, John. "Breaking the Boundaries." In *From Grierson to the Docu-soap: Breaking the Boundaries,* edited by John Izod, Richard Kilborn and Matthew Hibberd, 97-102. Luton, U.K.: University of Luton Press, 2000.

Chapter 4
On the Media Representation of Reality: Peirce and Auerbach—Two Unlikely Guests in the *Big Brother* House
Fernando Andacht

To Peptonize or Not to Peptonize the Real? That is the (Real) Question of Reality TV

What do Reality TV shows have to do with the real? What is the relationship between protean formats of Reality TV as a genre with the world out there, [1] the world as it is without any cosmetic makeover? To answer these questions, which have been discussed heatedly by a large number of media critics and scholars in the many countries where TV's *Big Brother* has been produced, I will use the theory of representation, in fact two versions of it. For the first one, I must go back in time, almost a century before Endemol launched its landmark product, in a small Dutch cable TV station.[2] In 1906, the man who came to be known as the American Freud, the eminent philosopher William James, gave a lecture at the Lowell Institute in Boston, whose content, with the passing of years, I believe has probably reached an audience as large as those achieved by *Big Brother*: "We may glimpse it [reality], but we never grasp it; what we grasp is always some substitute for it, which some previous human thinking has peptonized and cooked for our consumption. If so vulgar an expression were allowed us we might say that wherever we find it, it has been already *faked*."[3]

Through this perhaps not very alluring metaphor, James proclaimed the basis of a philosophical doctrine whose anti-representationalist tenets continue to persuade scholars of many stripes, more than a century later:[4] Anything that is represented whether verbally or (tele)visually is doomed to be digested by us and in the process, be utterly destroyed, simplified, altered beyond recognition,

37

so that we can grasp its meaning. Whatever survives of reality after its peptonizing—James's metaphor for the radical alterations that occur to representations of
the real, similar to the effects of cooking and digestion on food—which irreversibly transforms the texture, color, smells, and taste of the inputs we perceive, is what we naïvely believe to be reality, the truth, and the real. As partak-
ers in this life-long self-delusional banquet, the forlorn conclusion is that we
have to accept that our perception of the real, through whatever kind of representation it comes to us, is in fact a confidence game: ultimately we are contemplating a fake. I entertain a different epistemological belief, and representational
or semiotic theory, which claims that you can have both representations and the
world they (fallibly) convey. So, in a kind of analytical counterpoint, and in an
attempt to answer the questions about Reality TV that I formulated at the start of
this section, I will bring the views of a contemporary James who founded semiotic theory. Also using a metaphor, this time a meteorological one, Peirce offers
a more optimistic account of the mechanism of representation. He claims that
through representation humans are capable of both grasping and assimilating the
meaning of reality, in spite of the subjective and fallible nature of this endeavor:
"everything that is present to us is a phenomental manifestation of ourselves
(which) does not prevent its being a phenomenon of something without us, just
as a rainbow is at once a manifestation of both the sun and the rain."[5]

Based on Peirce's theory, every sign is by necessity a manifestation of both
the subjectivity of its agent and the world's otherness. The fact that a sign—
another name for "representation" in Peirce—can be related to the minds of both
utterer and interpreter, does not stop it from having an epistemic relationship
with elements that are outside of the mind. Peirce defines the real as anything
"whose characters are independent of what anybody may think them to be."[6] An
upshot of this definition is a non-dualistic principle which holds that human perception is both direct and mediated, and which is at the basis of Peirce's semiotic theory, as Ransdell explains it:[7]

> There is no immediate perception in the logical sense of the term 'immediate.'
> All perception is mediated in the sense of being representative. Hence what
> Peirce calls—and would usually be called, or regarded as—'immediate' per-
> ception would be better called 'direct' perception, which differs from 'indirect'
> perception as self-representation differs from other-representation.

This apparent paradox will be solved through the account of indexical representation, which will also serve to explain the longing of Reality TV viewers for an
unmediated access to reality in an overtly mediated environment. Peirce's theoretical claim of the independence of reality of any individual mind leads to a
social vision of representation and to the hope of the community to attain reality
through true representations. This is valid for both a group of scientists and for
mankind at large. Instead of considering the act of understanding reality—or of

grasping it, as James put it in 1906—as synonymous with irreversibly altering or degrading what we seek to know, I will adopt Peirce's model and claim that in spite of their incomplete and fallible nature, we have to rely on representations if we are to have a connection with any kind of reality, no matter how uncertain it may be. The boom of reality TV formats furnishes a good opportunity to test this claim, in spite of the overt manufacturing of the environment which we perceive in the construction of sets and interaction rules for shows such as *Big Brother*. Given the premise that all knowledge of reality is representational, in the rest of this text, arguments will be provided to describe both the kind of access to the real of the format and the expectations of its audience. Both aspects may be summed up in the trans-reality concept. A first, provisional definition of this central notion presents it as a complex blend of show business as usual with the kind of recording of actuality that is associated with the documentary genre. Thus the typical experience of trans-reality for the audience of Reality TV consists in attaining some shards of factuality which manage to come into view through the heavy layers of typical television production make-up.

The Peircean logical model of representation or semiotic has frequently been criticized: one such critique was formulated by Manning, who is disparaging about Peirce's triadic logic, which is inseparable from the pragmatic philosophical framework, describing it as an abstract model of signification. Manning argues that since Peirce was a logician, someone whose main concern was far from society's flux since his "sought-for prize was a code,"[8] this, in his view, makes any contribution of the semiotic to the social sciences irrelevant. Manning goes on to criticize the terminological complexity of Peirce's semiotic as "a vast confusing body of contradictory work that few understand, in part the cause of Peirce's uneven career."[9] He then claims that Peircean theory is individualistic and thus completely alien to all forms of social interaction. This objection presupposes that Peircean pragmaticism is a kind of positivism, or the kind of behaviorism practiced by Morris in his version of the semiotic, as Halton[10] puts it in his response to Manning's critique. It is useful here to recall that when Peirce wrote that: "Logic is rooted in the social principle,"[11] he meant that human beings, insofar as they are meaning-generating creatures, share far more with their neighbors than the notion of personality allows us to realize. This central idea of triadic semiotic has been developed in a book-long study of Peirce's approach to the self,[12] which includes a detailed account of the contrast between James's and Peirce's views of human identity in relationship with society.

Of course, we may err in our imperfect perceptions and interpretations of the world, but representations are all we have to rely on in order to gain some knowledge about anything out there or within ourselves. This non-skeptical but self-critical epistemological take on representation is the poor relation in current media studies. Such a state of things seems to be reproduced in the experience of many TV viewers, especially in the relentless scrutiny to which they subject the goings on in the many formats of Reality TV screened across the world. Between the extremes of total skepticism of the Jamesian, peptonizing kind, and a tentative but lively quest for representational evidence of the real within a Peircean spirit, there is the entire gamut of viewers' attitudes regarding this type of TV program, and the basic motives for watching it. For Peirce, wherever we find it, meaning is the kaleidoscopic, shifting interplay of three modes of representing the real: the iconic, the indexical, and the symbolic. Thus, images, facts, conventions make up our everyday semiotic environment; each type of representation reveals some partial and complementary aspect of the real. In Peirce's representational theory, reality is seen as continuous with its representation, in contrast to the reductionism of Cartesian dualistic oppositions, which pit as irreconcilable poles the authentic against the mediated, in life and in TV genres. The dualistic take on reality underlies the canonical discussions on the honesty of this media endeavor,[13] for critics, scholars, and its regular audience.[14]

The melancholy or bitter complaints about the absence of reality in the representations of Reality TV—and before that, in those of documentary films—are the (usually) unwitting outcome of a conviction that the upshot of representing anything out there is to alter it irreversibly and thus turn any truth it might reveal into a fake. It is a kind of latter day variation of the touch of King Midas: whatever we represent of the world, we turn into dross. I do not claim that there is any kind of direct or explicit influence of William James's thought on every enraged critic or scholar who has written disparagingly about the utter fabrication of every Reality TV format, let alone on the multitudes of viewers of these programs around the world. Nevertheless, the single question obsessing the people I interviewed,[15] and the critical discourse of the media I consider elsewhere[16] is the following: Are the people who appear in *Big Brother* true to themselves or is everything we watch only a huge fabrication? Since this kind of doubt does not normally arise in connection with other TV genres, this one feature makes Reality TV and its formats distinctive, something that does not fit into the category of traditional entertainment and which takes us to a new epistemological realm, what Corner aptly describes as "the post-documentary age."[17]

Based on Peirce's theory of representation, I argue that the claim to the real in Reality TV programming is not wholly unfounded, and this is not due to the good intentions or purity of the media producers, but simply because of the way that signs function, both on and off the screen. This raises the question of how reality is actually transposed into the narrow confines of a house that is surveilled twenty-four hours a day and is inhabited by a group of strangers. This relates to an aesthetic concern, namely, what are the specific narrative modes of representation that structure these TV formats? To help answer this second question, I call on the natural ally of semiotic theory, the philological study of the ways in which, throughout history, different literary genres have endeavored to imitate reality, to reproduce life through the adoption of different textual conventions. If we allow that a TV show, such as *Big Brother,* can be seen as a popular culture modern avatar of the traditional, realistic literary depictions of the past, then Auerbach's study of the modes of representing reality in Western literature, *Mimesis,*[18] can be seen as being useful to analyze the socio-cultural significance of Reality TV as a newcomer to the universe of contemporary media. The notion of "trans-reality" denotes the attempt to reunite what has been the lure of fiction for so many centuries, namely, the dramatic development of events guided by a carefully crafted ending, and the fly-on-the-wall kind of access to common people's everyday life, just as it unfolds before our eyes. Trans-reality is the outcome of blending a traditional way of producing the illusion of reality in Western literature with the fleeting revelations of reality in its three modes of representation: the qualitative (iconic), the existential (indexical) and the conventional (symbolic). The televised observation of everyday life set in an uncanny environment results in an unprecedented mixture of the colorful, crammed with superficial details, and the well-lit mode of representation, characteristic of the Greek epic on the one hand, and the soul-searching, psychologically perspectival depiction of existence brimming with muted, internal conflicts, typical of the mimetic mode of the Old Testament on the other. *Big Brother* can be construed as the commercially successful hybridization of the aristocratic, high mimetic epic mode, translated to a domestic and demotic setting, and the epiphanies of the spiritual or emotional in the lives of common people, steadfastly looked out for by the audience.

In this chapter, from a methodological viewpoint, I draw on these two notions of representation, the one derived from semiotic theory (sign mediation) and the other from literary analysis (mimesis of reality), to analyze some examples taken from my work on the *Big Brother* formats produced in Brazil and Argentina. The claim that in the overtly artificial, uncanny settings of domesticity manufactured for each glocal edition of *Big Brother* nothing of the real is represented and thereby revealed to the audience is untenable. In an always incomplete and fallible way, signs manifest some aspect of the real. From the present perspective, the term "trans-reality" refers to those aspects of the real which transcend the commercial entertainment aim, and reveal information about both the elaborate trappings of a contemporary TV show, as well as the hardships suffered by the subjectivity of those who agree to undergo the ordeals of the self. These shards of reality survive unscathed despite the mighty industrial media machinery employed in the creation of any format of Reality TV.

Searching for the Soul in Endemol's House: The Unfathomable Success Story That Is *Big Brother*

The new-fangled "effect of the real"[19] of *Big Brother* brings to mind an early meditation on a performance that was also based on human hyperbolic exposure to close scrutiny, and which was also surrounded by its loyal audience's unwavering skepticism. In *A Hunger Artist* (first published in 1922), Franz Kafka's nameless hero is a professional faster who resents the mere thought that he could ever cheat his devoted public, and that during his performance he would eat in secret, when no one was watching. Similarly, present day anonymous artists of privacy-deprivation resent any idea that they are not being themselves at all times, even when they are being plainly dishonest or are trying to deceive others into believing them to be what they appear to be. Like Kafka's martyr of the image, the artistes of *Big Brother* are honestly mischievous, authentically dissembling in their real self-enactment, in a house that never sleeps. Although the constant production of abundant bodily evidence from the housemates is as authentic as our sweat in hot weather, in Reality TV all is ultimately for the greater glory of an improvised *dramatis persona* whose single goal is to achieve popularity, to be allowed by the audience vote to stay on in the house, as part of a politics of the good image. To that extent, this audiovisual representation is as symbolic, that is, as conventional, as the politician's carefully rehearsed speech. From this perspective, the participants' behavior could be considered inauthentic. Eventually, every sign generated in the twenty-four hour observed house is interpreted according to the conventions of the medium and of the format; thus, even the body language becomes symbolic. The function of any kind of sign, whether spoken or expressed involuntarily, is to reveal fallibly and incompletely some aspect of the real.

We need to understand the complexity of the kinds of signs that are inseparable from the body and which represent the most basic, animal actuality—the blushes, the sweat, the tears—as well as the highly contrived, neo-folk art of being oneself in a place and a time which conspire violently against that very possibility. This semiotic issue is at the basis of the question that the audience wants answered by watching this program: the search for some truth amidst the rubble of cheap performance.[20] The production teams of any Reality TV format engage in a similar quest, but with a different purpose, hoping to retrieve some nugget of behavior that represents authentic-looking interaction, from a vast sea of mundane debris given off by those bodies in closely surveilled co-existence.

A decade has elapsed since the first broadcast in 1999 by a small-time cable station of what appeared to be a minor, European divertimento, a low cost experimental TV show that would surely not survive a season of local (Dutch) production. Against all expectations, this modestly produced program became a kind of media tsunami, if one is to heed both its wild, unheard of popularity, and the equally wild battery of attacks from the thinking professional minds of media reviewers and many communication scholars. In some cases, the latter chose to simply ignore the phenomenon. Many scholars did not dedicate any academic time or energy to accounting for what was becoming the most noticeable TV success for many years, even when it began to rival traditional genres, such as the daily soap opera, or mobilize large portions of the population.[21]

It seems important to analyze a media phenomenon which celebrated its tenth anniversary and which is still enjoying enormous popularity, which is in inverse proportion to the negative reactions engendered by Reality TV in general, and this format in particular. Of the ever growing range of media products included in that generic labelling Reality TV, I focus here on the format based on twenty-four hour surveillance of the enclosed existence of ordinary people, in the extraordinary circumstances produced by the strange architectural mix of airport terminal, shopping mall, show house and *Sims* video game, which is the *Big Brother* habitat. This televisual realm may be described as "the melochronicle of the interaction order."[22] The concept serves to emphasize the spectacular framing of the humble micro-sociological domain first described by the sociologist Goffman,[23] and the hybrid trans-genre which mixes the documentary recording of the minutiae of the existence of common folks with the melodramatic components associated with soap operas or dramatic sitcoms.

If we can account for the representational and narrative mechanisms of *Big Brother*, for the ways in which the house dwellers signify their existence and are interpreted by their massive audiences throughout the planet, this should contribute to explaining the difference that makes the difference[24] regarding this TV format. A distinctive element is what audiences look for, which then engrosses them and ensures their loyalty to a TV program. In the case of *Big Brother*, this involvement can go on for weeks or even months, with viewers following the routines of the increasingly less anonymous enclosed group of individuals, as the latter go about the house living, loving and, perhaps, lying. The eventuality of the participants' not telling the truth was what many of the viewers of the 2004 Brazilian edition of this TV format continuously tried to detect, as if they were improvised, self-styled *CSI* officers.[25]

Although there is widespread skepticism concerning the sincerity of the participants' behavior, the hope that truth will somehow shine through (false) appearances, in that most unlikely environment, sustains the public's interest. It is not in spite of, but because of this obsessive concern with revelations about the deepest level of human existence, namely, the soul or psyche, that audiences loyal to the format continue to watch in their quest for the ultimate reward or promise of the program, one of the particularly hard to find "regions" of the real, namely, the authentic. A very relevant distinction which constitutes the kernel in the meaning of this TV format is that between *reality* and *authenticity*. Corner proposes that *Big Brother* has modified the traditional documentary debate about "extracting the personal from the social (e.g., all those problems about authenticity in docu-soap) by building its own social precisely for the purpose of revealing the personal."[26] If the real, as Peirce wrote,[27] is a realm that is independent of any individual's opinions, the authentic refers to a subset of that universe. The "personal" referred to by Corner denotes the restricted domain of the self and, in the format, is revealed mainly by those signs that are closest to the body, such as tears, sweat, and blushes. I describe this phenomenon as the "index appeal" of *Big Brother*, to account semiotically for what Hill's empirical reception study of the British edition of the format refers to as its "moments of authenticity."[28] The recording and broadcasting of the mundane, including the minutiae of the human physiological functions, plus the abundant "phatic communion,"[29] that is, small talk about such things as the weather, which serves as the lubricant of existence, are not simple fodder—like the polite conversations satirized by Jonathan Swift in the 18th century.[30] This downpour of apparent triviality serves as privileged access to the bedrock level of humanity, to the participants' authentic self. The self-appointed task of the *Big Brother* audience is to search for these modest epiphanies by separating the nuggets of authenticity from the dross of faked appearances, the overt and glaring fabrications of everyday life. Such is the representational blend which constitutes the promised trans-reality, which is the goal of the loyal viewers of this television format.

A Representation Is Haunting the Globalized World—the Indexical Signs of the Real

Elsewhere I have studied the mechanism of meaning of factuality programming[31] in order to understand the signs that generate what Corner considers to be central to it, namely, that it is "common, real and honest, three attributes,"[32] that are the basis of the audience's appreciation. My approach allowed me to analyze how these three qualities are embodied in images thought to represent the national (e.g., of Argentina or of Brazil), as embodied in the participants, and particularly the winners of these TV programs. The title of this section paraphrases the beginning of *The Communist Manifesto* and alludes to the unsettling impact of a mode of media representation that has an existential link with the object that it represents, namely, the indexical sign or index. Instead of the classic question in the social sciences, "How is the real constructed?" my text assumes that reality is represented. The basic premise of social constructionism is "that any so-called reality is, in the most immediate and concrete sense, the mental construction of those who believe they have discovered and investigated it."[33] The theoretical and methodological framework I adopt, Peirce's semiotic model, posits a logical continuity between the real and its representation: "a realist is simply one who knows no more recondite reality than that which is represented in a true representation."[34] The type of representation that Peirce calls indexical is that of a sign "which fulfils [its] function by virtue of a character which it could not have if its object did not exist, but which it will continue to have whether it be interpreted or not."[35] Similar to footprints or fossils, two examples of indexes, the function of the signs given off by our bodies is not primarily to communicate anything, thus they can go unperceived insofar as they are produced sometimes accidentally, physiologically. Though peripheral to verbal production, indexes express moods, and attitudes, for instance, when we blush or sweat as we talk. Indexical representations furnish the material evidence of our bodily existence; they inevitably accompany what is said like a tangible halo on anyone who engages in communication. Indexical signs are our factual, tenacious shadows.

What distinguishes Peirce's semiotic model is the process-like, triadic functioning of representation that it postulates: besides the sign that we perceive and the object that it represents, there is still another sign which is generated in this process, namely, the interpretant. In that consists the *triadic* logical mechanism of semiotic representation. Therefore, the meaning of any sign is to be found in another, more developed sign of itself. In Peircean semiotic, meaning is the logical upshot of the sign-mediated object (equal to whatever is represented). Examples of interpretants are the critical reviews of *Big Brother* and the opinions of the public about the TV show, examples of which I gathered in previous field work.[36] A dynamical interpretant is the technical term for any historical, embodied interpretation or actually produced meaning, which is considered analytically apart from the interpreters who understand it. The distinctive feature of the "professional" dynamical interpretants produced by media critics is their status as influential public signs, which are thus prone to generating many other interpretants, once they reach their publics. Let us turn to a concrete example from the first edition of *Gran Hermano* (Telefé 2001), Argentina's version of the Endemol format, in which we can observe both the indexical signs that are the trademark of this Reality show, and also the kind of indexically-based opinions (dynamical interpretants) that are the response to those indexical signs.

In *Gran Hermano,* whenever the young attractive blonde woman, Tamara, was summoned by a masculine disembodied voice to the isolated room known as "the confessional,"[37] to fulfill her duty of nominating two candidates for eviction, she dissolved into tears. By the time she had reached the point of uttering the second name, a painful process that took a long time, the pretty, exotic features of Tamara had been replaced by a swollen, red face that was the very picture of grief. So, not only did she tell the disembodied voice that she felt like a traitor at that moment, but her intense weeping had disfigured her usually harmonious features; they had been transformed by her uncontrollable emotions. This very obvious physical change, in itself both an indexical sign of suffering, and a dynamic interpretant of a central rule of the format, produced sympathetic interpretants among the audience, which underlined the indexical and thereby authentic nature of her behavior in the house:

But in the very end, I felt sorry for her. I said, well, if Marcelo doesn't win, I want Tamara to win! (Female university student, *Gran Hermano* 1)

But that chick [Tamara] was like . . . really sensitive, she looked like . . . a chick . . . who really cared. She lived in a state of a . . . kind of . . . constant sensitivity. At every instant, she started to cry. (Male university student, *Gran Hermano*1)

Oh yeah! She was crying all the time, did you see her eyes what they looked like? (Female university student, *Gran Hermano*1)

The pre-eminence of this type of audience response in my studies, as well as the observation of the functioning of the TV format *Big Brother* in two of its regional productions have led me to posit as its specific semiotic feature the representational mechanism of *index appeal*. I can illustrate this further through the example of an elaborate ceremony that occupies a noticeable portion of *Big Brother Brasil*, shown on every second Tuesday during the run, that is, the day of "the firing squad line up" (in Portuguese: *paredão*). This metaphor was used by a participant in the first edition of *Big Brother Brasil* (2002), and alludes to the ritual eviction of one of the two chosen housemates. A key component in this ritual is the attaching of electronic gadgets to the bodies of the two would-be evictees, which gives a real time, exact reading of their heartbeats. Through an on screen visual device reminiscent of hospital operating room equipment, viewers of *Big Brother Brasil* receive live, precise information about the levels of anxiety in each participant as the threat of expulsion draws near. Rather than the attractive participant (icon), or a persuasive speech (symbol) such as we might expect from a well-rehearsed actor, what matters most in this example is the discharge of bodily indices as a form of "semiotic transpiration." The indexical representation of the semiotic object—the predictable unease of the potential soon-to-be-evicted participants—captures the public's gaze. The audience reacts as if it were under the influence of "a pointing finger [that] exercises a real physiological force over the attention, like the power of a mesmerizer, and directs it to a particular object of sense."[38] If we apply Peirce's definition of the indexical sign to the media realm, we can account for a kind of meaning response that is based on the physical rather than on the verbal (symbolic), and which I will call the "index-appeal" of Reality TV formats. This almost tangible representational effect is a basic component of the aesthetic of this Reality show.[39] The proposed term is intended to hint at and contrast with the kind of fascination exerted by the unreachable, Olympian divas of classic Hollywood, that is, iconically-based sex appeal. What the new-fangled reality TV formats represent through the index-appeal mechanism is trans-reality, that is, a mixture of an overtly fabricated TV show, of the kind which has been produced by the medium since the earliest sitcoms (*I Love Lucy*, 1951-1957) and talk shows (*The Tonight Show*, 1954-), together with body symptoms and interactional behavior which are perceived as the real thing, as the revelation of authenticity in the participants, despite the acknowledged staging and high artificiality of the TV production. Through the qualitative methodology of semiotic analysis of both the reality TV production features and audience response we can analyze this new mode of mediated representation which is trans-reality. The notion of a dominantly indexical trans-reality allows us to overcome the blind alley of dualism, which underlies James' opposition of faked (represented) vs. ungraspable (un)representable reality. It is not necessary to believe in the good intentions of TV-reality contestants or in the dubious honesty of the format producers to claim that the basic interest for the audience lies in the contemplation and interpretation of represented factuality. We must bear in mind that every indexical element—the body semiotic—is practically inseparable from a colorful array of theatricality (music, editing, subtitles, voice over, etc), which are the iconic and symbolic components of the representation. This is what constitutes the "melochronicle"[40] of this trans-reality, a hybrid of spontaneity and artificiality. The broadening of the traditional class of "discourses of sobriety," which corresponded to the category of the audiovisual chronicle, as in classic documentaries,[41] has brought attention to this mixture of the everyday with the utmost mundane, deprived of any visible kinship with politics or ideology, at least not in the classical manner (e.g., socialism vs. capitalism) which was depicted by documentaries through the twentieth century.

From the Index Appeal to the Para-tactile Interaction of Reality TV

The prevalence of indexes in the media representation of behavior of participants, such as Tamara in *Gran Hermano*, coupled with the growing interest of the audience in all forms of body-prints, such as Tamara's strong physiological, emotional reaction to the living conditions in the house, foster a kind of intimacy that is quite different from that produced from watching, say, a work of fiction. This distinctive media experience recalls Horton and Wohl's pioneering study of the kind of relationship established between the audience and the television presenters who migrated to that new medium from the radio, half a century ago.[42]

What these social psychologists described as "para-social interaction" with television denotes a feeling of imaginary intimacy between the viewers and the personalities of the then recent mass medium. I consider that the index appeal of programs like *Big Brother* is a development of this kind of imaginary intimate relationship. The relevance of Horton and Wohl's concept for my approach to Reality TV justifies the following lengthy quotation, which includes a reference to self-enactment, which is also part of this TV genre:

> In television, especially, the image which is presented makes available nuances of appearance and gesture to which ordinary social perception is attentive and to which interaction is cued. Sometimes the "actor"—whether he is playing himself or performing in a fictional role—is seen engaged with others; but often he faces the spectator, uses the mode of direct address, talks as if he were

conversing personally and privately. The audience, for its part, responds with something more than mere running observation; it is, as it were, subtly insinuated into the programme's action and internal social relationships and, by dint of this kind of staging, is ambiguously transformed into a group which observes and participates in the show by turns. The more the performer seems to adjust his performance to the supposed response of the audience, the more the audience tends to make the response anticipated. This simulacrum of conversational give and take may be called para-social interaction.[43]

For media representations that are based on index appeal, such as *Big Brother*, I propose that the relationship between audience and the self-enacting performers be described as a "*para-tactile* interaction." Instead of relying heavily on phatic verbal communication to create an imaginary bond with the audience (i.e., the para-social interaction as a magical divide that viewers can cross to feel that they are on a friendly basis with someone that they know that they do not actually know), *Big Brother* constitutes a semiotic "affordance"[44] for engaging in an imagined bodily contact experience. This TV program furnishes viewers with some "latent possibilities" of its structure to enable them to have the experience of almost touching the performers. In the case of "television personalities,"[45] para-social relationship or interaction is the result of the performance of someone who engages viewers in a simulated friendly, easy-going aside, while he or she interviews, is announcing or presenting the contestants (of quiz shows). This TV character engages in the kind of endearing small talk more usually experienced in exchanges with neighbors, relatives or work colleagues. For such a semiotic production to become effective, all backstage behavior[46] must be meticulously kept out of sight and out of hearing. In the case of Reality TV, the lure of its anonymous participants is based on the promise that the audience will have full access to the backstage of their lives, even the "deep backstage."[47] For this to happen, there must be constant displays of indexical signs, wherein lies the index appeal of the format. For this reason, we can construe the relationship between audience and format as one that is close to the skin of the participants, as in pornography, but without that kind of extremely narrow script and totally predictable narrative outcome. Instead, the audience expects some modest epiphanies, enabled by those indexes, which will point roughly but surely to that which is neither visible nor audible, the depth of the person's character, her true self.

Another element which contributes to the effect of *para-tactile* interaction is what I dubbed elsewhere "internal zapping,"[48] which is part of the *Big Brother* viewing experience. Instead of just switching channels via the remote control, viewers can modify the narrative line, they can interfere by favoring alternative diegetic outcomes by voting to evict someone, or by trying to persuade others to allow a particular participant to stay in the house to facilitate a budding love interest or allow development of a growing and potentially explosive rivalry. In a literal sense, this is a way of meddling in or of laying a hand on the development of the interaction order in the house. Although to vote for or against the permanence of a housemate is a very limited type of viewer participation, it is a significant change from being able only to move away from a program using the remote control. Previously, TV viewers have not had a say in plot development, apart from the cases of audience participation that are used in focus groups in the production of series and soap operas.

As a consequence of the index-appeal and para-tactile relationships, which are the main semiotic components of the *Big Brother* format, the audience entertains the illusion not of being acquaintances or friends of these persons—who are not TV personalities, in the sense discussed by Horton and Wohl[49]—but the belief of having gathered enough physical evidence to allow them to experience a kind of non-mediated contact with them. Viewers feel they have become so close as to acquire a kind of ephemeral but tangible carnal knowledge of the participants. By the end of an edition of *Big Brother*, these performers of themselves have wept, kissed, hollered, got drunk, said regrettable or opportune things, but more than anything, they have left behind an enormous number of body-prints, a term I use to refer to all kinds of physical evidence, and a broader category than fingerprints or other physical indexes. This semiotic perspiration is unique to this format. When we find its equivalent in the fictional domain, it is the outcome of a carefully written and directed effort which an actor must follow, according to her or his talent to make it more convincing, even memorable, as a fictional performance. This is not the case in Reality TV programs, even granting that most if not everything that the participants do is done purposefully, to create a good impression, ultimately to win in this gamedoc situation. There is no proper space or time for rehearsal, no deep recess of the house where the avid cameras and microphones will not be able to catch red-handed the housemate who tried to practize this dramaturgical trick, before enacting it in front of others.

If, as Corner[50] proposes, we are living in "a post-documentary age," one in which the most popular representation of factuality is that of "documentary-as-diversion," the para-tactile interaction may well account for the success of a media production characterized by "a performative, playful element." This development gives viewers access—maybe in a sort of regressive, child-like manner—to the kind of playing in which children engage when they handle toys, be they human-like or not. Touching is an essential part of the sort of playfulness that is inseparable from physical activity, and which thus involves the whole body. The practice of internal zapping enables viewers to physically and imaginatively participate in the choice of some narrative outcomes rather than others. This engagement with the format comes close to the playfulness involved in the Sims videogame, when the players build a house and choose a lifestyle for the members of that fictional family.

In Reality TV, there is not the "willing suspension of disbelief"[51] typical of fiction, but rather the opposite attitude: a mixture of astuteness, with a hunter-like disposition to collect evidence. Viewers behave like *CSI* officers on holiday, who are exercising their skills in a leisure-driven, non-criminal environment. The readiness with which critics and to a certain extent viewers in my research, refer to the housemates as "characters" betrays a willful blurring of the borders between fictional and factual entertainment, which may be more in the beholder's eyes and beliefs, than in the actual format of *Big Brother*. The index-appeal of this TV program depends to a large extent on the performance being a self-enactment. No doubt a great deal of spontaneity and unselfconsciousness is by necessity lost in attempting to carry out that very action. However, self-enactment is a basic tool in the kit that every participant must take to the house together with his or her clothes and the few precious belongings they are allowed. Also, the challenge of how to convince oneself and many millions of viewers is formidable. One must persuade everyone that the old self is still doing its thing, that it is acting in its previous-to-entry-to-the-house ways. And this task must be accomplished in spite of the Boschian (as in Hieronymus) surroundings that the body and its soul must inhabit with no chance of leaving the premises except by eviction, voluntary exit, or fainting. Even sleep is a closely controlled activity, since it may easily turn into an abrupt awakening, a fight, or an erotic encounter with another participant. Therein lays the uncanny, postmodern talent of these artistes of privacy-deprivation: they must persuade us bodily, not verbally, that their sacrifice of the social backstage[52] is both painful and necessary to attain the feat of the presentation of normality in the most abnormal conditions. That is precisely what Goffman[53] describes as the folk art of "self-enactment" in everyday life. Such as when we are going about in our normal, non-self-conscious way, say in a big city, late at night, or in the course of our habitual walk home, we might spot a potential threat, a silhouette that could reveal the presence of a dangerous criminal lurking and waiting to pounce on us, or it could be just more of the same, i.e., sheer normality, someone waiting for a bus, or taking the air. From that moment on, every step we take will be laborious, what was an automatic behavior becomes one of the hardest dramaturgic feats: to continue existing while pretending that nothing is out of order, when our alarm system has been fired, because we have spotted something in the vicinity that may—or may not—harm us. We are now performing our old, now longed for self, the normal appearance which was not just an appearance a short while before, but the faithful expression of our spirit, the emotion we show when there is no particular or strong emotion to be shown.

In order to illustrate the apparently impossible challenge of going from an unnoticeable self-enactment to a wild performance of the self, which, nevertheless, has enough violence and self-destructiveness to make the housemate bitterly regret what she or he has done, I describe below a peculiarly violent incident from the fourth edition of *Big Brother Brasil*, which involved a fierce quarrel between two women. It allows us to observe at close range the working of index appeal and the production of a para-tactile interaction based on such a representation, which becomes barely tolerable for the television viewers. The index-dependent impression of authenticity occurs regardless of the positive or negative impression that the scene produces on the audience, as they go from watching a paradigmatic instance of light sociability, a cheerful party, to witnessing the very epitome of deep backstage interaction, the exposure of raw anger through uncontrolled bodily signs and offensive words.

Near the end of the fourth series of *Big Brother Brasil*, there was a showdown that had racial overtones, between Marcela, a white upper-middle class woman, and Solange, a black lower class petrol station attendant. Everything was rolling smoothly at this Mexican party organized by the production team in order to entertain the few survivors, only five participants, and also to offer some light-hearted fun to the audience. Two of the women previously had won a visit to a very fancy restaurant, where neither was able to behave as was expected; they had thus transformed a luxurious dining occasion into a slapstick comedy. Now their colorful big Mexican hats and wide peasant skirts provided the touch of exoticism that the typical food and drink completed. Throughout most of the party, there had been the predictable outgrowth of phatic communion, which marks these occasions as a paroxysm of normality, a way of making visible and celebrating, in a Durkheimian manner, the very cement of society. After large quantities of heady tequila had been consumed, a politely contained grudge between Marcela and Solange, who had quarrelled in the house on many occasions, exploded, its viciousness in terms of its non-verbal and verbal violence exceeding the levels of argument in a typical episode. The fact that they were women, that they were visibly drunk, and that their race and social upbringing were overtly different did much to increase the impact of the indexes which were given off during that crisis in the interaction order.

After separating themselves from the rest of the group, and from the atmosphere of easy-going festivity, the women became involved in an escalation of ferocious aggression whose climax included an exuberant indexical duel. Visibly drunk, Solange pointed out that Marcela was obsessed by the idea of winning the big prize of that edition ($250,000). In a similar altered state, Marcela came up with a retort that seems difficult to surpass for its ferocity, especially because it was uttered when she was in that physical condition. What Marcela told Solange, as a reply to her accusation of being exceedingly greedy, was disturbingly tinged with barely disguised racism. Surprisingly, she first said she wished Solange, her rival, who was poor and uneducated, could win all of the money of the big prize. And then the shocking explanation of her "good" desire became apparent: "I wish you won all that money, because you are more stupid than a dog, and even that amount of money will just be no good for you!" So

strong was the index appeal of this much commented on and controversial episode, that the next day, the presenter, a prestigious journalist, made a curious
announcement. He said, as a form of warning which, of course, was also intended to whet the appetites of the viewers, that what they were going to watch
was something that made you feel ashamed for the behavior of the persons involved. Although he did not say as much, it was as if he were explaining that on
that occasion there had been just too much indexicality, that their animal selves
had got the better of the participants. It was not only the speech of hatred addressed to the other, which, of course, was problematic enough, it was also the
fact that these women had gone from the pleasant exchange of trivialities, which
enables us to interact smoothly with others, to a deep recess where symbols become too close to indexes, where raw rage replaces articulate anger. Once again,
the authentic as a specific and privileged manifestation of the real comes to the
fore, in what became for the public a memorable, even if a shocking instance of
index appeal, in the house of *Big Brother*. The reddened eyes, the trembling lips,
and the slurring of the words worked like an indexical uppercut for the viewers
that I interviewed in the south of Brazil. These women, according to viewers,
had been both authentic and unbearable: although what transpired seemed undoubtedly and disturbingly a revelation of the self of these housemates, these
viewers expressed their concern for insufficient symbolic mediation, which
would have stopped this outpouring from happening. There was great keenness
to discuss in some detail the purport of this unsettling moment in *Big Brother
Brasil* and, predictably, these two participants were soon evicted from the house.
Indexical signs furnish solid evidence of the authentic feelings of those who live
in the house, but this does not automatically entail an approval of what is thus
revealed of their self. In this case, the para-tactile experience was simply too
much to endure for the majority of the audience, as the producers realized,
which prompted them to have the presenter introduce that day's slice of life with
an unusual, apologetic meta-message. It may be opportune to quote Peirce's
pragmatic account of this controversial and crucial entity, the true self, which
constitutes a tantalizing prize for those who regularly watch *Big Brother*: "When
I speak of a man's Real Self, or true Nature, I mean the very Springs of Action
in him which mean how he would act."[54] To acquire reliable knowledge of the
authentic self amounts to grasping the real meaning of that person, to knowing
the way in which he or she would act in certain circumstances.

Big Brother as a Latter Day Avatar of the High Epic and Low Demotic Modes of Representing Reality

> The idea that everyday life is dramatically enthralling, that it is fascinating
> simply in its boundless humdrum detail, is one of the great revolutionary con-
> ceptions in human history, which Charles Taylor in *Sources of the Self* claims

as Christian in inspiration.[55]

Once upon a time, there was a narrator who could afford to engage in a kind of *"mythos interruptus."* He brought his story-telling to a halt, at the peak of its tension, and instead of continuing to build the suspense, he would wander away from its focus, and calmly invite the readers—originally listeners, since I am talking about Homer—to appreciate, in full detail, a well lit present time which depicted a remote landscape of people, places and events. We might as well follow here Auerbach,[56] from whose treatise on the representation of reality in Western literature this account is drawn, and quote Schiller on Homer's procedure. The Greek poet gives us "simply the quiet existence and operation of things in accordance with their natures."[57] Were we to change only a few minor details, such as depicting the quiet but altered existence of ordinary people according to their natures, or to what the casting specialists in the production of *Big Brother* deem them to be, we would have the basic formula of one of the most successful Reality TV formats of all time. I would like to bring out the rhetorical parallelism between what Auerbach presents as the two modes of rendering the real in terms of verbal art throughout the ages—his study goes from the *Odyssey* to the modernist narrative experiment of Virginia Woolf—and the mechanism of the television format *Big Brother* for representing realistically the plain lives of people whose task is simply to be in the company of strangers, while being filmed as if what they were doing and saying during ten weeks was worthy of recording for posterity. What used to be the privilege of the explorers and adventurers, the heirs of Odysseus, as they climbed Everest or plunged into the depths of the oceans, at the risk of their lives, has now become the acquired right of anyone willing to sign up for a collective confinement under the silent gaze of multiple cameras. Those who are ready to sacrifice what most people consider to be as precious as freedom, namely, their privacy, agree to hang around, sleep, love, and rage, not in the company of those they choose, or their families, but within a group of carefully picked partners, whose existence is more than likely to bring about conflict. Such is the fate of these artistes of privacy-deprivation.

In what has become a classic treatment of realistic, mimetic representation in Western literature, Auerbach presents two opposite ways of rendering the real. One involves filling the page with every little detail, no matter how mundane, concerning the daily existence of the fictional characters. Be they Olympian divine creatures or, much less frequently, modest shepherds, everyone whose life was illuminated by the epic narrative focus would become totally visible, because "Homer . . . knows no background. What he narrates is for the time being the only present."[58] I am tempted to refer to this high mimetic mode as "H," both for Homeric and for Hollywood: every formulaic blockbuster, as well as many of the most creative commercial products of that dream factory can be correctly characterized by that powerful narrative beam which leaves no feature in the dark, and which invites viewers to delight in the rich geography of studio sets and natural surroundings. Across the genres of commercial cinema that mimetic mechanism remains unchanged: the cameras and the sound devices will represent as vividly as is humanly and technologically possible, the minutiae of existence, in order to create the verisimilitude that we have come to associate with the Hollywood film factory, and then, in reduced dimensions, with television's series, sitcoms and all kinds of entertainment, including Reality TV.

At the other end of the representation spectrum, there is that eerily quiet realm which Auerbach presents through his analysis of the biblical episode of Abraham's blind obedience to God as he is about to sacrifice his only son Isaac.[59] While "Homeric style [leaves] nothing which it mentions half in darkness, to represent phenomena in a fully externalized form, visible and palpable in all their parts,"[60] the Old Testament leaves almost everything which is crucial unsaid, elliptical to the point of forcing readers to follow as the only possible route that of their imagination. What were these characters feeling and thinking, while they proceeded in such eerie silence to accomplish the terrible fate that had been ordained from above? This is a narrative chiaroscuro, a Rembrandt-like rendering of a terrible crisis in the life of Abraham, whose emotions, expressions and thoughts are completely concealed by the laconic text. In contradistinction to the "H" mimetic mode, which all takes place in the foreground and which privileges an absolute present, which even includes detailed references to long past episodes, this psychological kind of mimesis favors the perspective, the depth between the little that we learn from indexes, and all that we have to conjure as concealed symbols about this tragic episode.

I propose that the incidents of the interaction order represented by the Reality TV format are a mixture or hybrid of both mimetic modes, which accounts for its being a trans-genre. On the one hand, there are the signs of embodied existence, which are shown in such minute detail that only pornography has approached. On the other hand, there is a kind of self-exploration and of emotional upheaval of the participants which cannot but leave much for the viewers of *Big Brother* to imagine, to guess, to suspect. What is the truth in all the words said, in all the gestures displayed? What is sheer fabrication, deceitful behavior, to persuade viewers of something which is lacking in the participants—simulation—or of something that they want to conceal and which is there to discover—dissimulation? This intellectual and emotional activity of the audience is as much part of the experience of the program as the gossip about their scandalous behavior, as in the drunken quarrel of the two women in *Big Brother Brasil* described above.

In a provocative review of a recent re-edition of *Mimesis*, Eagleton[61]posits an ideological parallelism between two unlikely "romantic populists": Auerbach, the German philologist and the Russian theorist Bakhtin. In the critic's view, "the anti-Fascist poetics" of Auerbach, and "the anti-Stalinist one" of the other, make them construe "realism in the broadest sense [as] a matter of the vernacular. It is the artistic word for a warm-hearted populist humanism." Eagleton writes that rather than an epistemological or formalist analysis, it is a political position, a defense of moral values, which made Auerbach conceive of "realism [as] the artistic form that takes the life of the common people with supreme seriousness, in contrast to an ancient or neoclassical art which is static, hierarchical, dehistoricised, elevated, idealist and socially exclusive."[62]

I now recall an episode from the fifth edition of *Big Brother Brasil*, which blends the high and the low mimesis, by representing the lives of the common people, with a strongly demotic flavor, in contrast to the orderly separation of high and low, which is typical of the aristocratic epic genre of classical times. As in Eagleton's critical view of Auerbach's "populist humanism," I posit a new form of literary realism where we least expect it: in the depiction of the lives of common people in *Big Brother*, but not on account of the "supreme seriousness" of the producers, but because, like humidity in a house, that serious attitude present in people's lives may get through any kind of representational obstacle, and come to embody worthy values and ideals for the audience.

Shortly after the beginning of the fifth edition of *Big Brother Brazil*, the atmosphere in the house had become very tense because there was a radical division between two antagonistic groups. One of them had organized a thinly disguised homophobic conspiracy, which had Rogerio as its leader. He was a white, handsome, upper middle class doctor. From the participants in the "opposite faction," he had targeted the one he thought was the most vulnerable, a black, self-made university teacher from very humble origins, Jean Wyllis (who eventually won that edition), who made no effort to conceal his homosexuality. He began to fear for his future in the house, as he realized that the men and women in the other group were actively plotting his eviction. One evening, the audience saw him sobbing quietly, thus giving vent to his melancholy, as he lay on a couch in the garden. Jean was in the company of two rather marginalized women—one embodied the stereotype of the frivolous blonde, Grazie, a beautiful, rather simple, childish woman, who later was hired to take part in the Globo Network soap operas.[63] The other woman was a glaring transgression of the unwritten TV norms regarding acceptable appearance: she was a poor, uneducated middle-aged black woman, who wore no make-up and used none of the other front stage visual strategies. Instead of being admitted through the conventional casting procedure, Marielza, who came from a shanty town, had won her place in the house through a raffle organized by the production team for the readers of the *Big Brother Brasil* fanzine. (The fourth edition had been won by a poor young woman called Cida, who had similar characteristics to Marielza, and who had also gained admission to the house through sheer luck.) The scene was an involuntary sociological portrait of the inequalities and rare opportunities in that vast Latin American country.

Grazie and Marielza were sitting next to Jean trying, without much success, to comfort him. All of this changed, when Grazie, at the end of her tether, told Jean—supportively—that it was only he who felt the prejudice against gay people, a prejudice that he wrongly attributed to the others in the house. At that point, as if responding to a powerful inner call, Jean literally lifted himself out of his self-pity and, adopting a didactic attitude, which went well with his use and evident mastery of the Portuguese language, explained, softly but firmly, that the easy-going country which is Brazil could often be very gentle,[64] but also was prejudiced against people like him—poor, black, and gay. Thus, what began as a typical break-down scene, one those "money-shots" so sought after by the production team of the format, became a stirring lesson about equal rights that was broadcast from that most unlikely place in no uncertain terms.

Maybe Paulo Freire, whose work on the pedagogy of the oppressed[65] is well known in his own country and abroad, would not have found anything to complain about in this short but powerful speech by Jean. Besides, seldom can this kind of talk in defense of minorities have reached such a large audience as the one enjoyed by *Big Brother Brasil*. The scene could not have been more disturbing for a classic realistic canon: a university professor, who had just dried his tears of self-pity, caused by what he thought was his imminent expulsion from a TV program that is the emblem of all that high culture finds terribly wrong with mass media, had risen above his private and publicly exposed misery—which could well be a strategy to gain sympathizers, come eviction day—to articulate a relevant and well expressed defense of a non-dominant sexual orientation. This is a case of what could be called *neo-documentarism*: out of overt self-interest, a person, not a character unless in metaphorical and rather misleading usage, as he is not following a script, improvises words and gestures to express a strong emotion or a relevant idea, in a mediated and persuasive way.

In that episode in the fifth edition of *Big Brother Brasil*, there was a smooth blend of the two opposite mimetic modes described by Auerbach. On the one hand, viewers appreciated, through close ups and even subtitles when people were whispering, everything that transpired in the scene which was represented. No detail escaped the well-trained eyes and the attentive ears of the audience, which normally delights in the accents that participants cannot but display as they talk, and with the gestures that also reveal which region of that large country they come from. The same applies to culinary tastes, to the way the participants moved around the house, etc. Little is left to the imagination due to the extensive and thorough coverage typical of this TV format. However, there is also a psychological depth dimension in this narrative, one that corresponds to the opposite mimetic mode. It somehow resembles the representation mode of the Old Testament, which leaves so much unsaid and so much to be imagined by the reader. The unexpected leap from a purely emotional reaction, from the unmistakable signs of self-pity expressed by the body of Jean Wyllis, to his spontaneous testimony, which brought together his own personal ordeal with something that went well beyond it, to include the suffering endured by any person due to his or her social condition or race or sexual orientation, in Brazil. The coexistence of both mimetic modes in this scene is another clear instance of the complex nature of the trans-genre of this Reality TV program, as well as one of the reasons for its interest for world-wide audiences.

The journey from an overtly superficial display of emotions, small talk, flirting, and the self-enacted basic functions of human survival to the kind of self-enquiry which that young man embarked upon in that edition of *Big Brother Brasil,* constitutes a distinctive element of factuality programming. Without adopting a populist viewpoint that would celebrate the inclusion of the common people, it must be said that this episode is a representation of someone's struggle for his own voice, in a most unlikely place, for a person's emancipation. And yet, just as Auerbach points out that the single gesture of Abraham during that dark night of his soul is when he raises his eyes, as they are about to reach the terrible destination to which he is leading his only son Isaac, so this concrete attempt at saying what had to be said in a place overtly designed for other, lighter purposes, managed to create the kind of narrative chiaroscuro which inaugurated the modern, psychological novel, as a consequence of the mixing up of the humble and the sublime, the two opposite mimetic modes of Western civilization.

Representing Reality in the Age of the Index Appeal and of Para-tactile Interaction

What is the trans-reality involved in this glocal TV format called *Big Brother,* and in the many versions and variations that are at present filling so many hours of open and cable TV around the world? Through the semiotic effect of index appeal, the audience engages the format created by Endemol and its vast media progeny in a *para-tactile* interaction. This seems to be the next evolutionary step of the TV medium, following the illusory relationship of intimacy with the first television personalities, who unilaterally addressed their viewers by means of cheerful small talk. Thus, the television audience has gone from enjoying the kind of experience which is to be had with close friends, with the people who fall within the range of our phatic communion on a day to day basis, to an even closer, vicarious kind of intimacy. Through the reliance on mediated indexical signs, this globalized, alluring song of the body is displayed as the main ingredient of the represented interaction order of most Reality TV formats. It enables the audience to imagine an almost tangible contact with self-enacting performers who do not address it, but tacitly invite millions of people to watch closely the formerly restricted backstage of their lives.

Rather than concluding apocalyptically that the double, the simulacrum or the simulation of the real has finally and irreversibly substituted reality in contemporary mass media, as a changeling in the old legend of the stolen and exchanged infant, I believe that it is closer to the truth of the functioning of this kind of Reality TV to think that there is a different kind of access, of referential relationship, to the represented object, that of trans-reality. A kind of neo-documentarism of the mundane and common is sustained by vast amounts of freshly given off indexes, which are peppered with verbal signs, as in the case of Jean Wyllis's testimony against prejudice. But even in the case of that exceptionally—for *Big Brother Brasil* standards, that is—articulate housemate, it was the fact of his being there, of his lying on a couch, of his being seen crying softly in front of fellow participants, and of so many millions of Brazilian TV viewers, that gave his words such repercussion and which probably contributed to his winning that 2005 edition of the program. In other words, had the same person, with identical enlightened ideas, and even with his talent for expressing them,[66] spoken in the framework of a conventional educational TV program, he would probably not have had the same kind of impact on Brazilian public opinion. Such an effect was undoubtedly due to that speech having been formulated as this man was living and suffering, inside the house of *BB*. It is not only the sheer quantitative difference in the size of the audience, but also and decisively the fundamental and distinctive hegemony of the indexical signs in that program which gave his symbols—the words he uttered on that occasion—an entirely different, epic dimension: The lived experience of somebody who literally lifted himself from his abjection, in order to do what he felt had to be done, without the benefit of a backstage in which to rehearse his performance. Thus, the impression of having interacted with the true self of that person was the semiotic outcome of the representation of trans-reality by this TV format on that episode, and on many others.

Drawing on Peirce's sign model and Auerbach's analysis of the literary representation of reality, we can conclude that in some formats of Reality TV, such as *Big Brother*, there is a distinctive kind of semiotic functioning which results from the peculiar mixture of the two opposite modes of mimesis. They are based on the hegemony of two different kinds of signs which constitute this trans-genre. The epic or "H" mimetic mode depends on the foregrounding of indexical signs, which are staged only in the present, so that the factual components of our everyday life and environment may serve to identify us. The other mimetic mode, the one that favors the perspectival representation of human psychology, that modern avatar of the soul, depends for its work on our symbols. I will not denounce this new form of popular culture as the ultimate exploitation of the people. Neither will I praise it as a kind of redemptive folk art, an aesthetic production which gives a voice to those who never had it before on TV. It may be more productive, from an analytical viewpoint, to describe the basic effect of such television formats on the audience by means of an enriched theory of human representation. Thus, the index-appeal and the para-tactile interaction which I claim account for the trans-reality generated by these Reality TV formats, may contribute to our understanding of both their semiotic mechanism and their relationship with the TV audience. From this analytical perspective, a possible way to understand the concept of trans-reality in relation with Reality TV is that there is no abolition of the structural border between fact and fiction in this trans-genre, but a playful, imaginative engagement with the acquired social skill of self-enactment of both participants and viewers. Viewers, however, seem to practice such an activity for a serious purpose: the exploration of the self.

Notes

1. Concerning the conceptual distinction genre/format which I use throughout this text, the term "format" is to "genre" what Starbucks is to a coffeehouse. The former lives in its serial incarnation, as a letter type is embodied in its tokens, so that it can be easily identified wherever it occurs. The latter is a class, a general way of organizing an event, namely, the consumption of coffee and pastries, and its concrete instances can be quite heterogeneous. Such is the relationship between the globalized franchises of *Big Brother* and Reality TV as a broad TV genre.

2. "In 1994, the production companies of two major television producers in the Netherlands, Joop van den Ende and John de Mol, merged to become Endemol. This merger triggered the international development of the Endemol Group and since then Endemol has rapidly expanded to become a leading format creation and production company." (Information drawn from the History section of the official Endemol website, www.endemol.com/About%20Endemol/Default.aspx?fID=7129&rID=18.)

3. James, 109 (emphasis in original).

4. For a recent discussion and a critical definition of anti-representationalism in the work of James and other pragmatists, see Jones, 1604ss.

5. Pierce, CP 5.283.

6. Peirce, CP 5.405.

7. Ransdell, 58

8. Manning, 144.

9. Manning, 144.

10. Halton, 122.

11. Peirce, CP 2.654.

12. Colapietro.

13. Corner.

14. Andacht, 2005.

15. Andacht, 2004.

16. Andacht, 2005.

17. Corner, 98.

18. Auerbach.

19. Barthes.

20. Andacht, 2004.
21. Andacht, 2005.
22. Andacht, 2003a.
23. Goffman, 1983.
24. Bateson.
25. Andacht, 2004, 128.
26. Corner, 257.
27. Peirce, CP 5.405.
28. Hill, 335.
29. Malinowski.
30. Partridge.
31. Andacht, 2002; 2003a; 2003b; 2004.
32. Corner, xiii.
33. Saunders quoted in Turrisi, 122.
34. Peirce, CP 5.312.
35. Peirce, CP 5.73. The other two kinds of representation are the iconic one which is based on a quality, and the symbolic one which consists in a rule of general interpretation. In fact, sign action involves the three to different degrees. But semiotic analysis attempts to find out on each occasion which kind of representation is the dominant or hegemonic one.
36. Andacht, 2004, 133. The data for this audience research came from two focus groups (male and female students, eighteen to twenty-eight) held in Montevideo, to study the reception of the first season of *Gran Hermano* in the region of the Rio de la Plata, in 2001. For the Brazilian audience, the data come from three focus groups (male and female students fourteen to eighteen, and adults thirty to fourty-five) in the south of Brazil (Porto Alegre, Canoas and São Leopoldo), to study the reception of the fourth edition of *Big Brother Brasil*, in 2004. For a detailed discussion of the findings of this qualitative study, see Andacht 2003b.
37. This room is called *"el confesionario,"* and it corresponds to the diary room in the Anglo-Saxon versions of the format.
38. Peirce, CP 8.41.
39. Andacht, 2003a, 41-47.
40. Andacht, 2003.
41. Nichols, 1992.
42. Horton and Wohl.
43. Horton and Wohl, 215.
44. Gibson, 127ss.
45. Horton and Wohl.
46. Goffman, 1959.
47. Meyrowitz.
48. Andacht, 2003a.
49. Horton and Wohl.
50. Corner, 260.
51. Coleridge, 314.
52. Goffman, 1959, 106ss.
53. Goffman, 1971, 269.

54. MS 649, 36, 1910, quoted in Colapietro, 90.
55. Eagleton, 2003.
56. Auerbach.
57. Auerbach, 5.
58. Auerbach, 4.
59. Genesis 22, 1.
60. Auerbach, 5-6.
61. Eagleton.
62. Eagleton.
63. The powerful Brazilian TV network, which produces *Big Brother Brasil*, also produces the most popular "novelas," the daily soap operas that are shot during nine months in the Projac, outside Rio de Janeiro, a large lot which is very close to the place where the house of the reality TV format was built.
64. The Portuguese word which Jean uses is "*cordial*," which has traditionally been used to depict the national character.
65. Freire.
66. He went on to write a book about his experience in the house, and to do some journalistic work for some Globo Network talk shows.

References

Andacht, Fernando. "Big Brother te está Mirando. La Irresistible Atracción de un Reality Show global." In *Ética, Cidadania e Imprensa*, edited by Raquel Paiva, 63-100. Rio de Janeiro, Brazil: Mauad, 2002.

———. *El Reality Show. Un Abordaje Analítico de la Televisión*. Buenos Aires, Brazil: Grupo Norma Editores, 2003a.

———. "Uma Aproximação Analítica do Formato Televisual do Reality Show *Big Brother*." *Galáxia. Revista Transdisciplinar de Comunicação, Semiótica, Cultura* no. 6 (2003b): 245-264.

———. "Fight, Love and Tears: An Analysis of the Reception of *Big Brother* in Latin America." In *Big Brother International. Formats, Critics and Publics*, edited by Ernest Mathijs and Janet Jones, 123-139. London: Wallflower Press, 2004.

———. "Representaciones de lo Real Mediático en el Brasil Contemporáneo: Auto-imagen Nacional en la era del Reality Show." *Cuadernos del Claeh* 90, no. 28 (2005): 28-44.

———. "O Signo Indicial na Representação Televisiva do Real." In *Os Mundos da Mídias: Reflexões Metodológicas Sobre Produção de Sentidos Midiáticos*, edited by Antonio Fausto Neto, 199-220. João Pessoa, Brazil: Editora Universitária da UFPB, 2006.

Auerbach, Eric. *Mimesis: The Representation of Reality in Western Literature*, translated by Willard Trask. Princeton, N.J.: Princeton University Press, 1953.

Barthes, Roland. "L'Effet du Réel." *Communications*, no. 11 (1968): 84-89.

Bateson, Gregory. *Mind and Nature*. New York: Bantam Books, 1980.

Colapietro, Vincent. *Peirce's Approach to the Self. A Semiotic Perspective on Human Subjectivity*. Albany, N.Y.: State University of New York Press, 1989.

Coleridge, Samuel Taylor. Biographia Literaria. In *The Collected Works of S.T. Col-*

eridge, edited by James Engell and William Bate. Princeton, N.J.: Princeton University Press, 1983 (1817).

Corner, John. "Performing the Real. Documentary Diversions." *Television & New Media* 3, no. 3 (2002): 255-269.

————. "Foreword." In *Big Brother International. Formats, Critics and Publics*, edited by Ernest Mathijs and Janet Jones, xii-xvii. London: Wallflower Press, 2004.

Couldry, Nick. "Playing for Celebrity. *Big Brother* as Ritual Event." *Television & New Media* 3, no. 3 (2002): 283-293.

Eagleton, Terry. "Pork Chops and Pineapples." *London Review of Books* 25, no. 20, from www.lrb.co.uk/v25/n20/eagl01_.html (accessed March 3, 2004).

Freire, Paulo. *Pedagogy of the Oppressed*, translated by Myra Bergman Ramos. London: Penguin, 1972.

Gibson, James J. *The Ecological Approach to Visual Perception*. Hillsdale, N.J.: Lawrence Erlbaum, 1986.

Goffman, Erving. *The Presentation of the Self in Everyday Life*. Garden City, N.Y.: Doubleday, 1959.

————. *Relations in Public. Microstudies of the Public Order*. New York: Harper Torchbooks, 1971.

————. "The Interaction Order." *American Sociological Review*, no. 48 (1983): 1-17.

Halton, Eugene. "Manning to Earth." *Symbolic Interactionism* 31, no. 2 (2008): 119-141.

Hill, Annette. "Big Brother The Real Audience." *Television & New Media* 3, no. 3 (2002): 323-340.

Horton, Donald and Richard Wohl. "Mass Communication and Para-social Interaction: Observations on Intimacy at a Distance." *Psychiatry*, no. 19 (1956): 215-229.

James, William. "Pragmatism and Humanism." 1906. Reprint. In *Pragmatism and other Essays*, 101-117. New York: Washington Square Press, 1963.

Jones, Owain. "Stepping from the Wreckage: Geography, Pragmatism and Anti-representational theory." *Geoforum*, no. 39 (2008): 1600-1612.

Kafka, Franz. "The Hunger Artist." In *The Kafka Project*, 1922. www.kafka.org /index.php?id=162,159,0,0,1,0 (accessed October 10, 2007).

Malinowski, Bronislaw. "On Phatic Communion." 1926. In *The Discourse Reader*, edited by Adam Jaworski and Nikolas Coupland, 302-305. London and New York: Routledge, 1999.

Manning, Peter. "Minding and Dreaming: A Comment on Halton." *Symbolic Interactionism*, no. 31-2 (2008): 143-148.

Meyrowitz, Joshua. *No Sense of Place. The Impact of Electronic Media on Social Behaviour*. New York: Oxford University Press, 1989.

Nichols, Bill. *Representing Reality: Issues and Concepts in Documentary*. Indiana: Indiana University press, 1992.

Partridge, Eric. *Swift's Polite Conversation*. London: A. Deutsch, 1963.

Peirce, Charles Sanders. *Collected Papers of C. S. Peirce*, edited by Charles Hartshorne, Paul Weiss, and Arthur Burks. Cambridge, Mass.: Harvard University Press, 1931-1958.

Ransdell, Joseph. "On Peirce's Conception of the Iconic Sign." In *Arisbe, The Peirce Gateway*, 1997. www.cspeirce.com/menu/library/aboutcsp/ransdell/iconic.htm (accessed November 20, 2008).

Turrisi, Patricia. "The Role of Peirce's Pragmatism in Education." *Cognitio,* no. 3 (2002): 122-135.

Chapter 5
Reality TV and Reality of TV: How Much Reality Is There in Reality TV Shows? A Critical Approach

Anastasia Deligiaouri and Mirkica Popovic

Philosophical Contestations of Reality Challenging Its "True" Meaning

What is "reality" and which are the prerequisites for describing something as "real"? The philosophical question and analysis of reality have been contentious in social theory from its origins. We draw on the work of several great philosophers to try to unpack certain facets of this controversial concept.

On the philosophical battlefield the definition of reality is approached and analyzed using mainly two philosophical paradigms: idealism and materialism. These philosophical adversaries provide diverse explanations of reality and, thus, different ways of approaching this reality.

At the apex of idealism stands the "absolute idealism" of Hegel. The "absolute idea" is the Totality in which the "double reality" of Object and Subject is reconciled. Literally "what exists in Reality is the Subject that knows the Object or, what is the same thing, the Object known by the Subject."[1] The profound basis of the Hegelian approach is the dialectic methodology of "Thesis-AntiThesis-SynThesis." Thesis engenders AntiThesis and its dialectical overcoming leads to SynThesis. What is important in this procedure is that AntiThesis is not negated but, on the contrary, is preserved in the final SynThesis. In this way a "new Thesis" surfaces which essentially comprises all the elements of the movement toward it. For Hegel, "I" is an absolute mediation, a result of the interaction of the subject with others. This interaction is achieved dialectically and therefore his reality is essentially the "recognized reality," a hetero-defined reality.

History in its Hegelian perception has been understood as the dynamic movement of the spirit towards its liberation.[2] In this movement, the spirit, being self-estranged from its natural existence, molds, and embraces all that we mean by "culture." For "culture, looked at from this aspect, appears as self-consciousness making itself conform to reality."[3] This moment of objectification, when the spirit is being actualized, constitutes the rehabilitation of the balance between the spirit and materiality. Reality is the sacrifice and renunciation of spirit to essential reality.

The opposite paradigm materialism, basically represented by Marx and post-Marxist philosophers, insists on the social and historic determination of reality and underlines the complexity of its construction which, nevertheless, is dependent on an economic base. The Marxist reality is mind-independent, residing before and for the subjects, resting upon the production relationships in societies. According to Marx, "It is not the consciousness of people that define their being but it is their social being that defines their consciousness."[4] In this sense, reality is a quite predetermined situation which, in addition, appoints a particular position for people ("class") and their role in society. Also, reality addressed in this way, seems to deprive the subjects—at least to a certain degree—of their active role in constructing it. Reality is already there. Change of reality means change of production relationships. For Marx "the real of reality lies in the action."[5] The important point here is the historical-social definition of reality which has been understood and practiced only in relation to the material factors that exist in a specific society. Appraisal of reality cannot take place unless we take into account its particular historical framework. According to this approach, reality shows are the final co-product, the outcome of current social conditions plus the tendency to reification of humanity and human relationships into a new commodity. The Marxist doctrine that "it is only within social relations that man can develop mental and practical orientations"[6] simply inserts research into any social phenomenon into the network of social relations in which it is rooted.

Post-Marxist approaches that moderate the rigid structures of Marxism contribute to providing critical illuminations of social domination, such as Gramsci's and Althusser's concepts of "hegemony" and "ideological apparatuses."[7] Via social and political apparatuses dominant discourses are channeled toward the preservation of social consent. The post-Marxist philosophers underline the (beneath the surface) hidden strength and the disciplinary effects of such practices tending toward the creation of a feeling of freedom (as if everything depends from peoples' choices), while, on the other hand, discreetly trying to manipulate and control these choices more effectively. The media are functioning indisputably as the most common and central apparatus in contemporary societies, by maintaining the divinization of the image and its overwhelming "truth"; the core value of modern visual culture.

Helpful and epistemological inferences can be drawn from the previous short retrospective on the philosophical investigation of reality. It is obvious that reality can be confronted and explained from many different angles, but, at the same time, we cannot ignore that in the "living reality" there is a certain level of materiality that cannot be neglected. Even the Hegelian idealism does not overlook, rather it endorses the discipline of the spirit to what it calls "essential reality." Social and economic conditions always pre-exist in societies. Ideological apparatuses are also present and hegemonic mechanisms exist, having been established in any hierarchical and class-divided society long before people identify them as such. Media are interwoven in this social structure and sometimes their power over the masses reaches a critical point often exceeding even the legal framework. In our case of Reality shows, the media go beyond societal ethics and social values.

Certainly, the idealist approach that invests in the individual apperception of reality by the spirit, permits different interpretations derived from the diverse variables that determine this apperception: educational level, social environment, personal beliefs, one's society, etc. Any interpretation though, however vague and subjective it may be, is reflected and finally actualized in our everyday lives, in the way we address issues, problems, human relations, ourselves, etc.; all these actions are revealed in empirical forms that are very "material." People are condemned to live in empirical worlds, whether or not they regard them as "real."

To elaborate further on the issue of "interpretation," it is reasonable that the use of the same cognitive and experiential resources will result in similar interpretations. In communicative terms, the use of the same cognitive resources leads the subject to the convergent de-codification of a message and avoidance of cognitive dissonance. Today, our main "resource" for acquiring information and constructing our knowledge and experience banks, is media. Media in modern societies act as the predominant material of what is being believed to be real. Proximity to realness is essential for social cohesion and is forged by media discourses. Media are positioned as the central ideological forums from which ideology is disseminated to the public.[8] People need to stay close to the prevailing discourses of reality because the fear of isolation is always present and guiding their behavior.[9] "Common visuality" in western societies as the key constructive element, has granted to media the role of deciding what is and what is not real, investing it always with the truthfulness that is inherent in visual perceptions. "Common visuality" is our modern "common sense," which leads to common attitudes and aspects in our social world. A high level of coherence in masses makes manipulation mechanisms easier to pursue and maintain.

The struggle between idealism and materialism and the oppositional approaches to the concept of "reality" may possibly lead to the assumption that the concept of reality is an issue basically seen through an ideological prism. Apparently taking one approach or another simply leads to different conclusions. But is that so? Is the definition of reality only a philosophical matter, a matter of philosophical opposition? And if so, how can we measure our everyday life according to such uncertainty? Thus, the necessity to form a more safe conceptual and methodological ground emerges in order to estimate and characterize something as "real."

De-constructing Media Reality in their Discourses

In these conflicting interpretations of reality, we can find clues to how we can unravel the emergence of Reality shows and their correspondence, if at all, to reality, as alleged by their producers. Our wish is not to reconcile opposing philosophical views, but to derive from them useful tools for the understanding of Reality TV broadcasts. What was it that promoted such a rapid explosion of this sub-genre worldwide in TV programming? Why did producers decide to call it "reality" and why have audiences seemed to welcome it?

The approach in this chapter is grounded on the relativist approach in post modern and post-structuralist theories. Whenever necessary, we also take account of criticisms of the philosophical thinking outlined above. The deconstruction by Foucauldian theory denies any attempt to form a universal truth and a one sided reality. Therefore, different ideological readings of the same facts and things are always available. According to Foucault's point of view, a specific concept can be understood and be analyzed only by and within the discursive practices and rules that define the "silent existence of reality"[10] and formulate the "acceptable" statements of truth in relation to this concept. Consequently, "there are no mistakes, in the narrow sense of the term because the mistake can only be born and become acceptable within the context of a practice."[11] Reality is defined and, nevertheless, constituted only by this circuit of dominant discourses that are specific and appear in a historically oriented society. These discourses have acquired their truthfulness through their recognition and embedding in social life by the relevant dominant powers in society.[12] In these terms, truth is a social convention. As Howarth, commenting on Foucault, argues: "Truth is not outside power or lacking in power but a thing in this world which is internally connected to logics of power and domination."[13] Finally, these practices succeed in being internalized by subjects, thus defining what they believe or are made to believe as true. Foucault's deconstruction model proposes a way of analyzing facts and their nature by splitting them in their discourses, into their constituent elements, by studying the complexity of the cluster of relations that surround them and finally by re-constructing them.

Accordingly, following Foucault's methodology of analyzing the process of articulating discourses, in this chapter we try to analyze Reality TV as a resultant and constant repetition of specific discourses in everyday life, at the same time highlighting the danger of this practice and the illusions that may be produced by their uncritical acceptance. Media reality or media based reality, in this perspective, is the aggregation of well entrenched discourses and practices, which, within a specific social context, claim their closeness to reality.

More specifically, then what are these discourses in Reality TV and its reality show that construct their discursive environment? The main inclusive discourse is the media discourse, the discourse of visuality and the obvious truthfulness that the television camera has convinced us that it conveys. The media discourse is always a socially oriented and at the same time an ideological discourse. The *general*, we could also call them *external*, discourses of social fragmentation, individualism, commercialization, worship of technology and economic profit by any means, are the core of the phenomenon called Reality TV, which is the evolutional sub-genre of commercial TV, literally a trans-genre.[14] Therefore, the trans-reality of media is obviously related to the economic dimension of commercial TV and to the demands set by the harsh competition imposed by market rules.[15] This quite new-born genre of media, trans-reality, has succeeded in reducing reality to a reality that is "staged," with particular characteristics and procedures that can be easily controlled and guided, as the empirical part of this chapter demonstrates. Our realities, each individual's perception of reality, is subsumed and finally lost in the general "pool" of media reality. The paradox of trans-reality is that it does not belong to any of specific members of the audience, while, at the same time, it belongs to all of them generally, because each one can search and find something of his or her own in this collection and compilation of "realities." A "side" effect is that we are tempted to "perform" and "stage" our lives according to the media presented life.

Trans-reality has interfered to our common social space, has eroded the lines between the private and the public and introduced new tv-celebrities and ethics. Ordinary people "celebrate" themselves, share their very intimate moments with anonymous viewers and "exhibit" their right to privacy. Trans-reality protagonists carry the burden of providing "interesting" realities on TV that could attract peoples' attention. On the other hand, TV audiences, frustrated and tired of their real life, are looking for an alternative reality that is very close to theirs and that they can experience with no real personal cost. In a way, spectators are part of this "spectacle of the real" as well, since the rearticulation of reality in reality shows is well rooted in representations of their own lives. This new trans-genre also needs their approval in order to exist. Therefore trans-reality is a bipolar contructed reality where the need of participant's self-exposure is met by the need of spectator's self-alienation. In the confluence of these two needs, which are indicative of postmodern fragmented identities, trans-reality surfaces to encompass diversities, to align concepts that used to remain in opposition to each other (e.g., private and public) and finally, to establish the "realm of trans-real" where subjectivity is anticipated as objectivity and the transgression of reality is understood as the "true" reality.

In the reign of this trans-real, people, their feelings, their inner-selves, their private lives and their very intimate moments are sold at the command of larger spectatorship. People obey the principle of fast but temporary, and fragile publicity, since most of the time they hope to translate it into significant amounts of money or a career in the entertainment industry. Reality TV is one of the most representative examples of current popular culture; the culture of TV celebrities willing to be exposed in front of the camera sacrificing their right to privacy in the altar of spectatorship.

Until the appearance of Reality shows, TV generally relied on a belief in its visual truthfulness, even though it was common knowledge to the audiences that broadcasts were directed and edited. The revolutionary aspect of Reality TV is that it has managed to convince, opposing McLuhan's view that "the medium is the message," that the medium has disappeared; now you can have the message intact; henceforth, since interference from the mediator is absent, objectivity recovers.

Discourses referring to the media production of Reality TV (we can call them *internal* discourses) seem ontologically to resemble reality. Simulations of space and time, the "uncontrolled" actions of participants, real-life events, ordinary people participating; everything seems to be real "enough." The frequency of the broadcasts in weekly TV programs and the proximity and familiarity of audiences with the TV characters create this "hyperreality" and ultimately, yes, "the simulacrum is true."[16] Media reality has succeeded over time in being totally subsumed in society. In the era of "medialities" the prototype, the mediation and its reflection are inseparable. There is a unique inversion going on that is no longer understood as such; instead of questioning media reality and to what degree it is objective, we question whether our empirical reality complies adequately with its media equivalent. This alone is sufficient evidence that media are in a prominent position to define truth.

The constructive elements of media discourse, such as its "mythical character," symbolism, representativity, ritual, visual mystification, aesthetic elements, dramatization,[17] are inherent in Reality TV as a sub-genre of media reality, and are characteristics familiar to audiences of long ago. The intertextuality and the multimodality of the media discourse[18] render the result even more convincing. In fact, what Reality TV has achieved is a blurring of the boundaries between daily life and TV life. Perhaps one of the basic ingredients in this success is their daily screenings. Continuous watching of the same representations makes the mechanism of identification faster and more unconscious. Some viewers become so obsessed with watching these TV shows that they forget even quite significant things in their lives, such as appointments with friends, or neglect their children. Media reality overall is a well constructed discourse, solid and grounded in the pathologies of contemporary societies.

When Reality Becomes a Show

The term used to describe something, a fact, a phenomenon, anything, "speaks" its attributes and also "confesses" its ends. A close linguistic scrutiny of the term "Reality shows" proves that it is a construction and not a mere, non-mediated reflection of the real. The words chosen are always important and enlightening about the encrypted intention behind their selection.

"Reality show" as a phrase is self-confessing, at least to a degree, in terms of two things. First, from a linguistic, syntactical perspective the word "reality" stands as an adjectival determination of the word "show." The noun "show," then, does not stand alone but inevitably has attributes of the adjective "reality." Second, "show" as a media genre reflects a broadcast of exaggeration, whose content tries to fascinate viewers and achieves this usually by transforming facts to the level of the "spectacular." Consequently, Reality show is a show which, like any other show, is in the control of media experts in order to gain high levels of spectatorship. This etymological analysis leaves us with the conclusion that this is a show that aims to be perceived as real. Thus, it is either reality presented as a show or we have a "show" of reality, that is, with specific parts of the reality accentuated to produce a show.

Either way, Reality shows are obviously media shows that follow the rules of media production and are constructed in order to provide truthful representations of reality. Apparently, again, part of their representation is proportionate to empirical reality; otherwise identification for the audience would not be possible. But even when real things are happening on stage, the demands of dramatization will either amplify them or reduce them to an unnoticeable event. Nancy Day explains that:

> Today, Reality shows use on-the-scene video cameras to record real events. But they also use re-enactments. Even though they look like documentaries, reality-based television shows are as carefully photographed and edited as movies. Cinematic lighting, special effects, moody background music and narration are added to enhance the drama . . . Film footage of real events is mixed with scenes that have been recreated.[19]

The show begins: there are no professionals or actors, only ordinary people participate; we are shown real scenes between the participants, with only "appropriate" direction cuts, due to the time limits of the episodes. Audiences are constantly offered occasions to observe habits, characters, personal moments, everything. Live fights and personal dramas take place in front of the TV viewers, sometimes in real time. And in modern culture what matters is now, the ultimate triumph of "presentism." Keeping up with the actual moments' thrills makes the spectacle more real. Notwithstanding this, it remains a spectacle, an edited, staged reality that has the purpose of filling the gaps in our reality, or giving us a reason to be occupied with others rather than ourselves. Unfortunately or not, real life cannot be edited and cut to suit our needs while in TV reality "real life" can be handled and can offer pseudo-experiences at a low personal cost, since it is a distance-lived reality.

Why are these shows being aired? Is it the big profits from TV advertising that forces TV producers to re-invent and re-sell reality? From an economic perspective the Reality TV experiment has been successful. The definite coalition of media power and economic forces is a good evidence for the strong, inherent, political consequences in these "innocent" entertainment shows.

Let us take a close look at Foucault's model for analyzing power and the relationships that surround it. Foucault prefers the micro-level, the specific view of power rather than identification of the political power with its official and traditional locus, the "state." Sarup comments that: "For Foucault, conceiving power as repression, constraint or prohibition is inadequate: power produces reality, it produces domains of objects and rituals of truth."[20]

By analyzing discourses of power we find that the consecutive effect of power is to create knowledge. To this extent, knowledge is a dependent variable of power relations and the historical evidence leads to the conclusion that the main body of society is capable of knowing basically only what is allowed to know by the hegemonic power. Since we have already accepted a cognitive factor regarding the identification of reality, we can support the option that specific knowledge patterns lead to a specific acknowledgment of reality. Common knowledge and the perception of social events is a factor in the solidarity of public opinion. Even though people may not believe in the "real" premise of these shows they still watch them and receive common representations of world. If knowledge is the power to define others, then definitely media have the power to produce knowledge and define others' reality; our reality.

This model signals one of the basic arguments in this chapter, that media reality is basically a construction and a cognitive mechanism and not a simple mediation of reality. Media have the power and their practitioners have the knowledge to produce identical representations of reality, equal to the existing ones. Ideological horizons converge, and equally our views of the world are narrowed. The power of signification, the power of providing a specific meaning (signifier) to the signified is the key to exercising control, at least mind control. The rules of our perception, as mentioned above, are defined very much by media as the main source of our information. Moreover, when the rules are posed and practiced by the same source, media, their messages are bound to succeed.

Perhaps, this media power is not perceived as direct, and herein rests its pervasiveness. This can readily be seen in long-term observation, especially of children and young people whose socialization nowadays depends heavily on media discourses. The fear involved in trying to imitate behaviors and characters from TV, and the well known effects of media in creating idols, are—or should be—significant factors in our analysis of these shows. The long term effects and the power of these true representations lie in the fact that they are no longer identified as "effects."

The New Public "Panopticon"

Why then are the TV ratings so high for these shows? A psychoanalytic approach would provide useful illumination on this point. People identify with particular TV characters and see them as mirroring themselves. Watching these ordinary people suffering, being happy, arguing, taking revenge, in short, dealing with everyday situations, serves as "katharsis" to use an ancient Greek term. The psychology of the TV viewer is affected by the situations in which their TV heroes or heroines are involved. Somehow, they come to believe that these TV facts concern them, and that they should be occupied with them. This pseudo-experience sometimes can be a relief from the daily pressures, but in the end results in total distraction and a befuddled mind in terms of any evaluation of the spectacle being watched. Lack of time and insecurity are allies in the personal equating with TV characters. It enables the view to have "safe" confrontation with real life; the TV screen is always a self-protector. Whatever happens, true or not, it is "in there," behind the screen, not too close to us. The "deviation of keyhole"[21] is responsible for creating totally wrong social behaviors.

We might say that these shows are a new production of Bentham's "Panopticon"[22] which was utilized in Foucault's theory of surveillance. In the "old" Panopticon, prisoners could not see and they did not know when they were observed, but they behaved well because of the fear of punishment. As Foucault explains, the major effect of the Panopticon lies in its ability to induce in the inmate "a state of conscious and permanent visibility that assures the automatic functioning of power."[23] The Panopticon was also a laboratory that used "as a machine to carry out experiments, to alter behaviours, to train or correct individuals . . . to monitor their effects,"[24] a function akin to the social experiment dimension analyzed in the empirical part of this chapter.

The contemporary "Reality-Panopticon" has a unique innovation: the participants know that they will be subjected to observation and media exposure. It is a free will confinement and a deliberative imprisonment, which is the basis of its "legality." These people are aware of the game. The common defensive reply to public criticism of Reality shows is that participation is based on personal, free-will decisions to be exposed in the media. Here rests the significance of external discourses such as social ethics, referred to above. Perhaps even in the 1980s, when social conditions and social ethics were different, the success of such shows would be very dubious.

How, then, has surveillance become an acceptable act? Simple exposure in front of a camera convinces us that when a person knows that he or she is in a public sight the behavior changes. The adjustment of the participants' behavior to the staging rules of the Reality show is obvious and is reflected in the second part of this chapter. The modern power of the Panopticon, of surveillance, is based not on imposing limitations on subjects, but on inventing new forms of activity, quasi free-activity, which are manipulated at source. People here are not punished if they do something wrong, if they break the rules. On the contrary, we have seen participants remain in a show because of their unconventional behavior, which causes stress, drama, and spectacular outbursts of feeling. In "TV Panopticon" participants are not afraid of being watched when performing routine actions; they are afraid if they are *not* being watched, because a decline in audience ratings could mean an end to their short, but exciting new "careers."

The participants in these shows are the outcomes of these new forms of activity that insist on the premise of free will engagement with the rules of the game. However, it is amazing that freedom can become a form of imprisonment. To this extent, Foucault's methodology of deconstructing concepts to their historical discourses seems to be verified. What once constituted the values of freedom and private life are no longer very much appreciated. What Orwell assumed in *1984* is no longer a threat; contra wise it constitutes an acceptable logic. This is how Orwell's Big Brother is de-incriminated; now anyone can be the big watching eye, legally and acceptably.

And, because we have supported a synthesis about the mental and material conception of the reality and social facts, the next sections provide some empirical testimony to these theoretical elaborations.

The Empirical Evidence: Approaching the Players for Answers

Reality shows are the new loud marketplace; selling talent, and beauty, using real lives for momentary Warholian fame as an exchange currency, lives that under the terms of a contract can be directed and manipulated in any way the advertising directors and a team of audience psychologists suggest.

In order to get a better insight into the conduct of reality programming, we interviewed two Reality show participants, one from the Romanian version of *Big Brother* and one from the Greek *Survivor*.[25] The choice for these shows was based on their worldwide and ongoing popularity. The decision to use interviewees from different countries was aimed at getting closer to the spirit of the globalized standardization of this media product.

The research in this chapter can be characterized as both exploratory and analytical, as we conducted a detailed investigation into the lifes and habits of participants in a Reality show, and this determined our research methodology as well. Qualitative research methods, more descriptive as they are, strive to investigate and understand more in depth human interactions in society. Qualitative researches strive to uncover answers for their speculations, while quantitative research is based on strict hypothesis testing. Discussing the varieties of qualitative methods and techniques, Susana Horing Priest commented that "descriptive observation of another culture's rituals, interviews that use open-ended questions, and verbal analysis of the tone of the argument in a set of newspaper editorials are all examples of qualitative research."[26]

Qualitative interviews were the primary research technique as they provide more substantial data than questionnaires. Furthermore, interviews are useful for getting better insight into the personal experience of the participants. The interview allows one to perform more in-depth research by continuously asking follow-up questions. The format is not as strict and close-constructed as in the quantitative questionnaire; the beauty of the open-ended interview is that it can explore more aspects than originally planned, as there is always the possibility of stepping into uncharted territories. A set of questions was prepared for both interviewees, to allow for a better analysis of the data; nonetheless, there was room for asking additional questions that were not on the agenda and were provoked by the stories of the participants.

The logic behind having open-ended questions was that the participants could be seen, in part, as quasi-anthropologists, conducting ethnographic studies on experimental groups that represent society. In addition, they were part of a social experiment and a survey with closed questions would not do justice to their experience and insights. Thematically, the interviews focused on the reasons for taking part in the show, the living conditions, their behavior and the daily routines of participants throughout the show, and their understanding and general overview of the show and the changes it had made to their lives.

Both of the interviewees have been out of the Reality show spotlight for several years, and thus, involvement in the study was not affected by worries related to protecting a newly gained reputation. One of our interviewees had left after the first week's show; the other had made it to the final show, but did not take the winning title and financial reward. Thus, our study is balanced (but of course still small); two different Reality show participants, and different experience and strategies.

Reality and Performance

Turning a Mundane Routine into a Show

Earlier in this chapter we discussed the etymology of the phrase "Reality shows," arguing that the word "show" entirely alters the concept of reality. The noun "show" immediately recalls the entertainment character of television. O'Shaughnessy concisely characterizes entertainment as "easy, pleasurable, hedonistic and democratic, in that manner offering available pleasures in the face of the problems in real life."[27] Bearing in mind that for many the reality equals a daily struggle against problems, we might wonder why the audience, after living this struggle, should be so keen to watch its TV representation. Even more puzzling is the question of why someone would want to participate in a magnified version of his or her privations. One answer can be found in Ewen's argument that: "the dream of identity, the dream of wholeness, is intimately woven together with the desire to be known, to be visible, to be documented for all to see."[28]

Our interviews took place within the context of this puzzle. The interviewees were asked why they had decided to participate in a Reality show. The *Big Brother* participant explained:

> I was a senior at university and I was extremely bored and wanted to do something extraordinary to break my routine. A friend told me about *Big Brother* recruiting participants and that being on the show would enhance the chances of me getting a career in television.

Similarly, the *Survivor* interviewee drew attention to his conviction that the show would enhance his career:

> I was inspired by the catchy advertisement trailer for *Survivor* calling for participants. The specific way of life appealed to me—living on a deserted island in the middle of a lost paradise. In addition, I was convinced that if I did well on the show, it would help me progress in my career and earn a celebrity status. Let us be realistic, everyone wants to be famous and show off, even for a day.

The reasons for entering the Reality show are at odds with the concept of portraying reality. It is obvious that the participants were discontented with their lives and were trying to escape from or improve them through exposure to millions of viewers. Alongside Ewen's argument regarding dependence on public judgment of one's self image, what both players were seeking was to join the celebrity culture. This kind of fame, Geraghty suggests, derives from "exploiting the private life instead of a person's performing presence."[29] Holmes refers to Boorstin's definition of "acceleration of celebrity culture in which people are well known simply for their "well-known-ness," rather than for 'greatness, worthy endeavors or talent."[30] Belonging to the celebrity culture is clearly fulfilment of the uses and gratifications theory.[31] The need is a new, trendy reality and only those characters most capable of juggling with their looks, behavior, and willingness to play by the rules of the game, have the chance to become celebrities, stars, even though they might be expelled from the game in one of the early episodes.

The "Etiquette" of Reality Show

The most successful collaborations between cast and production team result from the desire for mutual exploitation. Revealing an abundance of personal and private detail equates with gaining more media attention, that is, increasing the show's ratings and augmenting the post-broadcast lifestyles and career opportunities of the participant. According to the interviewees, the behavior of participants is directly linked to audience and sponsorship interest, thus, a carefully planned strategy is crucial in order to succeed. The participants have to switch roles: before joining the show they have been active audience members and thus have learned how to decode its messages. As participants they become the encoders. Hall reminds that: "The consumption or reception of the television message is also itself a 'moment' of the production process in its larger sense, though the latter is 'predominant' because it is the 'point of departure for realisation' of the message."[32] Hence, it would be slightly naïve to believe that Reality show participants are left at the mercy of the constantly running video camera: quite the contrary, if we remember the Reality Panopticon and the newly developed fear of *not* being watched. The participants are educated within a TV culture and, therefore, are subconsciously well trained in terms of the camera's and the audience's demands.

Apart from their personal strategies, it was of research interest whether the production company provides participants with a guidebook on acceptable behavior. Both interviewees answered negatively, the *Survivor* interviewee adding that: "They wanted to see real reactions." However, while the reactions may be real, the directions in which they are cut in the editing room and then presented pose a dilemma for our hypothesis. This interviewee went on to say that:

> To be completely honest, one is a bit uneasy in the show regarding their behavior. You are not completely your true self. On the one hand, you are extremely exhausted by the lack of food, safe shelter, the usual commodities that one is used to in daily life. I remember we all came back home weighing 14kg less . . . On the other hand, Survivor is a strategic game, so you can't always act as you feel i.e., show your ultimate true self in front of the team players. One can't completely relax, everything is taped but there is no friendly audience voting for you over the phone or online. You depend solely on the preferences of your team.

Less life-threatening, but still unnatural were the living conditions in the Big Brother house. The *Big Brother* participant recalled that they were told minutes before the show began that they would be observed in private areas such as the restrooms and showers:

> Me, including two other girls disagreed to shower naked and wore our bathing
> suits. One of the girls had a cloak that she used to cover her body when taking
> showers, and soon I and some of the other girls started using it to take showers.
> Our refusal to show naked skin in the show was criticized by the public. At the
> same time, the media were overwhelmed by nude photos and videos of the par-
> ticipants showering naked. I remember the audience criticized our *Big Brother*
> sequel as too shy, whereas the next sequel was criticized for being too explicit.

Lastly, it seems that the core of Reality shows is to make judgements and to
criticize; participants' actions are examined through a microscope and popularity on the show equates with popularity among the audience and production
team. The *Big Brother* interviewee, who was the first person to leave that particular series, provided a detailed account of the reasons why she left. Characterizing herself as an introvert, she felt the production crew turned her into a
sociopath.

> I did not have good relations with the other eleven participants in the house. I
> disagreed with their manners and therefore decided it would be for everyone's
> well being to be distant from them. Politely enough, I did make small talk and
> greeted them and participated in all group activities, but I was remotely close
> only to one other participant in the show. What was shown on television, how-
> ever, was that I was alone at all times, did not participate in late night group ac-
> tivities, when in fact I was asleep as I cannot stay up too late and then wake up
> at the designated morning hour. So, the production team did not tell me how to
> act, but they used scenes from the way I acted to make me look just like they
> wanted in the eyes of the public.

According to the other interviewee, this participant's mistake was not to think
ahead and adapt her behavior toward what would be more likely to be popular.
In his opinion, participants are forced by the situation to choose and maintain
certain roles during the show, adjusting their characters to particular situations.
He confirmed this by saying that his friends often commented that they could
hardly recognize him in the show, saying that he was nothing like the person
they saw on the TV.

Thus, the participant who behaved like her true self was voted off *Big
Brother* after the first week's airing, whereas the participant who was more
flexible, adapting his character features, managed to get to the final of the show
that he was in. This actually mirrors real life: some people are flexible, capable
of maintaining good relations with everyone and thus are able to "progress" in
their social lives, while introverts are perceived and portrayed as difficult, in-
flexible characters and often are rejected or ignored in favor of more extroverted
people.

The participants' first reactions can be summed up as selecting a role to play in a small, constructed social drama. Reality shows resemble the social milieu of the characters, a feature that reveals another side of Reality TV: its similarities with the features of soap operas.

Among the several genres that emerged during the 1990s with the occurrence of Reality TV, is the docu-soap, which Hill described as "a combination of observational documentary, and character-driven drama."[33] The element of drama and performance is thus, legitimately an indivisible part of Reality shows. Moreover, the reality genre borrows from the soap opera as a genre the element of: "tension between the conventions of realism and melodrama."[34] This may be the key to the question of why Reality shows have had such tremendous success worldwide. Production teams become "editing teams" in their efforts to create a more interesting, more intriguing story for both audiences and advertisers. The *Survivor* participant interviewed observed:

> I saw "reality" in the episodes shown on television. There were cuts and edits of the interviews we were having with the production crew, and there were noticeable, guided stories toward a certain point, making someone the good or bad guy, showing sentiment, liking or disliking. I guess the show has to sell and if there is a romantic story evolving around a beautiful girl, why would they send her out and leave only three bearded men in the show? When you get out you understand how they are thinking. They drive the escalation of the situation according to audience's interest.

The *Big Brother* participant passed a similar comment:

> The technical team wanted to stress some things at a certain moment at least that is my view of it. For example, they knew exactly who was going to leave the house every week and they were showing this person's character flaws, with a direct, unhidden agenda to have him/her leave the house.

In a nutshell, this practice is a basic TV journalistic rule that applies to human interest stories: they must intrigue, must engender greater interest, with a drop of drama and tears in the mix.

Staged Realities

Control and Surveillance: Under the Microscope of the Social Experiment

The words most commonly used in both of the interviews to talk about the Reality show in which they had participated were "game" and "social experiment." Firstly, it is a game because a certain number of participants are competing for a prize, reminding us of the gladiatorial fights that entertained the public in Roman times. It is a game where the winner's destiny is decided by the results of the audience ratings, the charisma of the player, the adequacy of his or her strategy according to a specific society's standards reflected in phone and online votes, all of which are pre-determined by the edited TV images. Root characterizes this as the "spectacle of real emotion."[35]

On the other hand, Reality shows are a social experiment since they present society in miniature. They present a place where various social groups are included and portrayed, where conflicts are provoked, where romantic relationships blossom and are crushed, where people are constantly incited to demonstrate extreme temper. The *Big Brother* interviewee stated:

> Social experiment is the term the production crew used most often to describe the show. See what happens when you lock people inside a house. Automatically different characters will conflict. One can observe what happens with different social group members, uniting and dissolving.

The *Survivor* participant said that:

> If the point of *Big Brother* is observing what happens when people are under the pressure of the house they are locked in, the point of *Survivor* was to see people's reactions under the pressure of deprivation that is, lack of food, decent safe shelter, unpleasant weather conditions, dangerous animal world around for example, crabs, scorpions, snakes, etc.

The word "experiment" constructs the basic argument disputing the "reality" of these TV shows. Namely, an "experiment" as a research method is using an artificially controlled environment, with many controlled variables. The natural habitat is immediately altered simply by bringing a foreign object, such as a video camera, into the area, let alone reconstructing the habitat under artificial circumstances. Consequently, Reality shows as "social experiments" utilize staged events under controlled conditions in an artificial environment that supposedly tells the story of real society.

The controlled artificial nature is detected by the constant camera presence along with the atypical living conditions in the shows. Regarding the camera presence, *Big Brother* had twenty-four hour video surveillance throughout the house, including the restrooms and showers.

> Waking up was at 7 am and the day had activities planned beforehand, different arranged tasks we had to fulfill, etc. Some of the tasks were helpful, easing the acquainting process, bringing the participants together, but there were annoying tasks such as an alarm clock that rang every two minutes, and there had to be someone to turn it off otherwise we would have been punished for not doing what we were asked to. Other activities included dancing nights or dress up

night where we were given costumes and were supposed to pick one and wear
it all night long.

Most of the activities the *Big Brother* interviewee refers to were prearranged and
controlled. The concept of *Survivor* on the other hand, mainly due to the vast-
ness of the island, is different from *Big Brother*. The arranged spectacle is also
derived from daily interviews in which participants express their views on the
performances of the other participants' in the show and on the previous day generally. The main staged events were the competitions:

> The competitive games were the staged and directed moments. They do not last
> for ten or fifteen minutes as the viewers see them on television. It usually took
> four to six hours to complete the shooting of a competition scene. We had to
> rehearse where we were going to come out from, where we are going to stand,
> which trajectory we are going to follow, lights, microphones and cameras
> needed to be precisely set up. Apart from those scenes, we did have a fair lib-
> erty of moving around the island without being followed by cameras, but it was
> at night, after dark fell, when the camera crew would leave that we were enjoy-
> ing the actual reality. We would talk, discuss problems and emotions, cry,
> laugh, dance, sing, and just be ourselves without the camera pressure.

The other controlling factors were the unusual living conditions. Twelve strangers locked inside a house without a TV or radio, for four months, or twelve
southern European players surviving deprivation for two months on a desert island in Malaysia, poses a query about what exactly is realistic in these situations.
Bearing in mind that the participants' normal living conditions are completely
different, it is unlikely that these participants will act and react in the same ways
as they would do in their own environments.

Tincknell and Raghuram reflect on *Big Brother*'s surveillance tactics, mentioning that: "The webcams in the show produced lazy and unfocused images of
the private spaces of bedrooms and bathrooms which emphasised the sense of
gaining access to the forbidden, while the 'unedited' quality of the programme—however spurious—confirmed the sense of liveness."[36] What should
cause concern is the quick adaptability of the players to the presence of the camera; behaviors that initially might have emerged in response to the camera's ro-
tations quickly became part of the players' reality. If the show imitates life, at
the same time constituting human experiment, embracement of the surveillance
camera may be an indicator that society silently has embraced all forms of surveillance that ultimately serve marketing purposes. Just as audiences patiently
observe participants' actions in the shows, marketing companies observe the
everyday consumption of members of the public, perhaps not via a video camera, but via their consumption preferences. Couldry describes this "surveillance-
entertainment" phenomenon as both concerning and disturbing:

> Surveillance-entertainment has implications for everyday social relations . . .
> while the saturation of the public space with closed-circuit television is a matter
> of concern, the issue is more its effects on the quality of everyone's experience
> of public space, rather than the effects on how people might perform in front of
> the visible and invisible cameras.[37]

The Reality show is not just a forty-five-minute program on a specific TV channel, it is also accompanied by a vast number of commodities that can be consumed: magazines about the show, morning programs discussing the previous
day's action, tabloid newspapers, fan clubs, online, and phone voting, etc. The
fanaticism with the show reaches the point where people on their own initiatives, form support groups for their favorite characters and create their own mer-
chandise, such as tee-shirts, flags, etc. Feeding the show with attention turns it
into a successful commodity. What is more, our reality is benchmarked to an
edited forty-five-minute spectacle. "The everyday word for editing is cutting.
The key to editing is finding the precise point at which a shot starts and stops
being interesting. Of course, you also have to find a way of putting them all together to tell the story."[38] It is, as Gergen says when analyzing Debord, as
though "we live together increasingly in a world of appearances, experiencing
not life itself, but a negation of life."[39] Does this mean that our real life is no
longer sufficiently thrilling for us?

Dream-Producing Factories

Reality shows resemble dream factories. Ordinary neighbors become instant
celebrities. Putting long-term effort into achieving a specific goal seems no
longer necessary when Reality shows can achieve it so promptly and effectively.
Our *Big Brother* participant got the career in TV that he wanted and the *Survivor*
player was bathing in a pool of fame:

> It is a very strange, but beautiful feeling. For a certain period of time you are
> not able to do anything unnoticed by the media or audiences. Everyone knows
> you and your name. I still find it amazing how much power TV has over daily
> life, that is, I would watch myself sitting in a cage on the island during an epi-
> sode and the people on the table next to me were discussing the exact episode
> of *Survivor*, talking about me and the people I have lived the whole adventure
> with already months ago, in real life.

However this "shiny" dream can fade if the participant counts the cost of it. Participants can achieve their dream, but, in exchange, they have to give up their
private lives totally. Although, at first, the luxury hotels and media lights might
be dazzling, ultimately the paparazzi flashlights and scandalous spectacles may
become so blinding that the celebrity has to hide behind dark glasses.

A Controlled Reality with Uncontrolled Results

Audiences seem to continue to be eager to tune in to the pseudo-experience of Reality shows. Hill notes that "Reality shows managed to capitalise on the tension between appearance and reality by ensuring the viewers have to judge for themselves which of the contestants is being genuine."[40] But, what is the value or the pertinence of this judgement when the whole "reality" concept is mocking itself?

The trans-reality of television is trans(-)forming audiences and their lives to a "trans-life" where elements of reality are edited, manufactured and offered as convincing pictures of the "real." This unique obsession of television to be the irreprehensible witness of truth has offered new attributes to the ontology of "real" and a skepticism for how eager audiences may be to abandon their realities for a constructed one.

The issues that arise in relation to Reality shows also apply to the breaking of social taboos and how far the negation of social ethics can go. The reverse Panopticon of voluntary imprisonment that takes place under the public gaze also signals a change in the substratum of social life, dangerously blurring the boundaries between "private" and "public," between "freedom" and "illiberality." Even the engagement of the word "experiment" for humans goes beyond existing social norms. Can human beings be acceptably subjected to experiment? And what happens if the experiment "succeeds"?

In the spirit of consumerism we have accepted the interference in our lives from market professionals who provide "ideal" solutions and products. The stronger ideological apparatus used to channel these "interferences" was media. Based on previous success in proposing products, the media have moved to the next level; that of proposing and guiding a reality. Talking in communication terms, the art of persuasion can be well grounded on false representations that aspire to being conceived as real. After all, "Truth is an error that has become true."[41] The "reality effect" enforced by these shows should be considered more seriously from the point of view of their entertainment value.

We end this chapter by quoting Woody Allen: "Life doesn't imitate art, it imitates bad television."[42] Therefore, a lot more attention should be paid to the effects of constructed TV spectacles in order to avoid their imitation in our real lives.

Notes

1. Kojeve, 174.
2. For a brief analysis of Hegel's basic points of philosophy see: *Lexicon of Philosophy* by Theodosis Pelegrinis (in Greek) (Athens: Ellinika Grammata, 2004), 1296-1300.

For Hegel's "historical method," see, George Holland Sabine, *History of Political Theory*, transl. to Greek by C. Manthou (Athens: M. Pehlivanidis and Bros Publications, 1961), 676-681.

3. Hegel, 516.
4. Marx, 23.
5. Dagogne, 180.
6. Antonopoulou, 121.
7. See further comments in Mouffe, 168-204.
8. Deligiaouri, 2007a.
9. For a brief analysis of the "spiral of silence model," see Noelle-Neumann.
10. Foucault, 1987, 77.
11. Foucault, 1971, 25.
12. Foucault, 1971, 7.
13. Howarth, 128.
14. Berger, 387.
15. For genres of television and their economic dimension, see Sorogas, 33-50.
16. Baudrillard, 1.
17. For the analysis of characteristics of media discourse, see Deligiaouri, 2007b, 123-192.
18. Kress and Van Leeuwen.
19. Day, 67.
20. Sarup, 74.
21. Papadimitriou, 82.
22. Bentham.
23. Foucault, 1991, 195-228.
24. Foucault, 1991, 203.
25. Legal Statement: The interviewees remain anonymous in this article in respect to their participation in the Reality shows and any information and detail provided in this article is used only for the purposes of academic research and cannot be used or reproduced in any way for any other use.
26. Priest, 5.
27. O'Shaughnessy, 90.
28. Ewen, 197.
29. Geraghty quoted in Holmes, 119.
30. Boortsin quoted in Holmes, 131.
31. Katz et al., quoted in McQuail, 2000, 318.
32. Hall, 503.
33. Hill, 27.
34. Barker, 266.
35. Root quoted in Holmes, 123.
36. Tincknell and Raghuram.
37. Couldry.
38. Watts, 78.
39. Gergen, 201.
40. Hill, 70.
41. Kojeve, 189.

42. *Husbands and Wives.*

References

Antonopoulou, Maria. *The Classics of Sociology. Social Theory and Modern Society.* Athens, Greece: Savalas Publications, 2008. (in Greek)

Barker, Chris. *Cultural Studies: Theory and Practice.* London: Sage, 2000.

Baudrillard, Jean. *Simulacra and Simulation,* translated by Sheila Faria Glaser. Ann Arbor: The University of Michigan Press, 1994.

Bentham, Jeremy. *The Panopticon Writings,* edited by Miran Bozovic. London: Verso, 1995.

Berger, Arthur Asa. *Popular Genres.* Newbury Park, Calif.: Sage, 1992.

Couldry, Nick. "Teaching Us to Fake it: The Ritualized Norms of Television's 'Reality' Games." In *Reality TV: Remaking Television Culture,* edited by Sussan Murray, 57-74. New York: New York University Press, 2004.

Dagogne, Francois. *The Great Philosophers and their Philosophy,* translated by Maro Triantafyllou. Athens, Greece: Melani Publications, 2007.

Day, Nancy. *Sensational TV: Trash or Journalism?* N.J.: Enslow Publishers, Inc., 1996.

Deligiaouri, Anastasia. "Political and Ideological Dimensions of Contemporary Mass Media." In *Social Sciences Today,* edited by Kostas Zoras and Badimaroudis Philimon, 635-650. Aegean University, Athens-Komotini, Greece: Ant. N. Sakkoulas Publications, 2007a. (in Greek)

———. *Political Discourse and Mass Media. The Legal, Political and Sociological Dimension.* PhD Thesis, Thessaloniki, Greece: Aristotle University of Thessaloniki, 2007b. (in Greek)

Ewen, Stuart. *All Consuming Images.* New York: Basic Books, 1988.

Foucault, Michel. *The Archaeology of Knowledge,* translated by Kostis Papagiorgis Athens, Greece: Exantas Publications, 1987.

———. *Discipline and Punish; the Death of the Prison.* London: Penguin Books, 1991.

———. *The Order of Discourse,* translated by Minas Christidis. Athens, Greece: Iridanos Publications, 1971.

Gergen, Kenneth J. *An Invitation to Social Construction.* London: Sage, 1999.

Hall, Stuart. "Encoding-Decoding." In *The Cultural Studies Reader,* edited by Simon During, 2nd ed., 90-103. New York: Routledge, 1999.

Hegel, Georg Wilhelm Friedrich. *The Phenomenology of Mind,* translated by James Baillie, 2nd ed. New York: Humanities Press, 1977.

Hill, Annette. *Reality TV: Audiences and Popular Fiction.* New York: Routledge, 2005.

Holmes, Su. "All you've got to worry about is the task, having a cup of tea, and doing a bit of sunbathing: Approaching Celebrity in Big Brother." In *Understanding Reality Television,* edited by Su Holmes and Deborah Jermyn, 111-135. New York: Routledge, 2004.

Howarth, David. "An Archaeology of Political Discourse? Evaluating Michel Foucault's Explanation and Critique of Ideology." *Political Studies* 50, no. 1 (2002): 117-135.

Husbands and Wives. DVD. Directed by Woody Allen. New York: Sony Pictures, 2002.

Kojeve, Alexandre. *Introduction to the Reading of Hegel. Lectures on the Phenomenology of Spirit,* translated by James Nichols. Ithaca: Cornell University Press, 1980.

Kress, Gunther and Theo Van Leeuwen. *Multimodal Discourse. The Modes and Media of Contemporary Communication*. London: Arnold, 2001.

Marx, Karl. *Criticism of Political Economy*, translated by Fotis Fotiou. Athens, Greece: Themelion Publications, 1978.

McQuail, Denis. *The Theory of Mass Communication for the 21st Century*, translated by Katia Metaxa, Stelios Papathanasopoulos. Athens, Greece: Kastaniotis Publications, 2003.

———. *Mass Communication Theory*. 4th ed. London: Sage, 2000.

Mouffe, Chantal. "Hegemony and Ideology in Gramsci." In *Gramsci and Marxist Theory*, edited by Chantal Mouffe, 168-204. London: Routledge and Kegan Paul, 1979.

Noelle-Neumann, Elisabeth. "Public Opinion." In *The "Construction" of Reality and Mass Media*, translated by Tereza Kapelou, T. Kokkali, edited by Roi Rigopoulou, Pepi Panagiotopoulou, Myrto Rigou and Sotiris Notaris, 88-104. Athens, Greece: Alexandria Publications, 1996. (in Greek)

O'Shaughnessy, Michael. "Box Pop: Popular Television and Hegemony." In *Understanding Television*, edited by Goodwin Andrew and Garry Whannel, 88-102. New York: Routledge, 1990.

Panagiotopoulou, Roi, Pepi Rigopoulou, Myrto Rigou and Sotiris Notaris. *The "Construction" of Reality and Mass Media*. Athens, Greece: Alexandria Publications, 1996. (in Greek)

Papadimitriou, Zissis. *Postmodern Deadlocks*. Thessaloniki, Greece: Paratiritis Publications, 2002. (in Greek)

Pelegrinis, Theodosis. *Lexicon of Philosophy*. Athens, Greece: Ellinika Grammata Publications, 2004. (in Greek)

Priest, Susana Horing. *Doing Media Research: An Introduction*. New Delhi: Sage, 1996.

Sabine, George Holland. *History of Political Theory*, translated by Chr. Manthou. Athens, Greece: M. Pehlivanidis and Bros Publications, 1961.

Sarup, Madan. *An Introductory Guide to Post-Structuralism and Postmodernism*. Athens, Georgia: The University of Georgia Press, 1993.

Sorogas, Evangellos. *The Phenomenon of "Reality."* Athens: Kastaniotis Publications, 2004. (in Greek)

Tincknell, Estella and Parvati Raghuram. "Big Brother: Reconfiguring the 'Active' Audience of Cultural Studies?" In *Understanding Reality Television*, edited by Su Holmes and Deborah Jermyn, 252-269. New York: Routledge, 2004.

Watts, Harris. *On Camera: How to Produce Film and Video*. London: BBC Books, 1984.

Chapter 6
Trans-Professionalism Undone? The 2007 British TV Scandals
Matthew Hibberd

2007: Annus Horribilis for U.K. TV

Television viewers in the United Kingdom have been shocked by several recent admissions of "phone rigging" in relation to competitions on popular TV and radio programs, and the revelation that a trailer prepared for a BBC documentary film on the Queen was "manipulated" in order to engender controversy and boost audience ratings. It is calculated that between June 2007 and June 2008, fines issued by the U.K. media regulator, the Office for Communications (OFCOM), relating to these various TV and radio deceptions amount to almost £12 million. Few, if any, of the United Kingdom's top broadcasters have escaped these controversies and all five main terrestrial channels have been subject to fines issued by OFCOM. A public opinion poll conducted by ICM for the *Guardian* newspaper in July 2007 shows that public trust in the BBC fell sharply in the wake of the phone-in and "Queengate" scandals.[1] This poll also revealed "a wider crisis of public confidence in the broadcasting industry as a whole, with viewers strongly skeptical of what they see on television, even when they are told the scenes are real." Corrupt practices in TV and radio programs involving interactions with the public are not new: They were occurring as far back as the 1950s and constituted a feature of early popular entertainment television in many countries.[2] However, in this chapter we argue that the 2007 phone quiz and documentary "faking" scandals have eroded public confidence in TV producers and broadcasters. We also argue that producers are more and more willing to bend the rules, break programming codes and go against ethical mores demonstrating that new forms of power are being practiced, resulting in TV audiences, and especially participants in phone-in competitions, being duped or defrauded. This raises questions about whether we have entered into the stage of the post-professional, in which old professional norms have become devalued. In this chapter we trace the origins of these scandals and examine the extent to which broadcasting professionalism has been undermined in the United Kingdom. We show that although TV scandals have always been a part of the broadcasting environment, in an era of increasing commercialism, engagement with publics is becoming more an instrument of economic exchange in which publics are seen as consumers, and less a partner in the provision of a public service that celebrates and promotes the very best in human endeavor.

Trans-Professionalism in the Broadcasting Context

Broadcasting industries across the world have often been seen offering a professional opportunity which encourages the development of specialist program-making skills through on-the-job training and formal education and abidance with strict codes of conduct. The precise definition of a profession is tricky and there are longstanding debates on issues relating to professions and professionalism in sociology and management studies.[3] While debate over the definition of professionalism, who can be defined as a "professional" and what industries qualify as professional, there a number of basic attributes that are commonly ascribed to professionals:

> The professional has skills or expertise proceeding from a broad knowledge base.
> The professional provides a service based on a special relationship with those whom he or she serves.
> Professionals have a social function of speaking out on broad matters of public policy and justice, going beyond duties to specific clients.
> Professionals are often members of their particular industry association or trade union. Professional bodies often assert their independence from state or commerce and possess legal or moral authority to codify laws, discipline members and speak on behalf of the industry in policy and public debates.
> Professionals undergo formal processes of training and education.[4]

One problem with definitions of professionalism is that they do not often distinguish those occupations with key social functions where maintenance of professional mores remains especially important. The broadcast media, arguably, is one such occupation. Broadcasters often claim to promote values and beliefs essential to the maintenance of democratic ways of life and in providing comfort and support to those sections of society who often feel most isolated or withdrawn from economic and political life: the pensioner; the poor; the working classes; social groups living on the margins of societies. The broadcast media can argue that they do more than most institutions in alleviating the sense of alienation that modern social conditions can bring. In a recent book chapter McQuail develops the broader concept of public occupation, which he defines as:

> An occupation that takes on, or is attributed, some task with potentially wide public implications. Its activities are supported by and sometimes necessary to other social institutions. It is carried out with some degree of transparency and it is open to public scrutiny, without necessarily being carried out under public supervision or primarily for public benefit. There are a range of occupations that might qualify for the term, mostly in service industries or in the fields of justice, health, education and politics. The degree of "publicness" is quite variable. The concept is deliberately chosen to avoid reference to the narrower term of "profession," although the work of professionals is often of a public character in much the same sense.[5]

In relation to the development of European broadcasting, attaining high professional standards has often been closely associated with particular forms of public occupation, namely public service broadcasting (PSB) and a strong tradition in documentary film making. We discuss PSB first.

Although the term PSB actually goes back to David Sarnoff, the pioneer of the American commercial radio system, the concept is more commonly linked with John Reith, the BBC's first General Manager and Director General from 1922 to 1936, who developed a theoretical analysis and practical implementation of PSB. Reith believed, first, that a public service broadcaster should be a publicly-owned entity, but that it should remain independent from the state in order to provide a greater degree of autonomy and impartiality in its dealings with different political and commercial actors. Reith's position was therefore closer to Habermas's concept of public sphere than to classic liberal doctrine. The rational nature of this debate, in line with the wider beliefs of the Enlightenment movement, emphasized human progress in all spheres of life. Reith's second central idea was that a public service should provide cultural enlightenment that will inform, educate and entertain by providing everything that is best in every human department of knowledge, endeavor and achievement. An important part of the public service broadcasters' remit has been to educate and inform the public about a wide range of contemporary issues, and eliciting their opinions and securing the involvement of ordinary people has been seen as being in tune with this remit, especially in relation to political or social issues. It is one of the strategies used by program-makers and television executives to persuade and reassure the viewing audience that the programs on offer are relevant to their lives and concerns.

The development of PSB in Western Europe as a public occupation promoting professional ethics can be traced, above all, to the immediate post-Second World War period. The severe economic and social upheavals facing Europe in the wake of the war required urgent attention. Responsibility for this havoc was blamed on a series of political and economic failures in the 1920s and 1930s: the failure of parliamentary and democratic institutions to stem the tide of extremism throughout the 1920s and 1930s; the rise of authoritarian and totalitarian dictatorships that led to the occupation of large parts of continental Europe; the economic depressions of the 1920s and 1930s, largely created by the debacle of the Versailles treaties and the system of reparations; a situation that was made worse by antagonistic commercial policies causing so much bitterness and resentment; and, of course, the resulting social and economic inequalities during the period of the 1930s depression. The question, therefore, was how to reconcile the need for the nation-state as the primary focus for collective identity without arousing the kind of jingoistic noises associated with nationalism that had done so much to damage the continent. The subsequent policies adopted included a mixture of the following three elements: reconciliation that required and promoted selected amnesia of past events; promotion of "founding myths" for hope and renewal; and, enactment of state-led policy measures to encourage greater political, social and economic equity. But for such relations to emerge required semi-autonomous public institutions in order to inform and promote active citizenry. One such public institution was broadcasting. Although there was a common rationale of purpose behind public service—to provide information and to act as a forum for public debate—individual national systems developed in line with their own distinctive political, economic, social and institutional patterns but always promoting professional norms associated with broadcasting quality.

Another institution or public occupation which can be said to have influenced professional norms was the European documentary movement of the 1920s and 1930s. The influence of documentary film-makers, such as Jean Vigo, John Grierson, Germaine Dulac and Alberto Calvacanti, is regarded as seminal to the subsequent development of television as a public occupation in Europe in the post-war period. The influence of the British Documentary Movement and John Grierson is of particular importance in the context of the United Kingdom. Grierson directed his first film, *Drifters,* in 1928—a documentary that followed the lives of the fishermen of the Scottish herring fleet. This film exemplifies some of the key aesthetic features of the British Documentary Movement. *Drifters* was released in 1929 and shared a billing with Eisenstein's *Battleship Potemkin,* which was receiving its British debut screening (Grierson had been responsible for organizing the first American screening in 1925). The two films have many common features, as the British Film Institute (BFI) argues:

> Like *Potemkin, Drifters* employs montage in an expressive manner, creating dramatic tension in the absence of any psychological characterisation. Both films also use "types" (non-professional actors) instead of actors in order to create a more "authentic" reality, and both films make use of extensive location

shooting. Grierson, nevertheless, always stressed that he was keen to make a film with distinctively "British" characteristics, which he saw as moderation and a sense of human importance. *Drifters* is, therefore, slower paced than *Potemkin*, and focuses on more mundane, less inherently dramatic events.[6]

So, although *Drifters* does not employ *Potemkin*'s formal theoretical qualities, Grierson's film is still ideological insofar as it identifies and promotes the cause of industrial modernity as opposed to (pre-industrial) traditional fishing methods, representing progress and the readiness of the human spirit to embrace and adapt to change. *Drifters* was the first in a line of films whose key attributes can be summarized as documentary films focusing on social issues, where working class, non-professional actors were often brought to the forefront of the action and where a lot of the shooting takes place on location. These films can be classed as "progressive," insofar as they highlight the advances made in society while pointing toward the need for more political and social reform after years of war and conflict. Grierson's influence on key British and European documentary film-makers such as Alberto Cavalcanti, Norman McLaren and Basil Wright is well known. But this influence extended also to contemporary European film-makers whose films are invariably well crafted and shaped, and tackle social issues that relate to everyday lives; these are international film-makers who engage with their participants providing, arguably, a duty of care in soliciting public contributions that further PSB ideals. In the words of John Willis, a British documentary maker: "The history of the documentary is the celebration of the maverick, of the renegade, of the oddball—a range of attributes that television's candy floss culture surely need."[7] Here we see, in essence, the notion of trans-professionalism at work in the broadcasting context: the distinction between producers and publics or participants becomes more fluid, and emphatic relationships and partnerships are constructed. At the same time, the notion of professionalism remained a driving (and protective) force for these producers, and openness toward the "other" implied neither the abandonment of professional ethics, nor the negation of expertise.

Trans-Professionalism in the Postmodern Age

The development of broadcasting in the post-war as a public occupation with professional mores coincides with the period of late modernity in Europe. Anthony Giddens argues that in the period of modernity—defined broadly as the age of industrial capitalism—the concept of time-space distanciation has occurred: the separation of time and space through the intensification of worldwide social relations. Social relationships have to an extent become disembedded and disconnected from traditional face-to-face interactions. Instead, social relationships via communications and the mass media have become re-embedded across different social places and physical places.[8] The jump to a "postmodern condition" has occurred through the acceleration in the globalizing and unifying tendencies of monopoly capitalism. The rapid expansion of global capital accumulation, aided by instant telecommunications, and a supply of cheap, international labor, has resulted in a further distribution of social relationships across time and space. This has created conditions in which a new social order can emerge. The postmodernist claim is that this new economic, social and technological revolution has had an impact on how culture is made and remade, with the explicit assumption that the old concept of a "high" or national culture has been in part superseded by global cultures and a vast multiplicity of localized cultural identities. It is this pressure from above (global) and below (local) that has, arguably, threatened the stability of the nation-state. A prime example of this jump from the modern to the postmodern has been the reorganization of the European telecommunications and broadcasting industries in the past two decades. Broadcasting, especially, was not run on economic criteria but linked to political and cultural needs of the post-war settlement. While European economies were buoyant in the post-1950s period, advertising and marketing opportunities were underutilized. With the onset of economic troubles in the 1970s and 1980s, this situation began to change. Furthermore, by the 1980s social conditions were evolving fast and this impaired the ability of government to keep close control on the broadcasting industry. The post-war boom had produced very different social and economic conditions to those existing in the immediate post-war years. The thirty years from 1945 to 1980 saw massive social upheavals across Europe. The allocation of resources to fund welfare systems ensured that people, on the whole, were healthier and better educated. Economic growth had also led to significant increase in living standards. By the 1980s, therefore, there were numerous interlocking but distinct pressures in favor of broadcasting change: the advent of new distribution technologies such as cable, satellite and digital which led to the expansion of TV channels and the gradual fragmentation of audiences; the re-emergence of ideological thinking welcoming far greater commercial intervention; the demands of the public for more programming and services; and the constant search for economic expansion and renewal. Faced with so many compelling arguments for change, governments gradually dismantled the old broadcasting systems. With hindsight therefore it is hardly surprising that the public service would succumb to a commercial logic that would dominate broadcasting policy for the next two decades. That is not to say, however, that all broadcasting or public participation in post-war Britain and Europe was as highbrow or so strictly related to the information and educational aspects of PSB. Entertainment strands have always featured prominently in PSB radio and TV schedules, more so with the advent of commercial TV models influenced by the United States, and especially with the development of format or canned programming in the 1950s, which have had an impact on public and commercial European broadcasters in recent years.[9]

Since the early 1990s, coinciding with the reorganization of the broadcasting industries, there has been a rapid rise in the number of programs that involve participation of members of the public either on screen or by text, phone or email. Whether as participants in "reality" strands or docu-soaps popular in the late 1990s, or the latest Reality programs, public contributions have become a regular part of viewers' TV diets. Driven primarily by the economically-inspired recognition that more people-centered content would attract larger numbers of viewers and lead to lucrative spin-offs, such as phone competitions, and cheaper production costs, European broadcasters had begun to develop styles and formats of programming that gave ordinary members of the public greater visibility. Talk shows and Reality TV shows have become a ubiquitous feature of TV schedules, offering viewers the opportunity to view themselves, or others like them, apparently holding their own in the company of resident TV celebrities and presenters. The development of the various strands of Reality programming has likewise ensured that the activities of certain members of the public have become the focus of sustained media attention and has provided some participants with opportunities to build media careers as celebrities. The step-change in the development of new audience-centered formats took place at the end of the 1990s. Media companies by then were becoming increasingly globalized in their business dealings with activities including the trade of products and internationalization of corporate and program brands such as *Big Brother*, *Who Wants to be a Millionaire?*, etc. By 2004, the global format program business was worth some €2.4bn. The number of format hours broadcast in the United Kingdom had increased by 22 percent since 2002 and the United Kingdom was also the biggest-single exporter of formats: 32 percent of all format hours broadcast originated in the United Kingdom with Game Shows representing 50 percent of global format airtime.[10] With this development came the accusations that professionalism in broadcasting, which had been nurtured over many decades by public service broadcasters, was being gradually eroded in favor of franchised program formats, which could be exported in a similar fashion to hamburger restaurants. Critics pointed to two areas where broadcasting's social role was being damaged: young producers and documentary film-makers were no longer gaining tradecraft skills as they became increasingly employed on ready-made format programs; and the relationship between film-maker and participant was being compromised as the latter were encouraged to act up for the camera by the former in order to increase the entertainment value of programs.[11] But while critics deplored the rise of this "candy floss culture," others saw the potential of new formats to reach out and touch the lives of audiences as never before. Many of these arguments would be played out in the aftermath of the 2007 U.K. TV scandals, to which we now turn.

The 2007 U.K. Scandals

The kinds of corrupt practices that caused the 2007 U.K. TV scandals are not something new. Many popular forms of TV programs have been accompanied by controversy—and especially those involving public participation or offering large cash prizes—since the introduction of regular TV services in the 1950s. The United States witnessed a spate of incidents in the latter half of the 1950s when cheating was uncovered in *Twenty-One* and the *$64,000 Question*. One of the contestants complicit in the *Twenty-One* scandal, Van Doren, was later portrayed in the Robert Redford movie, *Quiz Show*. There have also been scandals connected with TV programming in the United Kingdom, most notably in October 1996 when the main commercial broadcaster, ITV, broadcast the Carlton TV documentary, *The Connection*, which purportedly provided evidence that there was a new drug supply route to the United Kingdom from Colombian drug cartels, and included an interview with a key cartel member. The documentary deceived viewers because the new drug route did not exist and the interviewee was played by an actor. Carlton was later fined £2 million, a record at the time, by the then U.K. regulator, the Independent Television Commission, for deception.[12]

But the 2007 scandals surpassed any problems that occurred in the late 1990s, arguably leading to a drop in trust among the general public and the arrival of multi-million pound fines for broadcasters.[13] The origins of the 2007/2008 scandals can be traced in part to the rapid growth of participation programs in the early years of the current decade and especially to a revival in the popularity of quiz and talk shows. With the development of digital television in many parts of Europe, and the rapid proliferation of TV and radio channels, the need to find cheaper popular forms of programming to fill the schedules was never so acute at a time of fragmenting audiences. Quiz channels have emerged, which has led mainstream broadcasters to revive this format, especially as appendages to popular talk shows. The widespread use of mobile phones and text messaging in European societies has allowed broadcasters to reach new audiences and develop a new and lucrative income stream in addition to advertising and sponsorship: premium rate telephone charges levied for real time quiz competitions encouraging public participation. And this practice has not been limited to commercial broadcasters. The BBC was happy to take advantage of an opportunity to generate income additional to the license fee. The timeline of the major events related to the scandals described in this chapter was late June 2007 to July 2008:

- June 2007: Media regulator OFCOM fines Channel Five £300,000 for faking the winners of a phone-in quiz on the daytime show *Brainteaser*.
- July: OFCOM becomes the first media regulator to fine the BBC

(£50,000) for a faked phone-in competition on its popular children's TV program, *Blue Peter*.

- July: Controller of the BBC's main TV channel, Peter Fincham, briefs journalists on the upcoming autumn schedule, showing clip from the RDF-made documentary *A Year with the Queen*, in which Queen Elizabeth appears to walk off "in a huff" after a photo-shoot. Within twenty-four hours, the BBC puts out press release making it clear that the clip was edited incorrectly. The BBC orders an enquiry which, when published in October 2007, criticizes the BBC and RDF for "misjudgments, poor practice and ineffective systems."
- September: OFCOM fines *Good Morning TV* (GMTV) over a series of fraudulent phone-in competitions in which some 18 million callers participated without there being a chance of winning.
- December: OFCOM fines Channel 4 a total of £1.5m for misconduct in the *Richard and Judy Show* contest "You Say We Pay," and the "Deal or No Deal" phone-in competition.
- May 2008: OFCOM fines ITV £5.675m—a new record fine—over the misuse of premium-rate phone lines in a host of prime-time shows. ITV made £7.8m from uncounted votes and some 10 million calls were affected.
- June: OFCOM fines GCap Media £1.11m for running a competition that listeners had no chance of winning.
- July: OFCOM fines the BBC £400,000 for unfair conduct in viewer and listener competitions across a range of TV and radio shows. The BBC had revealed that production staff passed themselves off as genuine viewers or listeners, or invented fictitious competition winners.

These fines were imposed following a number of high profile reports conducted by OFCOM and the BBC, drawing on research by consultants and accountants Deloitte and Pricewaterhouse Coopers. The main OFCOM report was written by board member, Richard Ayre, and published in June 2007, and examined the conduct of phone-in competitions in relation to compliance with media regulations and codes. The Ayre report and other enquiries into the failings by broadcasters and program-makers in 2007, makes it clear that much of the focus of debate revolved around compliance or adherence to rules and regulations. As Ayre reports in the opening section of his report:

> My terms of reference required me to consider:
> Consumer protection issues and audiences' attitudes to the use of PRS in television programmes;
> The benefits and risks to broadcasters in the use of PRS in programmes;
> The respective compliance and editorial responsibilities of broadcasters, producers, telecoms network operators and others involved in those pro-

grammes;
The effectiveness of broadcasters' and telecoms operators' internal compliance procedures, guidelines and arrangements to ensure compliance with OFCOM and ICSTIS codes.[14]

And the word "compliance" appears no less than twenty-one times in the report with Ayre's conclusions serving as a damning indictment of broadcasters' failures to adhere to their own rules. As OFCOM chief executive, Ed Richards, commented on publication of the Ayre Report, "programme-makers showed a total disregard for their own terms, conditions and broadcasting codes."[15]

Trans-Professionalism Undone? The Rise of the Post-Professional

There is a small but interesting section toward the end of the Ayre Report that outlines public attitudes to phone-in competitions. The results of a survey provide sober reading for media professionals, with 84 percent of the public blaming broadcasters or regulators for the phone-in scandals. Coupled with polls conducted in the aftermath of the scandals, which note public distrust in broadcasters and phone-in competitions, it has become clear that the key damage to broadcasters is in terms of reputation and trust rather failure in compliance issues. Some in the industry have commented on the necessity of restoring this trust, for example, the Chairman of the BBC, Sir Michael Lyons, argues that the corporation must rebuild its reputation and become a different place.[16] However, the broadcasters' main response has been to ban phone-in competitions, tighten the rules relating to program codes, and talk to each other, arguably a navel-gazing exercise that seeks to protect the industry rather than to provide a public engagement with skeptical audiences. It could be argued that the emphasis on framing these scandals as a lack of compliance with the rules and regulations and providing public demonstrations that the rules have been tightened, somehow diverts attention from the real key failings of broadcasters in 2007, and especially in the way they encourage participation in TV and radio and seek to engage with audiences.

There have been arguments from those within the industry that the implementation of fines and punishments will inhibit risk taking and excellence in broadcasting as producers and film-makers seek to protect themselves. As one former director of BBC radio recently argued:

> I have heard stories about things not making it onto air which really should not be caught by these [new] rules and regulations . . . The pendulum has swung a little bit too far on this occasion. It needs to swing back a bit to allow greater interactivity, which is the great strength of radio . . . There are too many rules and regulations, creating an "I can't be bothered" culture because it is too much trouble to go through the hoops.[17]

While not quite signaling the end of the maverick, odd-ball or renegade, over-reliance on regulations and rules backed up by punishments may inhibit engagement with audiences, which surely would be detrimental to public service ideals.

Another problem with a concentration on compliance is that it diverts attention from the misgivings expressed by academics, some industry figures and members of the public about the current range and nature of audience participation programs and the possibilities they offer for training the current crop of producers and film-makers. A recent example of this occurred in October 2008 when editorial staff cleared for transmission a pre-recorded edition of the weekly BBC *Russell Brand* radio show which included a series of lewd telephone messages left on the answer phone of a senior British actor, Andrew Sachs, by Brand, a comic noted for his edgy and risqué humour, and another leading BBC entertainer, Jonathan Ross. Sachs was especially upset by revelations of a sexual relationship between his granddaughter and Brand. The BBC received 36,000 complaints over the ten days following broadcast. The BBC, Brand and Ross all issued unreserved apologies to Sachs, but the damage had been done. Brand eventually resigned from his radio show along with the head of BBC Radio 2, and Ross, one of the BBC's most highly-paid entertainers, was suspended from all BBC radio and TV programs for three months. Again, much of the media and public debate surrounding "Sachsgate" concentrated on rules and regulations and lack of compliance with BBC editorial codes and why production staff had sanctioned the transmission of such exploitative material, especially when it is a criminal offense in the U.K. to make abusive phone calls.

The broad point we make here is that young production talent is not being taught how to meet basic production and editorial standards. In essence, are producers losing their public occupation or professional status as craft skills are marginalized in the pursuit of audiences and successful formats? Have they become post-professional? Or to paraphrase Kilborn, what are the implications of the current glut of entertainment-led phone in programs and Reality shows for factual and documentary making in general?[18] While documentary strands such as the BBC's *Storyville* continue to enjoy critical acclaim, even examples of carefully crafted programs such as *A Year with the Queen* can fall foul of misleading claims and dubious editing and marketing techniques designed to heighten their entertainment value.

Another danger in the current climate is that attitudes in general to public involvement in broadcasting will become more skeptical and cynical. I have argued elsewhere that there are two main schools of thought about the development of public participation programs in contemporary societies.[19] Optimists emphasize the potential of TV and radio to represent more fully and to strengthen groups and institutions of civil society and encourage greater public participation, especially among those groups that currently feel excluded or marginalized from the mainstream media (ethnic minorities and young adults). Greater public participation is seen here as a democratic good with academics stressing positive aspects of mediated participation via TV, radio and the Internet, where citizens can talk about their lives or state their views on political and social issues.[20] Audiences, too, so the argument goes, enjoy seeing fellow citizens take center stage, especially in the various strands of Reality TV, and "are neither passive nor voyeuristic in their viewing consumption."[21] Gamson, in relation to political talk shows argues that: "Mediated public participation, then, is meaningful for the outcome of the political process, for the individual self-development as a citizen, and for increasing the collective capacity of citizens to act on their own behalf."[22] Producers here are articulated as trans-professional, their professional identity being affected by the participatory process. But their mediating role does not imply the end of this professional identity, only its extension.

Pessimists, especially in light of the 2007 scandals, will question further the virtues of mediated participation suggesting that the rise of such programming has more to do with the commercial and entertainment imperatives of broadcasting and cultural industries internationally than any supposed democratic ideals.[23] They argue that these programs tend to be cheap and formulaic, and exploit real people's lives for entertainment value and profit. The producers of such programs are no longer seen as being driven by professional values and ethics, but rather are seen as exploitative and manipulative. From this perspective, they have become post-professional. Audiences, especially of the more lurid examples of Reality TV cited by critics, such as the *Jerry Springer Show*, are seen as passive voyeurs who have difficulty telling the difference between reality and reconstruction.[24] And the participants themselves can be seen as egoistic show-offs looking to launch/further their media careers. These programs are seen as modern day equivalents of the Victorian Freak Shows, whose educational or informational value was minimal or non-existent.

Clearly, the range of factual programs on offer in the United Kingdom and elsewhere means that neither optimists nor pessimists can claim total victory in pronouncing on the merits or otherwise of participation programs. Participants in *Big Brother* probably have little in common with contributors to a Paul Watson documentary examining the impact of Alzheimer's disease on family life. But the optimists will find little comfort in current trends and will hope that the continued commercialization of the market does not relegate professionalism and meaningful public participation to compliance issues alone, and that the trans-professional is not replaced by the post professional.

Notes

1. Glover, 2007.
2. Ayre; BBC; Glover.
3. L'Etang.
4. Quoted from Morrell.
5. McQuail, 48.
6. BFI.
7. Willis, 97.
8. Giddens, 1991, 3.
9. Moran.
10. Screen Digest, 2005.
11. Kilborn, 2000, 116-117.
12. Winston.
13. BBC; Glover.
14. Ayre, 3.
15. *Guardian*, 2008.
16. Glover.
17. Bannister quoted in Plunkett.
18. Kilborn, 2000, 116.
19. Hibberd in De Blasio, 134.
20. Livingstone and Lunt.
21. Hill, 132.
22. Gamson, 58.
23. Bourdieu.
24. Hill, 131-132.

References

Ayre, Richard. *Report of an Inquiry into Television Broadcasters' Use of Premium Rate Telephone Services in Programmes*. London: OFCOM, 2007. Available at: www.ofcom.org.uk/tv/ifi/prsinquiry/ayrereport/ (accessed November 22, 2009).

BBC. *Annual Report, 2006/2007* and *2007/2008*. Available at: www.bbc.co.uk /annualreport/ (accessed December 18, 2008).

Bourdieu, Pierre. *On Television and Journalism*. London: Verso, 1999.

British Film Institute (BFI). *Screen Online: The Drifters*, 2008. Available at www.screenonline.org.uk/film/id/439877/index.html (accessed December 18, 2008).

De Blasio, Emiliana., Guido Gili, Matthew Hibberd and Michele Sorice. *La Ricerca sull' Audience dei Media*. Milan, Italy: Hoepli, 2007.

Gamson, William A. "Promoting Political Engagement." In *Mediated Politics. Communications and the Future of Democracy*, edited by Lance W. Bennett and Robert M. Entman, 56-74. Cambridge, U.K.: Cambridge University Press, 2001.

Giddens, Anthony. *Modernity and Self-Identity: Self and Society in the Late Modern Age*. Stanford, Calif.: Stanford University Press, 1991.

Glover, John. "Poll Reveals How Trust in BBC Has Plummeted." *Guardian*, July 28,

2007.

Guardian. "ITV hit with Record £5.68m fine." 2008.

Habermas, Jürgen. *The Structural Transformation of the Public Sphere.* Cambridge, U.K.: Polity Press, 1989.

Hill, Annette. "Fearful and Safe: Audience Response to British Reality Programming." In *From Grierson to the Docu-Soap: Breaking the Boundaries*, edited by John Izod, Richard Kilborn and Matthew Hibberd, 131-144. Luton, U.K.: University of Luton Press, 2000.

Kilborn, Richard. "The Docu-Soap: a Critical Assessment." In *From Grierson to the Docu-Soap: Breaking the Boundaries*, edited by John Izod, Richard Kilborn and Matthew Hibberd, 111-120. Luton, U.K.: University of Luton Press, 2000.

L'Etang, Jacquie. *Public Relations: Concepts, Practice and Critique.* London: Sage, 2008.

Livingstone, Sonia and Peter Lunt. *Talk on Television.* London: Routledge, 1994.

McQuail, Dennis. "Journalism as a Public Occupation: Alternative Images." In *Democracy, Journalism and Technology: New Developments in an Enlarged Europe*, edited by Nico Carpentier, et al., 47-59. Tartu, Estonia: Tartu University Press, 2008.

Moran, Albert. *The Significance of Format Programming for PSB.* Keynote speech given to RIPE Conference, "Public Service Broadcasting in a Multimedia Environment: Programmes and Platform." Amsterdam, November 15-16, 2006. Available at: www.yle.fi/ripe/Keynotes/Moran_KeynotePaper.pdf (accessed December 18, 2008).

Morrell, David. "What is Professionalism?" *Catholic Medical Quarterly.* February, 2003. Available at: www.catholicdoctors.org.uk/CMQ/2003/Feb/what_is_professionalism.htm.

OFCOM. *Comments of Ed Richards on Release of Today's Ayre Inquiry to the Broadcasting Press Guild.* Press Release, July 18, 2007. Available at: www.ofcom.org.uk/media/speeches/2007/07/bpg07 (accessed December 18, 2008).

Plunkett, John. "Bannister Says Anti-fakery Regulations are Damaging BBC Output." *Guardian*, July 1, 2008.

Screen Digest. *The Global Trade in Television Formats*, 2005. Report accessed at www.screendigest.com/reports/gttf05/pdf/GTTF05_1-n/view.html (accessed November 22, 2009).

Willis, John. "Breaking the Boundaries." In *From Grierson to the Docu-Soap: Breaking the Boundaries*, edited by John Izod, Richard Kilborn and Matthew Hibberd, 97-102. Luton, U.K.: University of Luton Press, 2000.

Winston, Brian. "Making Connections: The European Convention on Human Rights, the Independent Television Commission and the Documentary." In *From Grierson to the Docu-Soap: Breaking the Boundaries*, edited by John Izod, Richard Kilborn and Matthew Hibberd, 209-220. Luton, U.K.: University of Luton Press, 2000.

Part 2
TRANS-POLITICS

Chapter 7
A Short Introduction to Trans-Politics and the Trans-Political
Nico Carpentier

These two concepts attempt to capture a process that transgresses the borders of politics (as an institutionalized system) or the political (as the broad ideological domain) by saturating it with a particular discourse. In contrast, the concepts of post-politics and the post-political, for instance, are reserved when these types of hegemonic projects manage to achieve a certain stability (albeit of course limited over space and time). The basic assumption behind the concepts of trans-politics, the trans-political—and even post-politics and the post-political—is that political realities are characterized by a diversity of uncommensurable discourses (or ideologies, positions, interests, values, norms, etc.), which, at the same time, often compete to become the univocal representation of these political realities situated simultaneously at the micro and macro level.

Permanently frustrated by the infinity of the political field of discursivity, there is no political project (or even discourse) that can uphold its claims to capturing the universal through the particular[1] or to essentializing a political reality, since there is always the possibility of a dis/re-articulation and dislocation of these political projects. At the same time, political projects sometimes have explicit or implicit strategies to hegemonize or normalize their discursive constructions of reality, with the objective of becoming a social imaginary that can benefit fully from being taken for granted, or that can be considered universal. In practice, these strategies can be based on (calls for) common sense, morality, expertise or (bureaucratic) management.

Although this hegemonic situation is unavoidably unstable and undecidable, and resistance will always occur, these strategies in some cases succeed to (temporarily) foreclose on the structural openness that characterizes the social, and remove conflict and difference from the political equation. In these cases trans-politics becomes post-politics, and the trans-political is turned into the post-political.

Although these transgressive processes can be seen to be at work at the level of institutionalized politics (which here we call trans-politics), they are not limited to this specific societal system. The democratic revolution over the past 200 years has gradually opened a diversity of societal systems to contestation and conflict. As pluralist-democratic and radical-democratic models argue, this broadening of the political playing field first of all affects the relationship between the world of institutionalized (or party) politics and other societal structures (such as civil society), which is producing the more fluid and networked structure of institutionalized (trans-) politics.

But power and conflict do not stop at the edges of institutionalized politics, however fuzzy these frontiers have become. The political pervades many more societal fields, which do not all link up necessarily to institutionalized politics. Ideological projects can be found in any realm of the social; this is exactly their objective when the project is being developed and their strength when the objective is realized. Given the importance of symbolic capital in contemporary societies, it comes as no surprise that media organizations are involved in these hegemonic struggles, not only distributing media products that (can) act as carriers for hegemonized discourses, but also strengthening hegemonic discourses through their own structures, practices, and cultures.

Note

1. Laclau.

References

Laclau, Ernesto. *Emancipation(s)*. London: Verso, 1996.

Chapter 8
Post-Democracy, Hegemony, and Invisible Power: The Reality TV Media Professional as *Primum Movens Immobile*
Nico Carpentier ·

Setting the Stage: The Identity of Reality TV's Media Professionals

Reality TV is often seen as a tool of empowerment, which gives "ordinary" people the opportunity to gain access to the sacral sphere of the TV system. As they become visible, they are offered opportunities to perform identity politics or simply enjoy the pleasure of presence. Paradoxically, they are at the same time subjected to high levels of management by a wide variety of media professionals, making Reality TV a site of power imbalance and participatory fantasies.

This chapter looks at the hegemonic identity of Reality TV's media professionals and how this identity legitimizes this strong power imbalance. The taken-for-grantedness and normality of these power imbalances raise especial concerns about the democratic potential of Reality TV. Although a wide variety of hegemonic and counter-hegemonic discourses and practices can be generated in the context of Reality TV, the power imbalance and the position of media professionals at the heart of the Panopticon remain almost impossible to contest and are structurally constitutive for many Reality TV programs.

Given this essentialist, universalized and hyper-consensual position of the media professional, we can link the production context of Reality TV to the notions of the post-political and post-democratic. In the post-political and post-democratic condition, we become entangled in an ultimate consensus that transcends political dissent, combined with a (state or media) system that has incorporated almost all powers for the exercise of governance. In this chapter these theoretical concepts are combined with a Foucauldian analytics of power and the Aristotelian (myth of) the first mover, which allows me to demonstrate the politics of invisibility in Reality TV. In order to further demonstrate the workings of the politics of invisibility, the management techniques of two seemingly very different programs—*Temptation Island* and *Barometer*—are analyzed as case studies.

The Post-Political and Post-Democratic Condition

In order to theorize Reality TV and the management culture of its media professionals, we can first turn to political theory, and more specifically to the work of Mouffe (and others such as Žižek and Rancière) on the post-political. The starting point is Mouffe's recent work, which focuses (amongst other issues) on the conditions of possibility of agonism. Echoing Connolly,[1] the agonistic model of democracy is built upon the distinction between antagonism (between enemies) and agonism (between adversaries). While the presence of an adversary is considered legitimate and his/her right to defend his/her ideas is not questioned, an enemy is (to be) excluded from the political community.[2] The aim of democratic politics then becomes to "tame" or "sublimate"[3] antagonisms, without eliminating conflict and passion from the political realm or relegating it to the outskirts of the private, and without denying the structural existence of antagonisms in society. Although agonistic struggle has been criticized by Žižek[4] for its inability to challenge the present-day, neo-liberal status quo, Mouffe believes that it can and should "bring about new meanings and fields of application for the idea of democracy to be radicalized."[5]

But, at the same time, Mouffe recognizes the tendencies of political actors to strive for hegemony. Already in 1985, in *Hegemony and Socialist Strategy*, co-authored with Ernesto Laclau, Mouffe made extensive use of the Gramscian (version of the) concept of hegemony. The ultimate objective of these hegemonic projects is to construct and stabilize the nodal points that can form the basis of a social order, the aim being to transform myths into a social imaginary, i.e., a horizon that "is not one among other objects but an absolute limit which structures a field of intelligibility and is thus the condition of possibility of the emergence of any object."[6] At the same time, these hegemonies can never be total, all-encompassing or unchangeable, as Mouffe also points out: "Every hegemonic order is susceptible of being challenged by counter-hegemonic practices, i.e., practices which will attempt to disarticulate the existing order so as to install other forms of hegemony."[7]

In her 2005 book, *On the Political*, Mouffe critiques the neo-liberal hegemony and its capacity to ignore the pluralist and antagonistic characteristics of the political, replacing it with an ethics of harmony and consensus. For Mouffe, the "context of conflictuality" remains crucial to our understanding of the political, and more specifically, the power conflict, and antagonisms are seen as the driving forces of contemporary political realities.[8] This position is hardly surprising, given Mouffe's post-structuralist emphasis on contingency and difference, starting from the idea that rearticulations and reconfigurations of the social are always possible. At the same time she recognizes that stability and fixity do exist, but the social is at the same time always structurally unstable and unfixed, as any kind of stability and fixity can always be destabilized and dislocated. From this perspective, harmony and consensus are seen as temporarily and spatially contingent, and cannot be seen as structural characteristics of the political. Although Mouffe[9] agrees that consensus is necessary, dissent remains an equally necessary *compagnion de route*. Her radical pluralism (whose development originated in her earlier work with Laclau)[10] articulates the existence of diversity and conflict as structuring forces of the political, which she contrasts with (a "dominant tendency within") liberalism, and the way it understands pluralism:

> The typical liberal understanding of pluralism is that we live in a world in which there are indeed many perspectives and values and that, owing to empirical limitations, we will never be able to adopt them all, but that, when put together, they constitute an harmonious and non-conflictual ensemble.[11]

The discourse of consensus thus becomes another strategy to hegemonize (or universalize, or essentialize) political projects that are intrinsically particular, a strategy that aims to mute the voices that find themselves outside the dominant social imaginary. Mouffe's work suggests that this hegemonic strategy uses "essentialist forms of identification or non-negotiable moral values"[12] to establish a consensus and disregard the possibility of dissensus. In this post-political configuration even the possibility of contesting these forms of identification and moral values becomes non-existent. In other words, the post-political is a political project that negates what structurally defines the political (namely the existence of antagonism, difference, and dissensus), and that posits a particular perspective on social reality as a universal and non-negotiable truth.

Mouffe's perspective on the post-political is similar to Rancière's concept of the post-democratic, although Rancière focuses more on the (hegemonizing) role of government.[13] However, there is also a more general formulation developed (when discussing "the communitarian miscalculations"), in which Rancière sees post-democracy as "the rule of the principle of unification of the multitude under the common law of the One."[14] His more specific formulation (relating post-democracy to government) resounds earlier critiques on the technocratization of the political and on competitive-elitist democratic theory, where democratic government becomes detached from popular participation (in whatever form), as illustrated by the following:

> Postdemocracy is the government practice and conceptual legitimation of a
> democracy *after the demos*, a democracy that has eliminated the appearance,
> miscount, and dispute of the people and is thereby reducible to the sole inter-
> play of state mechanisms and combinations . . . It is the practice and theory of
> what is appropriate with no gap left between the forms of the State and the state
> of social relations.[15]

Just like in the political, power plays a crucial role in the post-political and post-
democratic condition. Here, we can revert to Foucault's work and his analytics
of power. In his *History of Sexuality*,[16] he states that power does not belong to a
specific actor (or class), but cuts across human relationships. However, this mobile and multidirectional character of power does not mean that power relations
are equally balanced. Foucault expressly recognizes the existence of unequal
power relations, focusing on discipline (of the other and the self) in *Discipline
and Punish*.[17] Of course, the possibility of resistance and contra-strategies will
remain, and no actor will ever be able to fully realize his strategies and intentions, but, at the same time, hegemonic discourses and practices will still play
crucial roles in structuring the social. In some cases, hegemonic forces will
manage to establish a social horizon that "is not one among other objects but an
absolute limit which structures a field of intelligibility and is thus the condition
of possibility of the emergence of any object."[18]

Another metaphor that can be applied to analyze this condition of hegemony is Aristotle's concept of the first mover. In his *Metaphysics*, Aristotle claims
that the divine is defined by its capacity to generate movement without moving
itself. As what is being moved is intermediate, the first mover is "something
which moves without being moved, being eternal, substance, and actuality."[19]
Of course, the first mover metaphor is hardly capable of presenting a convincing
case of a divine existence. Nevertheless, it provides a good metaphor for the
intensity and rigidity of hegemony, where the first mover is perceived as the
source and origin of the emergence and movement of any object (to paraphrase
Laclau)[20], signifying its normality, taken-for-grantedness and indisputability. As
is the case with hegemony, the first mover can always be dethroned, denatural-
ized and de-essentialized, but usually the first mover does not yield lightly.
From a Foucauldian position, also the first mover cannot escape being implicated, being moved, pushing the first mover to the level of the mythical.

> Such is perhaps the most diabolical aspect of the idea and of all the applications
> it brought about. In this form of management, power is not totally entrusted to
> someone who would exercise it alone, over others, in an absolute fashion;
> rather this machine is one in which everyone is caught, those who exercise this
> power as well as those who are subjected to it.[21]

In the context of this chapter, special attention is paid to the notions of visibility
and invisibility in the exercise of power. Obviously, Foucault's (use of the)

metaphor of the Panopticon shows the importance of visibility and invisibility in the exercise of power, as the objects of the disciplining power are rendered visible to the disciplining gaze of the guards that wield power, while the guards themselves remain invisible. In her discussion on performance, Phelan formulates this as follows: "the binary between the power of visibility and the impotency of invisibility is falsifying. There is real power in remaining unmarked; and there are serious limitations to visual representation as a political goal."[22] Referring to Lacan, she continues: "Visibility is a trap it summons surveillance and the law; it provokes voyeurism, fetishism, the colonialist/imperial appetite for possession." To put this into a Foucauldian perspective: the objects of power have become more visible, while the exercise of power has become less visible. And to use the Aristotelian metaphor, the first mover becomes hidden, cloaking its operations, whilst what is being moved, becomes visible.

Media and the Post-Political

The question that arises is whether we can transfer this debate to the realm of the media and Reality TV. A theoretical argument that legitimizes this migration[23] can be found in Mouffe's broad definition of the political. In contrast to politics, Mouffe sees the political as a domain of the social, which can emerge in a wide range of social relations (as explicitly indicated in the definition rendered below). Moving into the world of trans-politics, this wide range of social relations would arguably include both mediated social relations and social relations within the media system itself.

> By "the political," I refer to the dimension of antagonism that is inherent in human relations, antagonism that can take many forms and emerge in different types of social relations. "Politics" on the other side, indicates the ensemble of practices, discourses and institutions which seek to establish a certain order and organize human coexistence in conditions that are always potentially conflictual because they are affected by the dimension of "the political."[24]

A second line of arguments legitimizing the migration of the (post-)political can be found in the extensive literature on media, participation, and democracy, showing the intimate relationship between media and the political. Here, it is important to distinguish between participation *in* the media and *through* the media. Participation *through* the media deals with the opportunities for extensive participation in public debate and for self-representation in the public sphere. Consensus-oriented models of democracy (and participation) emphasize the importance of dialogue and deliberation and focus on collective decision-making based on rational arguments in the public sphere, à la Habermas.[25] Other authors[26] stress more conflict-oriented approaches. They point to the unavoidability of political differences and struggles, and call attention to articulations of the media as crucial sites of the struggles for hegemony. Both consensus- and conflict-oriented models facilitate emphasis on the need for citizens' participation in the processes of dialogue, debate, and deliberation. Participation *in* the media deals with the participation of non-professionals in the production of media output (content-related participation) and in media decision-making (structural participation). These forms of media participation allow citizens to be active in one of the many (micro-)spheres relevant to daily life and to put into practice their right to communicate.

Alternative media have proven to be more successful in organizing more intense forms of participation in the media[27], but mainstream media have also attempted to organize forms of audience participation. The BBC's TV and web project, *Video Nation*, illustrates that many obstacles can be reduced effectively when the involved media professionals adopt an open, honest, respectful, process-oriented and (micro-)participatory attitude, based on a thorough analysis of the power processes and imbalances.[28] In Reality TV, we can find a number of arguments to support the participatory claims made by these programs, however diverse. First, Reality TV provides "ordinary" (and many other social categories of) people access to the TV system or to the machineries of mediation that renders their existence, practices and discourses visible to the outside world, and (in some cases) allows them to acquire celebrity status.[29] As Andrejevic phrases it: "the promise of Reality TV is not that of access to unmediated reality so much as it is the promise of the access to the reality of mediation."[30] This access renders "ordinary" people and their everyday lives visible, and signifies their importance. It resonates with what Lazarsfeld and Merton[31] called the status conferral function, and with Tuchman's[32] notion of (avoiding) symbolic annihilation, summarized by Gerbner and Gross as: "Representation in the fictional world signifies social existence; absence means symbolic annihilation."[33]

But the democratic importance of Reality TV cannot be reduced to mere access; this access also allows "ordinary" people to enter into interactions with a number of other participants, with media professionals, and with audiences, collaborating in the production of a televisional text. Through their presence they can at least assist in the production of a wide set of discourses, which have (sometimes strong) ideological and political signification. At the same time, Reality TV also produces discourses on participation and power, as we get to see a participatory process (and its failures and constraints). These screened interactions contain moments of joint decision-making, providing a stage via which we enter the realm of participation (in Pateman's strict definition).[34] As Ouelette and Hay remark: "To say that reality TV offers demonstrations in group participation and governance is to point out TV's little, everyday ways of instructing viewers about the techniques and rules of participation."[35] This also brings us to Hartley's[36] argument about democratainment, indicating that TV can indeed offer a combination of civic education and entertainment.

Of course, all is not well with the participatory process of Reality TV programs. Even if "ordinary" people are granted access to the TV system and to the TV screen, the question remains what kind of existences, practices and discourses are they allowed to generate. Access as such does not necessarily avoid symbolic annihilation, as omission is not its sole dimension. Tuchman[37] added two more dimensions to symbolic annihilation, namely trivialization and condemnation. In the case of Reality TV, and especially in the case of the Humiliation TV subgenre, "ordinary" participants could end up taking part in rather disadvantageous (self)representations that produce a "spectacle of shame" or a "freak show."[38] For instance, Palmer[39] argues that this "spectacle of shame" is intrinsically linked to a major part of the genre of Reality TV, while Hill maintains that humiliation plays an important role in Reality TV:

> Some of the most dominant types of Reality TV have been the reality gameshow . . . and reality talentshow. These formats, and their celebrity cousins, have concentrated on putting people in difficult, often emotionally challenging situations. Audiences have come to categorize this specific type of Reality TV as "humiliation TV."[40]

Also, the levels of interaction and participation are often problematic. One of the harshest critiques comes from Andrejevic,[41] who claims that Reality TV might not result in the demystification of TV, but rather might enhance the fetishization of TV. This line of reasoning is related to Couldry's[42] argument that a series of media rituals serves and strengthens (the myth of) the mediated center. This implies that (mainstream) media organizations not only attempt to hegemonize their key position in social reality, but also to hegemonize their embeddedness in capitalist economies, their organizational cultures of management, their internal power structures and their modi operandi. This media-centric perspective strongly impacts on the intensity of participation within the Reality TV genre, to a degree, which Andrejevic, for instance, refers to as the "democratization of access to publicity as public relations" as he ponders on the need to distinguish between transactional and democratic participation.[43]

A crucial factor limiting the participatory intensity of Reality TV is the specific position of its media professionals, given the skewed power balance between them and the "ordinary" participants. Media professionals are placed in hierarchically structured entities and attributed specific responsibilities for the professional production of specific media products. This responsibility is complemented by the notion of psychological property.[44] To realize the professional goals in a world dominated by routine and time—a "stop-watch culture"[45]— media professionals can make use of the production facilities that are owned (in the strictly legal sense of the word) by the media organization. Wilpert's[46] theory of psychological appropriation provides support for the thesis that control over these production facilities leads to a sense of property. It is precisely this combination of responsibility and (psychological) property that supports the articulation of the media professional as the manager of a diversity of resources, from technology, via content, to people,[47] which, in turn, legitimizes the management, surveillance and disciplining of the "ordinary" participants. Moreover, the combination of Reality TV's focus on "ordinary" participants, and the identification of the media professional as the manager of resources, often leads to their reduced visibility. They of course remain visible for the participants, but they also resort to on-site managerial strategies (like rules and contracts) that render their operations at least partially invisible. Secondly, they are often edited out of the programs so that audience cannot witness them actually managing the participants. Of course, at the same time, we should be careful not to attribute absolute power to these media professionals, which would eliminate the possibility that participants might resist their management.

The impact of the hegemony of media-centrality within Reality TV, strengthened by the dominant position of the media professional, brings us back to the debate over the post-political and post-democracy. Within Reality TV, the access and representation of "ordinary" people remains a possibility, and might have empowering aspects in cases ranging "from people overcoming accidents and illness, to inspiring examples of people experiencing new things, to tips and advice on gardening or buying a home, all of which can present a positive message to viewers."[48] But, at the same time—and even in the cases referred to above—the restrictions imposed on the participatory process, and the structurally unequal power relations between the "ordinary" participants and the media professionals, radically disempowers many Reality TV participants.

The post-political thus not necessarily enters the stage at the level of the produced discourses, which remain diverse and often contradictory (avoiding hegemonic closure), and where the political can still play. The post-political becomes very present at the level of the production process with its skewed power relations. Reality TV, in many cases, remains political because of the structural openness of the wide range of specific discourses it produces, but it is simultaneously post-political because the hegemonic and consensual positions of the media professional (and the capitalist media system in which the media professional is embedded) are normalized and almost impossible to contest. We do see many examples of resistant practices, but these practices are often characterized by their temporality and are quickly and easily incorporated within the televisional narratives and absorbed within the programs' power structures. The alliance between media system and media professionals generates a power-bloc that has managed to have its self-proclaimed centrality accepted, and has consolidated the legitimacy of its high levels of control as a societal horizon. This "paradox of democratic participation"[49] also renders Reality TV an illustration of post-(media)democracy, with the alteration that, in these cases, not the state, but the media system exercises extraordinary powers. In this sense, the Reality

TV production teams become first movers: they are not seen themselves to be movable, but they manage to generate the movements on which the TV program is constructed. And, especially in comparison to the powers they wield, their on-screen visibility is very limited (sometimes virtually non-existent); often, we can only establish their presence through the effects of their actions.

A First Case Study: *Temptation Island*[50]

As indicated in the introduction to this chapter, the workings of the management techniques, the normalization of the legitimacy of the media professionals to exert these techniques, and their politics of invisibility, are illustrated by two case studies. The first concerns the fairly traditional reality game show *Temptation Island*, which does not have an explicit democratic-participatory claim (in contrast to the second program in the case study), but is very much articulated as entertainment.

The Format

The Reality show *Temptation Island* was televised for the first time in 2001 on the Fox network in the United States. Many TV networks bought the rights to this format, and in Belgium and the Netherlands the local version was produced by Kanakna Productions for two SBS Network broadcasters, namely VT4 in North-Belgium and Veronica in the Netherlands. The first Dutch *Temptation Island* was televised in 2002, and there has been a new series produced every year since, with the sixth (the latest at the time of writing) series broadcast from March 2007. A seventh series was broadcast in 2009 by VT4 only.

The format of *Temptation Island* is relatively simple, based on a clear and quasi-impenetrable categorization of the participants. Eight couples, four men and four women, are housed separately in "resorts" on two tropical islands,[51] where they meet a number of so-called "singles" (or "tempters" and "temptresses"). The program format revolves around a relationship test, in which each partner receives the attention of the tempters or temptresses over two weeks.

The eight partners (and their tempters/temptresses) spend most of their time having fun, in smaller or larger groups, with every action filmed and recorded by (sometimes hidden) cameras and sound recording equipment, by the *Temptation Island* production team. Each episode consists of a montage of this footage accompanied by commentary, and interviews with the participants. The (group) interactions are alternated with two subformats. On the so-called "dates," which culminate in the "dream date," the partners choose one of the tempters/temptresses for a private date, during which they partake in a romantic activity or an adventure. In the second scenario the participants are shown video clips of their partners' escapades at the so-called "bonfires," while being interviewed by one of the presenters. The final meeting between the couples takes place during a bonfire. Both the dates and the bonfires are aimed at increasing the pressure on the partners. The final episode in the series consists of a visit to each of the couples some months after their *Temptation Island* stay, in which an inventory is made of the damage caused to their relationship.

Power, Surveillance and Temptation Island

Applying Foucault's analytics of power to *Temptation Island*'s production sphere shows that the actors effectively find themselves in unequal power relations, and confronting the post-political hegemony of the production team. On the one hand, the media professionals largely control the island context: they have developed (*in casu* adapted) the format, they have established the rules that must be followed on the island, they have chosen (*in casu* cast) the participants, they have drawn up their contracts. Also, their cameras (partly visible and partly hidden) are focused twenty-four hours a day on the participants, they ask the interview questions, and they select the footage and edit it into a cohesive narrative which is broadcast on their respective stations. On the other hand, the participants are not completely powerless. The entire format of *Temptation Island* depends on their willingness to commit to interaction with the other participants, to answer the interview questions, to live with microphones attached to their bodies, and to try to forget about the ubiquitous cameras and cameramen and behave as "normally" as possible.

The production team uses a number of sophisticated management techniques to place the partners under pressure, the most important of these is the unlimited trial. By basing the entire program concept on a relationship test to which the participants voluntarily subject themselves, the extreme interventions of the production team are legitimized. Based on the concept of the relationship test, *Temptation Island* becomes an unlimited trial, where not only the tempters/temptresses "do everything in their power to place as much pressure as possible on the women [and men]" (VT4 website[52]), but also the production team tries to influence the context in such a way that the relationships of the carefully selected couples are put under pressure, often (but not always) resulting in a break-up between the partners when the series ends. By taking part in a program with this format, the participants relinquish power over the nature and intensity of the tests to which they are subjected.

The basic mechanism of the unlimited trial as management technique is strengthened by the artificial setting, which is strongly reminiscent of a Panopticon. The participants are cleverly isolated by being housed on a distant tropical island, which offers a wide range of tourist (and sexual) attractions, but at the same time is strongly reminiscent of a prison (including the occasional "escape"). Within the imaginary walls of the so-called "resorts" the participants are subjected to numerous surveillance techniques by means of which (almost) all their activities are captured day and night. Moreover, *Temptation Island* is "safeguarded" by numerous rules, which are contractually enforced, and which direct and discipline the participants' behavior. Later, the images are edited by the media professionals and then shown to the viewers and to their partners. With the exception of the presenters, the production team is hardly ever visible in the episodes that are broadcast. Again, they remain hidden.

A third management technique is based on what Foucault[53] terms confessional power. *Inter alia,* through interviews, the participants are continually urged to describe their activities and emotional states, and to confess even slight "infringements" of the rules to the presenters and thus also to the viewers. The interview questions are (partly) enabled by the production team's Olympian perspective (due to the ubiquitous cameras). This not only results in an endless series of (self)revelation, not of course reciprocated by the presenters, it also makes the presenters the first witnesses (and judges) of the, often inevitable, "lapses" of the partners. The culmination of the confessional power is found in the subformat of the bonfire, where the partners are questioned about their reactions to seeing suggestive or explicit clips of their partners, and where they also confess their own "bad behavior." It is in particular at the last bonfire, where the partners are re-united and have to confess their "sins" to each other (and to the presenter and viewers), that the most intimate details are revealed, often leading to emotional outbursts.

There are two more aspects of the production team's management techniques that should be highlighted in this analysis. First, the power dynamics are more complex than described above, because the partners do try to support and protect each other, but they also discuss and make judgements about each other's behavior, during the interviews. Second, and more important, is the evident resistance to the management of the production team from many of the participants. Despite lack of opportunity, participants sometimes do manage to escape the cameras and microphones, for example, by swimming out to sea, thereby becoming invisible and inaudible, or simply by removing their portable microphones. Also, a refusal to participate in the interaction by them locking themselves in or "going to bed early," in some instances can be seen as resistance. Also, the roles of tempters/temptresses were sometimes not performed with as much enthusiasm as expected.

A Second Case Study: *Barometer*[54]

The second case study has a very different angle, as *Barometer* has (in contrast to *Temptation Island*) an explicit participatory-democratic claim. But as the case study will show, the actual production practices position *Barometer* more within the Reality TV genre than could be expected at first sight. The *Barometer* case actually shows how channel managers and the program's media professionals attempt to leave their post-political position, but are lured back into it, and end up producing a Reality TV program instead of an Access TV program.

The Format

Barometer is a North-Belgian Access TV program inspired by BBC's *Video Nation*. There have been two series with, respectively five and eight episodes, of this program which is produced by Kanakna, and broadcast on the TV1 channel of the North-Belgian public broadcaster VRT. Each twenty-minute episode of *Barometer* was based on six two and a half to three and half minute "video letters," produced by "ordinary" viewers. The topics of these video letters varied widely, as illustrated by the episode shown on April 30, 2002, which dealt with: (i) practicing firemen; (ii) a sixteen-year-old happy mom; (iii) a practical joke involving a traffic light; (iv) a mucoviscidoses patient receiving a pair of new lungs; (v) a complaint against rack renters; (vi) elderly skydivers.

The program and the video letters are introduced by Michiel Hendryckx, a (press) photographer, who was only later to achieve some renown for presenting a motorcycle/travel show (called *The Gang of Wim*). Rather specific is that Michiel Hendryckx is filmed in his own living room doing the *Barometer* introductions, which is designed to increase the authenticity and appearance of ordinariness. At the start of the first episode, the presenter explains this:

> Good evening, and welcome to *Barometer*, the new TV1 program. But also welcome to my home, and this is rather unusual—TV programs are only rarely produced or broadcast from somebody's home. But *Barometer* isn't an ordinary program, it is a program that is made by you, the viewers. (Michiel Hendryckx [presenter] *Barometer*, Episode April 30, 2002)

The program's production process is seemingly straightforward. The viewers are invited to send their video letters to the program's presenter, Michiel Hendryckx. As his introduction in the second episode suggests, he makes the selection, and the selected material is then broadcast.

> Good evening, and welcome to the second episode of *Barometer*. It has been a busy week, I've received many video letters, letters that were made by you. I have watched them with pleasure and, as usual, I have selected six. The first letter is from Keerbergen [a small Belgian city], and was made by Linda. Linda is a happy woman, the daughter of a farming family, who is afraid that the environment and scenery of her youth is about to disappear. (Michiel Hendryckx, *Barometer*, Episode May 6, 2002)

On other occasions, the presenter's intros and outros suggest a slightly more complicated production process, in which the production team supplies the camera and provides technical support. Nevertheless, the idea is that "ordinary" people can produce these video letters themselves, as explained by VRT's producer Wendel Goossens: "The idea was to give a half hour of our broadcasting time to our viewers. We want to be a forum for viewers, that they can go to, and where we as program-makers do not interfere" (interview with Wendel Goossens, VRT producer *Barometer*). If we compare the (public version of the) production process of *Barometer* to *Video Nation*,[55] two important differences emerge. In the case of (the televized version of) *Video Nation*, the participant support structure is extensive; the participants were able to keep the camera for a longer period of time, and a member of the production team was available to provide assistance when necessary. Secondly, as *Video Nation* was embedded in the ideology of the BBC's Community Program Unit, attempts were made to maximize the participant power base within the BBC's institutional context. In the case of *Barometer*, the support and the intensity of the participatory process were less developed.

One could question, of course, whether access programs such as *Barometer* and *Video Nation* can be labeled Reality TV. Both Dovey[56] and Biressi and Nunn[57] link *Video Nation* to the (post-) documentary tradition, but at the same time acknowledge its capacity to represent everyday realities and its influence on the Reality TV genre. For instance, Biressi and Nunn write that "the look of Video Nation . . . has become part of the new visual lexicon of 'real life' on television."[58] More importantly, the actual production process of *Barometer* (see below) renders it more Reality TV than Access TV, given the strong impact of the producers. The choice to include the relatively old *Barometer* as a case study in this chapter remains debatable, but in practice *Barometer* has become Reality TV.

Barometer *and the Hidden Production Team*

If we look at the management techniques used by the *Barometer* production team from a Foucauldian perspective, we can see that the power relations in the *Barometer* production process were not necessarily very balanced, although the managerial strategies that are used are relatively different. The media professionals intervened on a number of levels to facilitate the production process and to increase the "professional quality" of the video letters. Firstly, they contacted participants in advance, which allowed the production team to plan and structure the actual filming. Although the participants had a voice in this negotiation, the media professionals' culture had a strong impact on the negotiation and its outcomes. One of the producers explains this as follows:

What happens beforehand is a discussion over the phone; then we say: Yes, and how will we be able to do that? We'll start with you in the playground, and then we should go into the classroom to film, so all the girlfriends need to be there. And what class are we going to take? So we do create a structure beforehand, and then we explain how they need to operate the camera. Some of them can do it themselves, others can't and then we do it for them (interview with Wendel Goossens, VRT Producer *Barometer*).

Secondly, when filming had been completed, the raw material was collected and processed by the media professionals. After an initial screening, the producers took the material to a (professional) editor, to reduce the available material to a well-structured and short video letter, with music added. Although the VRT managers criticized Kanakna for "aesthetisizing the [video letters] too much, modifying them and adding sound to them" (interview with Frank Symoens, Production Manager VRT), and the presenter also expressed dissatisfaction with the addition of music, Kanakna refused to implement a "rough" editing style, supported by audience research. Kanakna's producer of *Barometer* articulated Kanakna's role as follows, again emphasizing the role of the media professional and the imposition of professional standards at the levels of both content and form:

It is something that these people have been working on for two hours; you can't broadcast the full version. It [the unedited version] is of no value to the viewer, so of course we have to edit it. It is our job, to reduce the length, and to make the story—how it is told by the person—as clear and specific as possible in the three minutes available. And that's the hardest thing of all, because these people are clearly having trouble saying clearly and concretely what it boils down to (interview with Isabel Dierckx, Kanakna producer *Barometer*).

But, arguably, the production team's most important intervention is at the level of selection. On this point, interviews were contradictory. Most people that were involved in the production process described the formal procedure as above. In one case, VRT's producer of *Barometer* refers to the lack of contributions, but then changes the conversation ("It wasn't the case that we got a gigantic number of . . . but let's look at the procedure"; interview with Wendel Goossens, VRT's *Barometer* producer). But it was the presenter—a press photographer and not a Kanakna employee—who described a different procedure, which was later (in 2008) confirmed by three other interviews.[59] In the interview, the presenter explains that Kanakna was not receiving enough contributions and decided to add some researchers to the production team, who could scan the newspapers and look for potential stories and participants.

I was led to believe that these people [the participants] contacted Kanakna themselves . . . but after the summer, during the second series, it turned out that almost nobody . . . They had to go and look for people. They searched the newspaper for articles, then they contacted the people, and asked them: Would you like to make a video letter? (Interview with Michiel Hendryckx, Presenter *Barometer*)

The above extract is not only an indication of the post-political and post-democratic condition within the media system, it also shows the invisibility of the power exercised by the production team. Again, with the exception of the presenter, who is not a formal member of the production team, the media professionals are not visible in the program. In *Barometer*, the presenter symbolically represents the production team (making the media professional seem visible on screen), but, at the same time, he is an outsider with little control (and rendering the "real" media professionals invisible). For instance, with one exception and despite the formulation of his introduction to the programs, which suggest otherwise, he has no say in the selection of the video letters. The presenter claims to have received the video letters only the day before his introductions are filmed. When asked who is responsible for the selection, he replies (rhetorically excluding himself from the production team): "The people from the production team do that. You'll have to ask them . . . I didn't . . . I only vetoed a letter once, but I didn't have a say" (interview with Michiel Hendryckx, Presenter *Barometer*).

The VRT's producer of *Barometer* confirms that the presenter was not involved in the selection process, and legitimizes this decision as follows: "It was certainly the impression that he [the Presenter] had something to do with it, and that he chose and selected the topics. It really didn't happen like that—but that is often the case with television programs: not everything is what it seems" (interview with Wendel Goossens, VRT's Producer *Barometer*).

Of course, the invisibility does not apply only to the persons of the media professionals in the TV program *Barometer,* it also applied to their interventions in the program. The most interesting case is the presenter's claim that he was— at least initially—unaware that people were invited to contribute by the researchers on the production team. The possibility that invited contributions were used was never mentioned during the program. Showing clear irritation during the interview, the presenter refers to a conversation he had with Wim Van Severen, the VRT channel manager of TV1, in which Michiel Hendryckx expressed his dissatisfaction with these management techniques. He not only problematized that these techniques were hidden, he also made it clear that he did not appreciate the fact that they contradicted what he said in his televized introductions: "I say [on TV]: 'Good evening, welcome to *Barometer*, I've had a tremendous number of contributions.' But I hadn't had any! You had to go and look for them, like idiots, for all kinds of people that might have something to say!" (Interview with Michiel Hendryckx, Presenter *Barometer*—referring to a conversation with Wim Van Severen, Channel manager VRT TV1.)

The Post-Political and Its Ethical-Democratic Questions

In this chapter, my major claim is that one of the democratic problems of Reality TV (in a broad sense) is the post-political and post-democratic nature of the position of their media professionals. Although a diversity of discourses can be generated through Reality TV, its practices of and discourses on participation and democracy remain problematic, due to the management of the media professionals involved, and the apparent impossibility to contest the unequal power relations that legitimize this management. Many identities, discourses, and practices in Reality TV can be contested, but the position of the media professionals, exerting their psychological property, is situated beyond (structural) contestation and has become a social imaginary, making the media professional a first mover. Their power position allows them to exercise the generative and repressive powers required to overcome resistance and to make things move.

This position raises ethical-democratic questions. In Reality TV's "paradox of democratic participation"[60] we see opportunities for empowerment (mainly related to the specificity of program discourses and practices) combined with a high likelihood of disempowerment when it comes to the production process and its televisional representation. In *Temptation Island,* whatever the touristic, relational, and sexual pleasures generated and whatever the celebrity status acquired, the deontological question that remains is how the members of the *Temptation Island* production team can justify such destructive treatment of other people. And whatever the limitations in terms of the technical and narrative skills of "ordinary" people in *Barometer*, and whatever the need for efficiency and production speed, the deontological question that remains is how to legitimize the unwarranted claims of the program's participatory intensity and the combination of participatory claims, with strong management. Even in the case of informed consent[61] one might wonder whether these subtle management techniques could be communicated sufficiently well to generate informed consent, and whether consent should ever be asked to be given for these kinds of techniques.

The two cases illustrate the strong presence (and impact) of these management techniques, and how the TV system manages, very effectively, to hide its power, and render the production team's management role largely invisible. As the production team's direct interventions are supposed to remain hidden, their control is translated into a system of rules, or into a set of procedures. In *Temptation Island*, the power of these media professionals is never directly seen in operation; we only see the results of this power imbalance. Despite a number of modest manifestations of resistance, the entire program radiates obedience. The participants are docile bodies, disciplined by the production team. *Temptation Island* is an alarming discourse of obedience, with participants prepared to let their relationships deteriorate for the sake of the rules of the game, and for the entertainment of the many. In the case of *Barometer*, the presenter becomes a visual representation of the production team, deflecting attention from the "real" production team's power, rendering them invisible. But their restricted definition of participation, and their lack of participatory attitude, leads to a specific operationalization of the participatory process into a set of procedures, which affects the entire program and the roles allowed of the participants.

There are of course differences: *Temptation Island*'s management is framed and legitimized by a lack of validation and respect for the participants, who have accepted the rules of the game, and will be subjected to the trap of the relationship test. In the case of *Barometer* the participants are validated more, although their lack of skills is sometimes held against them, but at the same time management is legitimized by the need for efficiency and speed within a capitalist media economy. Despite these differences, both programs are illustrations of the normalization of media (professional) power as an impassive mover, the *primum movens immobile,* that manages to hegemonize its own basic assumptions, cultures, practices, principles and procedures.

Notes

1. Connolly.
2. Mouffe, 1997, 4.
3. Mouffe, 2005, 20-21.
4. Žižek and Daly, 2004.
5. Mouffe, 2005, 33.
6. Laclau, 64.
7. Mouffe, 2005, 18.
8. Mouffe, 2005, 9.
9. Mouffe, 2005, 31.
10. Laclau and Mouffe.
11. Mouffe, 2005, 10.
12. Mouffe, 2005, 30.
13. Rancière's version of the post-democratic does not lament the demise of (representative) democracy, but theorizes hegemonic processes within (representative) democracies.
14. Rancière, 2007, 88.
15. Rancière, 1991, 102; quoted in Mouffe, 2005, 29, translation modified and emphasis in original.
16. Foucault, 1978.
17. Foucault, 1977.
18. Laclau, 64.
19. Aristotle's *Metaphysics*, Book XII, classics.mit.edu/Aristotle/metaphysics.12.xii.html.
20. Laclau, 64.
21. Foucault, 1996.
22. Phelan, 6.

23. An extensive case for the use of discourse theory in media studies can be found in Carpentier and Spinoy.

24. Mouffe, 2005, 8.

25. Habermas, 1974 (1964), 49-55.

26. Fraser, 56-80; Mouffe, 1994.

27. Bailey, Cammaerts and Carpentier.

28. Carpentier, 2003.

29. Biressi and Nunn, 148.

30. Andrejevic, 215.

31. Lazarsfeld and Merton.

32. Tuchman.

33. Gerbner and Gross.

34. Pateman's strict definition in *Participation and Democratic Theory*; see also Carpentier, 2007; Andrejevic.

35. Ouellette and Hay, 215 (emphasis in original).

36. Hartley.

37. Tuchman, 1978.

38. Dovey.

39. Palmer.

40. Hill, 197.

41. Andrejevic, 215.

42. Couldry.

43. Andrejevic, 218. Transactional participation refers here to the forms of participation that are promoted by the "interactive digital economy."

44. Wilpert.

45. Schlesinger, 83.

46. Wilpert.

47. Livingstone and Lunt; Carpentier, 2001.

48. Hill, 195.

49. Ouellette and Hay, 198-199.

50. See Carpentier, 2006, for a more detailed analysis of *Temptation Island*. This analysis is based on a qualitative content analysis of the 2005 series of *Temptation Island*, in combination with a reception study of the online debates about *Temptation Island*.

51. The television text makes hardly any reference to the locality of these resorts, disconnecting them from their (post)colonial realities.

52. At the time of writing, this website was no longer online.

53. Foucault, 1978.

54. This case study is based on the qualitative content analysis of all *Barometer* episodes in combination with eight interviews with the producers. I want to thank Ann Braeckman for her help with the analysis; David De Wachter, Geert Dexters, Faiza Djait, Adil Fares, Paul Lashmana, Sabine Lemache, Tine Peeters, and Yolanda Van Dorsselaer for conducting the interviews with Michiel Hendryckx (Presenter *Barometer*), Isabel Dierckx (Kanakna *Barometer* Producer), Wendel Goossens (VRT Producer *Barometer*), Noel Swinnen (Manager Kanakna), Frank Symoens (Production Manager TV1 VRT), Jean-Philip De Tender (Channel Adviser TV1 VRT); and Maaika Santana for her interviews with Eva Willems and Joke Blommaert (*Barometer* researchers). All interview and

program citations are translations from Dutch by the author.
  55. See Carpentier, "BBC's Video Nation as a Participatory Media Practice."
  56. Dovey, 121.
  57. Biressi and Nunn, 16-19.
  58. Biressi and Nunn, 19.
  59. In a 2008 *Facebook* exchange, Isabel Dierckx (*Barometer* Kanakna producer) confirmed that there were four researchers involved: Joke Blommaert, Eva Willems, Caroline Meerschaert and Koen De Blende (the last two were also involved in the filming). In subsequent interviews, Joke Blommaert and Eva Willems then confirmed the role they played in scouting for potential participants.
  60. Ouellette and Hay, 198-199.
  61. See Hibberd, Kilborn, McNair, Marriott and Schlesinger. See also www.ofcom.org.uk/static/archive/bsc/pdfs/research/Consent.pdf.

References

Andrejevic, Mark. *Reality TV. The Work of Being Watched.* Oxford: Rowman and Littlefield, 2004.

Bailey, Olga, Bart Cammaerts and Nico Carpentier. *Understanding Alternative Media.* Milton Keynes, U.K.: Open University Press, 2007.

Biressi, Anita and Heather Nunn. *Reality TV. Realism and Revelation.* London: Wallflower, 2005.

Carpentier, Nico. "Managing Audience Participation." *European Journal of Communication* 16, no. 2 (2001): 209-232.

———. "BBC's Video Nation as a Participatory Media Practice. Signifying Everyday Life, Cultural Diversity and Participation in an On-line Community." *International Journal of Cultural Studies* 6, no. 4 (2003): 425-447.

———. "Participation and Power in the Television Program Temptation Island." In *Researching Media, Democracy and Participation. The Intellectual Work of the 2006 European Media and Communication Doctoral Summer School,* edited by Nico Carpentier et al., 135-147. Tartu, Estonia: University of Tartu Press, 2006.

———. "Participation and Interactivity: Changing Perspectives. The Construction of an Integrated Model on Access, Interaction and Participation." In *New Media Worlds, Challenges for Convergence,* edited by Virginia Nightingale and Tim Dwyer, 214-230. Melbourne: Oxford University Press, 2007.

Carpentier, Nico and Erik Spinoy (eds.). *Discourse Theory and Cultural Analysis: Media, Arts and Literature.* Creskill, N.J.: Hampton Press, 2008.

Connolly, William E. *Identity/Difference: Democratic Negotiations of Political Paradox.* Ithaca, N.Y. and London: Cornell University Press, 1991.

———. *The Augustinian Imperative: A Reflection on the Politics of Morality.* Newbury Park, Calif. and London: Sage, 1993.

Couldry, Nick. *Media Rituals: A Critical Approach.* London: Routledge, 2003.

Dovey, John. *Freakshow: First Person Media and Factual Television.* London: Pluto Press, 2000.

Foucault, Michel. *Discipline and Punish: The Birth of the Prison.* New York: Pantheon, 1977.

―――. *The History of Sexuality. Vol. I: An Introduction.* New York: Pantheon, 1978.

―――. "The Eye of Power." In *Foucault Live: Collected Interviews, 1961-1984,* edited by Sylvère Lotringer, 226-240. New York: Semiotext(e), 1996.

Fraser, Nancy. "Rethinking the Public Sphere." *Social Text,* 25/26 (1990): 56-80.

Gerbner, George and Larry Gross. "Living with Television: The Violence Profile." *Journal of Communication* 26 (1976): 172-199.

Habermas, Jürgen. "The Public Sphere: An Encyclopaedia Article (1964)." *New German Critique* 3 (1974): 49-55.

Hartley, John. *Uses of Television.* London and New York: Routledge, 1999.

Hibberd, Matthew, Richard Kilborn, Brian McNair, Stephanie Marriott and Philip Schlesinger. *Consenting Adults?* London: Broadcasting Standards Commission, 2000. See also www.ofcom.org.uk/static/archive/bsc/pdfs/research/Consent.pdf.

Hill, Annette. *Restyling Factual TV: Audiences and News, Documentary and Reality Genres.* London: Routledge, 2007.

Laclau, Ernesto. *New Reflections on the Revolution of our Time.* London: Verso, 1990.

Laclau, Ernesto and Chantal Mouffe. *Hegemony and Socialist Strategy: Towards a Radical Democratic Politics.* London: Verso, 1985.

Lazarsfeld, Paul and Robert Merton. "Mass Communications, Popular Taste and Organized Social Action." In *The Communication of Ideas,* edited by Lyman Bryson, 95-118. New York: The Institute for Religious and Social Studies, 1948.

Livingstone, Sonia and Peter Lunt. *Talk on Television, Audience Participation and Public Debate.* London: Routledge, 1996.

Mouffe, Chantal. "For a Politics of Nomadic Identity." In *Travellers' Tales: Narratives of Home and Displacement,* edited by Georg Robertson, Melinda Mash, Lisa Tickner, Jon Bird, Barry Curtis, and Tim Putnam, 105-113. London: Routledge, 1994.

―――. *The Return of the Political.* London: Verso, 1997.

―――. *On the Political.* London: Routledge, 2005.

Ouellette, Laurie and James Hay. *Better Living Through Reality TV. Television and Post-Welfare Citizenship.* Malden, Mass.: Blackwell, 2008.

Palmer, Gareth. *Discipline and Liberty. Television and Governance.* Manchester: Manchester University Press, 2003.

Pateman, Carole. *Participation and Democratic Theory.* London: Oxford University Press, 1970.

Phelan, Peggy. *Unmarked: The Politics of Performance.* London: Routledge, 1993.

Rancière, Jacques. *Disagreement.* Minneapolis: University of Minnesota Press, 1991.

―――. *On the Shores of Politics.* London: Verso, 2007.

Schlesinger, Philip. *Putting "Reality" Together.* London and New York: Methuen, 1987.

Tuchman, Gaye. "The Symbolic Annihilation of Women by the Mass Media." In *Hearth and Home: Images of Women in the Mass Media,* edited by Gaye Tuchman, Arlene Kaplan Daniels and James Benet, 3-38. New York: Oxford University Press, 1978.

Wilpert, Bernhard. "Property, Ownership, and Participation: On the Growing Contradictions Between Legal and Psychological Concepts." In *International Handbook of Participation in Organizations (2), Ownership and Participation,* edited by Raymond Russell and Veljko Rus, 149-164. Oxford: Oxford University Press, 1991.

Žižek, Slavoj and Glyn Daly. *Conversations with Žižek.* Cambridge, U.K.: Polity Press, 2004.

Chapter 9
Punitive Reality TV: Televizing Punishment and the Production of Law and Order
Jan Pinseler

Crime and Deviance on TV

Images of crime are part of everyday media output. Each day a multitude of crime movies and series is broadcast on a multitude of channels. Both fictitious and real crime stories do more than just represent crime, they also provide us with knowledge about crime. Programs that claim to show real crime and deviance play a special part in this. Reality crime programs include crime appeal programs[1] such as *Aktenzeichen XY . . . Ungelöst* on German TV, *Crimewatch UK* on BBC and the Fox network's *America's Most Wanted*. As these shows have some common characteristics, we can treat them as one subgenre. Recently, there has been another addition to the Reality TV genre that deals with offenders. Re-education shows, such as the British and American *Brat Camp* and the German *Teenager außer Kontrolle*, show troubled teenagers who are sent to boot camps to be "treated." Crime appeal programs show unresolved criminal cases with the stated aim of getting viewers to help solve the crimes in question. Re-education shows show young offenders being transformed into "responsible" members of society. Both crime appeal and re-education shows are described here as punitive Reality TV (PRTV).

What is normal and what is deviant is contested in every society and the limits of normality are constantly fought over and in permanent flux. Since mass media depictions of social reality always deal with questions of normality and deviance, they not only represent the limits of acceptable behavior, but are actively involved in the debate on these limits. Therefore, to analyze media representations of crime and deviance we need to examine closely which techniques are used for these depictions and how these depictions are related to the social debates on normality and its limits, which are embedded in specific power relations. This, as I will show in this chapter, can be done by applying the concept of communicative genre to the analysis of PRTV as a mediated communicative genre. To describe PRTV as a mediated communicative genre also contributes to its being perceived as transcending traditional genre conceptions. It can be understood as a trans-genre since it incorporates characteristics of different genres and is defined by its specific relation to reality.

There is no such thing as an integrated theory of media representations of crime and deviance, although televisual images of crime are as old as TV. Only bits and pieces can be incorporated into an elaborate theory of media depiction of deviance. In this chapter I look at representations of crime and deviance on TV in general, and crime appeal programs and re-education shows in particular. I discuss theoretical approaches to televisual representations of crime and deviance. Using these approaches I outline my contribution to the theory of crime and deviance on TV, suggesting that it is helpful to understand certain crime programs as a genre. This genre could be called punitive Reality TV (PRTV). I use the concept of communicative genres to analyze a mediated communicative genre. Using this framework I discuss how the genre of PRTV takes part in the production of hegemony. Finally, depictions of crime and deviance on TV are viewed as going beyond being simply political, which raises the question of what makes this genre an illustration of the trans-political.

Different forms of crime and deviance are represented in the media all the time. For example, among German media output there are newspaper reports on teenagers running amok and children dying due to negligence, but also on "work-shy" recipients of social security benefits. Also, a great deal of TV programming relates to deviance, from courtroom dramas to reality crime shows, from daily crime series to crime appeal programs. In addition, there are several programs that focus on moral rather than penal deviance. This is true of shows such as *Supernanny*, but also soap operas and nearly every other form of drama. The message in those programs might not always be as explicit as it is on crime appeal programs, where good and evil are distinct alternatives that cannot be mixed up. Rather, representations of deviance will often imply certain ideas of what behavior is normal and what is deviant, what is good and what is evil. In an inventory of programs portraying fictional crime, Brück (1999) found that a total of 153 such programs were broadcast in just one week in 1994. In terms of afternoon and evening programming, in one week in 2007, the six most important German TV networks transmitted ninety-seven different shows dealing with fictional crime.[2] These figures indicate the enormous importance of crime fiction on TV, and how TV works as a moral institution by showing normality through deviance.

There are two distinct kinds of Reality TV formats that deal with crime and deviance: crime appeal programs and re-education shows. Crime appeal programs are one of the oldest and the most emphatic forms of reality programming. The—presumably—first ever criminal investigation program was aired in 1938 on Nazi Germany's trial TV program and could be seen by very few spectators in public viewing halls.[3] The current trend of enlisting TV to assist in catching people suspected of having committed a crime started in 1967 when the then new West German channel ZDF launched its program *Aktenzeichen XY . . . Ungelöst*.[4] In the first show, the presenter, Eduard Zimmermann, explained what, in his view, the program was all about: "To use the telescreen for fighting crime, Ladies and Gentlemen, is the aim of our new series *Aktenzeichen XY . . . ungelöst* that I will introduce to you today."[5] *Aktenzeichen XY . . . ungelöst* quickly became an international show when the Swiss German language channel and the Austrian television began to participate in its production and transmission. In the early 1980s, the BBC became interested in and developed the format into *Crimewatch UK*. The producers of *Crimewatch UK*, however, emphasize that, unlike the case of *Aktenzeichen XY . . . ungelöst*, they insist on total editorial independence, and no interference from police authorities.[6] Similar shows were introduced in other countries including the Netherlands, France, Hungary, and Israel.[7] Based loosely on the same format, the Fox network in 1987 introduced *America's Most Wanted*. To an extent, *America's Most Wanted* radicalized the genre by showing only clearly identifiable murder suspects. This format, in turn, was re-imported back into Germany and adapted for the local market. The resulting program was called *Fahndungsakte*, and aired on a commercial TV network between 1997 and 2000.[8]

Re-education programs differ from crime appeal programs insofar as they do not try to catch criminals, but rather try to "educate"—or, more precisely, discipline—deviant teenagers. The best known re-education show format is *Brat Camp*, which was originally developed in the U.K. by Channel 4 and has now been adopted by TV networks in several countries, e.g., the United States and Germany. *Brat Camp* shows a process of re-education that takes place in a U.S. boot camp, presented through the format of a docu-soap. The participants in the German version, *Teenager außer Kontrolle*, were "guilty" of heavy marijuana use, of continuous absenteeism from school, of all day partying, or of refusing to get involved in family activities. They were depicted as being "teenagers out of control"—the literal translation of the German title of the show—and as needing harsh treatment since every other attempt to get them to conform had failed. The youngsters featured in the program are subjected to harsh and mostly pointless discipline. At the beginning of their "treatment" on *Teenager außer Kontrolle*, they are—amongst other things—not allowed to leave a small stone circle, or to talk to each other. They are served horrible food. Once they have accepted this treatment for a certain length of time, without questioning or resisting it, they are transferred to the next level of the "treatment," but still under threat of being demoted back to the first phase.

Both crime appeal programs and re-education programs show images of crime and deviance, but also articulate certain norms and values as self-evidently normal. Using authenticity production techniques, images of crime and deviance are passed off as reality, thus rendering authentic the depictions of crime and deviance and also the representations of everyday life for ordinary people. Since they—allegedly—"re-enact" crimes as they "really happen," or show teenagers who in real life are deviant and receiving treatment, PRTV programs produce a moral discourse that portrays certain moral values as unquestionable and obligatory for every member of society. By showing people as deviant—publicly accusing them in the media—crime appeal programs not only propagate certain moral values but in addition take part in producing ideology. Based on an ideal-world pattern, they depict the rules with which members of society must abide if they do not want to be associated with the criminal world. Crime appeal programs give the impression that they are defending universal rights, even though the rights they defend, especially the right to private property (which is a precondition for a capitalist society), are in fact particular. These shows, thus, contribute to the successful production of hegemony and, hence, maintenance of the current social order.

Theories of Media Representations of Crime and Deviance

According to Ericson,[9] it is possible to distinguish between two different strands of researching media representations of crime: the media effects model and, what he calls the dominant ideology approach. To analyze media representations of crime, researchers in this first strand usually compare media images to reality, arguing that the media image is a biased one and does not reflect real crime.[10] The problem with this kind of research is how to measure "reality." Usually, official crime statistics are used, mistaking—or misinterpreting—these as reality. These studies usually conclude that violent crimes are over-represented and property crimes under-represented in the media.[11] Also studies within this approach do not look for meanings assigned to these media images of crime; instead they interpret crime statistics as being the reality of crime, ignoring the fact that crime statistics are just one interpretation of reality—different from media interpretations but not reality itself.[12]

The dominant ideology approach is quite different. Its development followed the critical criminology approach of the 1970s.[13] The main point in critical criminology research is that mass media prefer members of the ruling classes as the sources and interpreters of what is happening, thereby reinforcing the dominant ideology.[14] Hall et al.'s book *Policing the Crisis: Mugging, the State, and Law & Order*,[15] which was a collaborative work by researchers at the Center for Contemporary Cultural Studies in Birmingham, builds strongly on this approach combined with Becker's[16] labeling-approach. However, what triggered Hall et al.'s study was the obvious disproportion between some robberies committed by young, mostly black men and the resulting moral panic that in Britain came to be known as the mugging crisis.

It is almost impossible to summarize *Policing the Crisis*. This is, as Barker[17] put it, an "overwritten book." It tries to bring together everything that had been achieved until then at the CCCS in analyzing culture. *Policing the Crisis* is an empirical study of the mugging crisis in Great Britain in 1972-73. Hall et al. demonstrate that a moral panic has no relation whatsoever to statistical data (in this case the increase in street robberies). Rather, a moral panic is produced jointly by the police, the justice system, the media and politicians. For them, use of violence provides a differentiation between those who are part of society and those who are not. The use of violence also triggers the news value system, which makes these muggings newsworthy for the media.[18] Moreover, the media do not present different points of view but adopt the perspectives of the police and the justice system. Hall et al. describe a circuit of social and political power, in which the police, judges, the media and politicians build up a problem and subsequently demand a solution to it. The mugging crisis was an effect of the general political crisis in Great Britain in the 1970s. It resulted in black muggers becoming the symbol for everything that went wrong in Britain at that time, a symbol of Britain's social problems. The main achievement of Hall et al.'s study was that it portrayed the relationship between politicians, the media and crime, taking into consideration the social conditions under which they operated. It seems fairly self-evident to demand that research concerning media images of crime should always deal with their relation to the social conditions under which the media and politics are operating. However, thirty years after *Policing the Crisis* was first published, analyses of media representations of crime still mostly ignore the social contexts of the images of crime.

Ericson empathizes that mass media institutions work in a more complex network of social institutions than is implied in *Policing the Crisis*. In his view, mass media are more than just mechanisms of reproducing ideology and upholding hegemony. He calls for a detailed analysis of how mass media actually produce depictions of crime. Ericson accuses the dominant ideology approach of an oversimplification of mass media as ideological apparatuses. "Ideology researchers on the left and 'moral majority' effects researchers on the right" talked about ideology instead of social contexts of media productions.[19] He suggests an "institutional approach" to replace these "ideological" approaches. A free market, Ericson argues, pushes mass media organizations not to behave as instruments of ideological control: "Mass media economics in fact work against tight ideological control because mass media texts must articulate with the concerns of a diverse array of organizations and institutions in order to obtain a sufficiently broad share of the market."[20] Thereby, the same principles of free market economy would ensure that mass media do not promote the conservatism that lies at the root of this.

In hindsight, this seems a rather bold assumption, especially if one takes into account the position of the mass media in the United States after 9/11, which, as far as mainstream media are concerned, allowed almost no criticism of U.S. politics, at least until 2004. Rather, it seems obvious that "market mechanisms"—or the conditions under which media corporations function within a capitalist society, aiming for the highest possible profits—contributed to this absence of critique. These conditions include ownership of media corporations and the resulting conflicts of interest. Also, journalists' working conditions are far from perfect: they usually have limited time and resources to deal with particular topics. And they are obliged to yield to editorial guidelines and decisions.

Ericson published his "institutional approach" to the media representation of crime in 1991, at a time when the cold war had just ended, a prospering future for capitalism seemed to lie ahead and the "end of history" was declared.[21] This may explain in part his optimistic view in terms of how the media operate within a capitalist framework. For Ericson, the police, the judiciary, politicians and the media are not part of one and the same power bloc. Moreover there are basic contradictions between these groups. In their study of sources for media depictions of crime, Ericson, Baranek and Chan[22] show the production of crime news as a struggle for the control of meaning that is fought at each level of production of crime news. In terms of news sources, news organizations are very powerful in this struggle. This leads Ericson and colleagues[23] to conclude that Hall and his colleagues in the CCCS study[24] were wrong to claim that journalists could only generate secondary constructions of meaning, since meanings are pre-constructed by the police, the judiciary and politicians. But if sources—namely police officers—claim that journalists do not fully accept their interpretation of a certain event, this does not imply necessarily that journalists assign meanings that are contradictory to those assigned by their sources, only that they do not fully accept their view. Other authors support this. For instance Skidmore, and Schlesinger and Tumber[25] argue that the dominant ideology approach ignores how sources compete for their interpretations to be adopted by the media.

This critique seems blind to a basic assumption in Hall et al.'s analysis,[26] that media representations of crime and deviance are a means of the ruling power bloc's upholding of the hegemonic ideology. While Ericson, Ericson, Baranek and Chan, Skidmore, and Schlesinger and Tumber[27] see the current social order as natural and not to be researched, the dominant ideology approach argues that the social order and the current power structures should be included in any research on media depictions of crime. To some critics of the cultural studies approach, hegemonic ideology, in effect, seems to be reduced to politician's pronouncements. Therefore, a statement from anyone outside the ruling power bloc is seen as a non-hegemonic statement. This ignores the fact that—supported by the media—the dominant ideology seems to be natural to and is regularly reproduced by the subordinate. This was shown impressively by Hall et al. Therefore, if we want to explain what depictions of real crime on popular TV mean for a society, we need to take ideology into account, since we are dealing with the processes of inclusion and exclusion, of disciplining and punishment, of depictions of what constitutes normal, appropriate behavior and what does not.

Constructing the "Ideal World" on Crime Appeal Programs

There are very few studies of crime appeal programs. These programs are sometimes discussed within the context of Reality TV,[28] but mostly, they are treated as the "ugly stepdaughters" of Reality TV. This is rather surprising, since far from being strange relatives, crime appeal programs are the forefathers of Reality TV and are very much alive today, with shows in more than half a dozen countries.[29] As mentioned before, the authenticity claim plays a crucial role in the genre, and was already present in the earliest forms of reality crime TV. The production of authenticity can be seen clearly in the first show of the West German program *Aktenzeichen XY . . . Ungelöst* in 1967. This program—in one way or another—became one of the models for the crime appeal program genre. To be credible as programs allegedly aimed at helping the police to catch criminals, crime appeal programs' depictions of crimes have to be realistic. Authenticity can be understood as producing the impression of reproducing reality, rather than giving a specific version of reality. Markers of authenticity are quite common in all crime appeal programs. This obviously is due to the fact that these programs have to deal repeatedly with certain problems, that they show staged crimes modeled on real crimes and have to pass them off as images of reality. Following Hattendorf,[30] I draw a distinction between strategies of authentication on the one hand, and signals of authenticity on the other. Strategies of authentication are all means used to imply the authenticity of non-documentary material. Means which are used to explicitly or implicitly emphasize the authenticity of documentary material can be called signals of authenticity.

There are a few such means of producing authenticity, which I classify by highlighting groups of signals of authenticity and groups of strategies of authentication. Signals of authenticity are used to produce authenticity by testifying (e.g., by using private photos of victims), by locating and naming (e.g., by showing and naming a location, using a caption and/or voice-over narration), by emphasizing an ongoing threat to someone (e.g., by disguising a victim's or witness's face), by authority (personified mostly by policemen and policewomen who may even sit in the studio and take the phone calls), by making feedback visible (e.g., by showing the name and telephone number of the police department in charge of a case) or by emphasizing a personal shock (which can be expressed by the presenter or a member of the police). Strategies of authentication, on the other hand, are used to give staged depictions of crime the appearance of being true to reality. This can be done by mixing staged and documentary material (e.g., a staged "re-enactment" of a crime is mixed with pictures from a CCTV camera), by the adoption of certain types of staging (e.g., a home video style, giving the impression that the incident was coincidentally filmed by a witness) and—again—by authority, especially by the voice-over, where the narrator is the omniscient authority on what happened. Using these means of producing authenticity, crime appeal programs produce not simply reality, they produce trans-reality—that is, a form of reality that transcends traditional conceptions of reality. These shows do not trust in the actual signs of these crimes having been committed but use "reconstructions" to produce images of crime that are more real than reality itself. These trans-real images in turn help to shape the genre of PRTV as a trans-genre, one especially that transcends the boundaries of the real and the fictional.

In addition, all film on crime appeal programs deals at considerable length with the everyday lives of the victims before the crime. These programs do not restrict themselves only to showing the crime, but add a narration about the victim's life before the crime: on the one side there is an ideal world in which the victim lives, on the other, there is evil, crime. This pattern of depicting crime can be called the ideal world pattern.

I introduce one brief example. A crime appeal on *Aktenzeichen XY . . . Ungelöst* on March 31, 2000 dealt with an armed robbery at the house of an artist. Throughout the presenter's introduction to the film, there is a screen in the background showing the name of the city and the telephone number of the police department in charge. Later, this is replaced by a picture showing the living room of the victim. This eventually becomes the beginning of the film, which starts by showing a lower middle class idyll. A sequence of scenes shows the everyday life of the artist: He comes into his studio and starts working, chats with a friend about what music they want to listen to, watches TV. The film shows children playing in the street and a client arriving, for whom the artist casually develops an ingenious idea. Sporadically, the film highlights things that might shed some light on the crime in question. In general, however, the first part of the film is aimed at depicting a harmonious, everyday life, free of conflict.

While all this obviously happens during the day, within minutes the film changes: The lighting changes from high-key to low-key, the background music from light jazz to dramatic sounds, and the mood of the artist from relaxed to agitated. We see two intercut scenes, showing some men outside the house watching the artist inside, watching TV and calling friends. This part of the film ends with the narrator telling us what the artist had intended to do for the rest of the evening and hinting at what actually happened: "The artist had planned, later this evening, to see friends to play cards. But he will not be able to meet them." It is only now that the depiction of the crime starts. The men who had been watching outside ring the bell, force their way into the house, beat up the artist and empty his flat. The film ends with a picture of the artist, beaten up, lying in his workshop. This picture remains as a background to the studio presenter's introduction of the detective in charge of the incident.

The re-enacted scenes here are highly interwoven with markers of authenticity. But the longest part of the film is concerned not with the crime itself, but with the everyday life of the victim as it was before the crime occurred. Since crime appeal programs are allegedly aimed at helping to solve crimes, it is somewhat surprising that the film shown mostly concerns things that—at least as far as the viewer is concerned—do not help to solve the case. This applies to most films on *Aktenzeichen XY . . . Ungelöst* and—to a lesser extent—to quite a few films on other crime appeal programs. These films all deal with the lives of the victims before the crimes. Sometimes this is done through flashbacks; sometimes this part of the film is quite short, but there is always something about the victims' lives before the crimes were committed.

This ideal world has special characteristics: It is the ideal world of a small monogamous heterosexual family of West European descent. This world has no major problems. The people that inhabit it have ordinary problems but, all things considered, they are quite happy in their world. Often, the victims have just fallen in love or are especially happy for some reason or another, or become victims on an especially important day. At the same time, there are also recurring characteristics in the depictions of crime. Conspicuously, criminals come from outside and break into the ideal world. Coming from outside can mean that they come from outside the victim's house or that they come from outside the world of ordinary people, ethnically or socially. Often, criminals are depicted as encompassing both these conditions. Alternatively, the criminal is shown as being not normal, as a pervert, deviating mentally, who lives in our society and who must be expelled from the world of normality. By asking viewers to call in with any evidence they might have, they are being asked to help to restore this ideal world.

The importance of this ideal world pattern for the depiction of normality versus crime is highlighted in cases where the lives of the victims do not entirely resemble the ideal world as usually depicted in these programs. For instance, in the film about the artist being attacked, there is one obvious crack in this ideal world. The artist lives with a male friend, but what kind of relationship they have is never specified. This is striking especially compared to the usual depiction of heterosexual spouses, who play an important part in portraying the ideal world of the victims. We are not shown any touching, any physical contact, enabling the program to avoid a breach of the ideal (i.e., heteronormative) world. I call this strategy of repairing the ideal world normalizing. This strategy is recurrently used to re-establish the ideal world for those victims who do not fall within the usual crime appeal program depiction of a victim. There is another such repairing strategy, which I call exclusion. Using the strategy of exclusion, victims are expelled from the ideal world and their world is linked to the world of the criminal. Usually, the strategy of exclusion is connected to the strategy of normalizing by depicting an ideal world in which the victim lived long before the crime happened, but which he left due to his deviant behavior. Sometimes this ideal world is alluded to by showing the beauty of the landscape or the village where the crime took place.

Thus, in crime appeal programs, the world is organized into the dichotomous categories of Good and Evil, where a victim can never be evil, a criminal can never be good. If the victim's life does not entirely resemble this view of the ideal world, these programs use strategies of exclusion and inclusion to reproduce the pattern.

The Genre of Punitive Reality TV

Mediated Communicative Genres

To describe a TV (sub)genre in relation to social reality, it is helpful to go beyond simple genre analysis. Genres cannot be described by reducing them to representational patterns. Rather, they arise from the interplay of representational patterns on the one hand, and their perception by viewers on the other.[31] To describe the genre of PRTV, I use the concept of communicative genres[32] as a research program for analyzing mediated communicative genres.[33] While this concept of communicative genres initially was developed for genres of interpersonal communication it has proved fruitful for analyzing mediated communication. Luckmann[34] distinguishes between two structures of a genre: the interior and the exterior structure. The interior structure of a genre includes structural similarities which result from its relation to the basic function of the genre and to its material basis. It contains its typical elements, rhetorical means and representational patterns. The exterior structure includes the communicative situation in which a communicative genre is used and in which participants and communicative milieus use it. Therefore, the exterior structure of a genre is the level where communicative actions relate to the social structure in which they operate. Thus, communicative genres, as described by Luckmann, are recurrent and recognizable forms of everyday reconstructions of social reality which have become part of the social repertoire of knowledge and are solidified into cumulative patterns. This approach to genres avoids the problems of defining genres as described above; instead they are seen as patterns that are used by people interacting in specific situations. This includes the specific social situations in which communicative genres are utilized, which makes this definition useful for mediated communicative genres. To understand media forms as mediated communicative genres directs attention to the social conditions and contexts of their use. This, then, enables us to describe media genres not only in terms of their shared structural properties, but also with reference to the relations between communicative interactions within a genre and the social structure in which it is embedded.

If we transfer this idea to mediated communicative genres, we have to look at their interior and their exterior structures. The interior structure of mediated communicative genres is characterized by recurrent and recognizable patterns of representations which are typical of a genre. Unlike interpersonal communicative genres, mediated communicative genres have two levels of exterior structure. On the first level the media system can be understood as an exterior structure of mediated communicative genres, that includes the conditions of production, scheduling and the position of a show within a broadcasting network. But a genre cannot be understood without taking social contexts into consideration. Therefore, the social context constitutes the second exterior structure of mediated communicative genres, which contains the interior structure and the exterior structure I. These genres are produced in different ways within different formats. This model of mediated communicative genres is depicted in Figure 1.

Interior Structure	Exterior Structure I: Media System
Recurrent and solidified patterns of depiction	Conditions of production media context
Realization of the genre within specific formats	

Exterior Structure II:
Social Context of the Genre
Reference to social concepts, norms and values
social power relations

Figure 1. Mediated Communicative Genres

Punitive Reality TV as a (Sub)Genre

Early on in the development of the Reality TV genre, in the early 1990s, it became obvious that there is not just *one* genre of Reality TV. Rather, we need to
speak, as Wulff,[35] for example, suggests, of several genres or of a combination
of subgenres. Keppler[36] makes a distinction between narrative and performative
forms of Reality TV. The most remarkable characteristic of the latter is that they
not only re-enact real events, they also intervene and change the actual lives of
participants. Building on this distinction, Klaus and Lücke[37] define a whole battery of Reality TV genres within these two groups. They take crime appeal
shows into consideration and put them into the narrative Reality TV genre. This
attribution seems flawed on two counts. First, crime appeal programs intervene
in the lives of people in very direct ways. They reconstruct the sufferings of
crime victims, and they intervene in the lives of suspects. Therefore, these
shows make up an important subgenre of RTV. To describe PRTV as a mediated
communicative (sub)genre, one has to look at how this genre is constructed at
the level of its interior structure and its two exterior structures. Here, I can only
briefly describe the interior and first exterior structures, but I discuss more
deeply how PRTV as a genre interacts with social debates on deviance and
crime, because this is the level at which PRTV becomes an example of trans-
politics.

At the level of the interior structure, PRTV is characterized by the posing of
a problem. Disciplinary action and punishment are advocated as the solutions to
the problem. In crime appeal programs, this is done by showing how a certain
crime disrupts and destroys the world of "ordinary" people. The shows then appeal to viewers for help in catching the criminals responsible for the disruption
of these everyday lives. Criminals, the crime appeal programs implicitly argue,
must be brought to justice to restore normality. In re-education programs, the
problem is non-obedient youth. *Teenager außer Kontrolle*, the German version
of *Brat Camp*, starts every episode, for instance, by showing the deviant behavior of the protagonists in the opening credits and contrasting them with pictures
of these same kids as small children. Hereby, the problem and the solution to the
problem are depicted. The desired outcome is achieved through the "treatment"
of these youths in a boot camp, which constitutes most of the program.

While PRTV programs are produced for local media markets, most of the
formats of this genre are exported globally and only realized locally, with protagonists from the country for which a specific show is produced. Therefore, in
terms of the exterior structure of the media system, the PRTV genre is shaped by
the international markets in which this genre operates. In addition, they are
linked to other forms of reporting, especially to news and yellow press (sensationalist) reporting. These links are partly the result of other programs also reporting crime, that are featured on PRTV programs, but quite often TV networks

actively use cross-promotion strategies by discussing, for example, the protagonists in re-education programs on news shows.

Interior Structure	Media System
Posing a problem and advocating a specific solution to this problem	International formats Features in other forms, e.g., news programming
Realization of the genre within specific formats	

Social Context of the Genre
Naturalization of discipline and punishment as a power technique
Production of hegemony
Taking part in the enforcement of power

Figure 2. The Genre of Punitive Reality TV

But the concept of mediated communicative genres is especially useful and powerful when discussing what in this context is called the exterior structure II, that is, how the genre is linked to the social context. This allows the relation between a genre and the social debate that encompasses it to be understood as an integral part of the genre itself. PRTV discusses the limits of normality, and the definitions of deviance and crime as part of this social debate. Those who are able to enforce their conceptions of deviance are also able to enforce their conceptions of society. This process can be understood as producing hegemony. To ensure power in the long term, those in power have to ensure that those who are ruled view their power—at least to a certain degree—as useful for them. Hegemony, according to Gramsci, is realized in institutions of civil society, one of the most important of these institutions being the mass media.[38] PRTV builds on everyday conceptions of crime, links them to a hegemonic concept and lets them appear natural and unquestionable. In addition, this genre transgresses the usual boundaries between state institutions and mass media by not only taking part in producing hegemony but also by enforcing power. This renders it a case of trans-politics. In crime appeal programs this is achieved through participation in the process of criminal prosecution; in boot camp shows it is achieved by organizing punishment—or forms of discipline that are presented as education. This is supported by representational strategies, especially the production of authenticity, the dichotomy of good and evil and the constant references to the police or pedagogic authorities. PRTV becomes a genre, exactly because it constantly refers to social conditions that are naturalized in a specific way. These characteristics of the mediated communicative genre of PRTV are summarized in Figure 2.

Trans-Politics and Punitive Reality TV

Producing Hegemony

Given all this, what can we make of the role played by PRTV in social debates on crime and deviance? As mentioned above, studies of these programs are scarce. Cavender,[39] Donovan,[40] Fishman[41] and Bond-Maupin[42] point out that crime appeal programs on U.S. TV draw a clear distinction between good and evil. Contradictions are dissolved in favor of clear distinctions.[43] This is also true of German crime appeal programs, which produce a Manichean world by using the ideal world pattern described above. This pattern is supported by the use of means of producing authenticity. This has been referred to in different ways by Waldmann,[44] Russo[45] and Bauer.[46] The means of producing authenticity authenticate not only the staged depictions of the crimes, but also the depictions of normality. This is done not in an indirect way, as Linder and Ort suggest,[47] but in a very direct way, by depicting the ideal world that the victims inhabited before the crime. Crime-appeal programs do not limit themselves to showing the search for suspects as Milanés suggests:[48] The actual search for suspects rarely takes place in these programs. A basic characteristic of crime appeal programs is that they show the victims' life before the crime is committed, that this world is destroyed by the criminal and has to be reconstructed with the help of the program, the police and the viewer. Also, by showing the ideal world, crime appeal programs—contrary to Rath's assumption[49]—demonstrate a particular kind of ethics.

The way that Normality, that is, Good, and Deviance, that is, Evil, crime and criminals, are represented on crime appeal programs is at least of interest because these programs allegedly intend to enable viewers to help solve the crimes depicted. Depicting the victims' lives before the crimes were committed probably does not further this aim. Rather this pattern of portrayal positions crime against the background of the ideal world that it destroys. Crime is therefore depicted as something unbelievably despicable and not originating from the same world.[50] Using signals of authenticity and strategies of authentication, this image of crime is passed off as reality. It renders authentic not only the depictions of crime, but also the world of the victims, that is, the ideal world. It claims to be a pure re-enactment of reality, which is dichotomously divided into a world of good and evil without any grey shades. Thereby, crime appeal programs are able to participate in the ongoing societal debate on normality and deviance, crime and punishment, representing their specific views on the matter.

Power, as we know from Gramsci, in the long run cannot be based only on oppression, but has to be at least partly accepted by the oppressed. To achieve this, the ruling power bloc, to an extent, has to secure the consent of the subordinate classes by convincing them that its rule is in the latter's best interest. If the ruling bloc succeeds in doing this, the social order is taken for granted by the ruled. In the area of law and justice, PRTV programs play a role in universalizing particular interests. Thereby these shows contribute to the successful production of hegemony and, hence, maintenance of the current social order.

Representing Discipline

To analyze the trans-political nature of PRTV, we have to look into what it is that programs in this genre offer their viewers. We can find at least one significant difference from other forms of Reality TV if we compare shows such as *The Apprentice, The Swan* or *Pop Idol* on the one hand, and programs such as *Crimewatch UK, Aktenzeichen XY . . . Ungelöst* or *Brat Camp* on the other. *The Apprentice* shows (and stage-manages) contenders who compete for a real life job, *The Swan* shows young women undergoing physical changes to make them conform more to a dominant idea of beauty, and in *Pop Idol* singers compete for a recording contract. While all the participants in these shows take part on a voluntary basis, the programs nevertheless, as Thomas argues,[51] walk a thin line between getting the contenders on the program to discipline them and their being disciplined by so-called trainers and instructors.

This is a fundamental difference from crime appeal programs. Here the "participants" do not agree to take part in the program. While this might not constitute a major issue for crime appeal programs, it is for shows such as *Brat Camp* or its German equivalent *Teenager außer Kontrolle*, where troubled teenagers are put into "education camps" where they are subjected to severe forms of discipline in order to re-educate them and turn them into law-abiding members of society. The teenagers themselves have not agreed to join the camp and to appear on TV, their parents do this for them. But understanding their placement in the camp as helpful—or at least claiming to do so—seems to be a vital part of the submission process to which these youths have to be subjected. Therefore, these shows switch the focus from "participants" disciplining themselves, to their being disciplined. This switch is underlined by their not being able to leave the show, a last resort for contenders in lifestyle TV programs.

All forms of PRTV use styles of self-discipline and being disciplined, but the emphasis varies. Self-discipline means that the TV show contenders try to conform as much as possible to certain norms and values. Being disciplined, on the other hand, is the act of presenters, instructors, supervisors, wardens or the police using their powers to get the participants to do something that they otherwise would not do. In other cases, this also implies that the disciplining agent simply ignores what the participant would or would not do. While lifestyle formats still involve some form of voluntariness, crime appeal programs and *Brat Camp* rely solely on coercion. By using coercion as a means of discipline, the latter types of shows demonstrate what happens to those who refuse to discipline themselves and thereby internalize the limits and demands of a neo-liberal society. Those who deny this act of self-discipline are subjugated to being disciplined by others. The act of disciplining working on two levels can be understood as trans-political. On the first level, viewers are taught about hegemonic conceptions of normality and deviance through normality being exemplified by depictions of deviance, and what happens to those who dare to deviate. On the second level, people are shown being punished on TV. This punishment is staged for the TV camera and would not happen—at least not in that way—if it were not being produced for a TV audience.

This can be described as the trans-real nature of PRTV. As was discussed above, PRTV's claim to simply represent reality in an unmodified way is an effect jointly created by patterns of production and reception of these programs. Program-makers use techniques of producing authenticity and users take markers of authenticity in the films presented as indicators to understand PRTV programs as simple representations of reality. PRTV is, therefore, simultaneously real and unreal. It is unreal in its claim of representing reality but it is real in being successful in claiming this. These programs present a specific view on the reality of crime and deviance but they effectively pass off their version of social problems as not being ideological but the only version of reality there is, thereby excluding other possibilities of the social production of meaning. Therefore, PRTV does not only transcend traditional notions of the difference between what is real and what is fictitious, it becomes trans-real. It also limits the possible meanings that can be attached to the behavior depicted in these programs as deviant. This politics of law and order by proxy can be understood as trans-political.

Trans-Punitive Reality TV?

Analyzing media representations of violence, Fiske argues that "represented violence is popular (in a way that social violence is not) because it offers points of relevance to people living in societies where power and resources are inequitably distributed and structured around lines of conflicting interests."[52] Therefore, media representations of violence can be understood as symbolic examinations of social inequalities. Much the same is true of media representations of crime and deviance. These representations discuss fundamental questions of the social state of a society in which these programs are transmitted. Most importantly, these are questions about the limits of normality. Since normality usually cannot be depicted it has to be shown indirectly through depictions of deviance. As described above, a core characteristic of PRTV is that programs in this genre produce the impression of simply depicting social reality as it really is. This impression is achieved by using specific techniques of representation and by constant references to social and state authorities, especially legal and pedagogical institutions. These techniques are effective against a background of social conditions in an increasingly deregulated capitalist society. One core ingredient of capitalist ideology is that everyone forges her or his own destiny and, therefore, can achieve whatever she or he wants to, if only she or he tries hard enough. Hence, social status—according to this ideology—depends only on merit and effort, not on economic means. This ideology is conveyed by numerous Reality TV programs. PRTV, however, goes further by—on a first level—exhibiting how those who became deviant or criminal are disciplined or punished. And on a second level, and in addition, demonstrating the limits of normality, of what is tolerated by society. Thereby, it depicts specific ideas of normality and deviance as self-evident.

The genre of PRTV includes one of the oldest and one of the newest forms of Reality TV, namely crime appeal shows and re-education programs. These shows work on a different level from other PRTV programs since they discipline on two levels. On the first level—and in a very direct way—they discipline the participants or try to bring them to justice. On the second level, they teach viewers about what kind of behavior is tolerated and what is outside normality. In a time, when, as Castells puts it: "A considerable number of humans, probably in a growing proportion, are irrelevant, both as producers and consumers,"[53] there is a significant need to control those who are excluded from vital parts of economic, political and social participation.[54] This control can be more easily exercised by getting the excluded to internalize their control (as Foucault would put it) and by persuading them that society offers them a chance of climbing the rungs of the social ladder. But if this does not work, they have to be shown the discouraging consequences of not behaving accordingly. While lifestyle TV appears to be part of the former, PRTV is part of the latter. Hence, lifestyle TV and PRTV are two sides of the same coin, or—to use a different metaphor—where lifestyle TV is the carrot promising a lucrative career, PRTV is the stick, disciplining those who no longer believe in the carrot. What we have here are the two forms of punishment identified by Foucault,[55] the spectacle of punishment and the panoptic discipline. Jermyn argues that crime appeal programs incorporate not the spectacle of punishment, but the spectacle of witnessing the crime: "Rather than the spectacle of gross public torture and punishment, spectacular display now focuses on seeing the performance of the crime and in identification and/or apprehension of the criminal."[56] This ignores the fundamental difference between watching a crime and watching the criminal being punished for the crime. While crime appeal programs only inform us about whether a criminal has been caught, re-education programs show young offenders actually being punished. These shows allow us to "enjoy" the spectacle of punishment. But while this is not the gruesome, public, torturing to death described by Foucault at the beginning of *Discipline and Punish*, it nevertheless is public. Moreover, it is both public *and* put on for the TV camera. The inmates of *Brat Camp* are only there because of TV, they have to act for the camera and their humiliation is public. Therefore this kind of punishment is simultaneously a public spectacle and a Panopticon, putting PRTV on a level beyond the mere political—in effect making it trans-punitive.

Notes

1. I borrow this term from Jermyn, who uses it in passing.
2. Pinseler, 2008, 69-70.
3. In the program *Die Kriminalpolizei Warnt* (The Criminal Investigation Department Warns) the presenter talked to policemen about unsolved crimes. In the very first show, a policeman presented a coat that was linked to a crime and the camera showed the coat in detail, see Winker, 226-227; Zeutschner; Seeßlen.
4. This roughly translates as File Number XY. Unsolved.
5. *Aktenzeichen XY. . . Ungelöst*, October 20, 1967.
6. For the early history see the self-portrayal of *Crimewatch UK* in Ross and Cook and the—rather uncritical—account in Schlesinger and Tumber 1993, 1995.
7. For detailed accounts see the articles in Fishman and Cavender, 1998; for an overview, see Pinseler, 2006.
8. For a detailed analysis of German crime appeal programs see Pinseler, 2006; for analyses of other crime appeal programs, see e.g., Oliver 1994; Sears, Bond-Maupin, Donovan, Oliver and Armstrong 1998; Fishman 1999.
9. Ericson, 1991.
10. E.g., Bortner; Lamnek.
11. E.g., Dominick.
12. See e.g., Cremer-Schäfer and Steinert, 20.
13. E.g., Cohen.
14. For a summary, see e.g., Skidmore, 79.
15. Hall et al.
16. Becker.
17. Barker, 85.
18. Hall et al., 68.
19. Ericson, 1991, 221, 223.
20. Ericson, 1991, 223.
21. Fukuyama.
22. Ericson, Baranek and Chan.
23. Ericson, 1991.

24. Hall et al.
25. Skidmore; Schlesinger and Tumber.
26. Hall et al.
27. Ericson, 1991; Ericson, Baranek and Chan, 1987; 1989; 1991; Skidmore; Schlesinger and Tumber.
28. E.g., Cavender, 2004; Jermyn.
29. For details, see Schlesinger and Tumber; Brants; Cavender, 1998; Donovan; Dauncey.
30. Hattendorf, 73.
31. E.g., Schweinitz; Müller; Keppler, 2006a.
32. Luckmann, 1986; 1989.
33. A similar approach is used by Ayaß in analyzing weekly televized sermons, developed by Pinseler, 2006 for analyzing crime appeal programs and described as a research program by Keppler, 2006b.
34. Luckmann, 1986.
35. Wulff, 1995.
36. Keppler, 1994.
37. Klaus and Lücke.
38. See e.g., Turner; Marchart.
39. Cavender, 1998.
40. Donovan.
41. Fishman, 1999.
42. Bond-Maupin.
43. See especially Fishman, 1999.
44. Waldmann.
45. Russo.
46. Bauer.
47. Linder and Ort.
48. Milanés, 1998.
49. Rath, 1981; 1985.
50. This pattern has already been described in relation to news reports on crime and horror films. See Ericson, Baranek and Chan for news reports and Wulff, 1985 for horror films.
51. Thomas, 2007.
52. Fiske, 134.
53. Castells, 344.
54. Nogala.
55. Foucault.
56. Jermyn, 81.

References

Ayaß, Ruth. *Das Wort zum Sonntag. Fallstudie einer Kirchlichen Sendereihe.* Stuttgart, Germany: Kohlhammer, 1997.
Barker, Martin. "Stuart Hall, Policing the Crisis." In *Reading Into Cultural Studies*, edited by Martin Beezer and Anne Barker, 81-100. London: Routledge, 1992.

Bauer, Ludwig. *Authentizität, Mimesis, Fiktion. Fernsehunterhaltung und Integration von Realität am Beispiel des Kriminalsujets.* München, Germany: Schaudig, Bauer, Ledig, 1992.

Becker, Howard S. *Outsiders. Studies in the Sociology of Deviance.* New York: Free Press, 1966.

Bond-Maupin, Lisa. "That Wasn't Even Me They Showed. Women as Criminals on 'America's Most Wanted'." *Violence Against Women* 4, no. 1 (1998): 30-44.

Bortner, M. Andrew. "Media Images and Public Attitudes Toward Crime and Justice." In *Justice and the Media. Issues and Research,* edited by Ray Surette, 15-30. Springfield, Ill.: Charles C. Thomas, 1984.

Brants, Chris. "Crime Fighting by Television in the Netherlands." In *Entertaining Crime. Television Reality Programs,* 175-191. New York: Aldine de Gruyter, 1998.

Brück, Ingrid. "Verbrechensdarstellung im deutschen 'Fernsehkrimi'." In *Verbrechen—Justiz—Medien. Konstellationen in Deutschland von 1900 bis zur Gegenwart,* 489-502. Ubingen, Germany: Niemeyer, 1999.

Castells, Manuel. *End of Millennium. The Information Age. Economy, Society and Culture, Vol. III.* Oxford: Blackwell, 1998.

Cavender, Gray. "In 'The Shadow of Shadows.' Television Reality Crime Programming." In *Entertaining Crime. Television Reality Programs,* edited by Mark Fishman and Gray Cavender, 79-94. New York: Aldine de Gruyter, 1998.

————. "In Search of Community on Reality TV. 'America's Most Wanted' and 'Survivor.'" In *Understanding Reality Television,* edited by Su Holmes and Deborah Jermyn, 154-172. New York: Routledge, 2004.

Cohen, Stanley. *Folk Devils and Moral Panics. The Creation of the Mods and the Rockers.* Oxford: Robertson, 1980.

Cremer-Schäfer, Helga and Heinz Steinert. *Straflust und Repression.* Münster, Germany: Westfälisches Dampfboot, 1998.

Dauncey, Hugh. "'Témoin No. 1.' Crime Shows on French Television." In *Entertaining Crime: Television Reality Programs,* edited by Mark Fishman and Gray Cavender, 193-209. New York: Aldine de Gruyter, 1998.

Dominick, Joseph R. "Crime and Law Enforcement on Prime-Time Television." *Public Opinion Quarterly* 37, no. 2 (1973): 241-250.

Donovan, Pamela. "Armed With the Power of Television. Reality Crime Programming and the Reconstruction of Law and Order in the United States." In *Entertaining Crime. Television Reality Programs,* edited by Mark Fishman and Gray Cavender, 117-137. New York: Aldine de Gruyter, 1998.

Ericson, Richard. "Mass Media, Crime, Law, and Justice. An Institutional Approach." *British Journal of Criminology* 31, no. 3 (1991): 219-249.

Ericson, Richard, Patricia M. Baranek and Janet B. L. Chan. *Visualizing Deviance. A Study of News Organization.* Toronto: University of Toronto Press, 1987.

————. *Negotiating Control. A Study of News Sources.* Toronto: University of Toronto Press, 1989.

————. *Representing Order. Crime, Law, and Justice in the News Media.* Toronto: University of Toronto Press, 1991.

Fishman, Jessica M. "The Populace and the Police. Models of Social Control in Reality-Based Crime Television." *Critical Studies in Mass Communication* 16, no. 3 (1999):

268-288.

Fishman, Mark and Gray Cavender (eds.). *Entertaining Crime. Television Reality Programs*. New York: Aldine de Gruyter, 1998.

Fiske, John. *Understanding Popular Culture*. London: Unwin Hyman, 1989.

Foucault, Michel. *Discipline and Punish. The Birth of the Prison*. New York: Random House, 1975.

Fukuyama, Francis. *The End of History and the Last Man*. Toronto: Free Press, 1992.

Hall, Stuart, Chas Critcher, Tony Jefferson, John Clarke and Brian Roberts. *Policing the Crisis. Mugging, the State, and Law and Order*. London: Palgrave Macmillan, 1978.

Hattendorf, Manfred. *Dokumentarfilm und Authentizität. Ästhetik und Pragmatik einer Gattung*. Berlin: Ölschläger, 1994.

Jermyn, Deborah. "'This *Is* About Real People!' Video Technologies, Actuality and Affect in the Television Crime Appeal." In *Understanding Reality Television*, edited by Su Holmes and Deborah Jermyn, 71-90. New York: Routledge, 2004.

Keppler, Angela. *Wirklicher als die Wirklichkeit? Das neue Realitätsprinzip der Fernsehunterhaltung*. Frankfurt am Main, Germany: Fischer, 1994.

———."Konversations- und Gattungsanalyse." In *Qualitative Methoden der Medienforschung*, 293-323. Reinbek, Germany: Rowohlt, 2006a.

———. *Mediale Gegenwart. Eine Theorie des Fernsehens am Beispiel der Darstellung von Gewalt*. Frankfurt am Main, Germany: Suhrkamp, 2006b.

Klaus, Elisabeth and Stephanie Lücke. "Reality TV. Definition und Merkmale einer erfolgreichen Genrefamilie am Beispiel Reality TV und Docu Soap." *Medien & Kommunikationswissenschaft* 51, no. 2 (2003): 195-213.

Lamnek, Siegfried. "Kriminalitätsberichterstattung in den Massenmedien als Problem." *Monatsschrift für Kriminologie und Strafrechtsreform* 73, no. 3 (1990): 163-176.

Linder, Joachim and Claus-Michael Ort. "Zur sozialen Konstruktion der Übertretung und zu ihren Repräsentationen im 20. Jahrhundert." In *Verbrechen—Justiz—Medien. Konstellationen in Deutschland von 1900 bis zur Gegenwart*, 3-80. Tübingen, Germany: Niemeyer, 1999.

Luckmann, Thomas. "Grundformen der Gesellschaftlichen Vermittlung des Wissens. Kommunikative Gattungen." In *Kultur und Gesellschaft. Sonderheft 27 der Kölner Zeitschrift für Soziologie und Sozialpsychologie*, edited by Friedhelm Neidhardt and Rainer M. Lepsius, 191-211. Opladen, Germany: Westdeutscher Verlag, 1986.

———. "Kultur und Kommunikation." In *Kultur und Gesellschaft. Verhandlungen des 24. Deutschen Soziologentags, des 11. Österreichischen Soziologentags und des 8, Kongresses der Schweizerischen Gesellschaft für Soziologie in Zürich 1988*, edited by Max Haller, Hans-Joachim Hoffmann-Nowotny and Wolfgang Zapf, 33-45. Frankfurt am Main, Germany: Campus, 1989.

Marchart, Oliver. *Cultural Studies*. Konstanz, Germany: UVK, 2008.

Milanés, Alexander. "Akte X und Aktenzeichen XY. Über Formen der Inszenierung Krimineller Bedrohung im Fernsehen." In *Inszenierung: Innere Sicherheit. Daten und Diskurse*, 51-64. Opladen, Germany: Leske+Budrich, 1998.

Müller, Eggo."'Genre' als produktive Matrix. Überlegungen zur Methodik historischer Genreanalyse." In *7. Film- und Fernsehwissenschaftliches Kolloquium*, edited by Britta Hartmann and Eggo Müller, 116-122. Berlin: Verein für Theorie and Geschichte audiovisueller Kommunikation, 1995.

Nogala, Detlef. "Gating the Rich—Barcoding the Poor. Konturen einer Neoliberalen Sicherheitskonfiguration." In *Soziale Ungleichheit, Kriminalität und Kriminalisierung*, edited by Wolfgang Ludwig-Mayerhofer, 49-83. Berlin: Leske+Budrich, 2000.

Oliver, Mary Beth. "Portrayals of Crime, Race, and Aggression in 'Reality-Based' Police Shows. A Content Analysis." *Journal of Broadcasting and Electronic Media 38*, no. 2 (1994): 179-192.

Oliver, Mary Beth and Blake G. Armstrong. "The Color of Crime. Perceptions of Caucasions' and African-Americans' Involvement in Crime." In *Entertaining Crime. Television Reality Programs*, edited by Mark Fishman and Gray Cavender, 19-35. New York: Aldine de Gruyter, 1998.

Pinseler, Jan. *Fahndungssendungen im deutschsprachigen Fernsehen*. Köln, Germany: Halem, 2006.

———."Nur auf den ersten Blick ein Ganz Normaler Stadtpark. Konstruktionen von Normalität und Abweichung in Fahndungssendungen." In *Medien—Diversität—Ungleichheit. Zur medialen Konstruktion sozialer Differenz*, edited by Ulla Wischermann and Tanja Thomas, 69-86. Wiesbaden, Germany: VS, 2008.

Rath, Claus-Dieter. "Das unsichtbare Netz." *Kursbuch*, no. 66 (1981): 39-45.

———. "The Invisible Network. Television as an Institution in Everyday Life." In *Television in Transition*, edited by Phillip Drummond and Richard Peterson, 119-204. London: British Film Institute, 1985.

Ross, Nick and Sue Cook. *Crimewatch UK*. London: Hodder and Stoughton, 1987.

Russo, Manfred. *Die Sprache im Österreichischen Fernsehen*. Wien, Austria: Österreichischer Rundfunk, 1980.

Schlesinger, Philip and Howard Tumber. "Fighting the War against Crime. Television, Police, and Audience." *British Journal of Criminology 33*, no. 1 (1993): 19-32.

———. *Reporting Crime. The Media Politics of Criminal Justice*. Oxford: Oxford University Press, 1995.

Schweinitz, Jörg. "'Genre' und lebendiges Genrebewußtsein. Geschichte eines Begriffs und Probleme seiner Konzeptualisierung in der Filmwissenschaft." *Montage/av 3*, no. 2 (1994): 99-118.

Sears, John. "'Crimewatch' and the Rhetoric of Verisimilitude." *Critical Survey 7*, no. 1 (1995): 51-58.

Seeßlen, Georg. *Natural Born Nazis. Faschismus in der populären Kultur*. Berlin: Tiamat, 1996.

Skidmore, Paula. "Telling Tales. Media Power, Ideology and the Reporting of Child Sexual Abuse in Britain." In *Crime and the Media: The Post-Modern Spectacle*, edited by David Kidd-Hewitt and Richard Osborne, 78-106. London: Pluto, 1995.

Thomas, Tanja."Heidis Girls und Popstars-Mädchen. Inszenierte Lebensträume und harte (Körper-)Arbeit." *Betrifft Mädchen 20*, no. 3 (2007): 108-114.

Turner, Graeme. *British Cultural Studies. An Introduction*. London: Routledge, 1996.

Waldmann, Werner. *Das deutsche Fernsehspiel. Ein systematischer Überblick*. Wiesbaden, Germany: Athenaion, 1977.

Winker, Klaus. *Fernsehen unterm Hakenkreuz. Organisation, Programm, Personal*. Wien, Austria: Böhlau, 1994.

Wulff, Hans J. *Die Erzählung der Gewalt. Untersuchungen zu den Konventionen der*

Darstellung gewalttätiger Interaktion. Münster, Germany: MakS, 1985.

————. "Reality-TV. Von Geschichten über Risiken und Tugenden." *Montage/av* 4, no. 1 (1995): 107-124.

Zeutschner, Heiko. *Die braune Mattscheibe. Fernsehen im Nationalsozialismus.* Hamburg, Germany: Rotbuch, 1995.

Chapter 10
After Politics, What Is Left Is the Police: Police Videos and the Neo-Liberal Order
Jan Teurlings

Police in Popular Culture

Popular culture has a long-standing fascination with crime and police work. Independent of the medium of the day, popular culture has returned again and again to police officers and the criminals they prosecute. We find them in 19th century popular crime novels, comics such as *Police Comics* or *Batman*, countless films and numerous television series such as *Hill Street Blues* and *Miami Vice*. The historical perseverance of the police in popular culture invites ahistorical interpretations, but in this essay I want instead to situate one specific "police genre" in the socio-political context from which it originates. More specifically, I look at Reality shows that focus on police work and situate them within the wider context of post-political neo-liberalism, a term that we will soon unpack. First, however, some remarks on the particular type of Reality TV that is the object of this chapter.

The specific "reality genre" I have in mind are Reality shows such as *The World's Wildest Police Videos* (WWPV) in the United States, *Police Camera Action!* (PCA) in the United Kingdom, or *Blik Op De Weg* (BODW) in the Netherlands. These shows use police surveillance footage as their raw material, although it is often mixed with dramatized enactments and post-hoc interview material. The basic "form" is the car chase, but it is not only that. WWPV, for example, also includes images of hold-ups, riots, and so on, whereas BODW focuses exclusively on traffic violations.

This chapter looks at such shows as part of the gradual transformation, since the late 1970s, of most (if not all) societies toward the neo-liberal model. Indeed, it is no coincidence that reality TV as a genre boomed in the same decade that neo-liberalism started its heavy-handed attack on the welfare state. The reasons for this are straightforward: in Europe, neo-liberal policy "deregulated" state-sponsored monopolies, leading to an increasing number of broadcasters, ever-fiercer competition for advertisers' money and thus a downward pressure on the production budget. Reality TV was the perfect programming solution for the economic problems of the sector, since it is often (though not always) very cheap television.[1] But Reality TV and neo-liberalism are connected in more profound ways than the latter providing the political-economic backdrop against which the genre could flourish. These programs also carry a set of ideals that stimulate the type of subjectivity that neo-liberalism requires, and it is my intention to show how this works in two of these programs, the American WWPV and the Dutch BODW.[2] This article therefore contributes to a line of inquiry that connects reality TV to changes in the capitalist mode of production.[3]

Post-Political Neo-Liberalism

Although in recent years the appetite for neo-liberal orthodoxy amongst the ruling elites appear to be on the wane, it is nevertheless clear that neo-liberalism remains hegemonic, that is, it still is the common sense perspective from which all matters of policy are considered. Even crises are seen as temporary instabilities that do not affect the dominance (and legitimacy) of the neo-liberal model. It is for this reason that a number of scholars have adopted the term post-political to describe the current period. Their use of this term refers to "a politics which claims to leave behind old ideological struggles and instead focus on expert management and administration."[4] Francis Fukuyama's infamous claim that with the fall of the Berlin wall we had reached the *End of History* is an example of post-political ideology: Liberal democracy-*cum*-capitalism had beaten communism and thus proven its superiority.[5] Some fine-tuning was needed, but the big ideological struggles were a thing of the past.

The economic doctrine of the post-political era is neo-liberalism, the belief that the market is the best method for organizing just about anything in society. All human productive activities should take the form of private enterprise, even those that until the 1970s were the exclusive territory of the state, such as broadcasting, communication, law enforcement or even the army. Neo-liberalism presents itself as a frontal assault on the state, although we will see that this rhetoric obscures the many ways in which it combines market and state. It aims at undoing what it calls "the excesses of state intervention" of the New Deal and the Keynesian Welfare State era, and makes private enterprise the model society should strive for.

The standard interpretation of neo-liberalism is that it is a socio-economic doctrine. In recent years, however, a new approach to neo-liberalism has started to emerge, one that is less influenced by socio-economic categories, but looks at neo-liberalism as a specific "mode of governance." The so-called governmentality school is heavily influenced by the work of Michel Foucault and, more specifically, by his writing on governmentality and liberal modes of government—a quite short and specific period in his intellectual trajectory, that comes between the middle Foucault of *Discipline and Punish*[6] and *The Will to Knowledge*[7], but precedes his last two parts of the *History of Sexuality*.[8] His governmentality writings were originally scattered across several sites, and it is only recently that his lectures at the *Collège de France* have been published together as series.[9]

Governmentality and Liberal Modes of Government

The governmentality writings constitute Foucault's reply to the Marxist critique that was launched against him after he wrote *Discipline and Punish*. Your microphysics of power is an interesting read, the criticism went, but what about the role of the state? Your detailed analysis of power relationships in institutions such as the prison, the army, the school or the hospital, is powerful, but are you not in danger of neglecting the role of what is perhaps the most powerful actor in your network, namely the state? Don't you neglect the actor that is the organizing force behind the institutions you so meticulously analyze? Foucault's answer was a genealogy of the different modes of governing, in which he focuses on succeeding changes in the idea of governing itself. It was this critical interrogation of the idea of government that allowed him to respond to his critics.

In the governmentality lecture series Foucault argues that a crucial break happened around the end of the eighteenth century. In the sixteenth and seventeenth centuries governing was first and foremostly a question of meticulous and rigid planning by the state, best exemplified by the *polizeiwissenschaft* of the time, or the absolutist monarchs of the Ancien Régime in France. At the end of the eigthteenth century, however, we witness the emergence of a new governmental logic, one that allows things to follow their "natural" course, since their free play leads—after some initial turmoil—to desirable effects. Foucault gives the example of the physiocrats[10] in France, but Adam Smith's invisible hand is another example of a doctrine that explains how the free play of things leads to the desired effect.

Crucial to this new governmentality, then, is the idea of liberty. Foucault stresses, however, that this freedom has a precise *governmental* function in the liberal mode of government: one governs through the strategic use of freedom. Or, in other words, the state should govern less in order to govern more effectively. Hence, his reply to the Marxist critics, namely that governing is not something that is done only by the state, but that it takes place in a number of institutions across civil society, by a variety of actors, in a decentralized way: "It is in fact vain to look for the hand of the state everywhere pulling the strings of micro-disciplinary power in nineteenth-century societies. But on the other hand, these largely privatized micro-power structures none the less participate, from the viewpoint of government, in a coherent general policy of order."[11]

Three observations are important for what follows. It is clear that Foucault's analysis of liberalism differs from the standard idea of liberalism as a political or economic doctrine. For Foucault, liberalism is first and foremost a rationality of government, a "whole way of organizing society," in which the free play of things leads to desirable effects—liberty as a regulatory force, as it were. Second, Foucault stresses that within liberalism freedom is not given but it has to be organized. Liberalism is "not the imperative to be free but the management and organisation of the conditions under which one can be free."[12] But the latter also means that liberalism always entails the risk of its own undoing:

> At the heart of this liberal practice there is the problematic relationship between the production of freedom and that which risks limiting or destroying it because of this production itself. Liberalism as I understand it, this liberalism that is the new art of governing of the eighteenth century, implies a relationship of production/destruction with regards to freedom. With one hand one produces freedom, but this gesture itself implies that with the other one has to set up limits, controls, coercions, or obligations founded on threats, etc.[13]

Hence, liberalism has a utilitarian impulse, since utilitarianism provides the method and the principles for calculating the cost of liberty. At the heart of the liberal governmental problematic is the calculation and balancing of costs: the costs of intervening, the costs of not intervening, and the difficult balancing act between the interests of the individual and the collective.

Foucault also stresses that liberalism goes hand in hand with a culture of danger: individuals are constantly reminded of the dangers that lurk, in order to make them vigilant and avoid risky behavior. The nineteenth century thus saw the emergence of a number of initiatives that stressed the dangers that threatened individuals in everyday life:

> The campaign . . . for saving banks; you see the emergence of the crime novel and journalistic interest in crime from the middle of the nineteenth century; you see all the campaigns concerning illness and hygiene; look at everything which happens around sexuality and the fear of degeneration: degeneration of the individual, the family, the race, the human species. In short, everywhere you see the stimulation of fear, which is in a way the condition, or the psychological correlate and internal culture, of liberalism. No liberalism without a culture of danger.[14]

The Foucauldian approach to liberalism (and thus by extension, to neo-liberalism) is substantially different from the standard leftist critique.[15] Indeed, throughout the governmentality series Foucault keeps repeating that the left has not developed its own mode of governing, and that it therefore is not capable of countering the coming onslaught of neo-liberalism. The strength of liberalism for Foucault is that it is more than an economic doctrine: it also instills a certain type of subjectivity. Or, to put it more precisely, it is through the creation of socio-economic arrangements that neo-liberalism hopes to create certain types of self-governing subjectivities—which is also why liberalism is sometimes described as "governing at a distance."

This is also what distinguishes liberals from neo-liberals. For the latter, the market is not a state of nature, but a tool for fashioning people. Hence, the emphasis is on introducing market principles into institutions that are not capitalist enterprises *as such*. Blair's national health service (NHS) reform is a good example here. The introduction of market principles, such as competition between departments, individual entrepreneurship and personal accountability, aimed less at making the NHS into a capitalist enterprise and more at responsibilization and transformation of its employees' subjectivity.[16] Or, to use the Foucauldian phraseology, neo-liberal reforms are *technologies of the self*,[17] aimed not only at changing practices, but also at transforming subjectivities, making them more productive in the process. Moreover, neo-liberalism goes far beyond the purely economic; it is a "moral economy,"[18] linking the political to the ethical. This can be seen at work in the neo-liberal conception of citizenship, for example. The ideal neo-liberal citizen not only has the moral injunction to avoid dependency on others; he or she should also adopt "a 'prudent' relationship to fate, which includes avoiding 'calculable dangers and avertable risks.'"[19] The moralistic implications of the latter are clear: if risks are foreseeable, the victim is to blame for lack of foresight.

The Police Car Chase as a Neo-Liberal Project

We are now better placed to understand how police car chases form part of the neo-liberal project. Both WWPV and BODW not only aim to be entertaining pieces of television, they also claim an educational function, or even a practical utility. In the first episode of WWPV, for example, the voice-over states:

> This show will take you for a walk on the wild side . . . What we are going to show you might just save your life . . . These amazing videos show you what you need to know. Every person who has ever been swindled, or robbed, or the victim of a crime thought it would never happen to them. This is what you need to know. Because it can happen to any of us. Any time. But now we have a friend out there . . . the camera is running.

From the opening statement it is clear that WWPV wants to entertain us ("a walk on the wild side"); but it also has educational purpose. It explains, so the voice-over claims, what we should do at the moment we are "being robbed, or swindled, or [are] the victim[s] of a crime"—a manual for dangerous times, so to speak. But the program warns and educates us in a particular, a neo-liberal, way. First, we are talked to as individuals, not as members of a community, or a class, or even a gender—in other words, individuals are lifted out of the social bonds that constitute them and are addressed as unmarked "persons." Moreover, we are already placed in the position of the potential victim of a crime, not the perpetrator (nor, I would add, the potential victim of police violence). The "us" the voice-over invokes is positioned as a "good, law-abiding middle class citizen," whose personal safety is threatened by the danger that looms large, and that is always ready to attack when we least expect it. We should, therefore, watch the show very carefully, because it will teach us what to do when that inevitable confrontation with violent crime occurs. And, precisely because violence inevitably *will* shake up our lives, we will have no excuse if we do not know what to do: "We all think it never happens to us," the voice-over warns, "but don't say we didn't warn you!" And so, individuals should stay out of dangerous situations and be forever vigilant.

On the other side of the Atlantic, BODW adopts a less extravagant tone. This is due to the format: rather than showing spectacular police car chases, the show follows traffic agents as they record and document traffic violations. Actual car chases, though they do happen, are rare and the focus is on speeding tickets, violations of traffic rules, or just plain old uncivilized behavior. Despite these differences, however, BODW resembles WWPV in one important way: its educational tone. Take for instance the following blurb from the BODW website:

> The idea for *BODW* surfaced during the 1984-1988 period. Host Leo De Haas was on the road all the time due to his job as a cameraman, and was astonished by the traffic behavior he witnessed. In everyday contacts we might be friendly and cooperative, but once we get behind the steering wheel the beast comes out . . . De Haas thought it might be a good idea to record our driving behavior and confront the perpetrators later on with the evidence.[20]

This educational mission is really at the core of BODW's format: traffic violations are taped as they happen and, invariably, the police stop the perpetrators, ask them why they did it, and confront them with their driving behavior as registered on the police cameras. In this sense, the camera not only records and provides proof of bad behavior, it also acts as a tool for creating law-abiding citizens. However, although different in tone from WWPV, the same elements of a neo-liberal governmental program are discernible in BODW. First, individual responsibility is stressed. In BODW drivers are frequently stopped for speeding. When asked why they were exceeding the limit, drivers often try to offer excuses such as being late for work, or having an urgent meeting. Rather than engaging in a debate about excessive working hours, or the stresses of living under late capitalism, officers remain polite and understanding, but nevertheless emphasize that it is the driver who is ultimately responsible, thus treating the violation as a personal or individual problem, rather than a social one. The Dutch police officers are thus seen as implementing a politico-legislative system, which (through the emphasis on individual responsibility) strengthens the neoliberal project. However, because the police officers (and the show) claim to be beyond politics ("we are merely upholding the law, sir") they are a prime instance of the post-political ideology referred to earlier.

Second, the show constantly stresses the importance of risk-avoiding behavior. Here are some examples to illustrate this point: in the episode of January 16, 2007, which was dedicated to motorcycles, the camera zooms in on a group of motorcyclists driving well below the allowed maximum speed, respecting all the traffic rules. The voice-over comments: "Look at them enjoying the landscape. What self-control!" In comments like these the voice-over praises overly prudent and risk-avoiding behavior. A more telling example appears in an episode shown a month later. The patrol has been following a car traveling at slightly over the speed limit in a residential area. The driver is stopped and the police officer warns him:

> I strongly advise you to change your driving style, especially in certain areas. You were driving extremely fast in a residential area and downtown. Now, you were lucky there weren't many people on the streets, but there are some small streets that run into the main street. You could be so unlucky that just at that moment some kids come biking out of one of them . . . If I were to ride out of one of these streets with my kids I would be really angry. Better be careful!

The exchange is remarkable: the officer readily admits that the situation was not dangerous, yet the driver is reprimanded for something that *might* have happened. In other words, he was not thinking ahead, he was not anticipating potential dangers. This is the core of the neo-liberalism *culture of danger*: You are chastised not for doing something wrong, but because you did not anticipate. A final example occurs in the motorcycle episode. The camera follows a cyclist who has been involved in an accident, to interview him in his home (a rare occasion in BODW). The motorcyclist was wearing a protective suit and, despite sliding for several meters, only suffered a mild graze. Nevertheless, the interviewer, adopting a moralistic tone says: "So this summer you will not be wearing a tee shirt on your bike, right?" The moral of the story is clear: *This time* the driver was all right; but don't even think about not wearing a protective suit.

Which Neo-Liberalism?

The analysis thus far has connected both of our police car chase shows to neoliberalism. However, by doing so, it tends to assume that neo-liberalism is a monolithic, univocal ideology that is implemented everywhere with the same results. Wendy Larner contests this idea. She argues that: "There are different configurations of neo-liberalism, and that close inspection of particular neo-liberal political projects is more likely to reveal a complex and hybrid political imaginary, rather than the straightforward implementation of a unified and coherent philosophy."[21]

That neo-liberalism is not a unified paradigm or theory is clear when we compare WWPV and BODW. If both shows differ in their format, this is attributable not just to the maker's idiosyncratic choices; these differences stem from and embody different types of neo-liberalism. Thus, we need to focus on the differences between the shows.

Problematized Behavior

One of the most striking differences lies in what is considered to be "inappropriate behavior." We have seen that WWPV tends towards the spectacular: All the footage they use includes images of crimes that contain a considerable degree of violence, often involving several crashed cars, and even death. Often car chases start as part of routine control, but we get to see only those that lead to spectacular getaways or shootouts. WWVP problematizes acts of *violence*, and by doing so equates crime with violence. In the few moments where other inappropriate behaviors are discussed, for example, drunk driving, it is the possible violent consequences that are stressed.

BODW does not focus on violence. In fact, in an entire season there was not a single instance of violence, other than some minor verbal abuse. BODW focuses instead on infringements to the traffic rules, even very minor and not strictly defined ones. A driver can be stopped and pulled over because the police officer judges that he or she is driving "a tad too aggressively." In other words, BODW puts the spotlight on respect for the rules, regardless of the severity of the infringement. The result is not just a less spectacular show; it also leads to a different problematization. The true danger, so BODW tells us, does not come from the occasional nutcase who is willing to use violence. Rather, it is a disrespect for the rules, or the idea that the rules do not apply to *you*, that is the true menace to society.

Perpetrators

There are also considerable differences in the way that perpetrators are portrayed. In WWPV, the perpetrators belong to a different category from "normal society." They are invariably "crazed," "irrational," "desperate," "a wild beast." This othering is then combined with a complete lack of biographic context: we never get to know anything about the criminals, who they are or what were their motivations: what prevails is the violent act itself. As a result, crime becomes an inherently incomprehensible, irrational and totally unpredictable act, committed by evildoers, presumably just for the fun of it.

BODW takes a completely different approach. The "criminals" are not some fundamentally other category, as in WWPV: they are full members of a "normal" society. The perpetrators *are* the average citizens, the Dutch John Doe, who today happens to be in a hurry, or who has just bought a new bike and wants to see how fast it will go. In the Dutch program we are *all* possible perpetrators, but it is important that we realize that we have to play by the rules; if not society will fall apart. BODW reminds us that the rules are there for a reason, and that if everybody were to pursue their own freedoms, this would benefit no one.

This is also why BODW pays a lot of attention to the circumstances leading up to a misdemeanor. Often the officer conducting an interrogation is not satisfied with a confession of guilt: he wants to hear *why* the perpetrator did as he or she did. Take, for instance, the following interchange between an officer and a biker:

> Officer: What do you have to say about those 144 km per hour, that is 50 km per hour too fast. You probably have something to say about this, why you did this?
> Biker: I don't have to tell to you that it is irresponsible. But I borrowed the bike, and wanted to try it out.
> Officer: And why did you pass that car left of the central reservation?
> Biker: I don't know the bike well, so I thought it would be better to drive to the left rather than braking abruptly.

A conversation like this is impossible to imagine taking place in WWPV: criminals are taken out or punished, not talked to! But in BODW, where the "criminal" is "somebody like us" it is important to make him or her realize the possible consequences of their behavior.

"Treatment"

This last point brings us to the third and last difference between the two series, namely the way abject behavior is "treated" in these shows. In WWPV the solution is simple: the criminal is arrested, or shot down—in any case, he is punished for his criminal act. No attempt is made to get the criminal to confess, let alone repent: since we have just caught the criminal on tape there is no need for the former, and the latter is of no importance as long as justice has been served. In BODW, however, emphasis is put upon making people understand their bad behavior, and the consequences that could have followed. The video footage in BODW thus serves a double purpose: It not only provides legal proof of the misdemeanor; it is a crucial tool for responsibilizing the criminal (as well as potential criminals watching the show at home).

The differential treatment of the perpetrators goes alongside the different roles of the police officers in these shows. In WWPV, the police officer is essentially a guardian of civilian peace: If somebody disturbs it, the officer is allowed to use the repressive powers conferred by the on him (or her) and literally "take out" the criminal to ensure that he poses no immediate threat to society. The officer is the protector and avenger of society. In BODW police officers also have a repressive function (e.g., they hand out speeding tickets), but this is not so much in revenge for harm done to society, but includes an element of making perpetrators recognize their risky behavior. In this sense the Dutch officer is more of an educator, while the U.S. officer is the punitive guardian.

WWPV's Authoritarian Neo-Liberalism

While both these shows have clear neo-liberal governmental aims, the differences between them make it hard to speak of *one* neo-liberalism. Rather, we see that each show implements some basic neo-liberal values, but this is done in such a way that there are crucial differences in their application. Hence, we can distinguish between two neo-liberal models, which I will call respective authoritarian versus communitarian neo-liberalism, corresponding roughly to the difference between the U.S. and the European versions of neo-liberalism.

In WWPV we can see that crime is equated with acts of violence, and that criminals are "othered" by not providing any background or motivation. As a result, crime becomes an incomprehensible, "evil" deed. This makes the world, as represented by WWPV, a thoroughly Manichaean universe, composed of people who are by nature "good" or "bad," a post-political idea if there ever was one.

But WWPV also functions as a *technology of the self* toward the citizens it addresses. The prudent, risk-avoiding citizen needs to know what to do in case of an emergency, but (due to the essentially irrational character of crime) cannot be completely prepared for it. WWPV thus propagates a paranoid subjectivity, inciting us to monitor and scrutinize our surroundings, never sure of our lives or belongings. Moreover, viewers are encouraged to identify themselves with middle-class values, such as respect for order, authority and most of all property.

The neo-liberalism in WWPV is authoritarian because it is very much focused on repressive methods. If neo-liberalism needs a culture of fear, the authoritarian variant believes in providing security exclusively through repressive methods. The role of the police is to safeguard societal peace, and the perpetrators of crimes place themselves outside of society and hence need to be "taken out" so that they can no longer pose a threat to society. However, since the *choice* to do so was theirs, they have only themselves to blame.

BODW as Communitarian Neo-Liberalism

BODW propagates a different view of society, which I will describe as communitarian neo-liberalism. Since this is a neo-liberal doctrine, it stresses individual solutions to collective problems, as well as risk-avoiding behavior and, in true post-political fashion, it negates its own politics, but dresses them up in neutral, "value-free" language. But the nature of "crime" and "transgression" are fundamentally different in the BODW universe.

For instance, criminals are not the radically other, incomprehensible and irrational "evil doers"; they are ordinary men and women. The danger does not reside in somebody radically different; rather, it is "the beast in each and every one of us"—a metaphor that is often invoked in the program. This means that everybody potentially is a perpetrator of crime, including the police officers. Moreover, crime is defined as "transgression of the rule." The consequences of a transgression do not matter *per se*: it is the breaking of the rule that is the fundamental problem.

This brand of neo-liberalism is communitarian because it stresses the fact that living together requires rules. The individual might be tempted to think that the rules do not apply to him or her, but this would lead to unliveable chaos. Hence, breaking the rules, independent of the consequences, is essentially a breaking of the social contract, a crime against the community.

As a technology of the self, communitarian neo-liberalism is a much more strict and inward-looking technology than its authoritarian version. Ultimately, BODW tells its viewers that we are all potential sinners, and that we must control our desires not to follow the rules. In this sense, BODW is a true technology of the self, that is a technology aimed at the self-transformation of subjects. In authoritarian neo-liberalism on the other hand, the viewer is directed toward the outside, monitoring the environment, and preparing him- or herself for the inevitable moment when violence strikes.

Two Models of Neo-Liberalism and What That Means for the Future

This chapter has shown that neo-liberalism is not a unified doctrine that is uniformly applied around the globe. Rather, what happens is that a set of governmental doctrines are implemented within already existing conditions. They become articulated through the already existing traditions. In this sense, the emphasis upon repression and the use of force connects U.S. neo-liberalism to the neoconservative moment, although it cannot be reduced to it.[22] Moreover, neo-liberalism, American style, found a powerful ally in the libertarian tradition, since both take the individual to be the measure of things.

In the Dutch version of neo-liberalism, other social and intellectual traditions are at work. Neo-liberalism arrived in the context of a firmly established welfare state, and had to assume the latter's language in order to take better hold of it—hence the emphasis on living together, respect for the rules, etc. The result is a "neo-liberalization of the welfare state," or the introduction of neo-liberal principles within what essentially remains a welfare state. Measures like a limited (in time) access to social services, or the introduction of the no-claim reconstitution (if you do not make use of the health services in a particular year, you receive some reimbursement) are typically being sold to us by referring to the collective: "We are forced to make people more responsible," so the argument goes, "since otherwise the system is in danger"—a curious *collective* argument for pressing through neo-liberal reforms.

There is also a curious *protestant* streak in Dutch neo-liberalism, in its emphasis on introspection and confession, and its almost moralistic handling of the issues. In this precise sense the Dutch version of neo-liberalism is much stricter than its American counterpart, since it locks its subjects into an "iron cage"—not of rationality, but of the moralistic burden to do good.

If it is true that neo-liberalism had to adapt itself to local contexts and intellectual traditions, this also has consequences for our counterstrategies, in that there is no "one size fits all" strategy against neo-liberalism. Rather, the left should develop an acute awareness of the local variety of neo-liberalism, and devise its argumentative strategies from there on. This means that in a country such as the Netherlands, our arguments should point out to what extent neo-liberalism is detrimental to the collective, and we should not shun moralistic claims. In the United States, on the other hand, the key concept to advance is "justice"—with a socio-economic twist.

The true challenge for the future, however, goes much beyond the discursive strategies of how to convince people—the Gramscian problematic, if you will. If Foucault's governmentality work still has enough power to sway our imagination, it is because of his painful assertion that the Left does not have a proper way of governing. And even though the neo-liberal project seems to have lost some of its original impetus and attraction, the Left has not advanced one inch toward creating a very necessary alternative mode of government.

Notes

1. For two excellent articles on the political economy of Reality TV, see Magder; Raphael.

2. The analysis in this paper is based upon the first season of the *World's Wildest Police Videos*, broadcast for the first time in 1998. For *Blik Op De Weg*, which more or less continuously broadcasts on Dutch public television, I analyzed episodes between January 16, 2007 and May 1, 2007.

3. See e.g., Rapping; Ouellette; Andrejevic; McMurria; Ouellette and Hay.
4. Žižek, 40.
5. Fukuyama.
6. Foucault, 1991 (1975).
7. Foucault, 1990 (1978).
8. Foucault, 1990 (1984).
9. Foucault, 2004.
10. The physiocrats were a number of French economists who were opposed to the mercantilist tradition under the Ancien Régime. The main issue of contention with the latter was the issue of protectionism versus *laissez-faire*, which is why they are often considered to be the intellectual predecessors of classical economists.
11. Gordon, 27.
12. Foucault, 2004, 65 (my translation).
13. Foucault, 2004, 65 (my translation).
14. Foucault, 2004, 68 (my translation).
15. Many authors have opposed Foucault's governmentality writings to Marxist approaches, and have pointed to their intricate incompatibility. See e.g., Peters, 74-79; Bennett, 60-84; Larner. For an alternative interpretation, see Nealon.
16. See du Gay, 285-344.
17. Foucault, 1999.
18. Hay, 166.
19. Ouellette, 234.
20. *Blik Op De Weg*, "Hoe het begon." 2008. www.blikopdeweg.nl/Hoe_het_begon /hoe_het_begon.shtml (my translation).
21. Larner, 12.
22. For the relationship between neoliberalism and neoconservatism, see Brown.

References

Andrejevic, Marc. *Reality TV: The Work of Being Watched*. Lanham, Md.: Rowman and Littlefield Publishers, 2004.
Bennett, Tony. *Culture: A Reformer's Science*. Londen: Sage, 1998.
Blik Op De Weg. "Hoe het begon." 2008. www.blikopdeweg.nl/Hoe_het_begon /hoe_het_begon.shtml
Brown, Wendy. "American Nightmare: Neo-liberalism, Neoconservatism, and De-Democratization." *Political Theory* 34, no. 6 (2006): 690-714.
Foucault, Michel. *Discipline and Punish: The Birth of the Prison*. London: Penguin, 1991 (1975).
———. *The Will to Knowledge (The History of Sexuality 1)*. London: Penguin, 1990 (1978).
———. *The Use of Pleasure (The History of Sexuality 2)*. London: Penguin, 1990 (1984).
———. *The Care of the Self (The History of Sexuality 3)*. London: Penguin, 1990 (1984).
———. "Technologies of the Self." In *Technologies of the Self: a Seminar with Michel Foucault*, edited by Luther H. Martin, Huck Gutman and Patrick H. Hutton, 16-49. London: Tavistock, 1999.

————. *Sécurité, Territoire, Population: Cours au Collège de France (1977-1978).* Paris: Gallimard Seuill, 2004.

————. *Naissance de la Biopolitique: Cours au Collège de France (1978-1979).* Paris: Gallimard Seuill, 2004.

Fukuyama, Francis. *The End of History and the Last Man.* New York: Free Press, 1992.

du Gay, Paul. "Organizing Identity: Making Up People at Work." In *Production of Culture/Cultures of Production*, edited by Paul du Gay, 285-344. London: Sage, 1997.

Hay, James. "Unaided Virtues: The (Neo)Liberalization of the Domestic Sphere and the New Architecture of Community." In *Foucault, Cultural Studies, and Govermentality*, edited by Jack Z. Bratich, Jeremy Packer, and Cameron McCarthy, 165-206. Albany, N.Y.: State University of New York Press, 2003.

Gordon, Colin. "Governmental Rationality: An Introduction." In *The Foucault Effect: Studies in Governmentality*, edited by Graham Burchell, Colin Gordon and Peter Miller, 1-52. London: Harvester Wheatsheaf, 1991.

Larner, Wendy. "Neo-liberalism: Policy, Ideology, Governmentality." *Studies in Political Economy* 63 (2000): 5-26.

Magder, Ted. "The End of TV 101: Reality Programs, Formats, and the New Business of Television." In *Reality TV: Remaking Television Culture*, edited by Susan Murray and Laurie Ouellette, 137-156. New York: New York University Press, 2004.

McMurria, John. "Desperate Citizens and Good Samaritans: Neo-liberalism and Makeover Reality TV." *Television & New Media* 9, no. 4 (2008): 305-332.

Nealon, Jeffrey T. *Foucault beyond Foucault: Power and its Intensifications since 1984.* Stanford, Calif.: Stanford University Press, 2008.

Ouellette, Laurie. "'Take responsibility for yourself': *Judge Judy* and the Neoliberal Citizen." In *Reality TV: Remaking Television Culture*, edited by Susan Murray and Laurie Ouellette, 231-250. New York: New York University Press, 2004.

Ouellette, Laurie and James Hay. "Makeover Television, Governmentality and the Good Citizen." *Continuum* 22, no. 4 (2008): 471-484.

Peters, Michael A. *Poststructuralism, Marxism and Neoliberalism: Between Theory and Politics.* Lanham, Md.: Rowman and Littlefield, 2001.

Raphael, Chad. "The Political Economic Origins of Reali-TV." In *Reality TV: Remaking Television Culture*, edited by Susan Murray and Laurie Ouellette, 119-136. New York: New York University Press, 2004.

Rapping, Elayne. "Aliens, Nomads, Mad Dogs, and Road Warriors: The Changing Face of Criminal Violence on TV." In *Reality TV: Remaking Television Culture*, edited by Susan Murray and Laurie Ouellette, 214-230. New York: New York University Press, 2004.

Žižek, Slavoj. *Violence: Six Sideways Reflections.* New York: Picador, 2008.

Chapter 11
Hijacking the Branded Self: Reality TV and the Politics of Subversion
Winnie Salamon

Reality TV and the Present-Day Configuration

In the 1920s, painter/film-maker Fernand Leger considered making a documentary film that would record the lives of a man and woman over twenty-four
hours. Nothing would be omitted or hidden, nor should the couple ever become
aware of the camera's presence. In the end Leger decided not to make the film
primarily because he believed that such a blatant display of voyeurism would be
intolerable to watch.[1] Flash forward to the first decade of the twenty-first century and times have certainly changed. Never before have the boundaries between the public and private spheres been so unwaveringly blurred. Rather than
shuddering at the thought of witnessing strangers sharing their deepest, most
personal views and experiences, millions of viewers now tune in as these "ordinary people" volunteer to expose their bodies, commit sexual acts, bathe, go to
the toilet, cook, vomit, sweat, fart, cry and bitch for the cameras. While Leger
had planned for his potential subjects to be unaware of the filming process,
nowadays Reality TV participants compete against thousands of hopefuls for the
chance to take part. Competition is tough and only an elite few make the cut.

By contextualizing Reality TV within a specific theoretical framework
which views late modernity as a fluid, consumerist and individualist society, it
becomes clear that Leger was right to forgo the making of his documentary. It is
not that individuals have forgone the importance of privacy, as McQuire[2] suggests, or that we have somehow evolved into a global nation of peeping Toms or
rampant exhibitionists. What has changed is that a clear-cut definition between
the public and private spheres no longer exists, resulting in a transformation not
only of the concepts of public and private, but of what it means to be an individ-

ual. In Leger's era, before digital technology helped to transform the nature of communication, creating a globalized universe of constant change and uncertainty, a fly-on-the-wall documentary simply would not have made sense. With its underlying discourse of individual choice, personal responsibility and personal transformation, where the self becomes a commodity no different from a brand of shoe or a laptop computer, and where every point in time must be viewed as an opportunity for personal growth or a potential "big bang" moment,[3] Reality TV is an undeniable product of the late modern era, indeed a trans-genre that, like everyday life in late modern society, is reliant on a fluid version of individual self identity.

While it may be tempting to argue that identity within the commercialized world of Reality TV is primarily one of commodification, self-branding and conforming to the status quo,[4] to dismiss Reality TV programming as a mere by-product of an oppressive and capitalist culture industry, a place where there is no room for an alternative status quo, or even for the acknowledgement that the possibility of one exists,[5] is problematic. The politics of popular culture are the politics of everyday life. Gains made are progressive rather than radical, making do within the system rather than directly opposing it.[6] Nowhere is this more apparent than in the world of Reality TV. For a contestant to participate in a reality show with the aim of destroying a commercial television network as a protest against late capitalist consumerism is ridiculous and most probably impossible. But for a participant to appear on *The Biggest Loser* and highlight culturally constructed ideas of beauty and body image on the show, or appear on *Big Brother* in order to protest against the Australian government's refugee policy, has been proven possible. This chapter draws on a series of semi-structured one-to-one interviews with former Australian *Big Brother* and *Biggest Loser* contestants to examine the actions and experiences of subversive Reality TV participants, to demonstrate that political subversion is not only possible, but also prevalent, even within tightly controlled, consumer-driven products of the culture industry, namely the aforementioned Reality TV programs.

Victimized Dupes of Capitalism or Democratic Pioneers?

While there is no doubt that Reality TV, with its emphasis on individualism and personal responsibility, is a product of late capitalism, a phenomenon unique to late modernity, the so-far limited research into the unique experiences of Reality TV participants themselves has resulted in a top-down, paternalistic view of both these programs and the individuals who participate in them. The work of Theodor Adorno, with his perception of the "culture industry" as a capitalist creation that means that culture now follows the same rules of production as any other producer of commodities,[7] has been integral to the work of theorists who view Reality TV participants as a new kind of exploited labor force, underpaid by television networks that are making big profits.[8] Habermas's work on the public sphere and his vehement criticism of popular culture and subsequent denigration of the public sphere is also regularly cited, both in agreement[9] and dispute.[10] But while mass cultural theorists see popular culture as a process that subordinates, massifies and commodifies people into victimized dupes of capitalism, theorists such as Bauman, Fiske and Hall[11] argue that the liberal pluralist perspective—which perceives popular culture as a place to find consensual meanings where the production of social rituals can harmonize social difference[12]—is also problematic. The very nature of popular culture, and the varying roles played by both its consumers and producers is complex and layered. As Fiske[13] points out, popular culture is created by various formations of subordinated or disempowered people out of the resources, both discursive and material, that are provided by the very social system that disempowers them. So while people's subordination means that they do not have the tools to produce their own popular culture, they do make their culture from these resources.

When it comes to Reality TV, the feminist adagio, which famously declared the personal to be the political, has never been more apt. As Lumby succinctly points out, to confront this new, infinitely more personal public sphere, we must grasp the fundamental changes the mass media has wrought on the way we conceive of politics and culture. Politics can no longer be limited to traditional, Habermasian notions of the public and private spheres. Notions of public/private, local/global, right/left, media/real life are no longer applicable in the new media environment.[14] Reality TV, with its manipulated narrative formulas and exaggerated character traits, may not be "reality" in the everyday sense, but the bardic function played by the television means that it occupies the center of our culture and, perhaps inevitably, a much broader and inclusive political sphere which includes the life politics of the everyday.

Within this broader political context, it is essential to recognize the parallels between historical changes in first-person media and society as a whole. As Griffen-Foley points out, first person confessional media first boomed during the late nineteenth century, a time when the traditional idea of community was disintegrating.[15] Reality TV resides in a world that has never been so fragmented and where personal identity has never been so unsure. It is a world where choice is so abundant that the only choice we do not have is not to choose,[16] and where experts become commodities on whom we rely for advice on everything from weight loss to organizing our wardrobes. So, to argue that the rise of reality programming is purely economically based, is to dismiss half of the equation, ignoring the parallels between historical changes in first-person media and society as a whole. Reality TV may be cheap to produce, but it is only profitable when people want to participate and to watch.

As Anthony Giddens[17] argues, everyday life in late modernity inevitably involves what he refers to as the "endless project of the self"—a reflexive endeavor of self-realization that is enforced upon all individuals residing in late modernity. Expanding on the idea of individuals making choices, both empowering and disempowering, within the society in which they live, Giddens argues that in late modernity this "project of the self" is continuously, and consciously, being revised through lifestyle choice and daily activity.[18] Within the realm of Reality TV programming, we witness "ordinary" individuals, usually people with little or no media background, embarking on a magnified and accelerated project of the self where everyday lifestyle choices, such as the food they eat or the clothes they wear, become reflective of a particular, often changing, personal identity. As individuals participate in a Reality TV program they find themselves, within a relatively short period of time, transcending their everyday realities to become spokespeople for various lessons in social selfhood or life politics. Hence, while the power of network producers to manipulate the representation of these individual participants is undeniable, it is also essential to recognize that these power relations cannot be analyzed within the limits of linear structures. Reality TV, as a trans-genre, means that it is not only possible, but probable, that power relations will shift in various directions.

Drawing on interview-based studies, such as the exploration of women's magazine audiences conducted by Hermes,[19] my research into the experience of Reality TV participation involves a series of fifteen semi-structured interviews with former participants of *Biggest Loser* and *Big Brother*. It would be wrong to consider this research to be purely ethnographic, for as Leila Green points out, "the term ethnography is a slippery one." However, while I would consider my research to be more of a reception study involving in-depth semi-structured interviews,[20] I chose to adopt Green's open-ended, semi-structured approach and did not put a time limit on interviews, preferring to give each interviewee as much time as he or she wanted. It is also important to recognize that, as with any form of ethnography, this style of research is "not valid in the same way a scientific experiment would be,"[21] and that the interviewer is deeply embedded in the texts created and, therefore, is under a professional obligation to make him- or herself visible. As a former tabloid journalist who has worked closely with the Reality TV media machine over a period of several years, I felt it necessary to discuss my background experience openly with interviewees.

I also followed Garson's approach which argues that researchers should strive to avoid theoretical preconceptions, and instead induce theories from their observations and from the perspectives of the interviewees. They can then seek validation from the people they have researched.[22] This is similar to the "grounded theory" approach practiced by Hermes.[23] The audience (in my case, the participant) "given its voice as individuals in the ethnographic interview process, constructs and represents itself in collusion with the researcher."[24] For this reason I chose not to construct a formal hypothesis prior to conducting the interviews, preferring instead to ask open-ended questions, focusing in particular on the concept of the journey and the self, while allowing interviewees to speak freely, even, on occasion, going off on tangents.

The Politics of Subversion

Tens of thousands of hopefuls have auditioned for the Australian versions of *Big Brother*, *The Biggest Loser* and *Australian Idol*, with many returning year after year in the hope of making the cut. The successful candidates are chosen because of an implicit expectation that they will play out a particular role in the series. And usually they do. As former *Big Brother* contestant Krystal Ince, who was encouraged to audition for *Big Brother* by one of the program's producers, points out, "Everybody had a character that they were branded . . . I felt like a product but then I thought, it's your own fault, if you want to put yourself in that situation then that's what will come about." While Ince did not necessarily like the commodity she became—"Krystal with the big boobs or Krystal the blonde. So I got that and it was highlighted across Australia. And I thought that's not how I wanted people to see me," she came to accept, and somewhat exploit, this cartoonish version of herself, in time willingly succumbing to the commodity manufactured by *Big Brother*'s editors and producers. Post-*Big Brother*, Ince posed for the almost obligatory men's magazine photo shoot and found herself with, "a diary that was pretty full, pretty much from word go 'til, I think my [*Big Brother* engagements] extended out close to a year so I had a nice year off, leisure time, doing maybe one or two appearances per week . . . I can't say I didn't enjoy it, I very well did."

However, while it may be tempting to reduce the politics of Reality TV to economics,[25] Reality TV participants, such as *Big Brother*'s Krystal Ince, make it clear that when it comes to Reality TV, the line between exploitation and empowerment is always blurred. While Ince's *Big Brother* experience highlights the fact that it is possible to benefit from the commodified self that Reality TV participation creates, it also emphasizes why a potential participant's willingness to cooperate is so important for the network producers. The construction of "reality" on which these programs rely is not so much in the hands of the participants themselves, but of the network producers and the narrative and characters they wish to present; obvious problems can arise if a participant fails to live up to the preconceived notions producers have of them. The very fact that producers handpicked Ince and asked her to audition is indicative that they had a particular character in mind before the auditions even began, blatantly undermining the image of *Big Brother* as an organic product spontaneously grown from the personalities of the ordinary people driving the narrative. In this context, Andrejevic's argument that participants are invited to sell access to their personal lives in a way not dissimilar to how they sell their labor power,[26] makes sense. But while it may be problematic to argue that Reality TV is true democracy driven by "ordinary" people, it is also unhelpful to dismiss the concept of the "savvy viewer" or, in this case, participant taking part in this new democracy as completely false simply because producers are getting cheap labor for big profit.[27]

Of course, it would be more than a little naïve to believe a television producer who claimed that *The Biggest Loser* has nothing to do with ratings and economics and is simply a show produced for the benefit of overweight individuals struggling to find an effective weight loss strategy. Just as it would be implausible to claim that *Australian Idol* is about nothing more than giving talented young singers the break they deserve, or that *Big Brother* was created to give exhibitionists the chance to experience their dream and appear on television. In late consumer society, any sellable product, whether it be an indigenous art work, a literary novel or a handmade wooden toy, is going to be produced with an economic outcome in mind. But this does not mean such intended outcomes cannot be challenged and subverted. "Culture jamming," as Mark Dery argues in his pivotal essay, "Culture Jamming: Hacking, Slashing and Sniping in the Empire of Signs," is an intensely political act, "directed against an ever more intrusive, instrumental techno culture whose operant mode is the manufacture of consent through the manipulation of symbols."[28] Ultimately, culture jammers seek to "disrupt and subvert the intentions of the corporate producers,"[29] which, in the case of Pamela Wilson's *Big Brother* culture jammers, for example, involved a series of attempts by viewers to infiltrate the first season of U.S. *Big Brother* by delivering to participants clandestine messages to encourage them to stage a group walk out. While Wilson's participants, in spite of these messages, decided not to leave the show, Wilson argues that what resulted was a kind of "narrative activism" that proved that it is in fact possible for both audience members and reality show participants to challenge "the hegemonic control of the media giants by

As Ang makes clear in her study about the viewing practices and experiences of *Dallas* viewers, from the point of view of production, the product may be a commodity, but from the point of view of the consumer, the product features a particular use value.[31] The nature of this use value from the point of view of a Reality TV participant is particularly unique because it sits somewhere between the role of a producer and that of a consumer. It may be obvious that Reality TV participants are not simply consumers or even interactive audience members, because they play a significant role in the production of the program, but neither are they are professional actors or producers. Some, like Ince, play the game to their own advantage, while others may complain of what Andrejevic describes as exploitation. And then there are those, such as *Big Brother*'s Merlin Luck and *The Biggest Loser*'s Chris Garling, who failed to follow the explicit, or implicit rules inherent in Reality TV programming, thereby practicing a game of subversion with the potential to turn the "tolls of mass media against the corporate forces themselves."[32]

Luck, who had been raised in a New South Wales hippy commune, was a university student when he decided to audition for Australian *Big Brother*, 2004. He had never seen an episode of the reality show, and auditioned with the specific intention of staging a political protest and subverting what he describes as "mindless entertainment."

> I auditioned because I was basically frustrated by Reality Television. I just see it as being pretty base. I think it's fine that it exists . . . but having said that, I felt that it [should be] more reflective and more representative of [the general population], not just a bunch of middle-class white kids sitting around getting drunk and calling that Reality Television. I saw it as an opportunity, to I guess, culture jam. Hijacking a mainstream medium to deliver my own message. The message was partly about refugee rights . . . But more broadly speaking it was also about making a statement against Reality Television, saying this isn't reality. If you want some reality here's reality. Just catching people off-guard and making them question a little bit, dig a little deeper. (Merlin Luck)

On one level Luck adopts Ang's "ideology of mass culture" as a guideline for talking about *Big Brother*, a program he has still not watched a single episode of in its entirety. For Ang, the "ideology of mass culture" is an ideology that labels mass culture as bad, and high culture as good. It is much easier, argues Ang, to talk about mass culture in this way, especially when the lines between individual experience and social ideology are blurred, as was obviously the case for Luck. The "ideology of mass culture," Ang[33] argues, "makes a search for more detailed and personal explanations superfluous" providing, "a finished explanatory model that convinces, sounds logical and radiates legitimacy." When Luck refers to Reality TV as "being pretty base," or when he says his aim was to make audiences "dig a little deeper" he is ultimately talking about a program he has never actually experienced as an audience member, but that he can discuss legitimately by using as a tool the "ideology of mass culture." But, despite his disdain for *Big Brother*, Luck also recognized its potential as a "political platform" for raising audience awareness of Australia's refugee policy.

> It's an opportunity to voice an opinion. It's basically like, you think of public space, whether it's billboards or advertisements in magazines or on TV, it's public domain. If you go to a urinal in a bar these days they have an advertisement in front of you on the urinal. It's just stepping back and saying what gives this multinational company a right to this public space? And the answer is clearly money. They buy the right to that public space. So why should money determine who is allowed to deliver their message? To me, that doesn't make sense. Why should someone be allowed to deliver their message just because they have money? So I chose to deliver my message and unfortunately I

couldn't buy a minute of air time to tell Australia what I think of that issue, so I
hijacked a popular Australian television show to do it. (Merlin Luck)

When Fiske wrote that, "The people make popular culture at the interface between everyday life and the consumption of the products of the cultural industries,"[34] he was writing in the days before *MySpace* and *Facebook*, before *You-
Tube* and Internet blogging made it possible for individuals who would normally
have very little or no involvement with the creation of media products, to be
able to cheaply produce written and visual work for a potential audience of
millions. But while Luck could have recorded himself sitting in on his couch
with tape over his mouth and a sign saying "Free the refugees" and posted it on
YouTube in the hope that people would see it, it would have likely been lost
amongst the endless footage of drugged out celebrities, or teenagers dancing in
their bedrooms. However, to commit such an unexpected act during his eviction
night, his gagged mouth preventing him from being interviewed, on a
commercial television program, even for a few minutes, meant that Luck was
able to turn Andrejevic's top-down model of Reality TV on its head and take
control. No longer was Luck simply a commodity created by the *Big Brother*
franchise, but an "ordinary person"-cum-media producer, controlling a domain,
which, unlike Internet culture, cannot operate without industry professionals.
Luck may not have had the finances to legitimately run his message on prime-
time television, but if popular culture is structured within the opposition between
the power-bloc and the people, as Hall and Fiske assert,[35] then Luck suddenly
found himself with his foot in both camps and he did his utmost to utilize the
unique kind of power that potentially results from such a position.

Luck never considered himself to be a "typical" *Big Brother* participant.
Not only was he not a fan of the show, he had not ever watched it. He grew up
in a hippy commune, was proud of his left-wing politics and says that he never
would have auditioned for the show had he not been planning from the outset to
stage his "culture jamming" prank. But while Luck was no *Big Brother* expert,
like any media savvy member of late modernity, he knew his protest would
come at a price. As Bauman[36] points out, the society of consumers has the
capacity to absorb all and any dissent it inevitably breeds, "then to recycle it as a
major resource of its own reproduction, reinvigoration and expansion." Drawing
on Thomas Mathisen, Bauman refers to "silent silencing" as a stratagem used by
consumerist society to "nip in the bud the dissent and protest generated and
spread by the system, the attitudes and actions which in origin are transcendent
and integrated in the prevailing order in such a way that dominant interests
continue to be served. This way, they are made unthreatening to the prevailing
order."[37] Bauman argues that this dissent is also converted into a major resource
in the reinforcement and continuous reproduction of that order.

There is no doubt that the television network attempted to absorb and appropriate Luck's subversive behavior to its own advantage. While Luck claims

to have had daily political discussions during his six weeks "in the house," not a single one was aired. In fact, Luck came across more as a Bohemian ladies man than a political activist during the on-air show. So when Luck taped his mouth and held up his "Free the refugee" sign on the eviction stage, he compromised the entire narrative of the program, presenting a character in stark contrast to the one depicted on the daily show. To audiences, Luck's protest did not make sense. Who knew he even cared about politics? Ultimately, while Luck's protest may have helped draw mainstream attention to Australia's refugee policy, particularly amongst younger audiences, his actions did not do *Big Brother* any harm. In fact, it is probably no coincidence that in the following year another left-wing politically active "Bohemian" was cast as a housemate. While Luck had created an opportunity to make an en-masse political statement, he had also helped revive the flagging ratings of a program, which, after four years, was growing stale.

> For weeks they had several publicists working the media circuit for me. It was a really interesting dynamic because on one hand they were really angry that I'd undermined them, but on the other hand it was getting massive publicity and media attention for the show. The ratings got a massive boost out of it . . . It was sort of an implicit agreement that they would continue to arrange media for me through their publicist, manage my touring the country on that media circuit, so long as I didn't say anything explicitly negative about the show. (Merlin Luck)

Luck is adamant that he never intended to be critical of *Big Brother* and that his protest was not about *Big Brother*, or even Reality TV, but about Australian refugee policy. Post-*Big Brother* he spent nine months using his new found media profile to publicly campaign for refugee rights. Australia was preparing for an election and Luck was passionate about the need for change from a conservative to a more progressive government. But while Luck received overwhelming support for his actions, his gains were progressive, not radical.[38] The conservative government still won the election and *Big Brother* continued to be shown for another year, although in the subsequent series the network did air three political discussions about the Iraq war, a first in Australian *Big Brother* history. Luck's culture jam did not change the world. It did not even have a huge impact on the nature of Reality TV. But what Luck demonstrated was that the idea of the "savvy" participant is not dead. Reality TV is not simply a forum for the top down exploitation of participants. It is, in fact, possible for exploitation to operate in both directions.

In contrast to Luck, former *Biggest Loser* participant and winner, Chris Garling, had no intention of making any kind of political statement. Like Luck, Garling was not a fan of the program for which he auditioned, but aged twenty-three, Garling weighed 149.5kg and genuinely wanted to lose weight. On the face of it, he was a model competitor. Once on the show he watched his food intake and exercised obsessively—up to ten to twelve hours per day. Unlike many of his fellow participants, he did not react to stress by lashing out and abusing those around him and he made a conscious effort to avoid the petty politics that tend to consume *Biggest Loser* contestants thanks to the physically demanding, isolated, competitive and highly stressful environment the program creates. In this respect Garling should have been a *Biggest Loser* poster-boy. He simply did what the show asked him to do: lose weight. But the problem for *The Biggest Loser* production team was that Garling lost too much, dropping 70.1kgs to reach a BMI of 20.1, with 20 being medically considered underweight, according to Australian Government health guidelines.[39] From the point of view of the production team, Garling failed to promote the program's health conscious image because his transformation saw him evolve from fat and unhealthy to thin and seemingly malnourished. Garling admits that, in order to win the competition, he trained so obsessively and ate so little that he even had trouble walking during the season finale. While he may not have set out, as Luck did, to deliberately culture jam the program, he still, in the words of Naomi Klein, managed to "hack into a corporation's own method of communication to send a message starkly at odds with the one that was intended."[40]

The *Biggest Loser* makes clear that there are strict guidelines outlining what the "born again" body should look like.[41] The program's uber-fit and toned personal trainers act not only as health, fitness and "well being" counselors, but as examples of what constitutes a beautiful body. But while Bauman[42] argues that "Everything in consumer society is a matter of choice, except the compulsion to choose," *The Biggest Loser* fundamentally asserts that if one wants to live a healthy, happy and productive life, then being fat is not a choice. And, as Garling's dramatic weight loss indicated, being too thin is also not one. "Shopping is not just about food, shoes, cars or furniture items," writes Bauman. "The avid, never-ending search for new and improved examples and recipes for life is also a variety of shopping."[43] In many ways, participating in *The Biggest Loser* is like shopping for a new body, a new and improved version of the old self. Participants enter *The Biggest Loser* compound, or at least this is what the program encourages, with the expectation that they are, from Giddens's perspective, about to embark on the reflexive project of the self with the intention of actively constructing and controling the body.[44] By making the lifestyle choice to participate in a weight loss reality show, participants are looking for a life-changing transformation.

For *Loser* to be successful, a certain amount of spectacle is required: Participants must be willing to parade their bodies in unflattering outfits, be filmed exercising to the point of complete exhaustion and participate in a range of humiliating tasks that emphasize just how out of shape they really are. In order to make "good" television, *Loser* is reliant on the appeal of the thin aesthetic that dominates late capitalist culture. As Peter Stearns[45] points out, "Dieting, weight consciousness and widespread hostility to obesity form one of the fundamental themes in modern life . . . Fighting fat goes beyond fashion and even health." While *Loser* may advocate the kind of extreme dieting frowned upon by most health professionals, it also reflects, and exploits, the anxieties about weight that many, arguably most, individuals residing in late modernity take for granted as an everyday part of life. Part of the *Loser* spectacle is the transformation from the flabby, unfit body into the slim, fit and toned physique admired by late modernity. The very nature of *Loser* is structured to disadvantage those who do not conform. Set up as a weight loss competition to see who can lose the most weight, participants who look as though they may not be able to comply and achieve this dramatic and transformative weight loss spectacle are likely to be evicted early on.

In this sense *Loser* follows Adorno's view of television as reliant on clichéd and predictable formulas that work to identify with the status quo rather than challenge it. While *Loser* unarguably gives a mediatized voice to the experience of obesity, a rare occurrence in mainstream television programming, the effectiveness of the culture industry, or in this case *Loser*, "depends not on its parading an ideology, on disguising the true nature of things, but in removing the thought that there is any alternative to the status quo."[46] For *Loser* to be a successful program, participants and audiences must accept the dominant discourse of fat as problematic, and weight loss as an achievement, an example of Giddens's reflexive project of the self at work. They must believe that all the humiliation, and the physical and emotional pain the program inflicts on its participants, is worth it. By the end of the series, the program must present the previously overweight contestants, made over and glowing, in a better state than before. It is clear from the outset that being fat is not an alternative if one wants to reach the ultimate goal of consumer culture and become a sellable commodity.[47]

But while Bauman may be right in arguing that the consumer culture responsible for the creation of Reality TV programming may attempt to absorb the dissidence it inevitably breeds,[48] this does not mean that such attempts are always entirely successful. Garling was selected to participate on *Loser* as an "intruder," meaning that he exercised independently with a trainer for the first six weeks of taping, not entering the program until week seven.

> What happened is I got through the first round of interviews but when it came to the second round they said, oh sorry, we've got you in a reserve so if someone pulls out because of injuries . . . Then they called me and said, you're in, can you come in as an outsider? Basically they said, you'll come in, you'll be in there for probably a week, everyone will hate you and they'll kick you out after a week first chance they get . . . I was training as hard as I could 24/7 and they didn't get a chance to kick me out because I stayed over the line every

time. If the line wasn't there I think it would have been a different issue because I wasn't really playing the political game in there. I was purely putting
the hours in and that was it. (Chris Garling)

Unlike Ince, whose role in *Big Brother* was not apparent to her until after her
eviction, producers made it very clear to Garling what was expected of him.
Ironically, it was the very fact that he played the game by the rules, staying
above the "line" that indicates whether or not a contestant can potentially be
evicted, that made him impossible to "absorb."[49] Which is not to say the
producers did not try. Although Garling continued to lose enough weight to
remain in the "game," he was presented on the program as a character who was
obsessed, humorless, overly competitive and unliked by the other participants.
For a program that relies on emotionally open individuals whom producers can
present as having life-changing experiences as a result of participating in the
reality show, Garling's role in the narrative, according to producers, was to
come in, shake things up and then leave. He was not the kind of character who
makes a suitable winner. As Garling points out:

> Everyone on the show had a sob story going and I didn't really buy into it. Like
> some people you felt generally sorry for, but some people thought that the more
> sob story they made up, the better chance they had of getting in it. I thought, at
> the end of the day, you put on weight, you put on weight. That's pretty much it.
> The buck stops there. So I pretty much told the producers, I'm not big on sob
> stories, I don't have one. I put on the weight because I was eating junk and not
> training. And that's pretty much how I took it. (Chris Garling)

As Garling continued to challenge the direction in which the producers wanted
the show to go, it was made clear to him that his dramatic weight loss, his
refusal to play the role to which he was assigned, was unacceptable.

> It was almost like, towards the end they were saying, if you go underweight we
> will kick you off. I said, you can't kick me off the final three, you've got no
> chance. But they were like, well, we'll find something. So I made sure I stayed
> just about that 20 BMI . . . I made sure I was absolutely focused, I didn't want
> to leave any doubts, the whole of Australia could see on the TV that I definitely
> looked the skinniest out of anyone else there. That was my rationale for going
> so hard . . . (Chris Garling)

At the season finale, a hyped and supposedly "inspirational" event, Garling's
final weight loss results were skipped over because:

> They didn't want to show me beating them by that much because it wasn't what
> they were after . . . They didn't want to go from obese to anorexic. And I was
> pushing the fine line pretty closely. But I had the impression that if I didn't win
> by a lot, I'm not saying they would, but you never know, it could have been

cooked a little bit. (Chris Garling)

Of course, it is not surprising that the program's producers were none too pleased about Garling's victory. As he stood on the finale stage, his cheek bones prominent and his arms thin, Garling did not exemplify the picture of good health that *The Biggest Loser,* despite its extreme weight loss techniques, is supposed to present. Instead, he looked as though he had been exposed to something insidious, a self-help mantra that had gone too far.[50] Garling, though, left with $200,000, a new career in the health and fitness industry and, after a few months, had regained a much-needed 20kgs. But perhaps most significant of all, Garling had demonstrated just how easy it is for a participant to jeopardize the entire premise of a program like *The Biggest Loser.*

Life Politics and the Reclamation of Public Space

Culture jamming, Klein argues, "badly rejects the idea that marketing—because it buys its way into our public spaces—must be passively accepted as a one-way information flow." [51] While neither Luck nor Garling managed to make much of a dent in the traditional political sphere, like Wilson's *Big Brother* jammers, they reminded us that within corporate controlled media entities, producers need not have the final say in the outcome of a product. Like Dery,[52] who argues that, "the intertwined histories of feminism, the civil rights moment, multiculturalism and gay and transgender activism remind us that hacking the philosophical code that runs the hardware of political and economic power is crucially important," Luck and Garling made it clear that the personal can indeed become the political. By challenging the tightly controlled Reality TV genre, a place where rules are *not* made to be broken, Luck and Garling made it clear that subversion is not only possible, but also potentially powerful. While Luck's carefully constructed culture jam drew attention to a political issue that *Big Brother* producers would much prefer to sweep under the carpet, Garling's narrative activism challenged not only the entire philosophy of *The Biggest Loser,* but also the body politic of health and beauty.

It would be problematic not to acknowledge that Andrejevic's model of Reality TV as a financially driven and exploitative medium has at least some truth to it. The fact is, the financial benefit for television networks undoubtedly exceeds any financial rewards a participant can hope to receive. And perhaps individuals in our culture of consumers are, at least in part, driven to audition for Reality TV programs through a desire, as Bauman[53] puts it, to "'lift' themselves out of that grey and flat invisibility and insubstantiality, making themselves stand out from the mass of indistinguishable objects . . ." But it is also clear that not all, but I would argue most, Reality TV contestants do not enter into the Reality TV experience as a blank slate and unable to comprehend what they are getting themselves into. Krystal Ince may not have challenged the way in which *Big Brother* operates, but it did not take her very long to figure out that she was a pawn in the machine, and to turn the experience to her advantage, and one that was financially lucrative. The experiences of Luck and Garling, in particular, clearly demonstrate that sometimes there is a fine line between exploitation, empowerment and subversion. Somehow, Reality TV participants manage to dip their foot into all three camps.

Notes

1. McQuire, 188.
2. McQuire.
3. Bauman, 2007, 32.
4. Andrejevic; Hearn.
5. Adorno and Bernstein, 9.
6. Fiske, 1989.
7. Adorno and Bernstein.
8. Andrejevic; Hearn.
9. Abt and Sessholtz; Habermas, 1989, 1996; Staats.
10. Lumby, 1999; Lunt and Stenner.
11. Bauman, 2007; Fiske; Hall; Bauman, 2000.
12. Lumby, 1999; Probyn and Lumby, 2003; Starrs.
13. Fiske.
14. Lumby, 1999, 254.
15. Griffen-Foley.
16. Bauman, 2000, 73.
17. Giddens, 1991.
18. Giddens, 1991, 5.
19. Hermes.
20. Schrøder, 147.
21. Green, 135.
22. Green, 136.
23. Hermes.
24. Green.
25. Andrejevic.
26. Andrejevic.
27. Andrejevic.
28. Dery.
29. Wilson, 324.
30. Wilson, 324.
31. Ang, 23.
32. Wilson, 324.
33. Ang, 114.
34. Fiske, 6.
35. Fiske.

36. Bauman, 2007, 48-49.
37. Bauman, 2007, 13.
38. Fiske.
39. Channel.
40. Cited in Wilson, 2004, 324.
41. Bauman, 2007, 49.
42. Bauman, 2000, 73.
43. Bauman, 2000, 74.
44. Giddens, 1991, 7.
45. Stearns, ix.
46. Adorno and Bernstein, 9.
47. Bauman, 2007.
48. Bauman, 2007, 48.
49. Bauman, 2007.
50. Salerno.
51. Klein, 281.
52. Dery.
53. Bauman 2007, 11-12.

References

Abt, Vicki and Mel Sessholtz. "The Shameless World of Phil, Sally and Oprah: Television Talk Shows and the Deconstructing of Society." *Journal of Popular Culture* 28, no. 1 (1994): 171-191.

Adorno, Theodor W. and James M. Bernstein. *The Culture Industry: Selected Essays on Mass Culture*. London: Routledge, 1991.

Andrejevic, Mark. *Reality TV: The Work of Being Watched*. Lanham, Md.: Rowman and Littlefield Publishers, 2004.

Ang, Ien. *Watching Dallas: Soap Opera and the Melodramatic Imagination*. London and New York: Methuen, 1985.

Bauman, Zygmunt. *Liquid Modernity*. Cambridge, U.K.: Polity Press, 2000.

———. *Consuming Life*. Cambridge, U.K.: Polity Press, 2007.

Channel, Better Health. "Body Mass Index (BMI)." 2008. www.betterhealth.vic.gov.au /BHCV2/bhcArticles.nsf/pages/Body_Mass_Index_(BMI)?OpenDocument.

Dery, Mark. "Mark Dery's Shovelware: Blogs, Books, Articles." 2008. www.mark dery.com/.

Fiske, John. *Reading the Popular*. Boston: Unwin Hyman, 1989.

Giddens, Anthony. *Modernity and Self-identity: Self and Society in the Late Modern Age*. Cambridge, U.K.: Polity, 1991.

Green, Leila. "Attempting to Ground Ethnographic Theory and Practice." *Australian Journal of Communication* 30, no. 2 (2003): 133-145.

Griffen-Foley, Bridget. "From Tit-Bits to Big Brother: A Century of Audience Participation in the Media." *Media, Culture & Society* 26, no. 4 (2004): 533-548.

Habermas, Jürgen. *The Structural Transformation of the Public Sphere: An Inquiry into a Category of Bourgeois Society*. Cambridge, Mass.: MIT Press, 1989.

———. *Between Facts and Norms: Contributions to a Discourse Theory of Law and*

Democracy, translated by William Rehg. Cambridge, U.K.: Polity Press, 1996.

Hall, Stuart. *Representation: Cultural Representations and Signifying Practices*. London: Sage and Open University, 1997.

Hearn, Alison. "John, a 20-year-old Boston Native with a Great Sense of Humour: on the Spectacularisation of the 'Self' and the Incorporation of Identity in the Age of Reality Television." *International Journal of Media and Cultural Politics* 2, no. 2 (2006): 131-147.

Hermes, Joke. *Reading Women's Magazines: An Analysis of Everyday Media Use*. Cambridge, U.K.: Polity Press, 1995.

Klein, Naomi. *No Logo, no Space, no Choice, no Jobs: Taking Aim at the Brand Bullies*. London: Flamingo, 2000.

Lumby, Catharine. *Gotcha: Life in a Tabloid World*. St. Leonards, N.S.W, Aus.: Allen and Unwin, 1999.

Lunt, Peter and Paul Stenner. "The Jerry Springer Show as an Emotional Public Sphere." *Media, Culture & Society* 27, no. 1 (2005): 59-81.

McQuire, Scott. *The Media City: Media, Architecture and Urban Space*. Los Angeles and London: Sage, 2008.

Probyn, Elspeth and Catharine Lumby. *Remote Control: New Media, New Ethics*. Cambridge and Port Melbourne, Vic., Aus.: Cambridge University Press, 2003.

Salerno, Steve. *SHAM: How the Self-help Movement Made America Helpless*. New York: Crown Publishers, 2005.

Schrøder, Kim. *Researching Audiences: A Practical Guide to Methods in Media Audience Analysis*. London: Arnold, 2003.

Staats, Joseph L. "Habermas and Democratic Theory: The Threat to Democracy and Unchecked Corporate Power." *Political Research Quarterly* 57, no. 4 (2004): 585-594.

Starrs, D. Bruno. "Sara-Marie as Feminist Fairytale: From Big Brother to 'Big Sister.'" *Feminist Media Studies* 4, no. 3 (2004): 359-361.

Stearns, N. Peter. *Fat History: Bodies and Beaty in the Modern West*. New York: New York University Press, 1997.

Wilson, Pamela. "Jamming Big Brother: Webcasting, Audience Intervention, and Narrative Activism." In *Reality TV: Remaking Reality Television Culture*, edited by Sussan Murray and Laurie Ouellette, 323-343. New York: New York University Press, 2004.

Part 3
TRANS-GENRE

Chapter 12
A Short Introduction to Trans-Genre
Sofie Van Bauwel

The trans-genre is the body of formats that articulate the idea of the hybrid or flexible genre. The notion of trans-genre, therefore, questions format and genre boundaries and conventions, and also (even) the construction of TV and visual culture, and destabilizes our rather fixed conceptualizations of the viewer, the spectator, the audience and the media professional. As a concept, trans-genre is related to the economic dimension of commercial TV and the international television market characterized by the demands set by the harsh competition imposed by market rules.[1] Often firmly embedded in a neo-liberal global context, the trans-genre concept points to the various practices of formatting and continuous re-invention, which in turn are re-articulated and consumed by audiences.

Besides the economic context of the contemporary visual culture, a trans-genre can be understood as an incorporation of the characteristics of different genres and their specific transgressions of format and genre boundaries, for example, the transcendence of the boundaries between the factual and the fictional. Trans-genre points to the limits of the linear structures involved in analyzing contemporary television culture. Although genres are never totally sealed off, the trans-genre concept refers to high levels of fluidity in genre conventions. Genre is a way to organize narration, or, in an audiovisual context, can be considered "a class of programmes,"[2] which simultaneously co-exist. This clustering becomes fluid, not only through the workings of (media) industries, but also through its audience receptions.

The transgression of the traditional genre conception is situated at the level of production (global television market and formatting practices), on the level of the media text (incorporation of different genre characteristics and use of inter-textual practices) and on the level of decoding. The latter means that audiences participate also as agents in this articulation and re-articulation of the boundaries and transgressions of the boundaries. As Altman[3] in his film studies work points out, genre constructions are more than textual: they are contextual and constructed by the expectations of the audiences.

In short, trans-genre refers to the transgression of genre boundaries, which are constructed by production practices, textual features, and audience practices.

Notes

1. Allen.
2. Berger.
3. Altman.

References

Allen, Robert and Annete Hill. *The Television Reader.* London: Routledge, 2004.
Altman, Rick. *Film/Genre.* London: BFI, 1999.
Berger, Arthur Asa. *Popular Culture Genres. Theories and Texts.* Thousand Oaks, Calif.: Sage, 1992.

Chapter 13
Genre as Discursive Practice and the Governmentality of Formatting in Post-Documentary TV
Frank Boddin

Public Service Broadcasting and the Rise of Post-Documentary TV

Reality TV is a post-documentary (PD) genre that has become a self-evident feature of contemporary television (TV) culture. This chapter concentrates on the production context of post-PDTV within Flemish (North-Belgium) public service broadcasting (PSB).

The term "post-documentary" was coined by John Corner to signal the relocation of TV documentary in terms of its current practices, forms, and functions.[1] The genre of documentary has undergone radical changes over the last two decades in order to reconfigure itself within new economic and cultural contexts. The transition from documentary to PD implied an explosion of new, hybrid formats, such as the reality crime show, the confessional chat show, the docu-soap, the docudrama or the reality game-show, most of them designed primarily to entertain rather than to inform. Indeed, the traditional contrasting categories previously used to distinguish genres, such as education versus diversion or fact versus fiction, no longer apply in a context of PDTV.[2]

This hybrid character of PDTV has proven to be very productive for PSB, which now finds itself obliged to reconcile popularity and audience reach with other socio-cultural and educational goals. No longer able to rely on traditional ways of dealing with factual genres, PSB has been forced to rethink factual genres, and explore how those genres traditionally associated with a public service ethos, such as documentaries, and new hybrid, factual genres, such as Reality

TV, are to become inscribed in and/or reconciled with its public service objectives. It has toned down its traditional educational (Bildung) logic and re-articulated the very notion of public service, linking PDTV to the democratization of TV and public space, challenging established paternalisms,[3] and the rise of post-modern, cultural forms of citizenship and identity politics.[4] At the same time the production and programming of PDTV have allowed public broadcasting companies to reach large audiences and to survive economically within a fragmented, commercialized and highly competitive media environment.

Within production studies, one of the concerns raised about PDTV deals with the contemporary formatting context in which these programs are situated. PDTV genres nowadays are commissioned for particular slots on particular channels and, accordingly, are required to be made in a particular style and to deliver appropriately sized audiences.[5] Since the end of the 1980s, factual and documentary strands have become subject to intense scrutiny by broadcasters to establish whether "they are performing to their full potential,"[6] not least within public broadcasting companies.

In this context the notion of formatting has been used to indicate that, much more than in the past, documentary-makers are subject to rules and restrictions, and are required to tailor their work to broadcaster-imposed requirements. The impact of formatting on documentary-making, and the organizational culture of PSB more generally, is criticized, because these measures, initiated by the broadcasting management, are considered to result in bureaucratic systems that suffocate the freedom and creativity of cultural producers.[7] In these analyses formatting is very much linked to the disciplining (or un-freedom) of media professionals, while power likewise is very much defined as a repressive force.

The focus in this chapter, however, is rather different. Based on the work of the French author Michel Foucault, we emphasize the productive character of power. Rather than seeing formatting as a solely repressive and constraining logic, this study defines formatting as a frame which also allows media professionals opportunities to realize themselves, that is, to practice forms of freedom and to be creative. Instead of seeing power as something possessed by managerial echelons and exercised over media professionals, it is suggested that power is mobile and multi-directional, a dynamic interplay of strategies and counter-strategies, involving both dominance and resistance, acts of oppression and revolt, forms of government and forms of freedom.[8] Grounded in this Foucauldian perspective on power, it is argued here that formatting involves both the government and freedom of media professionals.

In his final publications, Foucault was particularly interested in the nature of freedom on the part of the governed individual.[9] He developed the term governmentality, which was later revisited and expanded by scholars such as Nikolas Rose, Peter Miller and Mitchell Dean, to indicate a form of power that is made operable through the liberties of those over whom it is exercised.[10] The governmentality perspective on formatting that underlies this study is grounded in the argument that formatting interacts with and draws upon the identities and creativity of media professionals involved in PDTV.

Formatting within PSB

The term formatting is used in this study to concentrate on how a public broadcasting company's broadcasting policies and corporate strategy are translated to the production process, and impact on the realization of a TV program. In production studies the term formatting is used somewhat differently: formatting mostly refers to how formats shape production processes, implying all kinds of prescriptive rules, frames, codes or techniques used by media professionals working within a specific format.[11] This chapter, however, does not deal with these micro aspects of program-making and defines formatting as the efforts and practices, usually initiated by managerial echelons, to align programming in line with the philosophy, organizational policy, and corporate strategy of the organization. For a public broadcasting company, more specifically, a variety of cultural and economic considerations are at play in formatting practices. Ameliorating the wider broadcasting ecology by setting standards for quality can be defined as one such consideration. Cultural-national considerations can play a role, since in Europe, PSB much more than commercial broadcasting, is responsible for preserving local culture, identity, and diversity, especially in smaller countries. Furthermore, more normative ideas are invoked during formatting practices, such as the correcting of market-failure or the broader socio-political, democratic, and economic benefits resulting from having a socially and culturally better informed public/electorate. Obviously, economic and corporate considerations also play an important role in formatting choices, as PSB nowadays finds itself in a fragmented and highly competitive media environment. Considerations related to ratings, market shares, prime-time logics and scheduling strategies are all weighed during formatting processes, as public broadcasting companies are obliged to reconcile popularity and audience reach with other socio-cultural and educative goals.

The analysis of formatting in this chapter draws upon a qualitative study of formatting processes within the Flemish public broadcasting organization (VRT). In 1995, a decree issued by the Flemish Community changed the radio and TV broadcasting environment. It stipulated that the public broadcaster's task was:

> to reach the widest possible audience with a diversity of programs . . . a quality offer of information, culture, education and entertainment. The institution's priority is to bring audience-oriented information and cultural programming . . . sports, contemporary education, domestic drama and entertainment.[12]

In the context of this decree and wider economic and political pressures, the consultancy company, Synovate Censydiam, was asked to conduct an in-depth audience study of the Flemish TV market in 1996. As the same time, the consultancy agency McKinsey and Company was conducting an audit of the organizational structure of VRT (then known as BRTN). Supported by the results of these audits, more performance- and audience-oriented policies, grounded in new public management discourses, were introduced within VRT. Formatting practices became linked to and understood as the auditing and evaluating of programs in terms of their performance. Furthermore, the reliance on marketing policies intensified within VRT and it began to rely on quantitative and qualitative audience- and market-research for evaluating programs. The burgeoning enterprise culture in which formatting became embedded, defines the wants and desires of the customer as the main imperatives for an organization and its employees.[13] The introduction of marketing put much greater emphasis on the positioning of channels in the market and on working with target audiences and brands. The first, generalist, channel, Eén,[14] was positioned as a "widening net," and was addressed primarily to three target audiences: the so-called "active discoverer," the "spontaneous enjoyer," and the "family viewer." It continues to have a reputation for aiming to satisfy the needs of those viewers who wish to "be in contact with the outside world in a relaxed, not-compelling way . . . a vibrantly happy and accessible TV channel, with a healthy dose of familial intimacy, that corresponds to the ideal image of TV according to 54 percent of the Flemish viewers."[15] The second channel, Canvas, was positioned as the "deepening net," that is "an informative, enriching and expert channel, [the net] aims to reach those people who are looking for added-value, competence and self-awareness."[16] Canvas is described as "an original and challenging channel, which avoids artificiality or banality. It brings critical information, sports and a broad range of interesting, cultural and educative programming, rotated with exciting high-quality fiction."[17] Like Eén, Canvas's programming has specific target audiences, in this categorized as the "seeker of added-value" and the "active discoverer."[18] The marketing rationality of working with brands and target audiences became an integral part of formatting in the 1990s. From now on programs were ordered for particular slots on particular channels and, accordingly, were required to be made in a particular style and to deliver suitably sized (target) audiences. Formatting thereby came to be seen as a tool to stimulate media professionals to become more productive and efficient, but also more entrepreneurial, innovative, and creative.[19]

Formatting and Power

Ethnographic studies have highlighted media professionals' resistance against formatting practices and the burgeoning enterprise culture within PSB. Scholars, such as Georgina Born, have criticized the impact of audits on the organizational culture of PSB in general, and documentary programming in particular. Media professionals involved in PDTV, it is argued, are being forced to tailor their work to narrow, ratings-led, broadcaster-imposed and marketing-based requirements. Formatting measures are seen to be resulting in bureaucratic systems, which suffocate the freedom and creativity of cultural producers. It is argued that the intensified auditing and evaluating of programs and channels, and the reliance on market research have resulted in a standardization of the creative production process. More demanding sub-genres, such as the essay form, observational and less narrative forms, and the experimental documentary, are said to be ignored by broadcasters that follow low-risk programming strategies. These formalization and standardization processes, so it is argued, constrain media professionals' creative selves, and the practice of formatting is considered as the imposition of restrictions on documentary-makers' professional identities. Similar critiques have been leveled in the context of the wider debates in many European countries on the quality and the so-called "lowest-common-denominator" characteristics of Reality TV.[20]

There are at least three important questions that can be raised in the context of these very negative accounts of formatting. Firstly, one could ask whether TV documentary production has not always been characterized by tight regulatory frameworks and bureaucratic procedures that impact on media professionals' work and identities. TV documentary production has always involved specific protocols, norms and conventions and, very often, has been dependent on formatting and scheduling contexts, and the politics of organizational structures and financing, especially in the early decades of PSB.[21]

Secondly, one could question whether formatting has led to less creativity or to less innovative forms of program-making in the context of PDTV. Scholars, such as Richard Kilborn, have suggested that the currently more competitive context of broadcasting in which PDTV is embedded, has forced producers to become more creative and innovative.[22] Program-makers have experimented with (the crossing of) generic boundaries, combining traditional modes of documentary with styles associated with other genres. It would be wrong to consider all PD formats dull or imitative. PD genres to a certain extent are characterized by innovative adaptation and creativity, in terms of both topics, narrative forms and scopic appeal. Some scholars, such as Brian Winston, have even argued that TV documentary is experiencing a revival, as the success of popular factual entertainment has re-activated audiences' interest in more traditional forms of documentary.[23] The question of whether PDTV has driven out more traditional modes of documentary is complex and has not been fully answered.[24] Thirdly, one could criticize the negative conception of power underlying most critiques of formatting. In these critiques, the notion of formatting is linked solely to the disciplining or un-freedom of media professionals. Recalling the

Frankfurt School critiques, formatting is considered a reduction of the media professionals' subjectivity and creativity, which can be acted upon by a broadcasting corporation embedded in a commercialized environment. Power is linked to broadcaster-imposed restrictions, and defined very much as a repressive force (power as dominance). The subjectivity, freedom or autonomy of the media professional is described then, to put it bluntly, as existing only in a space not yet colonized by capitalism. It is argued here, however, that media professionals' forms of subjectivity, agency and will are not antithetical to power. Rather they form an integral part of power. Starting from a Foucauldian understanding of power, formatting is examined here as a frame which *also* allows media professionals' opportunities for self-realization and creativity, and thus presupposes the production of forms of subjectivity, agency, and will.

How then to understand a form of power that is productive rather than solely repressive, in the context of formatting? Although power relations in an organization are always to a certain extent dependent on the institutional and managerial structures of the corporation, power is examined here from a more culturalist perspective. Power produces cultural orders, types of knowledge, and frames of common understanding,[25] what Mark Allen Peterson has called the cultural epistemologies and social heuristics in the context of media production processes.[26] One such framework is the system of formatting, through which programs, genres, schedules, and the totality of TV output become culturally defined, interpreted and evaluated.[27] All actors and occupational groups involved in formatting to a certain extent draw upon common understandings, and their actions, intentions and identities are simultaneously constituted by, and constitutive of, these broader common understandings. Thus, although formatting is initiated by the management of the corporation, its underlying power relations involve a more complex interplay of strategies and counter-strategies of various actors and groups. Power is not something possessed by sovereign managers (or missed by documentary-makers in lower echelons). Power is dynamic and works through the multitude of different actors' intentions, actions, and revolts. It produces simultaneously forms of dominance and resistance, oppression, and revolt, government and freedom.[28] Grounded in this Foucauldian perspective on power it is argued here that formatting is very much about both the government and freedom of media professionals.

Formatting and Governmentality: Freedom, Government and the Conduct of Conduct

In his latter works Foucault was particularly interested in the relations between rationalities of government and practices of freedom. He developed the term governmentality to indicate a form of power that operates through the liberties of those over whom it is exercised.[29] One of the moments when Foucault uses the notion of governmentality is in his genealogy of post-war (neo)liberalism, its underlying practices of government and the welfare state.[30] Foucault defined neo-liberalism as a specific form of government, a theory later revisited and elaborated by scholars such as Nikolas Rose, Peter Miller and Mitchell Dean. This strand of Foucault's work is useful to the analysis of formatting here, because of the rather distinct conceptions of government and freedom developed within it. More specifically, the use of governmentality as a conceptual tool to examine formatting in this study is grounded in three arguments.

Firstly, Foucault argued that programs of government operate through subjects and therefore presuppose, rather than repress, the freedom of the subject. Power, Foucault suggested:

> is exercised only over free subjects and only insofar as they are free. By this we mean individual or collective subjects who are faced with a field of possibilities in which several ways of behaving, several reactions and diverse comportments may be realised. Where the determining factors saturate the whole there is no relationship of power.[31]

Secondly, Foucault also suggested that programs of government depend on the willingness of individuals to exist as particular subjects. This implies, he argued, that the exercise of freedom will always be dependent on the disciplining effects of specific social and cultural orders that have developed over time. Individuals can learn how "to practice" their freedoms by being embedded within these orders. Formatting can be seen as a program of government that allows media professionals opportunities to practice forms of freedom.

Thirdly, in his final publications, Foucault particularly explored his interest in the nature of the freedoms of the governed individual.[32] He suggested that in liberal forms of government, subjection is connected to the identities of those who are governed. He argued moreover that individuals voluntarily constrain themselves through their own desires, wants, hopes, and aspirations.[33] He believed that a liberal program of government relies on an intimate relationship between processes of subjectification and processes of subjection: one becomes an individual while simultaneously being produced through the program of government. This idea later has been elaborated and empirically examined in a range of studies of organizational power and governmentality.[34]

Formatting as a Program of Government: Governing a Site of Discursive Struggle

Following Foucault, it is argued here that formatting connects to, rather than constrains, media professionals' identities, in order to make formatting practices subjectively meaningful for those media professionals working with them. This belief stems from the observation that formatting as a practice of government is grounded in the aforementioned discourse of enterprise.[35] Formatting is associated with a broader organizational enterprise discourse that argues that work should provide a meaningful experience for those performing it and ultimately function as a source of identity. Formatting is involved with the production of "subject positions" with which media professionals can identify. How then to understand these subjects' positions, and where can we situate their discursive production?

Formatting is the moment when various (cultural) rationalities are balanced with the need for audience-orientation, especially in a PSB context. Formatting is the moment when genres become the object of diverse discursive practices: they are linked to assumed audiences, but also to cultural values and hierarchies, ethical aspects or social functions, and priorities.[36] It is argued here that during the processes of formatting genres become the subject of a discursive struggle between market-oriented discourses (which emphasize audience-responsiveness) and public service-oriented discourses (which emphasize cultural aspirations, civic education and social responsibility).

Traditionally, documentary genres were associated with the pedagogical production of "worthy citizens." Grounded in discourses of social responsibility, documentary TV's *Holy Grail* was seen as providing audiences with the knowledge, language, and tools to participate in democratic processes and interact with state authorities.[37] Today, this public service idea of speaking to the public/citizens has had to make room for discourses emphasizing listening rather than speaking to audiences/customers. Current formatting practices, as mentioned in the previous section, are situated within an enterprise culture which defines the customer as the main imperative for an organization and its employees. The wants and desires of the viewers are important benchmarks against which media professionals' work and identities are judged today. This transition has been debated for many years in relation to PSB,[38] but also in the context of PDTV and the rise of Reality TV. John Corner, for example, expressed his concerns about the idea of "the public" being threatened by the increasing emphasis on market systems and values within contemporary broadcasting environments, and their broader neo-liberal political, managerial and economic contexts.[39]

Formatting is deeply involved with this changed discursive formation and its underlying discursive struggles. As a program of government it aims to promote audience orientation, in Foucauldian terms: to produce an audience-oriented media professional. In order to produce subject positions with which all types of media professionals can identify, formatting has to deal with potential forms of resistance against audience orientation. Program-makers, especially older generations of documentary-makers traditionally working in a public service environment, might hesitate or refuse to become more audience oriented, as this often implies becoming more market oriented. The governmental character of formatting depends on the bridling, or the containing, of the struggles between audience orientation and other rationalities of government. It is argued here that formatting anticipates these struggles and potential forms of revolt from media professionals by co-articulating its market-oriented audience rationale with other public service objectives. In order to manage these struggles, formatting encapsulates them and turns them to account to its very governmental functioning. Moreover, this co-articulation introduces ambiguities and contradictions within the very practice of formatting: it promotes audience/market orientation while simultaneously leaving openings and possibilities for the articulation of other rationalities. More specifically, program-makers are stimulated to subject themselves to scrutiny in terms of how they combine audience orientation with other considerations, such as quality, aesthetics, ethics, and social responsibility. Thereby, formatting allows and even invites media professionals to be creative in dealing with formatting guidelines. From this perspective, formatting is a frame that offers program-makers opportunities ("freedoms") to take responsibility for their self-organization. Its governmentality then is successful to the extent that program-makers come to experience themselves, their identities and their work through this framework.

Case Study: Formatting within Flemish Public Broadcasting

The theoretical frame elaborated in the previous section was applied in a case study of formatting processes in the Flemish public service broadcaster VRT. The broader aim of this study was to scrutinize the degrees of freedom for media professionals allowed within these formatting processes. Using governmentality as a conceptual frame, the study examined how the formatting practice aims to produce a governable, audience-oriented media professional.

The case study concentrated on the formatting of human interest programming within VRT. Human interest is a genre that centers around (ordinary) people, their (everyday) lives, interests, and problems, and how they deal with the various troubles and opportunities they encounter in their lives. The genre was rather prominent on Flemish public TV in the 1980s and the early 1990s, with popular documentary programs such as *NV De Wereld* (*The World Inc.*) or *Kwesties* (*Issues*). Generally associated with public service objectives, human interest documentary aimed to show how the possibilities and limitations of people's everyday lives are defined by broader socio-economic circumstances. In the 1990s the traditional human interest documentary genre developed into a variety of factual formats dealing, in one way or another, with "human interest stories." The human interest approach became a popular method of documentary-making, applied to very diverse PDTV programs, such as the mass of Reality TV formats, in the course of which its public service objectives were redefined and re-interpreted. In the context of some controversial Reality TV shows on commercial channels, such as *Big Brother* and *Temptation Island*, the notion of human interest became re-articulated in terms of voyeurism and exploitation, and disarticulated from any public service ideal. In other genres, however, the human interest approach was celebrated in public service terms for its engaging, democratic potential. Human interest is a trans-genre, its method, over time, being continuously re-invented throughout various hybrid reality TV formats, and (re-)articulated within diverse discourses and rationalities in a PDTV context.

For VRT, the rise of Reality TV implied a popularization of the traditional human interest documentary, what VRT called their "social frequency." As other factual frequencies began to experiment more and more with human interest, the social frequency experienced difficulties in profiling and positioning itself, both in-house and within a Flemish media market over-populated with Reality TV programming, and VRT was forced to rethink its social frequency. Its social frequency programming was increasingly audited and evaluated in terms of success and failure. During this period, the broadcasting management tightened its assessment and formatting practices, intervening at different production levels from the redistribution of programming slots, to continuous evaluations of program series, to the distribution of formatting guidelines through production manuals.[40]

Within VRT the most important aspects of formatting are the processes of ordering new programs (the "briefing") and of evaluating programs (the "debriefing").[41] The (de)briefings are initiated by the broadcasting management and addressed to media professionals at the production level.[42] The briefing includes guidelines regarding the formatting of programming, such as recommendations regarding adjustments to the format or the re-positioning of a program in line with the channel's brand and/or schedule, the cancelling of a program and the ordering of a new program, or the rethinking of the concept of a program or a whole slot or strand.[43]

The empirical data drawn on for the case study were the (de)briefing files used for evaluating the social frequency from 1995 until 2005, a period when the use of formatting practices intensified.[44] The study had two main aims: first, to scrutinize the promotion of audience-orientation within formatting practices. More specifically, a first phase of analysis focused on whether and how audience-considerations are embedded in the formatting practice, whereby both the structure and content of the (de)briefing files were analyzed. Second, we wanted to examine the relationship between audience-orientation and other rationalities in the texts. Therefore, clusters of similar recommendations were inductively labeled on the basis of a repertoire analysis. This enabled a mapping of the variety of economic, cultural, civic, ethical, and narrative considerations used to evaluate the programs.[45]

Balancing Market and Public Service Rationalities

The case study showed how different rationalities and their underlying governmental discourses work together in the (de)briefs and come to govern the work of the media professionals. More specifically, it highlighted that, on the one hand, marketing is the dominant rationality within the (de)briefs and, on the other, that civic and cultural rationalities are mobilized to imbue this dominant frame discursively. This promotes two media professional identities: the "market-oriented" media professional and the "public-service-oriented" media professional. The next section describes how these two identities are promoted in the (de)briefs and how their co-articulation aims to subdue potential conflicts between them and their underlying governmental discourses.

Producing the Market-Oriented Media Professional

Analysis of the (de)briefs showed that formatting within VRT was a largely marketing-based procedure in the ten years between 1995 and 2005. It showed that the lay-out and structure of the (de)briefing files are aimed at facilitating and promoting a marketing rationality. The debrief usually consists of two parts. The first part deals with delineation of the assumed target audiences (or "motivational groups") for the program, and description of how these target audiences deal with TV, followed by descriptions of the target audiences' perceptions of the program. The second part deals with the question of whether the program connects with the brand of the channel on which the program was scheduled ("channel identity"). It asks whether the target audiences' perceptions and appropriation of the program align with the channel identity. The briefing files, similarly, comprise two parts. The first provides a quantitative delineation of the market and scheduling contexts, and a more qualitative explanation of the target audience. It elaborates about how the target audiences use TV and what they expect from the genre and the particular program under consideration. In addition to a detailed, quantitative overview of presumed audience reach and market share, both brief and debrief usually conclude with a range of recommendations regarding (re)alignment of the program's format in relation to motivational groups and channel identity.

This marketing rationality is grounded in a range of broader governmental discourses that aim to regulate media professionals' work. Firstly, it is grounded in a discourse that emphasizes predictability and measurability. The measurement of audiences' wants and satisfactions is aimed at what Ang calls "objectification"[46] of the audience, characterizing a broader evolution in broadcasting towards scientification.[47] Media professionals are stimulated to think of their work in terms of measurable targets or outcomes, such as market shares or demographically delineated target audiences. The case study showed that the (de)briefs never refer to more intangible or indirect objectives or impacts of PDTV (or PSB for that matter), such as collective socio-political and democratic benefits to society, for example. Secondly, marketing starts from audiences' uses and gratifications grounded in a discourse of consumer-sovereignty. The formatting practice encourages media professionals to scrutinize how to translate or mold a program in line with the motives, wants and lifestyles of a specific target audience, and how to engender commitment to the program on the part of these motivational groups. Furthermore, the discourse of consumer-sovereignty emphasizes listening rather than speaking to the public. Approaching the audience in terms of *Bildung* is discouraged in the (de)briefs, and mostly dismissed as being a too "elitist" or "paternalistic" position, as illustrated by the following quotes from an evaluation of the program *Kwesties* (*Issues*): "an intelligent, in-depth informative program that deals with human interest in a nuanced, serious and in-depth way (serious, *but not inaccessible or intellectualistic!*),"[48] and "one expects explanation and direction (*but not patronizing, educating or boring*)."[49] Throughout the (de)briefs the very genre of human interest is approached in terms of target audiences' uses and gratifications of this genre, whereby target audiences' assumed use of TV is always the first consideration. For example, the target audiences of the first channel Eén—the "active discoverer," "spontaneous enjoyer," and "family viewer"—are said to use TV "as an instrument to enlarge and enrich their own lives," although TV in the first place means "an accessible, easy, fun and varied form of entertainment,"[50] especially for the latter two groups.

Producing the Public-Service-Oriented Media Professional

The case study showed that although formatting is a marketing-based procedure, the guidelines to media professionals in the (de)briefs are not explicitly about marketing. Instructions in terms of a marketing repertoire are rare in the (de)briefs and requests to (re)orientate a format in line with channel identity or target audience appear only occasionally. For example, in an evaluation of the program *NV De Wereld* (*The World Inc.*) the recommendation is to "reorient the format, the choice of topic, the tonality and form towards the needs of, in the first place, the 'Receptive viewers' (2/3 of the target audience of the widening channel) and, second, the 'Active discoverers'."[51] Occasionally a marketing repertoire is used to argue for more homogeneity within a format in order to create recognition and commitment on the part of viewer, but is usually in the form of a general recommendation at the end of the (de)brief. The majority of the guidelines in the (de)briefs do not tackle marketing considerations; rather, they tend to relate to various civic, cultural or ethical considerations. The analysis highlighted actually that, although marketing is the dominant frame in the (de)briefs, civic and cultural rationalities are mobilized to imbue this frame discursively at the level of recommendations. More specifically, the so-called "motivational groups" and "channel identities" are constructed on the basis of repertoires associated with a PSB ethos. This public service ethos is grounded in governmental discourses aimed at stimulating workers to understand and deal with human interest programming in terms of cultural aspirations, civic education and social responsibility, whereby the role and potential of PDTV is defined as the cultural and social enriching of audiences and the building of citizenship.

These public service values are used in the (de)briefs to construct target audiences' expectations, uses and gratifications in relation to human interest programming. In other words, through the very construction of target audiences' genre expectations, a public service ethos is *attached* to or perhaps *inserted* into a marketing logic: the "public service oriented" media professional is produced through the promotion of a market-oriented media professional. The public service oriented media professional is produced firstly through the repertoires used in the (de)briefs to define and evaluate VRT's human interest programming. A variety of recommendations for media professionals are couched in terms of repertoires associated with a public service ethos. In the context of the first channel Eén, human interest programming is linked to the formation of cultural citizenship and processes of identity politics. The public service value of the genre is linked to audiences' cultural understanding and negotiation of identities in the private, domestic worlds of lifestyle, choice and preference, as, for example, in the docusoap *Huis Te Koop* (*House For Sale*), which follows ordinary people's search for a new house, or the decision of couples to adopt a child in *Het Leven Zoals Het Is: Adoptie* (*Life As It Is: Adoption*). A repertoire of democratainment is also used to define the narrative requirements of human interest on Eén: Viewers expect "to learn something in an entertaining way."[52] For example, the role of a human interest genre such as the Eén docusoap series *Het Leven Zoals Het Is* (*Life As It Is*) is defined as "stimulating amazement, curiosity and surprise. Stimulating engagement by revealing a mysterious side of a familiar world."[53] Indeed, especially familiar recognizable stories of everyday life are defined as important, but the genre is also linked to local identity and community building:

> The widening channel fulfils its educative and cultural role by providing "service" and "information" which are relevant to viewers' everyday lives, and are presented in an attractive form . . . the widening channel offers recognizable and engaging cultural programming and concentrates in particular on the own, Flemish culture . . .[54]

Also in the context of the second channel, Canvas, repertoires associated with a public service ethos are used to define human interest programming. In terms of human interest, Canvas is expected to be a frequency that deals with abstract, complex and distant social themes in an informative and in-depth way, although

identifiable stories are also defined as an important requirement for these programs, as the following quote from the debrief for the program *Document* illustrates:

> He/she [the viewer of Canvas] aims to get access (to learn more about) the
> daily lives and realities of certain groups living in other life conditions . . . The
> viewer of Canvas desires a complete picture of a particular
> situation/problem/development, in which actors' inner motivations are dealt
> with, apart from external conditions (social conditions, regulation, . . .).[55]

A debrief for the program *Kwesties* (*Issues*) notes: "the satisfaction [offered by
Kwesties] is situated at the level of learning . . . and . . . secondarily at the level
of excitement or immersion."[56] The identity of the public service oriented media
professional is also promoted, through the constructing of a distinction between
human interest on VRT, and other forms of human interest on other commercial
channels. A range of contemporary debates about PDTV genres, such as recent
moral panics about the sensationalist, voyeuristic, and exploitative nature of
some controversial Reality TV formats, or critical questions about staging or
manipulation, resound throughout the recommendations in the (de)briefs. The
case study shows how repertoires associated with a public service ethos are
mobilized in the (de)briefs in reaction to these kinds of public discourses about
PDTV.[57] Repertoires of distinction, articulating values such as "respect,"
"neutrality" or "reliability," are used to underline how VRT defines and
evaluates human interest. These are used to emphasize the distinctive character
of human interest programming on VRT, for example by opposing a "proper"
attitude of the genre to the sensationalistic, voyeuristic, and manipulated Reality
TV shows produced by competitors. Ideas of neutrality grounded in a public
service ethos, for example, are used frequently to define human interest
programming: "No position-taking, it is about the opinion of the viewer."[58] The
notion of authenticity also appears frequently: "Authenticity: a representation of
reality without manipulation, scripting or exaggeration. Dignity and respect: no
freak-show, dealing with 'experience experts' representing a certain social
phenomenon, who are portrayed respectfully."[59] Likewise, in a debriefing for the
program *De Wereld van Tarantino* (*The World of Tarantino*) human interest as
portrayed on Canvas is put forward in terms of public service values: "For the
viewers of Canvas this program is clearly Canvas. The program is defined as
heavy, realistic, experience-oriented, engaging, respectful, objectively critical.
In this sense it [the program] corresponds perfectly to the values of Canvas."[60]

Formatting, Governmentality, and the (Un)Freedom of the Media Professional

What does this analysis mean in terms of the governmentality of formatting? The production of a governable media professional through formatting (and the practices of freedom allowed within formatting) are dependent on the discursive mechanisms described above. The target audiences and brands of the two channels, Eén and Canvas, offer media professionals opportunities for self-realization while simultaneously enforcing self-regulation. The "motivational groups" and "channel identities" used by VRT are constructed in terms of repertoires associated with a public service culture, translated as sets of rather open values and guidelines. The very fact that the governmentality of formatting is dependent on the co-articulation of a marketing rationality and other public service rationalities means that there are ambiguities, contradictions and tensions within the very formatting practice. This co-articulation provides openings for media professionals, giving the formatting practice a productive rather than a repressive character. Formatting presupposes and perhaps even encourages creativity on the part of the media professionals, both in terms of their work and in terms of how they deal with formatting. Media professionals are allowed considerable space for creative interpretation and negotiation of the values and guidelines articulated in the (de)briefs, which allows them to project their own aspirations onto these governmental repertoires. They are encouraged to scrutinize how they can creatively translate their wants and aspirations into the programming schedules of Eén and Canvas by interacting with these channels' target audiences and brand identities.

At the same time they are encouraged to think in terms of target audiences and brands when scrutinizing the most effective ways of getting their creative work broadcast. It is here that the constraints of the formatting practice are situated: Brand and target audience are the first considerations. Furthermore, as brand and target audience are the only vehicles of public service repertoires allowed within formatting practice, these repertoires become encapsulated in a logic of scientification, measurability and consumer-sovereignty. Questioning these logics and their very marketing rationality thus is discouraged. Moreover, the case study shows how these hegemonic processes aim to work through the very selfhood of media professionals by allowing a space of freedom. The target audiences and brands can be used by the media professionals as what Michel Foucault called "technologies of the self"[61] in order simultaneously to practice forms of freedom and to govern themselves.[62] Indeed, in terms of government, formatting is not only about the disciplining of others, but also about the disciplining of oneself, what Foucault implied in his view of government as the "conduct of conduct."[63] Moreover, as the public service oriented media professional is produced through the promotion of a market-oriented media professional, potential forms of revolt against the marketing-based rationality of formatting are produced as a part its very governmentality. The question, then, is to what extent is this governmentality successful? Obviously formatting is but one (top-down) process within the production context of PDTV. Although a program of government, as Mitchell Dean has argued, produces forms of freedom and practices of the self, it does not constitute them.[64] The subjectivities promoted through the governmentality of formatting will always interact with the subjectivities produced throughout other contexts and production processes in which media professionals are situated. Media professionals thus may resist, subvert or negotiate the subjectivities or identities ascribed to them by the formatting logic. The results of the case study of formatting within VRT described here urge for further research into how media professionals experience the practices of freedom allowed within contemporary formatting practices of PDTV. In some cases program-makers might experience their work and themselves through the recommendations of VRT, which would indicate an "ideal form" of governmentality, when practices of freedom and practices of government presuppose each other. In other cases, media professionals might be looking for openings or contradictions within the recommendations, and searching for ways to strategically balance and negotiate these guidelines in line with other intentions and creativity. Moreover, it is not unthinkable that well-known or established program-makers will succeed in side-stepping formatting practices, exploiting their symbolic capital and drawing upon their intellectual-professional networks.

The multiple ways in which media professionals' interact with formatting practices makes the current Reality TV format a trans-genre that is continuously being creatively re-invented and discursively re-articulated within diverse rationalities. Arguably, it is this multitude of creative practices that in part explains the plurality of contemporary popular Reality TV formats on public TV in Flanders (as well as the very trans-generic character of human interest TV), as diverse groups of media professionals, both traditional documentary-makers and younger generations of program-makers, are allowed their space of freedom to practice creativity. This observation, at the same time, highlights that the governmentality of formatting promotes a trans-identity for these media professionals, that is a professional identity defined in terms of self-entrepreneurship and responsibility. The case study indicates how the burgeoning enterprise culture has impacted on and impacts on public broadcasting organizations and the professional identity of program-makers involved in PDTV. Formatting in this context is a frame used within PSB that offers program-makers opportunities to take responsibility for their self-organization and self-management, while at the same time encouraging discipline and self-governance.

Notes

1. Corner, 2002, 263.
2. Dovey.
3. E.g., Bondebjerg, 43; Van Zoonen; MacDonald, 80; Dovey, 83.
4. Hartley, 154-165; Brunsdon et al., 29-30.
5. Roscoe, 288; Kilborn, 1996, 141-143.
6. Kilborn, 1996, 147.
7. E.g., Jakobowicz; Born.
8. Foucault, 1977, 135-190; 1978, 81-102.
9. Foucault, 1988, 1-20.
10. Dean, 9-39; Rose, 15-60.
11. E.g., Boddin and Vandenbrande, 2-14; Carpentier; Cottle; Kilborn, Hibberd and Boyle, 2001; Leishman, 1-3; Teurlings; Ytreberg, 2004; 2006.
12. Flemish Community, "Decrees Concerning Radio and Television Coordinated on 25 January 1995," Art. 4 § 1 and 2.
13. E.g., Rose, 56; 102-103; du Gay, 51-74; 178-193.
14. The name "Eén" can be translated as "First" (referring to the first net), but also as "One" (referring to "becoming one" and the idea of social cohesion and community building). The baseline of Eén, "everyone his proper Eén" (or "Eén for everyone"), refers to both the idea of connecting people, and the attractiveness of the programming of Eén for everybody.
15. Internal and External Communication VRT-tv, "Basis info Eén 2005" (VRT, September 19, 2005): 3.
16. VRT Website, "Canvas." n.d. www.vrt.be/vrt_master/merken/vrt_merken_canvas/.
17. VRT Website, "Canvas." n.d. www.vrt.be/vrt_master/merken/vrt_merken_canvas/.
18. VRT Internal and External Communication TV-jvv, "Informatiebrochure Canvas—1 April 2006" (VRT, March 30, 2006): 2.
19. Peter Suetens, former Program Manager Documentaries, interview with author (February 6, 2008); Bettina Geysen, former strategic advisor television and channel-manager Canvas, interview with author (February 18, 2008).
20. Born, 2003: 75-76; Born, 2004, 302-372; Jakobowicz, 45-62; Kilborn, 1996, 147; Debrett, 2004, 7.
21. E.g., Palmer, 3-20; Corner, 1995, 79-85.
22. Kilborn, 1998, 215.
23. Winston, 1-53; 157.
24. E.g., Corner, 2002; 262.
25. Foucault, 1978, 81-102.
26. Peterson, 161-198.
27. E.g., Bolin, 2005, 5; Mittell.
28. Foucault, 1977, 135-190; 1978, 81-102.
29. Foucault first used the term "government" when he studied how the problem of government was thought about and dealt with in the sixteenth century. He saw government as the shaping of the general conditions of the daily life of populations through the detailed managing, administering and rationalizing of their conduct. This in order to attain the health and wealth of these populations and the broader State (Foucault, 1980).

Later he combined a macro-focus on government (of whole populations and the state) with a micro-interest in practices of self-governance (Foucault, 1988, 1-20). The meaning of government was broadened and became understood as any "conduct of conduct" (Foucault, 2000), that is, the multiplicity of ways through which a particular domain of activity is managed (e.g., television production, in the case of this chapter). The notion of governmentality then refers to "how we think about governing others and ourselves" (Dean, 212) within this domain of activity. Following from the above it is clear that the Foucauldian notion does not refer to the Government or the State. Although the terms government and governance are often used as synonyms in governmentality studies, the term government will be used in this study, in order to avoid associations with administrative decision-making.

30. Neo-liberalism, Foucauldian scholars argue, attempts to construct a world of individuals who are "free" and self-entrepreneurial. Individuals' interests or choices hereby are defined as faculties that must be rendered calculable, so the exercise of liberties becomes productive (e.g., Dean, 157, 164-165). This work later inspired scholars such as Peter Miller and Nikolas Rose in analyzing neo-liberalism as a liberal form of government and the rationalities of government in organizational contexts and economic activity (e.g., Miller and Rose, 1-31).

31. Foucault, 1998, 221.

32. Foucault, 1988, 1-20.

33. Foucault, 1988, 1-20; Dean, 11.

34. E.g., Knights and Willmott.

35. E.g., Rose, 1990, 56.

36. The idea that broadcasting contexts, such as formatting, shape generic discourses aligns with Jason Mittell's plea to examine genre from a cultural-discursive perspective (e.g., Mittell, 2001, 8-11; 2004, xii-xiii).

37. E.g., Palmer, 1-19.

38. E.g., Bardoel, 2003, 81-96; Bardoel and Brants, 2003.

39. Corner, 2002, 265.

40. Catherine Wilmes, former strategy advisor Canvas, VRT, interview with author (October 9, 2008).

41. Sebastiaan Nollet, strategic advisor Canvas, VRT, interview with author (October 3, 2008).

42. The evaluation of programming via (de)briefs is in the first place an in-house procedure at VRT. However, norms, rules and guidelines communicated through (de)briefs are also used within the collaborations between VRT and external partners. In the 1990s VRT introduced outsourcing policies, making PDTV no longer a solely in-house activity dominated by a network of established documentary-makers. Various independent production companies have mushroomed from the early 1990s onwards in reaction to the VRT policies of outsourcing, a phenomenon also witnessed in other European countries (e.g., Bolin, 2004, 280-286). The (de)briefs in this context are a tool used by VRT to safeguard their "quality standards," especially since much of its PDTV programming is being produced by independents that make programs for both public and commercial broadcasting.

43. Catherine Wilmes, former strategic advisor Canvas, VRT, interview with author (October 9, 2008).

44. In the case study twelve (de)briefing files dealing with quantitative and qualitative evaluations of fifteen programs were analyzed (*Document, NV De Wereld, Spijkers, Kwesties, Zwarte Vijvers, De Wereld is Klein, Sportkwesties, Spots, Ieder Zijn Wereld, Een Wereld van Verschil, Het Leven Zoals Het Is, De Believers, Dieren in Nesten, Stories* and *De Wereld van Tarantino*). Citations from the (de)briefing files in this chapter are the author's translations.

45. The repertoire analysis allowed distinguishing between different rationalities (or clusters of similar recommendations). The notion of *repertoire* used in the study aligns to the concept of interpretative repertoire which finds its origin in discursive psychology and allows for a micro-focus on how actors mobilize particular frames of understanding when interacting with others, i.e., when discourses are embodied in concrete speech acts and other linguistic practices (e.g., Whetherell and Potter).

46. Ang, 15-38; 153-170.

47. E.g., Born, 2004, 306.

48. Debriefing *Kwesties*, 1998: 8; emphasis added.

49. Debriefing *Kwesties*, 1997: 1; emphasis added.

50. Briefing *NV De Wereld*, 1997: 7.

51. Debriefing *NV De Wereld*, 1997: 2.

52. Debriefing *Het Leven Zoals Het Is*, 2006: 23.

53. Debriefing *Het Leven Zoals Het Is*, 2000: 13.

54. Briefing *NV De Wereld*, 1997: 12.

55. Briefing *Social Frequency*, 2004: 20-22.

56. Debriefing *Kwesties*, 1998: 8-9.

57. E.g., Biltereyst, 2004a.

58. Debriefing *Kwesties*, 1998: 8.

59. Briefing *Social Frequency*, 2004: 21.

60. Debriefing *De Wereld van Tarantino*, 2004: 37.

61. Foucault, 1988, 1-20.

62. These technologies also play a role on a broader level, being part of the broader promotional discourses of VRT and the corporation's strategies for creating trust, as e.g., Daniël Biltereyst has suggested, see Biltereyst, 2004b.

63. Foucault, 2000, 326-348.

64. The work of Mitchell Dean revisits and complements the originally rather structuralist view of governmentality developed by Foucault himself, e.g., Dean, 13.

References

Ang, Ien. *Desperately Seeking the Audience*. London: Routledge, 1993.

Bardoel, Jo. "Back to the Public? Assessing Public Broadcasting in the Netherlands." *Javnost/the Public* 10, no. 3 (2003): 81-96.

Bardoel, Jo and Kees Brants. "From Ritual to Reality. Public Broadcasters and Social Responsibility in the Netherlands." In *Broadcasting & Convergence: New Articulations of the Public Service Remit*, edited by Gregory Ferrell Lowe and Taisto Hujanen, 167-186. Göteborg, Sweden: Nordicom Göteborg University, 2003.

Biltereyst, Daniël. "Televisiegenres, Reality-tv en Mediapaniek. Over Reality-tv als Genre, Metagenre, Tendens." In *Film/TV/Genre*, edited by Daniël Biltereyst and

Philippe Meers, 171-194. Gent, Belgium: Academia Press, 2004a.

———. "Public Service Broadcasting, Popular Entertainment and the Construction of Trust." *European Journal of Cultural Studies* 7, no. 3 (2004b): 341-359.

Boddin, Frank and Kristel Vandenbrande. "Go for the Characters and their Stories. The Regulation of 'Ordinary People' and Media Professionals in Docusoap Production." Presented at the Sixth Annual Meeting of the Cultural Studies Association, New York, May 22-24, 2008.

Bolin, Göran. "The Value of Being Public Service. The Shifting of Power Relations in Swedish Television Production." *Media, Culture & Society* 26, no. 2 (2004): 277-287.

———. "Television Stories. The Approximation of Factual and Entertainment Narration." Presented at the MIT4 Conference, Cambridge, Mass., May 6-8, 2005.

Bondebjerg, Ib. "Public Discourse/Private Fascination: Hybridisation in 'True-life-story Genres.'" *Media, Culture & Society* 18, no. 1 (1996): 27-45.

Born, Georgina. *Uncertain Vision. Birt, Dyke and the Reinvention of the BBC*. London: Secker and Warburg, 2004.

———. "From Reithian Ethic to Managerial Discourse. Accountablity and Audit at the BBC." *Javnost/the Public* 10, no. 3 (2003): 63-80.

Brunsdon, Charlotte, Catherine Johnson, Rachel Moseley and Helen Wheatley. "Factual Entertainment on British Television. The Midlands TV Research Group's '8-9 Project.'" *European Journal of Cultural Studies* 4, no. 1 (2001): 29-62.

Carpentier, Nico. "Participation and Power in the Television Program Temptation Island." In *Researching Media, Democracy and Participation. The Intellectual Work of the 2006 European Media and Communication Doctoral Summer School*, edited by Nico Carpentier, Pille Pruulmann-Vengerfeldt, Karl Nordenstreng, Maren Hartmann, Peeter Vihalem and Bart Cammaerts, 135-148. Tartu, Estonia: University of Tartu Press, 2006.

Corner, John. *Television Form and Public Address*. London: Edward Arnold, 1995.

———. "Performing the Real. Documentary Diversions." *Television & New Media* 3, no. 3 (2002): 255-269.

———. *The Art of Record: A Critical Introduction to Documentary*. Manchester: Manchester University Press, 1996.

Cottle, Simon. "The Production of News Formats: Determinants of Mediated Public Contestation." *Media, Culture & Society* 17, no. 2 (1995): 275-291.

Dean, Mitchell. *Governmentality. Power and Rule in Modern Society*. London: Sage, 1999.

Debrett, Mary. "Branding Documentary: New Zealand's Minimalist Solution to Cultural Subsidy." *Media, Culture & Society* 26, no. 1 (2004): 5-23.

Dovey, John. *Freakshow: First Person Media and Factual Television*. London: Pluto Press, 2000.

du Gay, Paul. *Consumption and Identity at Work*. London: Sage Publications, 1996.

Foucault, Michel. "Interview with Michel Foucault." In *Power: Essential Works of Foucault, 1954-1984*, edited by James D. Faubion, Robert Tr. Hurley and Paul Rabinow, 239-297. New York: New York Press, 1998.

———. *Discipline and Punish: The Birth of the Prison*, translated by Alan Sheridan. New York: Pantheon, 1977.

————. *The History of Sexuality Vol. I. The Will to Knowledge*, translated by Robert Hurley. New York: Pantheon, 1978.

————. "The Subject and Power." In *Michel Foucault: beyond Structuralism and Hermeneutics*, edited by Hubert L. Dreyfus and Paul Rabinow, 208-226. Brighton, U.K.: Harvester Wheatsheaf, 1982.

————. "The Ethic of the Care of the Self as a Practice of Freedom." In *The Final Foucault*, edited by James Bernauer and David Rasmussen, 1-20. Cambridge, Mass.: MIT Press, 1988.

————. "The Subject and Power." In *Power: The Essential Works of Foucault, Vol. 3*, edited by James D. Faubion, 326-348. New York: The Free Press, 2000.

————. "Technologies of the Self." In *Technologies of the Self: A Seminar with Michel Foucault*, edited by Luther H. Martin, Huck Gutman and Patrick H. Hutton, 16-49. Amherst: The University of Massachusetts Press, 1988.

Hartley, John. *Uses of Television*. London: Routledge, 1999.

Jakobowicz, Karol. "Endgame? Contracts, Audits, and the Future of Public Broadcasting." *Javnost/the Public* 10, no. 3 (2003): 45-62.

Kilborn, Richard and John Izod. *An Introduction to Television Documentary*. Manchester: Manchester University Press, 1997.

Kilborn, Richard, Matthew Hibberd and Raymond Boyle. "The Rise of Docusoap: The Case of Vets in Practice." *Screen* 42, no. 4 (2001): 382-395.

————. "New Contexts for Documentary Production in Britain." *Media, Culture & Society* 18, no. 1 (1996): 141-150.

————. "Shaping the Real. Democratization and Commodification in U.K. Factual Broadcasting." *European Journal of Communication* 13, no. 2 (1998): 201-218.

Knights, David and Hugh Willmott. "Power and Subjectivity at Work: From Degradation to Subjugation in the Labour Process." *Sociology* 23, no. 4 (1989): 535-558.

Kuypers, Gijsbert. *Beginselen van Beleidsontwikkeling B*. Muiderberg: Coutinho, 1980.

Leishman, Christine. "People Know Me Really Well. Jane Macdonald and the Construction of Authenticity in The Cruise." *Ecloga*, n.d., www.strath.ac.uk/ecloga/ (accessed September 15, 2008).

MacDonald, Myra. *Exploring Media Discourse*. London: Hodder Arnold Publication, 2003.

Miller, Peter and Nikolas Rose. "Governing Economic Life." *Economy and Society* 19, no. 1, 1-31.

Mittell, Jason. "A Cultural Approach To Television Genre Theory." *Cinema Journal* 40, no. 3 (2001): 3-24.

————. *Genre and Television*. London and New York: Routledge, 2004.

Palmer, Garreth. *Discipline and Liberty: Television and Governance*. Manchester: Manchester University Press, 2003.

Peterson, Mark Allen. *Anthropology and Mass Communication: Media and Myth in the New Millennium*. Oxford and New York: Berghahn Books, 2003.

Roscoe, Jane. "Television: Friend or Foe of Australian Documentary?" *Media, Culture & Society* 26, no. 2 (2004): 288-295.

Rose, Nikolas. *Governing the Soul: The Shaping of the Private Self*. London: Routledge, 1990.

————. *The Powers of Liberty*. Cambridge: Cambridge University Press, 1999.

Teurlings, Jan. "Producing the Ordinary: Institutions, Discourses and Practices in Love Game Shows." *Continuum: Journal of Media & Cultural Studies* 15, no. 2 (2001): 249-263.

Van Zoonen, Liesbet. "Desire and Resistance: Big Brother and the Recognition of Everyday Life." *Media, Culture & Society* 23, no. 5 (2001): 669-677.

Whetherell, Margaret and Jonathan Potter. "Discourse Analysis and the Identification of Interpretative Repertoires." In *Analysing Everyday Explanation*, edited by Charles Antaki, 168-183. London: Sage, 1988.

Winston, Brian. *Lies, Damned Lies and Documentary*. London: British Film Institute, 2000.

Ytreberg, Espen. "Formatting Participation within Broadcast Media Production." *Media, Culture & Society* 26, no. 5 (2004): 677-692.

————. "Premeditations of Performance in Recent Live Television. A Scripting Approach to Media Production Studies." *European Journal of Cultural Studies* 9, no. 4 (2006): 421-440.

Chapter 14
Trans-National Reality TV: A Comparative Study of the U.K.'s and Norway's *Wife Swap*
Gunn Sara Enli and Brian McNair

The Trans-National Travel of Formats

Since the beginning of this century the global television industry has become more dependent on format trade, with the Reality TV genre responsible for a large share of this growth[1]. Reality TV formats are particularly suited to the global market, because they employ formulas that are highly adaptable for national contexts. Social experiment Reality TV formats, such as *Wife Swap,* can be flexibly applied to domestic cultures.

Although Britain and Norway are culturally and geographically close to each other, both being western European countries, there are major differences between the two nations in terms of socio-cultural aspects such as gender and class equalities, and industrial aspects such as the size and traditions of local TV production. This chapter investigates the trans-national travel of social experiment Reality TV with *Wife Swap* as a case. In this chapter we ask: what are the main differences between the British and the Norwegian versions of *Wife Swap?* To what degree are socio-cultural factors reflected in the respective versions of the *Wife Swap* format? To what degree was the trans-national travel of the format a success in terms of reception in the import country?

We draw on close readings of six episodes of both the British and Norwegian versions of the format produced in 2003 and 2004, as well as document analysis and statistics of ratings. The reason for selecting the United Kingdom and Norway for a comparative study is that they represent on the one hand a large country (60.8 million population) with a considerable format industry (ranked as the world's biggest exporter of formats in 2009). And on the other hand, a small country (4.6 million people) with only marginal exports of formats (only one successful format sale, *71 degrees North*). Moreover, as we will see in the analysis, the countries represent socio-cultural diversity within the European TV market, and illuminate major obstacles for the trans-national flow of formats.

Researching the Global Format Industry

Previous research into the trans-national travel of formats may be divided into three main strands. First, there is a traditional strand of research focusing on the *globalization* and standardization of content. The TV "format" is defined as the "fixed structure of a programme which is repeated week after week, giving the programme its character, dramatic movement, identity, and incidentally, its marketability."[2] The standardization of content is thus a natural consequence of the fast growing industry of format trade. Export of media content and socio-cultural differences has been widely debated in the research literature, and has often been related to concerns about the adverse impact of cultural "imperialism" or U.S.-led globalization on local cultures and identities. The increased global exchange of popular TV formats has renewed debate about the extent to which local media industries and cultural traditions are threatened by formats originated elsewhere and then imported.[3] The global format trade might be regarded as a threat to the local television industry, and reduce the degree of innovation and experimentations within the national production cultures. Even though there has always been exchange of ideas across borders, and a more informal "borrowing" of program ideas from the major TV markets, the recent formalized and standardized format trade has a more massive impact on local production cultures across the world. However, this has not reduced the degree of culture clash in global format exchange. The rise of TV exports from several regions, such as Europe, does not change the fact that there are inequalities in the flows of television, and that the major TV markets still have a dominance internationally.[4] For small countries, the format trade might result in an orientation of television production toward the successful formulas on the international market, and thus reduce local creativity.

A second strand of research is concerned with the need for "cultural proximity,"[5] meaning that the TV audiences prefer narratives that incorporate familiar phenomenon and recognizable dilemmas. As pointed out by Silvio Waisbord:[6] "A dozen media companies are able to do business worldwide by selling the same idea, and audiences seem to be watching variations of the same show. At another level, however, formats attest to the fact that television still remains tied to local and national cultures." Consequently, Waisbord argues that TV is simultaneously both global and national, "shaped by the globalization of media economics and the pull of local and national cultures." Global format trade is dependent on adjustments to national identities, cultural taste, consumer culture, and socio-cultural specificities.

Historically, and ever since the emergence of TV, there has been an intimate relation between TV and everyday life; from its early integration into the everyday rhythms of everyday life of the domestic sphere, to its long-standing interest in capturing events in real time. Television is a medium of everydayness, and compared to the movies, TV content is consumed in the settings of the home, and thus communicates recognizable narratives of the everyday life of the local audiences. In contemporary programming, reality-TV is a culmination of its long history, seeking to finally embed itself in everyday life.[7] In makeover Reality TV formats, the aim is to impose social transformations on individuals (*The Swan, Total Makeover* etc.) or family units (*Renovate My Family, Supernanny* etc.). A striking feature of these formats is their actual intervention in reality; the goal of the formats is not just to represent a certain reality in contemporary culture but to impose changes on present reality. These shows thus require fundamental insight in the domestic culture in which they will impose transformations, and one might expect local adaptations of makeover formats to be more challenging than for example game shows.

While adaptations of highly structured quiz shows, such as *Who Wants to Be a Millionaire?* have an almost identical style and aesthetic as the British original (except for a local host, local contestants and variations to questions to reflect local knowledge), Reality TV formats such as *Wife Swap* permit more scope for adaptation: "With something like *Wife Swap* the real skill lies in production of that show: the casting, the filming and the editing."[8] The production process involves selecting participants from the general public and, thus, is shaped by the socio-cultural context of the particular country. *Big Brother,* for example, resulted in controversy and even violent protest when adapted in Middle Eastern and Asian countries.[9] In 2004, *Arab Big Brother* provoked riots in Bahrain through its attempt (quickly abandoned) to place male and female Muslims in the same *Big Brother* house. A format that had been controversial even in the liberal, multicultural west[10] was regarded as an insensitive violation of Islamic religious norms. The success of a format adaptation is not guaranteed, since, for various reasons, localization may not always be possible without undermining the features that drove the success of the format in its original market.

Third, there is a strand of research focusing on *industrial factors* such as economy, regulation, and production culture. Recent research on the adaptation of reality formats has been concerned with how the local media environment influences production. Pia Jensen's[11] comparative study of format adaptation in Denmark and Australia demonstrates how the different history and traditions of these two broadcasting systems are reflected in the style and content of adapted shows. For Jensen, the factors that shape this localization are related primarily to the local media environment:

> Specific format adaptation processes are more dependent on the competitive
> conditions, funding, content regulation, media policies, audience demographics,
> history and ownership of the players in a national television market than on
> vaguer cultural concepts such as national mentalities and cultural tastes.

The use of formats is related to the television industry's desire to achieve
successfully in the market without a high investment or a high risk of failure.
The format trade is a sufficient way to, at least in theory, secure investment for
the TV channels; the formats are already developed by their creators, and all the
costs related to the innovation of the format are covered by the format owners.
Recent growth in the global trade for TV formats has run parallel with the
emergence of Reality TV since the 1990s.[12] Moreover, the format is already
tested in their home markets, and in many cases also in various export markets,
and the format buyer will be presented with a proven track record of the format.
In sum, the industrial benefits from importing formats, and particularly in small
markets, are significant, and the opportunity to adopt a finished product with
impressive track records seems like a highly welcomed deal for broadcasters
operating in commercial markets with tight budgets. Not least the significant
proliferation of channels and a total expansion of airtime has resulted in a
greater demand for content to fill the schedules. Given that locally produced
content generally is generating higher viewing numbers than imported canned
programs,[13] the benefits from format trade seems obvious; well-tested formulas
are implemented in new markets with expectations that their success will be
replicated, and with an added touch of national identity through the casting of
local participants and the filming on locations in the import country.

Wife Swap—the Format

The format under examination in this study, *Wife Swap*, takes the form of a
social experiment involving two families swapping wives for a limited period,
exposing contrasts between family values and lifestyles. These contrasts are
typically linked to such factors as social class, gender roles, and ethnicity, in
addition to other determinants of lifestyle. During the first week of the swap, the
new wife must adhere exactly to the rules and lifestyle of the wife she is
replacing. Each wife provides a house manual which explains her role in the
family and the duties she holds. During the second week, the wives are allowed
to establish their own rules, and their new families must adhere to these new
house rules. At the end of the two weeks, the two couples meet for the first time,
and evaluate their experiences.

Wife Swap was created in 2003 by the U.K. television production company, RDF media, a company that is also format holder of the television format *Ladette to Lady* (ITV), based on an idea of transforming "ladettes" (meaning: loud, foul-mouthed, and uncultured young women) into "ladies." This transformation project has a clear aspect of a traditional historical British *class* system and thus illuminates how social experiment formats are often based on local socio-cultural characteristics of their origin countries.

Export and sale of programs has become increasingly important in the British TV industry,[14] and *Wife Swap* has become a global format, produced in more than fourteen countries in Europe, Australia, North America, South America and the Middle East. The format's key feature of pitting contrasting lifestyles against each other has been used as a means to comment on local debates and thus be more relevant to local audiences. The Israeli version of *Wife Swap*, for example, added a political twist by swapping wives between Arab and Jewish families, taking the format to the frontier of the country's long-running conflict.[15] The U.S. version added a host who introduced the program and mediated the discussion between the participating couples at the end of the show. The reason for this adjustment, according to Steemers, was that "viewer tolerance for extremes is lower in the US, particularly on network prime time."[16]

In Reality TV the construction of contrasts between participants is a key formal element. In *Wife Swap*, for example, contrasts are created through the selection of participants from very different social backgrounds and lifestyles, and narratives build around the encounter between these differences. The participants in *Wife Swap* are subjected to life-altering circumstances for a short period, and the format might more precisely be defined as a "life experiment." In line with many Reality TV formats, *Wife Swap* is profoundly hybrid, and includes a combination of social experiment and observational documentary with melodrama.[17]

Criticism has been leveled at the allegedly melodramatic qualities of *Wife Swap*.[18] This is often linked with condemnation of the genre's banality, exploitation of participants and encouragement of voyeurism in its audience.[19] Some have identified the growth of Reality TV as one manifestation of the late twentieth century's fascination with confessional culture, or the "cult of reality,"[20] amounting to a progressive democratization of televisual culture in ways that might be educational and therapeutic as well as entertaining. A key function of the format of *Wife Swap* is to permit public access to the hidden worlds of private family life. It can thus be seen to express the feminist slogan "the personal is political." The format is important in its way of illuminating the family, its routines, division of labor and personal relations. As Anthony Giddens suggests, the family is "the site for the democratisation of intimate relationships . . . the major platform on which debate about moralities and ethics gets staged."[21]

The producers of *Wife Swap* lead on the key social, economic and cultural divides in a society, and the format can thus be viewed as a prism which illuminates how these divides are articulated in different countries. First, class distinctions are highly visible in Reality TV, whose construction permeates on a number of different levels. Palmer points to evidence of traditional middle class-ness bringing apparently effortless "good taste" to the new and more insecure classes, and argues that Reality TV helps to mold and legitimize class membership.[22] British society is internationally known for the sharpness of its class divisions. A recent survey of attitudes to social class in the United Kingdom confirms the widespread perception that Britain is a highly class-divided society.[23] Norway, on the other hand, is known as an egalitarian and social-democratic country where economic and social differences between rich and poor are less articulated than in Britain.[24]

A second important starting point for staging conflicts in the format is the gender roles and the difference between the roles of men and women in the home context, and in the public sphere. At this point, the two countries examined in this study are highly divided; Norway is more advanced than many European countries in terms of equal rights for men and women, while Britain is among the less advanced in this respect. Third, the format relies on tension between different ethnic groups in a country, and also on this point there is an important difference between the two countries; Norway has fairly recently become a multi-cultural nation in which immigrants from non-western countries are playing an important role. It is a relatively ethnically homogeneous society. Britain, on the other hand, has a long history as an ethnic "melting pot," with a large population of immigrants and their descendants. However, Norway is a country with noticeable divides between urban and rural lifestyles, and between modernist and traditional cultural values. Based on these theoretical reflections, the focus for the textual analysis is class, gender, ethnicity, urbanity, and modernism.

Wife Swap: United Kingdom

In the United Kingdom *Wife Swap* aired on Channel 4, a public service broadcaster funded by advertising. Channel 4 had an almost nine percent market share in 2007, ranks as Britain's third largest channel, and has obligations as a public service broadcaster (PSB). Channel 4 has followed the example of the BBC in defining Reality TV as a genre of PSB.[25] Channel 4's PSB remit includes phrases such as "innovation, experiment and creativity," "culturally diverse society," and "educative value."[26] These obligations are seen as being compatible with the Reality TV genre in the United Kingdom, at least in terms of the public service channels' categorization of such formats as documentaries. "As such," argue Dover and Hill, "they are presented as public service programmes documenting social issues, and are not explicitly associated with lifestyle features."[27] Channel 4 had already achieved huge success with Endemol's *Big Brother* format (allowing the channel to cross over from being a niche channel to attracting a mainstream audience), and *Wife Swap* reflected the channel managers' desire to benefit further from the trend in televisual culture toward reality formats. *Wife Swap*, as already noted, has been a success for Channel 4, and was part of its scheduling at the time of writing (2008). The format was Channel 4's biggest hit in 2003, regularly attracting more than five million viewers. *Wife Swap* is particularly popular among fourteen-to-thirty-four-year-olds, with a market share of 38 percent in this highly sought after market segment.[28] It has been developed into a *Celebrity Wife Swap* strand, and a trans-national strand, in which British families swap wives and lifestyles with families in Germany and Spain.

As noted above, the format is based on contrasts, achieved by the producers through strategic selection of participants. The families involved in the swap are selected on the basis of their differences, which set up potential conflicts related to parenting and lifestyle, and provide the show with its dramatic tensions. For example, in the episodes viewed for this essay, families with eight children were contrasted with families with only two, pet lovers were contrasted with those who hated animals in the house, and working mothers swapped with full-time homemakers.

Underpinning these contrasts in the U.K. version of the format are the recurring themes of *gender*, *class* and *ethnic* differences. Every episode viewed for this study addressed one or more of these elements, from which flowed other differences in taste and lifestyle within the participating families.

If confrontation between different lifestyles and approaches to family management is the immediate aim of this device, and provides the entertainment value which has contributed to *Wife Swap*'s ratings success in the United Kingdom, the presentation of contrasts also has a public service rationale. Channel 4 as a PSB is obliged to justify its programming in relation to the broader social good. The format is thus presented as a vehicle for exploring competing approaches to child rearing, the sexual division of labor within the home, attitudes to ethnicity and race, class differences, and so on. Moreover, it presents these competing approaches in a way that seeks to educate and improve the participants in the program and, by extension, the viewing audience. At the beginning of each episode the narrator makes this explicit through statements such as:

> The partners hope that swapping children and lifestyles will help them reflect on how they do things. (Episode 1, Series 1)

> What can they learn about their lives? (Episode 2, Series 1)

This context invites the audience to engage with the program, and to relate the conflicts between the participants to their own challenges in the private arena.

We now present a close analysis of selected scenes in the U.K. version, which draws attention to societal issues related to gender, ethnicity, and class.

Gender

In an episode that exemplifies the U.K. production's focus on gender and sex roles, the viewers are told that participants are also hoping to find out "how the experience will affect their relationship." In this respect, *Wife Swap* is explicitly packaged as a form of televisual relationship counseling, in which certain attitudes to sex and gender roles are highlighted and criticized (usually, though not exclusively, those of the male partner). In one episode, Michelle, the eigthteen-years' married wife of a professional gambler and all-round "geezer," Barry, looks forward to swapping her husband for hard-working "New Man" Peter, because: "Barry never does anything [around the house] . . . I wanna see what it's like to live with a real man." (Episode 2, Series 1)

Barry, we are told, does not allow Michelle to go to the pub unaccompanied. He is clearly and unapologetically a domestic tyrant, and a patriarch of the old school. As the episode unfolds we see Michelle, exposed to how things are done in this other family, begin to understand that her own married life is deeply flawed, and that other kinds of relationships are possible. At one point the narrator says, "Michelle is beginning to imagine life without Barry." And so she should, the viewer is invited to think.

But then comes the twist (a common feature of the format), in which our expectations as viewers are overturned. Having gone from a household where she is required by Barry to do all the housework, while also working full time outside the home, and looking after the children, to one where husband and children share domestic tasks in a progressive, post-feminist manner, Michelle announces: "I can't get used to not having to do anything . . . I'm bored with the fact that I can't clean up. It's strange. I feel guilty." (Episode 2, Series 1)

Finally, Michelle concedes that "it's in me"—that is, the life of apparent domestic drudgery to which she has become accustomed, and that this is what she wants, deep down. The viewer is presented with an ambivalent outcome, which says that there are different ways of managing marriages and relationships, and that for some people, at least, the old ways where men were men and women knew their place are the best. Or at least are valid.

These kinds of gender and sex role conflicts arise throughout *Wife Swap*, and also take in issues around parenting. Some wives come from families where children have every moment of their day regimented with military precision by parental control freaks; others are laid back, allowing their children to do and say more or less what they please around the house. At the climax of one episode, as two couples meet to assess their experience, one (liberal) wife calls the other "an evil cow" for forcing her daughter to eat vegetables. The producers generally avoid making overt value judgements, however. The overarching message of the format is the inevitability and legitimacy of difference in parenting styles. Every style, we see, whether tough or tender, is compatible with loving relationships between parents and children. We are urged to accept that no one style is necessarily better than any other.

There are some exceptions to this moral neutrality, however, when the wrongness of a particular individual is clearly signaled. In this case, the counseling function of the format is emphasized. In one episode we encounter Jason, who never plays with his children and happily admits that he spends all his free time in the evening in front of his computer (we are told by the narrator that in eleven years, Jason has never been alone with his two children). We see his son yearning for father-son contact, and "new wife" Jane, who comes into the house appalled at what she finds, trying to encourage the father to become more involved in his son's upbringing.

Jason's own wife, Nicola, meanwhile, in the course of her swap comes to see the failures of Jason's parenting style (and his husbanding—he is in the habit of paying her for everything she does in the house, including sex), to the extent that by the time she is due to return home she says "I can't live this life any more" and threatens to leave him. Jason, confronted with the possibility of marital breakdown, resolves to change his ways. At the end of the episode, Jason and Nicola agree that: "We've come out of it learning what we need to learn." (Episode 3, Series 1) This comment illustrates the frequent emphasis of the producers of the U.K. series on the potential learning aspects of the format, including viewers in this quasi-therapeutic exercise.

Ethnicity and Racism

Wife Swap also explores broader social attitudes, and airs socially unacceptable prejudices, such as racism, with a directness that other TV genres are rarely able to achieve. The program frequently presents what might be regarded by the typical Channel 4 audience (relatively young, affluent, socially liberal) as a dysfunctional and bigoted family, or one whose attitudes to parenting and gender roles, and to other social issues, leave a lot to be desired. For example, in one episode from Series 1, a white woman, Dee, swaps with a wife from the Afro-Caribbean population. Dee, when asked about her expectations of the swap, from the outset declares: "Worst thing, if they're black, I will have a problem." (Episode 1, Series 1)

As this demonstrates, racism is addressed quite directly in the U.K. version of *Wife Swap*. The white woman openly displays xenophobic attitudes in front of the camera team. And this and similar kinds of politically incorrect statements are regarded by many producers within the genre as "the money shot."[29]

Class and Social Status

In this same episode, the central contrast between ethnicity and attitudes to race connects to a narrative about class. The black husband, Wayne, when asked what he most fears in his temporary new wife (whom he has not yet seen) replies that she will be a "fat, ugly, slob." Dee, coincidentally or not, is certainly overweight, rather unattractive and is living on benefits. Thus, the program counterpoises two common prejudices—based on ethnicity and class respectively—before an audience who may or may not share them, but are expected to know better (because this, after all, is Channel 4, a radical, cutting edge channel dedicated to innovation and the representation of marginalized groups). A key challenge of the episode is to see how these prejudices are managed and, if possible, overcome in the course of the two weeks that these very different people are required to live together. The entertainment value provided by the confrontation is combined with the educational aim of exploring racism and what we might call "fat-ism" or body fascism (there is no word in English for prejudice against obesity and slobbishness). Dee hates the fact that Wayne smokes cannabis in the house (he sees "weed" as his due for a hard day's work); Wayne hates Dee's untidiness around the house.

In this particular episode, exceptionally, there is seen to be no progress toward overcoming prejudice or improving mutual understanding. Wayne says at the end that "I haven't learned anything," while Dee, while denying that she is a racist, reacts to the news that her opposite number, Sonia, is proving very popular as the new "wife" in Dee's household: "So I've got to paint myself black? I'd better go and get some boot polish." (Episode 1, Series 1)

Class, then, is a core theme in much Reality TV, and in *Wife Swap* it shapes the economic circumstances and lifestyles of the participating families. One family is on a high income, living in an expensive home with sophisticated consumer tastes; another is living on state benefits and eating takeaway food. The producers do not mock the lower class participants, however. On the contrary, the message about the inevitability of difference, and the legitimacy of contrasting lifestyles is consistent. Class is explored, and prejudices aired, but no judgements are made about class. And, indeed, the prejudices and idiosyncracies of the liberal middle classes are exposed to scrutiny. No one, the program seems to be saying, has the ideal happy marriage, regardless of wealth or status. Happiness is not about money or professional status. In this respect, like many reality formats, *Wife Swap* has a redemptive, socially-inclusive tone which fits well with the public service ethos of Channel 4.

Wife Swap: Norway

In Norway, *Wife Swap* was produced under the title "Konebytte" by the production company Rubicon and broadcast on TV3. The PSB environment of Channel 4 stands in sharp contrast to the commercial channel TV3, which transmitted *Wife Swap* in Norway. When TV3 was launched in 1987, it was Scandinavia's first commercial TV channel and marked the very beginning of an era of deregulation and commercialization in the Nordic countries.[30] TV3 has a unique regulatory position in Norway because the channels are broadcast from the United Kingdom and thus are excluded from the strict advertising rules that apply locally. TV3 in recent years has been a driver of the adoption of Reality TV formats such as *Survivor* and *Extreme Makeover.* During the studied period, TV3 had a five percent market share in 2007, and is thus the fourth largest TV channel in the Norwegian market.

The format was produced for two seasons, in autumn 2004 (seven episodes) and spring 2005 (six episodes), and achieved a ten percent market share. TV3 had previously (autumn 2003) shown the British *Wife Swap* and achieved relative success in attracting viewers; it had thereby prepared the Norwegian market and tested the format's appeal. A frequently used strategy in the adoption of international formats in smaller markets such as Norway is to give the audience a preview of the original version, in order to test their interest before money is invested in domestic production.

Success in the British home market was used as a marketing strategy to promote the format in Norway: "When shown on British Channel 4, the series reached a new viewer record with 6.5 million viewers, only beaten by the *Big Brother* final."[31] The producers expected considerably higher ratings for the Norwegian version of the format; but although the locally produced version achieved higher ratings than had the British format shown in Norway, numbers were not high enough to encourage TV3 to continue the production for longer than two seasons. Compared to other national versions of international reality formats produced for TV3, such as *Survivor*, Norwegian *Wife Swap* was a short-term visitor to the Norwegian TV schedules.

In contrast to the U.K. version, the possibility of learning from the experience was not emphasized in the introductory voice-over to the Norwegian version. The participants' motivations for taking part in *Wife Swap,* and the producer's goals in terms of a social experiment were not touched upon in the programs. This difference perhaps was because the British Channel 4 had public service obligations while Norwegian TV3 is a strictly commercial company. The Norwegian version's relative lack of success might also be explained by factors in the media environment, such as regulatory factors and market position, and in textual features of the program. How was the family unit portrayed in the Norwegian version? How does it comment on social issues such as gender roles, ethnic conflicts and class divergence?

Gender

The division of housework and gender roles is a recurring theme in the Norwegian *Wife Swap*. The majority of the episodes viewed for this study included a degree of tension between the man and the woman in the household. In one of the episodes, the producers underlined the uneven division of labor in the house with a scene showing the wife vacuuming the living room while the husband watches TV. She has to vacuum around him, and asks him to move his legs. This scene might be seen as a visualization of the statistical fact that women do more housework than men even if both also work outside the home. In this particular episode, the producers contrasted a working mother with two teenage children, with a housewife with six small children. However, in both cases, the wives were seen to have the main responsibility for the housework. The housewife says that she likes to have control and to take responsibility of the household: "I do about 95 percent of all the housework." (Episode 3, Series 1) The working woman also admits to doing the bulk of the housework, saying that the husband just occasionally "helped out" in the house. She argues that she is too "kind," and avoids conflicts with both her husband and her teenage children over helping more in the house. The husband's job involved a huge amount of traveling, and when he was at home he enjoyed watching TV: "When he is home, he likes to sit in his chair and watch TV, from when he comes home, until he goes to bed." (Episode 3, Series 1)

The program displays no explicit political edge in terms of advocating women's rights or pinpointing inequalities in society. Gender roles do not contribute to any dramatic culture clash or conflict scenes, although the two wives made quite different lifestyle choices and had different ways of organizing daily life. Part of the explanation for the lack of culture clash was that producers had chosen two families who already knew each other and lived in the same district.

Urbanity and Rurality

Compared to the United Kingdom, class conflicts are seldom articulated in Norway, which has a historical and political tradition as an egalitarian society. Economic differences between the different social groups are relatively minor, although they have grown in recent years. However, the differences between postmodern urbanity and rural traditionalism include not only lifestyle differences, but also elements of cultural division.

In the episodes of *Wife Swap* that were analyzed, the contrasts between lifestyle were first and foremost related to differences in the rural way of life in the outskirts of the city, and the urban city lifestyle. One episode of the Norwegian version illustrates this. For the purpose of analytical clarity, we use the terms "urban wife" and "rural wife" in the following discussion.

A narrative device often used by *Wife Swap* to underline contrasts is the "fish out of water" metaphor, which, especially in the scenes where the rural wife (who lives on a farm) shops in the city, is played as comedy. For instance, we are invited to laugh when she is confused by the variety of different products and the choices thrown up by contemporary consumer culture. Also, in negotiating the traffic in Oslo she is portrayed as a clumsy stranger in town. She obviously does not know about traffic rules, and walks straight out into a street busy with buses and trams. The scene is shot in an area of Oslo that has very high buildings and a totally urban look, so that she seems particularly out of her element. Likewise, the urban wife is portrayed as a "fish out of water" when she has to feed the farm animals and milk the cows. She behaves unnaturally and is ill at ease with the challenging tasks and the wilderness environment. In one episode the children visited their mother in her "new" home, and the urban children comment on the bad smells coming from the animals, and are shown as uncomfortable with life in the countryside.

Additionally, the choices of location highlight the contrast between urban and rural. The primary locations are the city apartment and the farmhouse, and their respective surroundings. The open landscape and fresh air of the countryside are contrasted with the narrow apartment and indoor lifestyle in Oslo. In the introductory scenes, the urban home is presented as a particularly small flat in an apartment building, and the wife complains about the limited space for a family which on some week-ends includes six people. The rural wife expresses harsh skepticism toward the other family's home when she arrives in the city: "This flat is very tiny and narrow. I would become claustrophobic living like this" and in contrast, idealizes life in the countryside, describing her home as situated on "the top of the world."

This statement refers to the advantages of living in an open landscape suitable for outdoor activities and a healthy lifestyle. The farmhouse is presented through overview pictures of nature and wildlife, and the indoor setting is characteristically traditional with a large living room and old-fashioned interiors. During the car ride to the farmhouse, the urban wife expresses unfamiliarity with her new environment: "Oh, they are taking me out of . . . civilization!" (Episode 1, Series 2) Her preference for urban life is emphasized in the "new rules" she presents to the rural family, which include going to a café in the nearest city with her "new" husband. The rural husband agrees to go to the café with her, although very reluctantly ("I'm not used to that") and when at the café makes an ironic remark about the "café latte trend," which has become an icon of the urban lifestyle.

The fact that Norway has been transformed relatively quickly, from an agricultural to a post-industrial society, has raised questions related to values and life choices. Traditional values from Norwegian agricultural society have been challenged by industrialization, globalization, urbanization and a change toward a more consumerist lifestyle. These influences have not impacted equally on the whole country, however, and the contrast between urban and rural lifestyles is among the main cultural and social divides in contemporary Norway. The producers exaggerate certain aspects of the rural and urban characters, and the portrayal of difference is based on stereotypes of life in the city and life in the country.

Traditionalism and Modernism

Norway is an ethnically homogenous society despite the recent growth in the immigrant population, which has raised some political concerns, especially from the populist right-wing parties. In general, however, Norwegian society has not changed dramatically, and is still quite traditional and conservative. The influence of the immigrants has contributed to new cultural trends, for example, exotic food and music. The Norwegian *Wife Swap* made no comment on the tensions between immigrants and Norwegians that have surfaced in some areas, because the producers did not select any families who were not indigenous Norwegian. However, the general tensions between Norwegian traditionalists and changing modern values were addressed.

In an episode from the second season of the Norwegian version, a wife with eccentric and alternative values was contrasted with a traditional and pragmatic wife. This contrast resulted in a scene where the traditionalist wife muses on the modern wife's beliefs in reincarnation and UFOs, and her involvement in healing, meditation and rhythm therapy as extremely strange. The traditionalist wife shows no interest in searching for a deeper meaning or contemplating extraterrestrial beings. Rather, she lives a simple life, involved with everyday concerns, and believes in honest hard work. Another scene that illustrates the differences in the families' lifestyles is where the modern wife—a vegetarian—reads the traditional wife's house manual. The urban wife exclaims sarcastically: "These people are meat-eaters!" (Episode 1, Series 1) Conversely, when cooking a vegetarian meal for her "new" family, the traditionalist wife characterizes the "fake" (i.e., reconstituted from soya or some other plant) meat, in an oral dialect typical of rural Norway: "This meat isn't real meat." The traditional wife lives in a farmhouse in the country, and her family has a traditional nuclear structure (mother, father and children), while the urban wife lives in Oslo, and has a typical "postmodern" family comprising a couple and their respective two children from previous relationships, who live with them part-time. The Norwegian version of *Wife Swap* illustrates the ongoing tension between traditional family values and those of the modern urban-dweller. The program provides participants with an opportunity to inhabit a different part of the Norwegian culture and, thus, to get a glimpse of how a family from a culturally different part of their country lives its life, and experience the challenges it faces.

Harsh Confrontation in United Kingdom, Cozy Conversation in Norway

The life experiment of *Wife Swap* could lead theoretically to changes in the participants' lifestyle and values. However, by the end of the show, in both the British and the Norwegian versions, the differences between the families often seem to have been reinforced, and the alliances between the original couples strengthened by the "intruders" having challenged their everyday lives and tried to impose changes on their routines.

The *Wife Swap* format typically includes a scene of closure when the two families meet and discuss their experience of swapping wives for ten days. At the end of each episode when the two couples come face-to-face and review their experiences it is evident that neither of the "wives" has been through any transformation, though many declare that they have learnt something. In general, the couples express pleasure in a new experience and at having been through a challenge. The conclusion of the program signals that the original couples will return to their own homes, and continue life as before, perhaps with some small adjustments after reflecting on what they have experienced. The conversation at the end of the episodes includes an evaluation of the life experiment, where they generally conclude that they belong in their "natural environments." This might be seen as a reinforcement of the class structures and social divides in society, underlining the fact that although people are offered the possibility to change, they are reluctant to cross the boundaries of class, gender or ethnicity because of their strong sense of belonging to certain social groups.

So far, the U.K. and the Norwegian versions of the format have followed broadly the same pattern. However, the tone and style of the closing scenes of the two versions show significant divergence; British *Wife Swap* often offers an explosive climax to the narrative, while Norwegian *Wife Swap* concludes with polite conversation and a light-hearted evaluation of the life experiment. The U.K. series often descends into personal insults and has degenerated into physical violence at least once in the life of the format. Arguments are common, and frequently heated, leading to accusations such as "trollop," "evil cow" and "fucking bitch!" (The program goes out after 21:00, which is the watershed for U.K. broadcasters, after which adult content is permitted.)

In the Norwegian version, the couples talk about their experience in a friendly manner, which involves funny remarks and lots of laughter. In the episode on urban versus rural living, the husband living in the city comments to the husband living in the countryside: "Thanks for letting me borrow your wife!" And in the same episode, the rural wife is genuinely surprised that her husband agreed to visit a café and comments: "You, at a café!" (Episode 1, Series 2) This denouement usually takes place in the house of one of the families or on "neutral ground," such as in a restaurant or a café. In the urban-rural episode, the two couples meet up in the large farmhouse. They sit with their original partners, opposite one another, as if in two teams, evaluating a contest on everyday living. The couples seem relaxed in the company of their original life-partners, and relieved to finally return to their own homes and lifestyles.

Trans-National Reality TV

Recent tendencies of *globalization* of the business model of television, and a following *standardization* of the content contrasts television's tight connection to *everyday life*, in particular local and *national* cultures.

This chapter has investigated the paradox between the trans-national travel of formats and the need for television to communicate with its local audiences. Drawing on a case study of the U.K. and Norwegian versions of the British format *Wife Swap*, the chapter has demonstrated that a format with a track record in the original market is not a guaranteed success in other countries, and that the lack of "cultural proximity" can become a key reason for the failure in a new market.

The comparative study of the Norwegian and U.K. versions of *Wife Swap* documented that the formula were similar in the two productions: the casting of polarized couples, the dramatization of differences between their lifestyles; and the closing reinforcement of each couple's status quo. This reflects the format's adaptability to different national contexts, and supports arguments that formats can travel across different countries because they relate to general aspects of being human and contemporary dilemmas: "The DNA of formats is rooted in the cultural values that transcend the national."[32] The fact that the format has had only modest success in the Norwegian market, and ran for only two seasons while the U.K. equivalent was a formidable multiple-season ratings hit, is a reflection of significant differences between the two national contexts within which *Wife Swap* was produced and consumed. The U.K. version of *Wife Swap* focused on extreme contrasts related to gender roles, class and race, while the Norwegian version focused on urban-rural and traditional-modernist divisions. The British version permits greater confrontation between participants. We may hypothesize that this made it more entertaining and "TV-friendly" than the version produced by the more emotionally repressed Norwegian society. As shown in the comparative analysis, the Norwegian version did not include harsh confrontations or name-calling, while these elements were central in the U.K. version.

In addition to the lack of "cultural proximity," the trans-national travel of *Wife Swap* included a move from a channel with PSB obligations and also experience in the production of hybrids of observational documentary and Reality TV. The public service obligations of the U.K. Channel 4 in terms of "representing cultural and ethnic minorities" have had an impact on the production values and institutional functions of the format; *Wife Swap* U.K. was not meant to be pure entertainment, but also to enlighten the viewers. The U.K. version of the series addresses societal conflicts and tensions in today's United Kingdom seriously, but also spectacularly and controversially. The Scandinavian TV3 has no public service remit, and thus did not have to "justify" their involvement in Reality TV,[33] and thus did not include genre conventions from documentaries such as the educational voice-over. The creative, symbolical and industrial investments in the Norwegian versions were not high enough to engage the public with a style and content of cutting-edge societal relevance. Quite paradoxically, a public service remit may be argued to permit a more direct engagement with societal conflicts and tensions, but also more spectacularly and controversially, than a commercial channel with no obligations.

The study demonstrated that trans-national travel of social experiment Reality TV formats is shaped by differences between national media environments, diverging socio-cultural factors, local cultural heritage and national identity. These formats can, and have been, successfully adjusted to a local socio-cultural environment, but the process of adaptation might require a high degree of research into the national culture and planning of the production based on socio-cultural factors. The trans-national travels of realities in these formats might come in conflict with the national realities in the new markets, and thus hardly connect with the domestic audience. In some cases, it might even be more economically efficient to avoid the trans-national formats and their imported realities, and trust the potential of the locally produced narratives, at least as a supplement to the imported DNA of formats.

Notes

1. The trans-national adaptation of popular television formats is not a new trend, but the global market in formats is now very substantial (an estimated €2.4 billion in 2004—Jensen, 2007a).

2. Lane, 2002, 6.

3. Moran, 2006.

4. Biltereyst, 2004; Golding, 1989; Waisbord, 2000.

5. Straubhaar, 2007.

6. Waisbord, 2004, 360.

7. Bratich, 2007, 7.

8. Cited in Rouse, 2003, quoted in Steemers, 2004, 176.

9. Mathijs and Jones, 2004.

10. Biltereyst, 2004, demonstrates that the Reality TV debate took a quite different direction on the European continent, and that the degree of moral panic and public anxiety

varies among countries. *Big Brother*, e.g., caused riots and public controversy in France, Germany and the United Kingdom, while debate quickly dissipated in most Northern European and Scandinavian countries.

11. Jensen, 2007a.
12. Hill, 2005, 2007.
13. Waisbord, 2000.
14. Steemers, 2004.
15. www.timesonline.co.uk, published July 5, 2006.
16. Steemers, 2004.
17. Dover and Hill, 2007.
18. Steemers, 2004.
19. SMRI, 2000.
20. McNair, 2002.
21. Giddens, 1999, 165.
22. Palmer, 2002, 178-189.
23. Thomas and Dorling, 2007.
24. Hofstede and Hofstede, 2005.
25. Channel 4 originally legitimized its production of *Big Brother* in public service terms, and the 2007 *Celebrity Big Brother* scandal concerning Jade Goody and her alleged racism toward Bollywood star, Shilpa Shetty, was defended by the channel as valid engagement with the racism issue.
26. Communications Act 2003.
27. Dover and Hill, 2007, 26.
28. Media Guardian, October 8, 2003.
29. Grindstaff, 1997.
30. The first company to adapt *Wife Swap* was the distributor and broadcaster Viasat, owned by the Swedish media conglomerate MTG, broadcasting from London. The target markets of Viasat are the Nordic and the Baltic countries, and its umbrella channel TV3 has become an established trans-national brand.
31. www.kampanje.com, August 18, 2004.
32. Waisbord, 2004, 368.
33. See Hill, 2007.

References

Biltereyst, Daniël. "Reality-TV, troublesome pictures and panics; reappraising the public controversy around reality-TV in Europe." In *Understanding Reality Television*, edited by Su Holmes and Deborah Jermyn. London: Routledge, 2004.

Bratich, Jack. "Programming Reality. Control Societies, New Subjects and Powers of Transformations." In *Makeover Television. Realities Remodelled*, edited by Dana Heller. London: I.B. Tauris, 2007.

Dover, Caroline and Annette Hill. "'Mapping Genres': Broadcaster and Audience Perceptions of Makeover Television." In *Makeover Television. Realities Remodelled*, edited by Dana Heller. London: I.B. Tauris, 2007.

Enli, Gunn Sara. "Redefining Public Service Broadcasting." *Convergence* 14, no. 1 (2008): 105-120.

Giddens, Anthony. *Runaway World: How Globalisation is Reshaping our Lives*. London: Profile Books, 1999.

Grindstaff, Laura. "Producing Trash, Class and the Money Shot: A Behind-the-Scenes Account of Daytime TV Talk Shows." In *Media Scandals: Morality and Desire in the Popular Culture Marketplace*, edited by James Lull and Stephen Hinderman. Cambridge, U.K.: Polity Press, 1997.

Hill, Annette. *Reality TV: Audiences and Popular Factual Television*. London: Routledge, 2005.

———. *Restyling Factual TV: The Reception of News, Documentary and Reality Genres*. London: Routledge, 2007.

Hofstede, Geert and Gert Jan Hofstede. *Cultures and Organizations: Software of the Mind*. New York: McGraw Hill, 2005.

Holmes, Su and Deborah Jermyn (eds.). *Understanding Reality TV*. London: Routledge, 2003

Jensen, Pia. *Television Format Adaptation in a Trans-national Perspective: An Australian and Danish Case Study*, unpublished Ph.D. thesis, Aarhus University, Denmark, 2007a.

———. "Danish and Australian Television: The Impact of Formation Adaptation." *Media International Australia*, no. 124, August (2007b): 119-133.

Lane, Shelley. "Format Rights in Television Shows: Law and the Legislative Process." *Statute Law Review* 13 (2002): 24-49.

Mathijs, Ernest and Janet Jones (eds.). *Big Brother International. Formats, Critics, Publics*. London: Wallflower Press, 2004.

McNair, Brian. *Striptease Culture: Sex, Media and the Democratization of Desire*. London: Routledge, 2002.

Moran, Andrew. *Copycat TV. Globalization, Programme Formats and Cultural Identity*. Luton, U.K.: Luton University Press, 1998

———. *Understanding the Global TV Format*. Bristol, U.K.: Intellect, 2006.

Palmer, Gareth. "Producing Incivilities-Neighbours From Hell." In *Television Discourses and the Real*, edited by James Friedman. New Brunswick, N.J.: Rutgers University Press, 2002.

———. "*Extreme Makeover: Home Edition*: An American Fary Tale." In *Makeover Television: Realities Remodelled*, edited by Dana Heller. London: I.B. Tauris, 2007.

Steemers, Jeanette. *Selling Television. British Television in the Global Marketplace*. London: British Film Institute, 2004.

Stirling Media Research Institute (SMRI). *Consenting Adults?* London: Broadcasting Standards Commission and Independent Television Commission, 2000.

Straubhaar, Joseph. *World Television: From Global to Local*. London: Sage, 2007.

Thomas, Bethan and Daniel Dorling. *Identity in Britain: A Cradle-to-Grave Atlas*. London: Policy Press, 2007.

Waisbord, Silvio, Watchdog Journalism in South America,: News, Accountability, and Democracy. New York: Columbia Univeristy Press, 2000.

———. "McTV: Understanding the Global Popularity of Television Formats." *Television & New Media* 5, no. 4 (2005): 359-383.

Part 4
TRANS-AUDIENCE

Chapter 15
A Short Introduction to Trans-Audience
Nico Carpentier

The notion of audience is one of the most pervasive in the field of mediated communication. It circulates within the media organizations that are desperately in search of it[1]—within our everyday lives and, of course, within communication and media studies. In some cases, it has achieved the status of a living entity, as something that thinks, wants and desires, "a huge, living subject."[2] But the ubiquity of the audience concept does not contribute to the establishment of a consensus on its definition, nor does the multitude of media technologies and media organizations (leading to so-called audience fragmentation and strategies of constructing target audiences) assist in capturing this concept.

Different strategies have been developed to deal with the overabundant definitions of audience, and its shifting meaning. One approach is to chart these numerous definitions, for instance, by linking them to specific research traditions or core dimensions;[3] another approach is to energetically defend a specific articulation. A radical strategy is to abandon completely the "outdated" concept of audience, since we are being confronted with the so-called "breakdown of the referent for the word audience in the communication research."[4] As the audience concept aims to capture a very real, but also very specific type of human activity (namely the attention that people attribute [up to a certain extent] to a specific medium, or to a component of that medium), it would make little sense to abandon the concept for reasons of articulatory complexity.

But at the same time, we should recognize that the audience concept is highly reductive in terms of how it incorporates a wide variety of human identities and practices within one signifier, privileging media-related behavior and consumption, and serves the agenda of media-centeredness. Arguably, this hegemonic strategy functioned reasonably well, until the frontier with its constitutive outside, the media professional, crumbled. While originally audience activity was limited to the possibilities for active interpretation and signification (situating audience activity mainly at the idealist level), the activities of audience members increasingly are entering the field of material practices. Although one should be careful about assuming that material audience activity is entirely new,[5] this type of material audience activity has become mainstreamed.

These transgressions into the territory that once almost exclusively belonged to media professionals, merits the use of the trans-audience concept, as this captures the conceptual hybridity that is triggered by the contemporary audience praxis. Although these active audiences remain audience members, they also become participants or "produsers,"[6] which is a structural transgression of their status as "ordinary" audience members (as exemplified by the notion of user-generated content).

Notes

1. Ang.
2. Ang, op. cit., 61.
3. Carpentier.
4. Biocca, 127.
5. See, e.g., the activities of non-professionals in alternative or community media.
6. Bruns.

References

Ang, Ien. *Desperately Seeking the Audience*. London and New York: Routledge, 1991.

Biocca, Frank A. "The Breakdown of the 'Canonical Audience'." *Communication Yearbook* 11 (1988): 127-132.

Bruns, Axel. *Gatewatching: Collaborative Online News Production*. New York: Peter Lang, 2005.

Carpentier, Nico. "The Identity of the Television Audience: Towards the Articulation of the Television Audience as a Discursive Field." In *Het on(be)grijpbare publiek / the ungraspable audience: een communicatiewetenschappelijke exploratie van publieksonderzoek*, edited by Nico Carpentier, Caroline Pauwels and Olga Van Oost, 95-122. Brussels: VUBPress, 2004.

Chapter 16
Trans-Audiencehood of *Big Brother*: Discourses of Fans, Producers and Participants
Mikko Hautakangas

Public Discourses on Reality TV

In public discussions ranging from the statements made by political and religious elites to discussions in tabloid papers and workplaces, the *Big Brother* format has been used to symbolize a broad array of current cultural phenomena. And academic interest in the subject is similarly wide and many-sided.[1] From the media studies point of view, there are many issues that make *Big Brother* interesting; one could even say that most trends and characteristics of contemporary (TV) entertainment production feature in it.

One of the most studied aspects of *Big Brother* is reception. The high level of audience interaction in this multimedia format has provoked discussions about the new, more participative role of audiences. Alongside the simultaneous growth of the Internet and the emergence of so-called "Web 2.0," or "social media,"[2] the huge audience participation in *Big Brother* and other so-called "Reality TV" formats suggests that in the current media culture, the lines between production and consumption are blurring and audiences are becoming more and more able to voice themselves. Many scholars have pointed to the potentially democratizing effects of such developments, and even proposed that they could provide the basis for more transparent political decision-making and knowledge production practices.[3] The phenomenon has also prompted questions about the possible need to rework the cultural studies' view of active audiences, as the "audience activity" is not limited to potentially "resistant" decoding processes ("reading against the text"), but also includes actual intervention in the text.[4]

There are other aspects that make *Big Brother* stand out as "new" and a "sign of the times." For instance, the display of "ordinary people" in *Big Brother* has inspired some re-thinking of the premises of celebrity studies.[5] *Big Brother* is also a prime example of the international format trade and novel product placement practices.[6] But, despite its innovations, *Big Brother* can also be studied within the more traditional framework of the "culture industry": it is produced and broadcast within the economic and political structures and conventions of commercial TV production and from that perspective, the roles and power relations between production and reception are far from being completely new or transformed. From a critical point of view, it is possible to see the participatory aspects of "new media" as an ever more efficient way of producing subordination and "false consciousness"[7]: it can be argued that by foregrounding the surface level of volatile participation and the freedom of (consumer) choice, the structural power relations and the ideological "interpellations"[8] are masked. This critical approach avoids overemphasizing the democratizing and "empowering" effects of participatory entertainment and reminds us that many interactive elements, such as voting or online discussion forums, are incorporated at the surface level of the media products in order to increase audience commitment; in other words they work as marketing tools. From this viewpoint participation in media culture, no matter how well-informed and media-literate, "doubles" for participation in maintaining and re-producing the existing system and power relations.[9]

In my view, this focus on the level of structures is a useful reminder of the limitations of "participation" within the constraints of the commercially-driven hegemonic "culture industry." However, it runs the risk of deeming *all* participation in media culture as ultimately non-democratizing, and undermining the overall (social and cultural) significance of a personal *sense* of agency, that is, the subjective experience of belonging to a culture and society. While the participation mechanisms in popular culture products, such as *Big Brother*, *Pop Idol* and the like, may not be revolutionary in terms of the power structures of media production, they can be studied as symptoms of larger socio-cultural attitudes and potentials. Instead of celebrating the "new media democracy" of increased audience involvement, we need to recognize the framework that steers and controls this participation (for both audience and producers); similarly, instead of dismissing interaction and changes in audience-production relationships as superficial and ultimately politically void, we need to place these dynamics in their socio-cultural contexts, as lived experiences.

The relationship between media production and consumption is often pictured as being between "the inside" and "the outside," or between "above" and "below." Even if audiences are treated not as passive masses but as active individuals, often the production is still seen as faceless "machinery." So, perhaps understanding the subjective experience of being involved in the production could provide new aspects on "active audiences" and "hegemony in practice."

It is important, therefore, to add to the theoretical discussion by way of specific empirical analysis. As Jane Roscoe puts it: "Debate cannot be moved along if an idealized, consolidated formation of *Big Brother* is simply conscripted onto an already formed position, as an exemplary text put into the service of a highly political argument."[10] Although there is a great deal of academic interest in *Big Brother*, empirical analyses focus primarily on the reception processes—the audience experience, and pleasure, fan culture and participation, and multimedia use,[11] while studies on the production "and on the participants are scarce."[12]

In this chapter, I continue the study of Reality TV audiencehood by examining both the audience experience and the relationships among the three "core actors" in Reality TV: the producers, the participants and the audiences.[13] The aim is to map the experiences of these people most intensely involved with the *Big Brother* media event. In particular, I am interested in how these people with different statuses negotiate their subject positions and describe their different viewpoints on authorship and power.

I exploit the rich empirical research material that was gathered in a research project during the first season of *Big Brother Finland* in 2005-2006.[14] The primary material for this study consists of interviews with representatives of each of the three core groups: individual theme interviews with members of the production team (including the executive producer, casting director and script writer, and editors and production assistants); similar theme interviews with the twelve housemates; and focus group interviews with audience members (seven groups of three-to-five people). The audience representatives can also be described as fans, since they were very active followers of the format, although the intensity of participation via the interactive elements varies among interviewees. Interviews were carried out in autumn 2005 and spring 2006,[15] and in the course of them, all interviewees talked about what they considered the central events of their personal *Big Brother* experience, about their understandings of the concepts of "reality" and "ordinary," and about their relation to the other two "core actor" groups.[16]

This interview material was supplemented by information obtained from an on-line survey, similar to those carried out by Janet Jones on British *Big Brother* audiences.[17] I also conducted discourse analysis of Internet discussions on the show's official discussion forum, and I also use these findings as a reference point.[18] By these means, I depict the differing yet intertwined experiences and participation of *Big Brother* fans, production team members and housemates.

Tracing Trans-Audiencehood

As a theoretical basis for studying the subject positions that contribute to the formation of *Big Brother*, it is useful to see them as complex "discursive articulations": social practices (in this case, "producing" or "consuming" media) cannot be explained definitively by the system structuring them, and corresponding identities are not fixed, rather these practices and identities are co-determined and negotiated in the discursive field.[19] As Stuart Hall stresses, this should not be seen as total independence of material reality, but the idea of discursive subjectivity does avoid the unifying or deterministic interpretations of cultural activity.[20]

This chapter follows the line of thinking, supported by prior analysis of the empirical material, that the different agency positions of *Big Brother* also are interrelated and co-determined. The different agencies of producers, participants and audiences could be depicted as intertwining and overlapping spheres that "leak" into each other, allowing the core players to move between multiple identities in the discursive space of the *Big Brother* experience: the audience and the producers are sometimes subjected to gaze alongside the housemates and become "part of the text"; the producers and the housemates observe the real-time unfolding of events with fan-like enthusiasm; and housemates and audiences partake in the production and progression of the show.

It is suggested here that this multi-positional subjectivity of belonging to the *Big Brother* discourse can be referred to as trans-audiencehood, since the practices of "audiencing"—observing, watching, keeping track of, and being affectively engaged—are central to the *Big Brother* discourse and experience. It is important to note that this trans-audiencehood is not limited to the format's sphere, as it enters into contradictory relationships with an "other": audiences, producers and housemates alike intensively follow the surrounding media publicity and public talk. This echoes Couldry's idea of media as an "exemplary center" of contemporary society: media are perceived as an access to the naturally existing social world, as a mythical center where meaningful social life is condensed. Couldry suggests that reality show participants are motivated by a wish to reach this mythical center.[21] Taking into account the fluidity of the positions described above, it would seem plausible to extend this idea of striving toward this "mythical center" to producers and audiences, as they are also "participants" in *Big Brother*.

From the point of view of "audiences" in the conventional meaning of the word, *Big Brother* means a major shift in the understanding of "active audiences"; it means a switch in the focus from what audiences "do with the texts" to the interrelations between audiences, texts and production.[22] This leads to a re-evaluation of the positions of production and text: the production becomes the management of content, relations and images (rather than "encoding"), while the "text" expands to cover not only the represented text, but the entire media coverage. In the case of *Big Brother*, the object of interest is not only, or even primarily, the events occurring in the house, but includes the whole unfolding of the season, the casting, the production decisions, the audience response, the media attention, and so on.

The "fluidity" of the subject positions must not be interpreted so that the three core groups are "one happy family," who are similar, or whose differences do not matter. The "conventional" positions of producers, participants and audiences are clearly distinct and particular, and these positions—or "roles"—are well acknowledged and internalized by the interviewees in our study. Certain characteristics can be distinguished in terms of how these subject positions are reproduced discursively in the interviews. All three actor groups describe their own viewpoints and experiences as "the real/true ones," "truly their own" or "central to the format"—in other words, the sense of active agency is strong in each of these discourses. However, the method of realizing this agency differs among the groups. The participants emphasize their *authenticity* and their first-hand subjective experience in the house, stating that the "true course of events" cannot be reached via the mediated representations.[23] The producers foreground the story that builds up under their strong *control*, that is, how everything "plays out" and how it is packaged by the means of production. Finally, the audiences stress that ultimately the reception and the audience relations are the key issues in *Big Brother*, and audience *participation* and feedback inevitably define the format's success or failure.

So, the core discourses around the three agency positions can be distinguished as authenticity, control and participation.[24] For a better understanding of the suggested trans-audiencehood of *Big Brother*, I now analyze these three discourses and illustrate their interrelatedness.

That's Just the Way I Am: Discourses on Authenticity

By definition, the "authenticity claim" is an essential part of Reality TV's attraction and promise. As many researchers have noted, the authenticity of manufactured TV "reality" is first and foremost located in the "real people" who appear on the shows.[25] The authenticity of participants lies, on the one hand, in their "ordinariness," that is, in their being peers of their audiences,[26] and on the other hand, in their willingness to "be themselves" on TV, to reveal their inner feelings and thoughts.[27]

In place of a lengthier discussion on the relationship between TV and "real" in general,[28] suffice it to say here that there is a recurring, naturalized understanding in the very core of the *Big Brother* discourse that "it is impossible to keep up an act in *Big Brother*"—that continuous surveillance and public display make it impossible for the housemates to hide their "true selves." However paradoxical this idea of inevitable authenticity under extremely artificial circumstances, it serves to legitimize *Big Brother* as an "interesting social experiment." It also appears to be taken for granted by audiences, producers and housemates alike. As a result, the assessment of authenticity and "truth" is central to the sense of power and "being in control" of *Big Brother*.

The interviews with Finnish *Big Brother* audiences support Annette Hill's[29] much cited argument that the evaluation of participants' personalities and the watching out for "moments of truth" are a significant part of the pleasure in watching reality TV, and "being true self" is valued:

> And I also liked [a female housemate], although every now and then I doubted whether she was being real. I suppose I fancied the ones who I thought were being real. (Audience focus group member (f), January 2006)

> . . . I admit that I have studied psychology, so I've always been keeping an eye on that kind of stuff, so I would say he was holding back . . . (Audience focus group member (f), December 2005)

This position of being at the center of authenticity production also seems to be well internalized by the participants. While audiences may feel in control when evaluating the authenticity of what they see on screen, the participants put primacy on their first-hand experience. The Finnish *Big Brother* housemates are aware of the questions of authenticity and performance embedded in the *Big Brother* format, but the borders between these two concepts are blurred and take on new meanings in the *Big Brother* context. The seclusion and the rules of the house, the presence of the other housemates and awareness of the TV audience create an extraordinary setting, making participants act very differently from "real life." Yet this is not conceived as "inauthenticity": all the housemates stress that they were not deliberately posing as something they were not, but that a degree of "performing" was a taken-for-granted part of the experience—they were "acting as themselves." Some also stated that, at times, they had been surprised by their behavior and feelings. This would seem to support the format's basic, marketed idea of the *Big Brother* house as a social experiment, a "human rat lab," where the effects of an unusual controlled environment on the human personality can be observed.

> I just became a zombie there, totally . . . I felt like I'm not really like this, but it just means that I've never been in a situation like this before and I'm really like this in this kind of situation. (Participant (m), June 2006)

The members of the production team without exception seem to agree with the housemates' claims of being "authentic in an inauthentic situation," and this seems to apply to *Big Brother* producers across the world;[30] they also denied any possibility of deliberate or manipulative performances from the participants.

> Do you think these people don't perform? [interviewer]
> Yeah they cannot perform . . . Once in a while when they've maybe been drinking a little they try to perform, they try to get attention in a way, but if you then

think about it, and, how do we really act in a party . . . So if that's performance, yes, then we perform all the time in the life, and then it's natural that people perform, but you can't actually play a role. (Production team member (m), September 2005)

Interestingly, the producers observe the events in the house, and watch for "moments of truth" as avidly as do the fans at home. However, the producers place themselves above the audiences based on their "behind the scenes" knowledge. They emphasize a kind of psychological understanding of the housemates' group dynamics and individual psyches, and seem to suggest even that they understand the housemates better than the housemates themselves.

It surprised me that people hate [a female housemate 1] so much. And that she was such a covert manipulator. And the way she manipulates is difficult [to detect], well you can see it from the reality shows, but it's not that she's bossy but she's manipulative, and that's interesting . . . Maybe it's just a coincidence that in this group she's behaving like that. What if she didn't have a follower like [a female housemate 2] whom she's manipulating all the time, full force . . . And [2] doesn't notice it herself. It's a bit sad. (Production team member (f), October 2005)

The online survey that audiences of the first season of *Big Brother Finland* responded to also displays the myth of "moments of truth": about 85 percent of respondents agreed that it would be impossible to continuously keep up an act. This is not to say, however, that they would watch *Big Brother* as a documentary depiction of reality. *Big Brother* is first and foremost entertainment, and audiences want to be entertained. The survey revealed that while the majority of respondents (84 percent) did indeed want to see the "most authentic" housemate win, many appreciated greatly housemates who they thought were simultaneously "playing the game to the full" and "being authentically" himself/herself; that is, they liked housemates who managed to keep in mind the artificiality, and the game and entertainment aspects of their situation, without especially faking or pretending.[31] So the desire for entertainment value does not rule out the meaning of authentic personality, it is just more demanding of the housemates' personalities.

Maybe there could've been more, like, controversial stuff, more different people, now they all were very much alike . . . Once or twice they had a bit of sparks flying and that was it. (Audience focus group member (f), January 2006)

It is worth noting perhaps that the issue of nationality recurred in both the audience interviews and the Internet discussions.[32] Many of the audience members interviewed had previously seen foreign versions of *Big Brother*, especially the British seasons 1 and 2 which had been broadcast by SubTV (the network that aired *Big Brother Finland*), so when analyzing the Finnish realization of the format, comparisons are abundant. Nationality relates to authenticity and a sense of power in the way that audiences judged the housemates and their actions as "typically Finnish" (or not), and then compared them to some kind of imagined ideal of *Big Brother*.

> I've been watching the English *BB*'s, and been hooked on them badly . . . but I don't know if it's the Finnish character, sitting alone and quietly in the corner . . . [in the English version] they were really able to talk and shout at each other, maybe it's the Finnish character. (Audience focus group member (f), January 2006)

When discussing the perceived authenticity of the housemates, several audience members remarked (like the production team member cited above) that all real life social situations require a certain amount of "role playing."[33] However, as the audiences had no personal contact with the housemates, their approach to and evaluation of this "role playing" is different from that of the participants and the producers. Comparisons between the participants' screen characters and the "real life person" remain speculative, and the question of authenticity is always mixed up with the question of representation. It is not just whether the housemates are being their "true selves," but whether the representation created by the production is an accurate picture of what goes on in the house. Audiences are wary of the kind of manipulation of characters that reality programs are often accused of.

> I'm a bit skeptical, because . . . knowing that they are being manipulated, that the production team does everything possible to make it look to the viewers completely different than what actually happens, so sometimes it made me wonder if [a housemate] is actually like that or if she is just being portrayed in certain light, being a bit difficult . . . (Audience focus group member (m), January 2006)

The centrality of casting is also well recognized by the audience, and the housemates are first and foremost evaluated with respect to their roles in the social drama and the group dynamics within the *Big Brother* house (thus, not too dissimilar from how the credibility or "realism" of the characters in any TV drama is assessed).

> [There had been talk that] the production company has aimed at creating a certain role for each of them which is not necessarily truthful at all, like by editing it is easily possible to create, and by choosing [theme songs in a dance contest task] and all that, they can manipulate a little. (Audience focus group member (f), January 2006)

So, for audiences, authenticity is a question not only of whether or not they "trust" the housemates, but also of whether they trust the producers. Their awareness and skepticism provides audiences with the feeling of seeing behind the moments of truth in both the performances of the housemates, and the performances of the producers—audiences strive to "control the controllers," so to speak.

We've Been Heard: Discourses on Participation

Multi-platform audience activation is an important part of the *Big Brother* format. Different parts of the *Big Brother* entity refer to each other constantly, and invite the audience to participate, via different channels, in as many ways as possible.[34] The opportunities for interaction and for affecting the outcome are emphasized continually (e.g., the marketing for the third season of *Big Brother Finland* [2007] revolved around the slogan "Use your power!," and informing audiences that they would have "even more control over the *Big Brother* house and its inmates than before").

But perhaps audiences are not so easily fooled. When the audience members were asked in an interview about whether they believe that audiences could influence the course of *Big Brother*, the most common answer was—a hesitant—"Yes and no." Overall, viewers seem rather skeptical about the means of interaction embedded in the format:

> Sure, if one bothers to vote like 100 times . . . (Audience focus group member (f), January 2006)

> I never thought that I could personally in any way influence the show, I saw myself as just a viewer . . . It is clear that the production team must probably think about the reactions that they get from certain things and mold the show according to that, but I never thought that I would be one of those reactions that the production team would monitor. (Audience focus group member (m), January 2006)

However, when it comes to less direct means, there is a strong sense of some level of influence; there is an especially strong belief in the collective power of the discussion forum. The forum became the center and symbol of the audience activity when talking about the actions and responses of audiences (constantly referred to by audiences as well as production team members and housemates), and its role in the *Big Brother* entity continued to grow in the later seasons.

> [The audience can affect] indirectly, but not directly, only when like fifty people attack the production company on the discussion forum, then at best something may happen. (Audience focus group member (m), January 2006)

> I remember reading [on the discussion forum] that somebody wrote that hey people, keep on commenting here, our opinion has been heard. (Audience focus group member (m), January 2006)

Some audience members had had suggestions submitted to the discussion forum actually taken up and enacted in the *Big Brother* house. These were clearly very significant personal moments for these people, but nevertheless they seemed uncertain about whether they had been "heard" or if it was just coincidence.

> I once . . . suggested an army task, wrote a really long message there [on the discussion forum] saying that they could do this and that . . . OK, it wasn't until three or four weeks later that [the task took place] and it was a bit different, but those are the things when one can't help thinking that maybe somebody read it, maybe they got the idea from there . . . (Audience focus group member (m), January 2006)

> And then there was this thing with the chicken; I namely called the Espoo police station when there was this terrible storm and the chicken were just running around [on the *Big Brother* House yard], and they couldn't get into their nest, so I called the Espoo police at 3 a.m., in the middle of the night! . . . then I e-mailed the Helsinki animal rights authorities, and they started to take action, the following night they [the housemates] had to put the chicken in, and I thought the whole time that I have made this happen, when they had to run around chasing the chicken to get them into the nest. That was memorable. (Audience focus group member (f), December 2005)

The female viewer cited above also mentioned that other participants in the discussion forum remembered her for this event, which, in turn, signals the importance of recognition: as the discussion forum is an important part of the *Big Brother* experience for those who actively use it, she became another "star of *Big Brother*" among her fan community—not quite achieving the celebrity of the housemates, but becoming somewhat extra-ordinary nevertheless.[35]

When asked about the possible influence of the audience, the housemates initially were surprisingly nonchalant, just mentioning the possibility to vote. From their perspective, audiences are rather "traditional"; they are first and foremost spectators. The housemates of the first Finnish *Big Brother* did not emphasize the importance of appealing to the audience or the possibility of viewers voting with a view to creating tension and drama inside the house (a strategy that has manifested itself in the behavior of some of the housemates, and has sometimes been referred to explicitly in later seasons). The participants' thinking seems to focus primarily on life inside the house and the group dynamics, rather than how the story plays out on TV. This seems to indicate that because the first season's housemates in Finland had no prior experience of audience reception of *Big Brother* and no idea about possible viewing ratings, the imagined audience may not have affected their Big Brother experience as significantly as one might assume in Reality.[36] They were conscious of being watched, but could not be sure of the ways in which they were being watched.

Although the housemates do not necessarily recognize or mention the Internet discussion forum as a form of audience participation, its influence often emerged as a side note. After eviction, all the housemates became aware of this active "fan community." Some decidedly refrained from reading the discussions after their eviction; others joined the discussions and, by doing so, punched one more hole in the imaginary screen separating the "media" from the audience. In any case, the housemates again prioritize their first-hand knowledge of the "truth" of the events.

> Well, when one reads the stories [on the discussion forum] one really has to laugh that how could they possibly interpret something in that way? And then you see that someone had written something and then someone [else] reads it and has not even seen [the situation in question], for example, because it's been on 24/7. And then those stories escalate, like the snowball effect, and become totally ridiculous. (Participant (f), March 2006)

At the same time, audience participation and especially voting is crucial as one benchmark of success for the production company and the channel—and this was often mentioned in the production interviews. But success is not just related to numbers, it has emotional aspects as well—audience approval is a clear sign for the producers of "good TV." On the day of the Season Finale, when the first Finnish *Big Brother* had proved a ratings success, a production team member reflected in a nostalgic and slightly self-congratulatory manner:

> Now that I read the Internet [discussions] and when they are starting to say goodbye to each other, they still have tomorrow and then [the discussion forum] will be shut down, it's like for real, we've had a great influence in many people's lives, many people have spent their autumn with [*Big Brother*]. We are about one hundred [production team members] here but there are so many people who have been at home watching, voluntarily, and written [in the Internet] and they've had a magnificent emotional experience. (Production team member (m), December 2005)

It is also interesting that for the fans, the sense of being "in control" of their own *Big Brother* experience often arises from resisting the offered channels of interaction. These interactive services are often seen as tricks to rip off money, and therefore, not spending any money on the services is an important source of gratification for many:

> I kind of drew the line with my *Big Brother* fandom there that I won't do anything that will cost extra, that I didn't order any fan merchandise or else . . . at

some point I thought about subscribing to the web camera, but then I thought,
no, it's not worth the price . . . (Audience focus group member (f), January
2006)

Although the fans are skeptical about the influence of voting on the actual
outcome, it was seen as central to participating, and was usually the first thing
mentioned in relation to audience participation. It should be remembered that a
decision not to vote can also be an important affective investment, while, on the
other hand, many said that they had voted regularly although they had not
thought it would make much difference. For these people, voting obviously
served to symbolize their pleasure and fandom. The media-literate audience is
aware of the system "behind the scenes" and recognizes the media business
logic, which then seems to justify their succumbing to that system with an ironic
wink. These findings are in line with Mark Andrejevic's statements about savvy
TV audiences participating online: in a sense, audiences feel empowered by
their own understanding of and involvement in the media system, by their
awareness that any participation through the means of interaction provided is
already "part of the script." Simultaneously, through that double sense of having
and lacking control, they are subordinated into the "system" ever more
thoroughly.[37]

In sum, the discussion forum is recognized as an important location of
audience participation, power and even direct influence, by all three core actor
groups and, also, by audience members who did not participate in the
discussions. As the forum provided an open and less-controlled platform for fans
to express themselves and "join their forces," it was the most immersive and
rewarding way of participating for many fans. And, perhaps for the same
reasons, it was the scariest and most negative part of the *Big Brother* experience
for many housemates.

That's the Name of the Game: Discourses on Control

In spite of all the participatory elements, the interviewees in large part agree that
the production team has the ultimate power in controlling the overall story, "the
big picture." And there are no great objections to this: these interviewees had
chosen to participate in the *Big Brother* format in one way or another, so they
had all accepted at least the basic "rules of the game." Indeed, this metaphor of
game and rules is repeated over and over in the *Big Brother* discourse, not just in
the obvious sense of the *Big Brother* game where the last housemate standing
collects the prize, but also in the sense of the *Big Brother* format as part of the
commercial media and publicity game. Doing well in this game is the main objective for all interviewees, no matter their position in the whole. It is remarkable that the producers also feel that they are playing this game. Their "oppo-
nents" are anyone watching *Big Brother*—because "watching *Big Brother*"

means not just following the events of the house, but also watching and assessing the actions of the production team.

Indeed, those who actively follow *Big Brother* and compare the televized broadcasts and the live feed, appear to find the most pleasure from unmasking the strategies of the producers and engaging in savvy discussion about the possible motives behind those strategies. A significant feature of *Big Brother* in this respect is that it offers the possibility to view unedited footage through the real-time "24/7" streaming video service. This gives the audience the power to evaluate how well the production team performs, and those who follow the live video feed repeatedly refer to it as the "true and whole picture" of the events.

> Well I thought that especially near the end [of the season], following the 24/7, one could tell when watching [the edited TV show] that what had been like, edited out of context and sometimes put in different chronological order . . . so one got a more truthful picture by following the 24/7. (Audience focus group member (m), January 2006)

The production team members themselves engage in a dual layered discussion about their agency. Naturally, they are aware that they are commonly accused of manipulation of "reality" for their own purposest.Therefore, true to the acclaimed nature of *Big Brother* as the ultimate fly-on-the-wall reality show, members of the production team downplay their role in controlling the production. The team works in shifts on around the clock monitoring of events, but in interviews this is several times referred to as a boring task—as if to emphasize the non-invasiveness of the job. Many refer to the production as a documentary or an experiment, in which some intervention is necessary in order to achieve the most accurate results:

> We edit the reality show out of twenty-four hours. It's always a choice, one way or another, that's clear. It's a TV program. I've thought all the time that we can't do anything else except put [the housemates in the house] and observe what they do and throw carrots at them and see which one they catch and what happens next and then react. A documentary might use slightly different tricks, but we're not far away from [documentary-making]. (Production team member (m), November 2005)

Although part of the production team's job is to come up with tasks for the housemates, they maintain that the core production team claims that moments of conscious directing are rare. The following comment by a production team member illustrates that one of the female housemates had decided to quit the show, and "Big Brother" involved another housemate in persuading her to stay:

> Yesterday it happened for the first time, a conscious manipulation from our part . . . It was like the last straw, that we asked [another housemate] to come to the

diary room and asked her that have you all now talked to [the housemate who was planning to leave], you are a community, you are responsible. So we didn't tell her to go to talk to her but we let her understand that very strongly. (Production team member (f), October 2005)

While the direct manipulation and the controlling role is played down by the producers, the position of being in charge is nevertheless present in the producers' discourse. They feel that they are "on top of *Big Brother*" due to their professional capabilities and psychological understanding of the dynamics in the house (as referred to already in in relation to the authenticity of housemates). To recall the game metaphor, the producers did not invent the rules, but they are the most experienced players.

A similar distinction between two different levels of control can be found in the audiences' comments on the control and power of the production, which has clear morally normative overtones. First, the production's control over the people and the events in the house is seen as an essential part of the format, since the basic premise is that the housemates are like "human lab rats" who have to obey the voice of "Big Brother" and tackle the challenges. In fact, it was a commonly expressed view in the discussion forum that production should have used its power to control the circumstances in the house *more,* in order to create more pressure and "action" in the house. The audiences are to be served and entertained and, if they are not satisfied, this is due to a lack of effort or competence on the part of the production team, and not so much because ordinary people are just dull to watch. In fact, when criticisms were made about the housemates being "too ordinary" and thus boring, even this was seen generally as a failure on the part of production in the casting phase.

The housemates also assign this understanding of production control as part of the "game," even when it is not favorable to them.

I think it was easy to see, it's really normal, this is supposed to be, like, business . . . It's so easy to direct [the program], well yes, pretty good possibilities to influence [the program] and that's why I'd like to, at some point I was thinking that I'd like to go to work for *BB*, or Metronome [the production company] I mean, to work on something on the other side of the wall [of the *BB* house]. (Participant (m), June 2006)

But then I have talked with them, I think it was with the script writer? And he said that toward the end he wanted to make me a kind of dictator. And at that point I thought, like, how could you possibly do that? . . . And then I thought that it would have been so funny if he would have managed to portray me like that. (Participant (f), March 2006)

These interview extracts again reflect Couldry's idea of media as the mythical, coveted center: understanding the rules and involvement in the game is what matters the most, and even defeat is better than being left out. In fact, "working on the other side of the fence" in the media appears to be one of the most common outspoken motivations of the Reality TV participants.

But the less transparent forms of production control, the control over representations by technical means, such as montage editing, use of voice-overs and biased writing of *Big Brother* news bits on the Internet page, are often referred to as "manipulation" in a strongly negative sense. For example, one of the housemates, who felt that she had been "edited out of context" and portrayed as the villain of the house, states:

> Of course they [the producers] will give people what people want to see, that's the name of the game and I knew it. But it irritated me a bit when I was in that emotional turmoil [after being evicted]. And it irritated my family so much that they called the producers and they were like, cursing, but in a civilized manner, that is this really necessary? (Participant (f), March 2006)

These two forms of control, one even desirable and the other not acceptable, relate to the discourse of authenticity: it is all right to "play the game" in so far as this is done by being real, "playing fair" as opposed to "cheating." This paradox of manufactured authenticity could perhaps be compared to the use of staging and makeup versus computer retouching in photography.

What to Make of Trans-Audiencehood, Then?

To summarize, by analyzing *Big Brother* fans, production team members and participants and their interrelations, it is possible to point to the discursive practices that characterize each of these positions. The analysis of these discourses illustrates different sites of negotiating power in *Big Brother*. Defining authenticity and "reality behind the scenes" is one such negotiation. In particular, participants express their sense of being in control in this respect by emphasizing their first-hand experience. But audiences also take part in the quest for authenticity by searching for moments of truth when the facade breaks down, be it related to the performance of the housemates or the actions of the producers. The producers in their turn foreground the power of the format as inevitably revealing the "true personalities" of the housemates, as well as their psychological understanding and control of the situation.

Another site of negotiating power is the ability for audiences to take part in the *Big Brother* text via various interactive services (and in more spontaneous ways, due to the real-time event-like nature of the format). The "deceitfulness" of the commercial motives in offering opportunities to participate are fairly well recognized by audiences, and they gain pleasure and a sense of control from this recognition: they feel that they know how "the game" works, and so they feel comfortable about participating in it, either by spending money on vote-outs that they do not altogether trust, or by making it a matter of principle not to spend anything on *Big Brother*. But the true sense of participation and "power of the people" is located within the online discussion forum where their comments are seen as the voice of public opinion, to which the producers must pay attention. This power is played down by the participants, who consider audiences ignorant of the "reality" that is happening in the house. The influence of the fan community is recognized, nevertheless, as the public opinion that matters, as "the word on the street." The producers keep track of the online discussions and the media publicity, and try to manage the audience power to produce an outcome that they regard as "good TV": entertaining, emotional and profitable.

The producers have the most direct control over Big Brother authorship, which subjects them to public surveillance, assessment and questioning. The actual production team members are clearly aware of the risks—of being accused of manipulation and exploitation—and they do their best to downplay their authorial role and to emphasize the "managing the reality" aspect. The participants may sometimes feel that they have been used, and falsely depicted, which may be a source of distress and disappointment, but this is mostly accepted as "the name of the game"—they volunteered to join the rule set of commercial entertainment, where creating drama is a top priority. For the housemates, doing well in the game, handling the pressures and remaining "their true selves" are the ultimate goal and reward: their success proves that they have sufficiently strong personalities to survive within the "mediated center of society" of media. The audience, in turn, wants the production to exercise its authorial power, as they too emphasize the demand for drama and emotional highlights. Audiences place themselves in the position of customers, and the customer has the right to demand quality. Yet it seems important to distinguish between the "psychological control" of what goes on in the *Big Brother* house, which is seen as a part of the format, and the more negatively toned "manipulation" of the representation, which is seen as akin to cheating. It seems that the latter is seen as jeopardizing the myth of authenticity, and the power of "revealing" that this myth offers for the audience.

Fans, housemates and production team members are all "insiders" who have a similar critical yet co-dependent relationship with the "fourth core actor": the surrounding publicity. As *Big Brother* as a cultural phenomenon is widely and constantly discussed in numerous public contexts, any active engagement with it produces a sense of being simultaneously a spectator and an object of gaze. So the experience of (watching/participating in/belonging to) *Big Brother* is formed in the dynamics and interrelations between the three core positions (it is not the mere producing and consuming of a text). The positions of the producers, participants and audiences of *Big Brother* are essentially hybrid due to the discursive mobility that certain characteristics of the format allow and invoke[38]—these discourses are not exclusive, but can be simultaneously or alternately joined by members from all of the core actor groups. Producers, fans and participants all seem to experience some control over the production and formation of the show; they all participate as audiences; and they all see themselves in the text/object position. This multi-positional engagement is trans-audiencehood.

Although the underlying structures, such as commercial interests, format rules and international connections, are well recognized and are reflected upon by all the interviewees, the format itself is seldom criticized. Individual production decisions are sometimes questioned, but the *Big Brother* format and the logic of commercial entertainment media are not challenged. Rather, it is seen as a given rule set to which everyone, including the producers, has to comply. After volunteering to participate, one simply has to accept one's part and—to borrow a phrase from another game show—try to "outwit, outplay and outlast" the competition.

It is exactly the understanding of and playing along with this "game" that seems to provide the most pleasure from any of the positions analyzed. So a discursive practice characteristic of trans-audiencehood would be an emphasis on a kind of "media-literacy"; extreme awareness of, and playing with, the media system and media publicity, both inside and outside the sphere of the format. All three groups seek to find the "mythical core"; all are a part of it already; and all simultaneously criticize it.[39]

While it is beyond the scope of this chapter to discuss in depth the wider social, cultural or political articulations of trans-audiencehood, let me sketch some connections. In his writing on TV fans actively participating on a Internet site called "Television Without Pity" (TWoP), Mark Andrejevic states that "[i]n contrast to the image of television as a mind-numbing addiction that promotes a culture of passivity, that of TWoP-enhanced TV is one of active participation, self-improvement, and actualization, even creativity, the benefits of which, it might be added, redound on the producers by increasing the value of TV content without in any way realigning the relations of production." He concludes that "spectators take pleasure in knowing—with the insiders—just why things are as bad as they are and why they could not be any different."[40] My findings in the case of *Big Brother Finland* are similar to those presented by Andrejevic. The different actors in *Big Brother* are empowered to the extent that they feel like insiders in the media system—as long as they accept the rules as given.

However, in my view, this does not signify that things "could not be any different from bad." It is clear that there is no reason to exaggerate the significance of practices around a particular format or its likes. But these practices have not emerged either from a vacuum or into one, rather they depict a certain historical situation, in both TV as a medium and in culture more generally. Although participation in popular TV seems to be weak in producing media democratization or social empowerment, it is not impossible to believe that the practices of participation and knowledge-sharing that have been familiarized by the popular media could resonate in other contexts—where the experience of "belonging to the inside" perhaps might be more inspiring than frustrating. If voluntary and active audience participation doubles as exploitation in the discourse of commercial media, could it not also double as contribution in other discourses?

The critical point here is how the given "rule set" is negotiated and reproduced or re-worked. The relationships between production and consumption, or between providers and users, and the common understanding of the role of public participation play an important part. For instance, John Hartley[41] argues that in the digitalized media world, the metaphor of media production as "industry," where producers produce goods and, in linear fashion, distribute them to audiences for consumption, fits poorly; instead (post)modern cultural production could be described better as "social network markets" and "creative industries" where agents, networks and enterprises interact within complex and open systems. Similarly, Jenkins[42] suggests that the increase in audience participation facilitated by the Internet has added to the cultural significance of "grassroots creativity" and changed the dynamics of the traditional top-down corporate production system: producers must increasingly keep their eyes, ears and minds open to the alternative interpretations and re-workings of "their" cultural products, and accept these re-makes as valid culture. Often implicit in such discussions (either optimistic or pessimistic in tone) is the potential to open up new models for consumer-citizenship and public participation;[43] as trust in traditional institutional party politics wanes, perhaps more direct means of political engagement and citizen activity could provide an alternative?

In these debates multi-positional trans-audiencehood could provide insights into the changing interrelations between (subjects formerly known as) producers, texts and audiences, without undermining the discursive power of ideological structures.

Notes

1. See Van Zoonen and Aslama.
2. "Web 2.0" is a popularized catch-phrase for interactive internet services with user-created content, such as *Myspace, YouTube, Facebook, Blogger* and so on. See O'Reilly. www.oreilly.com/pub/a/oreilly/tim/news/2005/09/30/what-is-web-20.html (accessed November 12, 2008).
3. E.g., Jenkins, 2006; Van Zoonen; Hartley.
4. E.g., Tincknell and Raghuram; Holmes, 2004; Andrejevic, 2008, 24-25.
5. Holmes, 2004; Holmes, 2005; Holmes, 2006.
6. Fredberg and Ollila; Raphael; Magder.
7. See Adorno and Horkheimer.
8. See Althusser.

9. E.g., Andrejevic, 2008; see also Carpentier's chapter in this book.

10. Roscoe, 474.

11. E.g., Hill, 2002; 2005; 2007; Jones. For Finland, see Hautakangas.

12. However, see Roscoe; Aslama, 2009.

13. On "core actors," e.g., Richard Johnson's "circuit of the production, circulation and consumption of cultural products."

14. I warmly thank Minna Aslama for permission to use the interview and survey material that she gathered during the research project on the first season of *Big Brother Finland*. I also thank her for the extensive collaboration that initialized the writing of this chapter, and for her comments which helped to give it form. See also Aslama, "Playing House."

15. The first season of *Big Brother Finland* was aired in August to December 2005. The production team members were interviewed during this period, and follow-up interviews were conducted in spring 2006. Fans were interviewed soon after the series had ended, in December 2005 and January 2006. The housemates were interviewed a few months after the end of the series, in February to June 2006, so the most intense period of media publicity was over.

16. See also Aslama, Lehtinen and Toivanen, 2006; Aslama, 2007.

17. See Jones. The respondents to this survey were invited through a link on the official *Big Brother* website that was up for three days in November. Total number of respondents was 7,311, 84 percent of whom were women.

18. See Hautakangas: on the basis of extensive follow up to and primary analysis of the online discussions; 160 discussion threads on different subjects were collected for in depth analysis. Each thread contained postings numbering from only a few to hundreds.

19. See e.g., Laclau and Mouffe, 2001, 105-114.

20. In an interview commenting on Laclau and Mouffe's views on articulation; Laclau and Mouffe, 1996, 145-147.

21. Couldry, 2003, 116; also Couldry, 2004; 2006, 9-31. See also Aslama, 2007, 9.

22. Tincknell and Raghuram; Jenkins; Hartley.

23. See Aslama, 2007.

24. These three aspects appear to reflect issues often stressed in popular public talk about *Big Brother* (and Reality TV more generally): the role of "ordinary people" as objects of gaze; the manipulation and "abuse" carried out by the producers; and the voyeuristic role of the audience in creating demand and success for such formats in the first place. This is perhaps unsurprising, since the people involved in *Big Brother* that we interviewed are naturally familiar with the popular discourses. See e.g., Biltereyst, 2004; Holmes, 2005.

25. E.g., Hill 2002, 175-176.

26. It should be noted that the people cast on TV shows cannot be entirely "just like anyone else," but rather they are extra-ordinary in their potential to provide an entertaining TV character. However, they are nevertheless "on the same level" as the audience, as opposed to being "real stars"—people on reality shows are mundane celebrities. See also Aslama, 2007.

27. Andrejevic, 2002, 261; Aslama and Pantti, 2006; Priest.

28. See e.g., Corner, 2002; Killborn, 2003.

29. Hill, 2002, 334-335.

30. See e.g., Couldry, 2002, 287.
31. The answer options in the survey originally had these two alternatives listed separately, but many had answered "both of the above" or something to that effect in the open slot provided for "other reason."
32. See Aslama and Pantti, 2007.
33. See Goffman, 1959.
34. Fredberg and Ollila, 64-65; Rasimus, 11.
35. See Andrejevic, 2002, 36-37.
36. E.g., Holmes, 2005, 221-222.
37. Andrejevic, 2002.
38. The most central elements facilitating this discursive mobility are the "peer" quality and "authenticity" of the participants; audience interactivity and participation; the nature of the format as a ubiquitous real-time multimedia event (especially for the active follower, *Big Brother* is a "live event" rather than a distinct piece of text; see Couldry, 2002; Scannell); and the monitoring and challenging of production control that is enabled by the aforementioned characteristics.
39. I want to thank Minna Aslama once again for conversations on the three "core positions" of *Big Brother* and their relationship to the media publicity as the "mythical center."
40. Andrejevic, 2002, 35; 40-45.
41. Hartley.
42. Jenkins, 131-168.
43. See Van Zoonen; Andrejevic, 2002; 2007.

References

Adorno, Theodor and Max Horkheimer. *Dialectic of Enlightenment*. London: Verso, 1979 (1944).
Althusser, Louis. *Essays on Ideology*. London: Verso, 1984 (1970).
Andrejevic, Mark. "The Kinder, Gentler Gaze of *Big Brother*." *New Media & Society* 4, no. 2 (2002): 251-270.
———. "Faking Democracy: Reality Television Politics on *American Candidate*." In *Politicotainment: Television's Take on The Real*, edited by Kristina Riegert, 83-108. New York: Peter Lang Publishing, 2007.
———. "Watching Television Without Pity: The Productivity of Online Fans." *Television & New Media* 9, no. 24 (2008): 24-46.
Aslama, Minna and Mervi Pantti. "Flagging Finnishness. Reconstructing National Identity in Reality Television." *Television & New Media* 8, no. 1 (2007): 1-19.
———. "Talking Alone: Reality TV, Emotions and Authenticity." *European Journal of Cultural Studies* 9, no. 2 (2006): 167-184.
Aslama, Minna, Pauliina Lehtinen and Meri Toivanen. "Kaksitoista Totuutta *Big Brotherista*: Osallistujien Kokemuksia tosi-tv:stä." *Tiedotustutkimus* 4 (2006): 7-23.
Aslama, Minna. "Playing House: Participants' Experiences of *Big Brother Finland*." *International Journal of Cultural Studies* 12, no. 1 (2009): 5-20.
Biltereyst, Daniël. "Reality TV, Troublesome Pictures and Panics." In *Understanding Reality Television*, edited by Su Holmes and Deborah Jermyn, 91-110. London and

New York: Routledge, 2004.

Corner, John. "Performing the Real: Documentary Diversions." *Television & New Media* 3, no. 3 (2002): 255-269.

Couldry, Nick. "Playing For Celebrity: *Big Brother* as Ritual Event." *Television & New Media* 3, no. 3 (2002): 283-293.

———. *Media Rituals: A Critical Approach*. London and New York: Routledge, 2003.

———. "Teaching Us to Fake It. The Ritualized Norms of Televisions 'Reality' Games." In *Reality TV: Remaking Relevision Culture*, edited by Susan Murray and Laurie Ouellette, 57-74. New York: NYU Press, 2004.

———. *Listening Beyond the Echoes. Media, Ethics and Agency in an Uncertain World*. Boulder and London: Paradigm Publishers, 2006.

Fredberg, Tobias and Sanne Ollila. "*Big Brother*: Analyzing a Media System Around a Reality TV-Show." In *Growth and Dynamics of Maturing New Media Companies*, edited by Cinzia Dal Zotto, 55-72. Jönköping International Business School Research Reports (no. 2005-2), 2005.

Goffman, Erving. *The Presentation of Self in Everyday Life*. Garden City, N.J.: Doubleday, 1959.

Hartley, John. "'Reality' and the Plebiscite." In *Politicotainment: Television's Take on The Real*, edited by Kristina Riegert, 21-58. New York: Peter Lang Publishing, 2007.

———. "From the Consciousness Industry to Creative Industries: Consumer-Created Content, Social Network Markets, and the Growth of Knowledge." In *Media Industries: History, Theory and Methods*, edited by Jennifer Holt and Alisa Perren, 231-244. Oxford: Blackwell, 2009.

Hautakangas, Mikko. "Aktivoitu yleisö Suomen *Big Brotherin* internet-keskustelupalstalla." *Tiedotustutkimus* 4 (2006): 24-40.

Hill, Annette. "*Big Brother*: The Real Audience." *Television & New Media* 3, no. 3 (2002): 323-340.

———. *Reality TV: Audiences and Popular Factual Television*. London and New York: Routledge, 2005.

———. *Restyling Factual TV. Audiences and News, Documentary and Reality Genres*. London and New York: Routledge, 2007.

Holmes, Su. "'But This Time You Choose!': Approaching the Interactive Audience in Reality TV." *International Journal of Cultural Studies* 7, no. 2 (2004): 213-231.

———. "'All You've Got to Worry About Is the Task, Having a Cup of Tea, and Doing a Bit of Sunbathing.' Approaching Celebrity in *Big Brother*." In *Understanding Reality Television*, edited by Su Holmes and Deborah Jermyn, 111-135. London and New York: Routledge, 2004.

———. "'Starring . . . Dyer?': Re-visiting Star Studies and Contemporary Celebrity Culture." *Westminster Papers in Communication and Culture* 2, no. 2 (2005): 6-12.

———. "It's a jungle out there! Playing the Game of Fame in Celebrity Reality TV." In *Framing Celebrity: New Directions in Celebrity Culture*, edited by Su Holmes and Sean Redmond, 45-65. London and New York: Routledge, 2006.

Jenkins, Henry. *Convergence Culture: Where Old and New Media Collide*. New York and London: New York University Press, 2006.

Johnson, Richard. "What Is Cultural Studies Anyway?" *Social Text*, no. 16 (Winter 1986-

1987): 38-80.

Jones, Janet. "Show Your Real Face." *New Media & Society* 5, no. 3 (2003): 400-421.

Killbom, Richard. *Staging the Real: Factual TV Programming in the Age of "Big Brother."* Manchester: Manchester University Press, 2003.

Laclau, Ernesto and Chantal Mouffe. *Hegemony and Socialist Strategy: Towards a Radical Democratic Politics.* London and New York: Verso, 2001 (1985).

Livingstone, Sonia and Peter Lunt. *Talk on Television. Audience Participation and the Public Debate.* London and New York: Routledge, 1994.

Magder, Ted. "End of TV 101: Reality Programs, Formats, and the New Business of Television." In *Reality TV: Remaking Relevision Culture*, edited by Susan Murray and Laurie Ouellette, 137-156. New York: NYU Press, 2004.

Morley, David and Kuan-Hsing Chen. *Stuart Hall: Critical Dialogues In Cultural Studies.* London and New York: Routledge, 1996.

O'Reilly, Tim. "What Is Web 2.0? Design Patterns and Business Models for the Next Generation of Software." 2005. www.oreilly.com/pub/a/oreilly/tim/news/2005/09/30/what-is-web-20.html.

Priest, Patricia. *Public Intimacies. Talk Show Participants and Tell-all TV.* Cresskill, N.J.: Hampton Press, 1995.

Raphael, Chad. "The Political Economic Origins of Reality-TV." In *Reality TV: Remaking Relevision Culture*, edited by Susan Murray and Laurie Ouellette, 119-136. New York: NYU Press, 2004.

Rasimus, Mari. "*Big Brother* Saapui Suomeen ja Johti Monimediaalisuuden Jäljille." *Tiedotustutkimus* 4 (2006): 58-70.

Roscoe, Jane. "*Big Brother Australia*: Performing the 'Real' Twenty-Four-Seven." *International Journal of Cultural Studies* 4, no. 4 (2001): 473-488.

———. "Watching *Big Brother* at Work: a Production Study of *Big Brother* Australia." In *Big Brother International: Formats, Critics and Publics*, edited by Ernest Mathijs and Janet Jones, 181-193. London: Wallflower Press, 2004.

Scannell, Paddy. "*Big Brother* as a Television Event." *Television & New Media* 3, no. 3 (2002): 271-282.

Tincknell, Estella and Parvati Raghuram. "*Big Brother*. Reconfiguring the 'Active' Audience of Cultural Studies?" *European Journal of Cultural Studies* 5, no. 2 (2002): 199-215.

Van Zoonen, Liesbet. *Entertaining the Citizen: When Politics and Popular Culture Converge.* Lanham, Md.: Rowman and Littlefield, 2005.

Van Zoonen, Liesbet and Minna Aslama. "Understanding *Big Brother*: An Analysis of Current Research." *Javnost—The Public* 13, no. 2 (2006): 85-96.

Chapter 17
Reality TV and "Ordinary" People: Revisiting Celebrity, Performance, and Authenticity
Su Holmes

Ordinary, Real and Authentic

> Ordinariness is not much in demand [on television] any more. Even reality TV
> shows claiming to explore the lives of the unfamous turn their subjects into
> stars, [producing] . . . fodder for heat magazine. The genuinely ordinary—the
> sort of people who might wear skirts with elasticated waists, eat fish fingers for
> tea and worry vaguely about fungal infections on their feet . . . are beneath
> general notice.[1]

Geraldine Bell's description in *The Guardian* of "ordinary" people, indicates
how responses to "ordinary" people on TV are couched within discourses of
(class) taste. The references to "elasticated waists" (*read* unfashionable, cheap
clothes) and "fish fingers for tea" (*read* unfashionable, cheap food) are far from
neutral. But Bell also points to what she sees as the effective disappearance of
the "ordinary" person on TV—a statement which necessarily implies that TV's
relationship with "ordinary" people and fame has entered a new age. Bell nods
toward the suggestion that Reality TV has developed an appetite for the type of
"ordinary" people that can guarantee something close to a semi-professional
performance, or as press critic Ian Parker puts it, "the real person who can not
rustle up a heightened TV persona is asked to step aside."[2] This resonates with
broader popular assumptions about the newness of Reality TV-programming
which has offered new TV roles to "ordinary" people, and which has fostered
"new" relationships between celebrity, "ordinary" people and fame. In particular, the quote suggests an underlying anxiety about an increasingly blurred line

251

between "ordinary" people and celebrity, as well as "ordinary" people and "performers." After all, and in historical terms, "ordinary" people have more often been conceptualized as *viewers*,[3] and the drawing of a symbolic line of distinction here has functioned to legitimate a hierarchical separation between the "media" world and the "ordinary" world.[4] In this sense, the apparently changing role of "ordinary" people as performers is of central concern to the concept of the "trans-audience" explored in this book—speaking as it does to the cultural and conceptual blurring of the line between "audiencing" and "performing."

The fact that TV's portrayal of "ordinariness" may differ across genres, or that it appears to be changing over time, foregrounds its status as a media construction: something which is brought into being *by* TV. But there remains a question about the role of the historical here. In 1999, John Corner observed how TV studies had worked with a "frantically contemporary agenda."[5] Although TV historiography has since become a vital part of TV scholarship, the dialogue between TV studies and TV history remains limited. Helen Wheatley refers to "the short-sightedness of [TV studies] . . . that often claims so much for the new without rigorous investigation of the apparently 'old.'"[6] Wheatley's conception might well be applicable to conceptions of "ordinary" people on TV. That said, the purpose of this chapter is not to deny change, but to point out that while it may seem that TV "has entered the age of the ordinary,"[7] we have comparatively little sense of the historical contours of this sphere, which, in turn, impact upon how we conceptualize its political possibilities. In particular, this chapter examines the discourses of selfhood which produce the construction of "ordinary" people on TV. It seeks to explore how (primarily British) Reality TV mediates contemporary fame, while drawing certain comparisons with program case studies from the past.

So What's New? Reality TV, "Ordinary" People and Explanations of Fame

Reality TV has often been invoked to epitomize shifts in modern fame. This has been couched in both negative and positive terms, depending on whether the speaker is promoting the thesis of "cultural decline" (in which Reality TV is invoked as the epitome of regrettable shifts in the crisis of value in celebrity culture), or subscribing to the "populist democracy" position (in which a previously more elite route to fame has been "leveled down").[8] Although academic analyses have offered more nuanced judgements than those promoted by the popular press, Reality TV has nevertheless often been conceptualized as the ultimate manifestation of the fabrication and manufacture of fame. With contemporary celebrity understood as a function of the globalized economies of multi-media (and trans-national) industries,[9] Reality TV is seen as representing TV's particular production of celebrity within a post-Fordist economy. Graeme

Turner describes how Reality TV represents TV's accelerated desire to manufacture celebrities from famous scratch, turning this process into the "outcome of a programming strategy."[10] Turner sees this as a bid to exert more control over the economy of celebrity, in so far as it seeks to contain some of the contradictions and struggles which usually mark out the relationship between a celebrity and the entertainment industries. Furthermore, this structure offers a repeatable economic and cultural framework which is integral to the turnover of TV formats within the contemporary TV landscape. As Turner comments of *Big Brother*:

> [I]t is essential that each crop of . . . housemates are easily replaced by the next if the format is to successfully reproduce itself, series after series. In this regard, television's production of celebrity can truly be regarded as a manufacturing process into which the product's planned obsolescence is incorporated.[11]

The discourse of manufacture is thus seen as openly permeating both the construction and reception of Reality TV stars: in referring to Jade Goody, British TV's first "Reality millionaire" (who shot to fame when she appeared as a contestant in the 2002 [U.K.] series of *Big Brother*), Tom Mole observes how she is not simply "famous for being famous," but she is "famous for *having been made* famous."[12] Reality TV pivots on what Mole conceptualizes as "hypertropic celebrity" in which "the structure of the apparatus has become as much an object of fascination as the individuals it promotes."[13]

The political economy of celebrity is only one way in which the social significance of fame, and especially fame originating from Reality TV, has been explored. A second approach focuses on how celebrity is a cultural framework that is replacing more traditional resources for social interaction and selfhood in late modern culture. Reality TV fame has been investigated by academics and cultural critics as the ultimate means of self-validation in contemporary society. While Couldry[14] theorized the concept of the media/ordinary hierarchy (in which the media world is presented as both the central site for accessing social "reality," as well as a higher form of reality than the everyday), others have investigated how Reality TV has functioned as a new horizon of contemporary self-realization—both naturalizing, and catering to, the desire to have one's existence validated through televisual observation.[15]

Given that both Reality TV as a form (the apparent "trivialization" of factual programming), and especially Reality TV celebrity ("Trash TV" fame) have been seen to dramatize crises of cultural value, it is impossible to separate such conceptions from the low cultural regard in which TV fame has long been held. Canonical and influential conceptions of TV fame have emphasized a close identification between persona and role: TV personalities give the impression of being just "themselves."[16] As John Langer asserts, "television personalities 'play' themselves . . . [P]ersonalities are [also] distinguished for their 'will to ordinariness,' to be accepted, normalized, experienced as *familiar*."[17] Although this now needs to take account of the increasingly self-reflexive nature of celebrity culture across all media forms (and the potentially more "savvy" reading strategies adopted by celebrity consumers), Langer's perception of an elision between on/off-screen is implicitly saturated with judgements of cultural value. After all, if TV personalities are seen as largely playing "themselves" (no "skill" or effort required), it is little wonder that TV itself has been foregrounded as the totemic medium in the "famous for being famous" debate.

More recent work on TV fame is beginning to challenge these assumptions.[18] But it was nevertheless the case that early scholarship on Reality TV and fame[19] debated and explored the extent to which such programming represented an extreme illustration of these paradigmatic conceptions of TV fame. In deliberately shrinking the dimension between the self that is "on TV" and "not on TV" (and in referring back to canonical conceptions of TV fame), in 2004 I asked: "what better format for the medium [of TV] than one in which people are precisely encouraged to 'play' *themselves*?"[20] This question remains important given that, in the programs themselves, the concept of successfully "being oneself" within a hyper-reality environment continues to be validated, praised and pursued. The fact that there are differing constructions of Reality TV fame reflects the differing investments involved in the production of discourse on celebrity (from Reality TV producers, celebrity agents, to cultural commentators and academics). But given that, for us, celebrity exists only *within* representation, the contradictory range of discourses which make up the construction of modern fame should perhaps give us cause to question the idea that there have necessarily been meteoric and "seismic" shifts in this field.

In this regard, it is worth considering the significance of Gamson's[21] work on the history of celebrity construction. After studying celebrity discourse in popular magazines, Gamson demonstrates how two key explanations of fame have historically engaged in a cultural struggle. On the one hand, there are meritocratic, "mystifying" myths of fame which emphasize the "unique," "innate" *nature* of the talented, inner self. On the other hand, there are the seemingly antithetical discourses of manufacture (hype, publicity, exposure). Since the Second World War, a number of economic and cultural shifts have enabled the manufacture-of-fame narrative to be "greatly amplified. It has become a serious contender in explaining celebrity."[22] Crucially, however, older narratives of fame are not rendered redundant, and the two explanations *jostle* for cultural legitimacy in the same space. In fact, Gamson suggests that by the late twentieth century, it was possible to discern strategies intended to cope with the increasing disjuncture between the two claim-to-fame narratives (which may pose a threat to the economic enterprise of celebrity). He points to the increased emphasis on the apparent exposure of the fame-making process, the construction of an ironic, mocking perspective on celebrity culture, and the increased emphasis on the power of the audience.

As I have argued elsewhere,[23] the global formats of the Reality pop shows, such as *Pop Idol*, *Fame Academy* and *The X-Factor*, are in many ways paradigmatic of this fusion. First, it is immediately clear that the invitation to go "behind-the-scenes" of fame productions, combined with an emphasis on the power of the audience, comprise the central narrative structure of these shows. Part of their claim to "reality" is that they are motored by a bid to "display" the cultural power of the "behind-the-scenes" impresarios, who once were hidden from view. The shows are undoubtedly produced for the scrutiny of a media-aware audience, a public conversant in the concept of "image" production and construction and entirely at ease with the economic logic which fuels them. We can openly see the strategies of image styling, notably quite literally the trying on of elements of a new "image" week after week, as well as occasions when the contestants are clearly dissatisfied with the "enforced" nature of this process. The audience becomes implicated in the professional knowledge, thus apparently transcending the frontiers between audience and media professionals, producing trans-audiences. Indeed, it is worth noting here that, while articulating ideologies of individualism in many other respects, these programs do not trade upon the mythic ideology of fame as "an act of individual, personal transcendence."[24] They resolutely display the collective nature of this work, and thus the Taylorist division of labor inherent in the process of image production.

However, given that the manufacture discourse ultimately represents a threat to the commercial enterprise of celebrity, these programs provide exemplary evidence of how the two claim-to-fame stories continue to jostle for legitimacy and cultural visibility. There is a clear emphasis on manufacture, but this is constantly chased by a parallel insistence on "specialness." Here, we are offered mythic constructions of the unique, authentic and *gifted* self. In terms of insisting upon an indefinable sense of "specialness" and "charisma," the use of such phrases as "you've got the 'X factor'" or "star quality" have become a convention in themselves (leading to the subsequent self-conscious title of *The X Factor*). In their emphasis on "ordinariness," "lucky breaks," "specialness," and "hard work," they are paradigmatic of Dyer's description of the "success myth" which gained mass currency in the years of classical Hollywood cinema.[25] Although not the exclusive province of stardom, the success myth is central to ideologies of democracy in capitalist society: It promises that there may be power relations and hierarchical structures, but all individuals have the potential to "transcend social constraints and reach the top."[26] In inviting the audience to shape this trajectory this perpetuates and normalizes the belief that life has its winners and losers, and that is only "natural."

It could of course be objected that such textual constructions cannot be equated with audience reading strategies—especially given the extent to which, in becoming a highly lucrative global franchise, these discourses are repeated and conventionalized, thus further drawing attention to the *process* of celebrity construction, rather than the individuals themselves. To be sure, the fact that the stars are made highly dependent on the format which produced them, exemplifies the economic logic of planned disposal: There must be room for the next crop of "product" to move in. In this regard, it is notable that relatively few of the winners of these shows (with exceptions such as Will Young [U.K.], Leona Lewis [U.K.] and Kelly Clarkson [U.S.]), have gone on to achieve any real longevity of musical fame on an international scale. Yet, given the TV popularity of these shows, as well as the huge record sales engendered by their winning artists, it would be difficult to argue that they are simply being enjoyed and consumed "ironically." But although it is not my intention here to explore or speculate on questions of audience reception, it is worth noting Gamson's[27] argument that such a representational paradigm (the articulation of contradictory explanations of fame within a framework that foregrounds the "exposure" of the fame-making process, as well as the increased power of the audience), at least *seeks* to contain such an overly "resistant" distance.

Big Brother may not be so invested in the mystifying myths of capitalist fame, and the concept of work is self-consciously understood as being evacuated from the program's construction of celebrity. But it clearly conforms to other aspects of Gamson's paradigm—not least the discursive emphasis on irony (which is less present in the pop programs). For example, in the eighth series of the U.K. *Big Brother*, contestant Kara-Louise, sitting in the house garden, muses that:

> I know you get to be some kind of minor celebrity after being in here, and it is a celebrity that is looked down upon. But, actually, I do think you deserve recognition as, watching it on TV, people don't recognize how hard it is . . . I think you do deserve the celebrity in return: it's hard work . . . I think it is an accomplishment.[28]

This excerpt was replayed on one of the format's ancillary shows, *Big Brother's Little Brother*, while the host, Dermot O'Leary asks rhetorically: "Kara-Louise—what were you thinking? It isn't coal-mining!,"[29] which solicits laughter from the studio audience. Yet such ironic distance evidently sits alongside more ideologically traditional conceptions of selfhood which serve to shore up, rather than deconstruct, the economic and cultural hierarchies which are always naturalized by fame.

"Chantelle—*you've* changed": Ordinary/Celebrity

This was dramatized particularly self-consciously by the 2006 series of the British *Celebrity Big Brother,* a series that differed from previous years in so far as the producers inserted an "ordinary" person amongst the celebrity guests. Chantelle Houghton, a "ditzy," blond, Paris Hilton look-alike and promotions girl from Essex, was required to assume the identity of a celebrity, posing as a singer from a fake girl band called Kandy Floss ("with a K"). Her task was to fool her fellow housemates into believing she was already a celebrity—a concept which exploited the vastly different levels of fame associated with the celebrities in the house (not everyone already knows everyone else), as well as the mass expansion of fame in the cultural landscape (with so many famous people populating the media climate, it is "impossible" to keep up). If Chantelle successfully fooled her housemates, Big Brother promised to grant her celebrity status *proper,* and the ultimate test involved the housemates lining up in order of fame ranking. If Chantelle managed to convince her housemates that she was *not* at the bottom end of the fame ranking, she would succeed in her secret mission. Chantelle was successful, and was told in the diary room that she was now a "genuine celebrity (you can stay)." She was asked how she would like to address her "fans," and whether Big Brother could have her autograph, before being released back into the house to enjoy a "celebrity inauguration party" with her fellow housemates (who were now aware of her secret mission and real status). As Chantelle exits the diary room the voice of Big Brother says "Chantelle—*you've* changed," to which she replies "What do you mean—what, my clothes . . . ?" while the other housemates laugh as they watch the sequence on a plasma screen.

On one level, the program literally dramatizes and exposes the synthetic nature of celebrity performance and identity: Chantelle had been able to "fake it," despite her disastrous attempt to sing what was meant to be one of Kandy Floss's pop songs. Intriguingly, her ability to offer a convincing celebrity persona was also primarily related to her display of a conventionalized celebrity (female) appearance (blond hair extensions, fake tan, designer clothes), which is itself the product of a synthetic consumer culture. The "fake" song she had tried to sing ("I Want It Now") was played at her inauguration party: this enabled the program to play out its own self-reflexive "hot-housing" of celebrity, while flaunting (it was, after all, less than tuneful) the elision of "talent" or work.

Yet on another level, and returning to the struggle between narratives of fame, this episode, and the program as a whole, remains deeply invested with the mythic "specialness" of celebrity. The entire Chantelle scenario functions to shore up what Couldry terms the media/ordinary hierarchy. Even though the media world is *not* separate from the "ordinary" world—it is part of the same world that is dedicated to mediating it, making the distinction is purely sym-

bolic[30]—the Chantelle sequence insists on the existence of a boundary: We literally "see" her cross it. This is also something of a double ideological bluff:
Chantelle is already famous simply by being mediated (she has at this point been
in the house for several days), yet *Big Brother* perpetuates the idea that fame is
mythically bestowed or conferred. Furthermore, *Big Brother*'s ironic playfulness
is at times received rather differently by Chantelle. When called to the diary
room to be given the results of her mission, *Big Brother* says "As you know, you
entered the *Big Brother* house as a non-celebrity, a nobody," and Chantelle simply listens and agrees ("Yes"). When asked if she thinks the other housemates
will still accept her she clearly hopes for their understanding: "Like you said, I
was a nobody—I hope [my fellow housemates] . . . think back to the time when
they were a nobody." Chantelle's apparent inability to comprehend the irony
which structure's *Big Brother*'s use of language here might well be seen as fit-
ting with her "dumb, blond but lovable" persona. Yet her response really only
attests to the naturalization of such hierarchies in the real world—a world in
which, to be a celebrity is to "really exist," to be rich in "symbolic and material
capital," while to exist outside mediation becomes a form of symbolic disempowerment.[31] Chantelle immediately acknowledges this hierarchy, and is only
too eager and grateful to shift across the symbolic boundary presented to her.
Finally, her winner's interview with host Davina McCall also makes recourse to
highly traditional ideologies of the self, which are in many ways more pre-
modern than modern or postmodern.[32] She not only makes frequent references to
her status as "just little old me," but when asked by McCall as to whether she
thinks she "has changed" or will change—the question previously asked with
ironic playfulness by Big Brother—she is vehement and earnest about the fact
that "I never will—I don't know *how* to change!"

As discussed earlier, Reality TV continues to insist upon the value of a constant, stable and unified self. After all, in the U.K. version at least, nobody has
ever won *Big Brother* for playing a "good game." In fact, despite the fact that it
is a game show, the concept of the game-player represents the ultimate form of
vilification in the discourse constructed by (and surrounding) the program. In the
U.K. context, this discourse of judgement remains most famously and visibly
associated with contestant Nick Bateman in series 1 (2000). When it was revealed that Nick had been seeking to influence other contestants' nominations
by writing names down on pieces of paper, he was shamed on TV by his other
housemates, and then promptly ejected from the house. Although this reflects
the opprobrium heaped on the identity of the "cheat" (especially in the context
of traditional scripts of British national identity which pivot on "fair play"), this
did not appear to be Nick's key "crime." Rather, in ideological terms, and in the
context of the social meanings of Reality TV, Nick highlighted the panoptic
weaknesses in the house's surveillance system (how had we not *seen* this going
on?), while he also embraced the concept of the multi-faceted self which can be

adapted to suit the context at hand.

It is important to emphasize that debates about authenticity have for long structured the circulation and reception of "ordinary" people as performers on TV. Writing before the explosion of Reality TV, both Jane Root[33] and Karen Lury[34] explored this fact. Lury, for example, speaks of the "uneasy ambivalence" that can structure our reception of the ordinary performer on TV. The "otherwise accepted duality of character and actor is made problematic when we witness real people perform. For if real people convincingly 'put on an act' where can sincerity, authenticity and real emotion be located with any conviction?"[35] While Reality TV may have crystallized concerns about "ordinary" people and authenticity, it can be seen that these debates are not new. A famous precursor in this regard is clearly represented by the American Big Money shows of the 1950s programs which found themselves at the center of the quiz show scandals.[36] As is well known, certain contestants were trained as "actors," and required to perform roles within a pre-planned (rigged) narrative outcome. Although the quiz show scandals invariably propagated an image of "ordinary" people as the victims of merciless broadcasters, any examination of how "ordinary" people are constructed as performers is always an examination of agency and power. As Jan Teurlings argues, while "people who appear on TV are not freely expressing their true selves," neither "are they the helpless objects of exploitative broadcasters."[37] According to Teurlings in his analysis of Love Game Shows, it is crucial to recognize that participants play a role in producing "constructions of the 'ordinary' *themselves*,"[38] even if not done on an equal terrain. Teurlings draws attention to the importance of what he calls the "structured and managed setting" in which "ordinary" people perform. This setting includes:

> Strategies of selection (through which the production crew aim to find the "right" participants for the show); strategies of form (aimed at directing the "communicative" behaviour of the participants); and strategies of content (intended to enhance the production of desirable discourses and performance of identities).[39]

This usefully points to the possibility that the scandals offered an exaggerated example of the "structured and managed setting"[40] which *always* shapes the televisual contexts in which "ordinary" people perform.

To be sure, there are certainly generic (as well as format) specificities here which remain important. For example, while Root's comments that TV employs people "*to be* ordinary" (my emphasis), and that part of "the real person's job is to be just like those watching, to act as viewers momentarily whisked to the other side of the screen,"[41] are still applicable to many traditional quiz and game shows, this is not what is required of Reality participants. From *Big Brother* to *Pop Idol* to *The Apprentice* to *Wife Swap*, Reality TV is eager to find "ordinary" people who embrace mediation, and who are only too willing to meet the camera's gaze head on. Far from accepting the medium as an unquestioned source of authority, many no longer feel that they are "too ordinary" to take part.

Reality TV and the Reflexive Self

But in terms of the extent to which Reality TV circulates discourses of authenticity concerning the construction of "ordinary" people, what is different is that this has become more fervently and anxiously centered on questions of selfhood—especially the dialectical relationship between interiority and exteriority. Much of the work on a confessional or therapy culture positions its arguments in relation to the modern conditions of the social within advanced capitalism. The loosening of "traditional anchors" in our lifecycles and social structures, such as family, work, community, gender divisions, class identity and national culture, has been a symptom of, and has helped to cultivate, the increasing emphasis on individuality.[42] In a culture where it is up to individuals to produce their own sense of ontological security, Anthony Giddens[43] famously described how we are thrown back on the resources of the self, positioning the concepts of reflexivity, individualization and embodiment as key dimensions of contemporary identity.[44] The combination of individuality and reflexivity in late modernity, as Momin Rahman explains, is "fundamentally dependent upon the increasing concern with interiority,"[45] and the expansion of therapeutic discourse has been pinpointed as exemplifying the increasing connection between discourses of reflexivity and individualization, and media culture.[46]

The concept of the reflexive self has been linked to discourses and images of the self in both make-over[47] and Reality TV.[48] Although the currency of the reflexive self has more often been linked to make-over TV (in which "labors of reinvention" are literally channeled into work on the physical self), it has also been seen as having a discursive currency in Reality TV. In an early analysis of *Big Brother*, for example, Gareth Palmer described the contestants in the first U.K. series thus:

> It should be clear that these individuals were chosen because they are symptomatic of an age in which enterprising selves utilize experience to further their ambitions . . . They see their lives as projects and work consciously on them like dieters or keepfitters or autodidacts in a night class.[49]

The concept of the entrepreneur of the self also dovetails with the wider social emphasis on flexible workers within a "flexible economy"—a culture that demands "strategic" self-fashioning and remaking, and a subject who can adapt and respond to change at will.[50] Given that this concept of a continual process of "becoming" compliments the conception of femininity as an on-going process,[51] it is no coincidence that often it is *women* who have been foregrounded as epitomizing the "ills," possibilities and "excesses" (depending on the perspective of the observer) of Reality TV fame. Indeed, whilst receiving loud cheers from the *Celebrity Big Brother* crowd when she promises not "to change," Chantelle is also encouraged in her final winner's interview to "go on and live the dream!" This transition was documented in a separate Reality show called *Chantelle: Living the Dream* (C4, 2007) which followed her newly burgeoning consumer lifestyle (by this stage she was romantically involved with fellow celebrity housemate/singer Preston from the band the Ordinary Boys), which included modeling and magazine shoots, and TV presenting auditions.

Yet precisely because Reality TV fame essentially seeks to collapse the division, at the level of selfhood, between "on TV" and "not on TV," it remains crucial for Reality TV stars to maintain a continuity of self after leaving the format/program from which they emerged (and this issue is further discussed below in relation to Jade Goody). Certainly, as Richard Dyer's earlier work reminds us, the appearance of sincerity and authenticity are two qualities that have been "greatly prized" in stars, not least because they suggest a person who bears witness to "the continuousness of [the self]."[52] But in the context of Reality TV this indicates how the emphasis on the stable self often functions to regulate (and limit) investment in the entrepreneurial, malleable and therapeutic self.

One of few analyses to acknowledge and explore this dialectic is Rachel Dubrofksy's article, "Therapeutics of the Self: Surveillance in the Service of the Therapeutic,"[53] which primarily focuses on examples from *The Bachelor* franchise. Dubrofsky is interested in examining how discourses of the therapeutic are transformed by the centrality of surveillance in Reality TV. Although traditional models of the therapeutic pivot on a desire to change the self alongside the impetus to accept or affirm the existing self,[54] Reality TV's investment in surveillance "builds on the popular trend in therapeutic culture in which subjects are constantly incited to work on (change) the self, but adds a layer in that the impetus is to assert a consistent (unchanged) self as therapeutic."[55] So successful participants are often seen to affirm the image of Reality TV's investment in "a consistent (unchanged) self across disparate and social spaces"[56] while—and this is especially true of the U.K. *Big Brother*—the idea of a "journey" is also valued (a dialectic exemplified by the case study of Chantelle). As Dubrofsky concludes, whilst much current scholarship constructs the discourse of the therapeutic as recasting social issues as the essentially private problems of the individual, her analysis both reframes and builds on such observations:

> Now therapeutic subjects can be content with who they are *and* with the state of the world around them. There is no impetus to change anything, but rather, people are invited to learn to become comfortable with things as they are.[57]

In this case, and as developed in more detail below, it might be a case of old ideologies in "new" packages.

Back to *The Family* (1974): Now and Then

As discussed at the start of this chapter, there is comparatively little historical research into TV fame, and this is especially true of the British context. Trajectories of TV fame, particularly in terms of its "ordinary" person modality, are frequently ignored, or painted in very broad strokes, as being based on canonical flashpoints or junctures. One such flashpoint was the twelve-part British documentary serial, *The Family* (BBC, 1974, Paul Watson), which is perceived as a British version of the American program, *An American Family* (PBS, 1973, Craig Gilbert). Although rarely examined in detail, or at the level of archival research, *The Family* has been positioned, in both popular and academic discourse, as the key precursor to Reality TV. Thus, it is not unusual to see the working-class Wilkins family, who appeared in the serial, conceptualized as Britain's "first Reality TV stars."[58]

Certainly, one of the most obvious links to today was the expression of distaste for what, in relation to Reality TV, Corner has since described as the "bad ordinary"—people who, "in certain dominant views [are] inclined towards the vulgar and the personally disappointing in ways [that are] unsuited to national visibility," yet are "being enjoyed by quite a large number of other ordinary people."[59] Seen as "nose-wiping, vacantly back-scratching, often inarticulate, always . . . overcrowded,"[60] the Wilkinses became a highly visible repository for the specter of class prejudice, and often found themselves rejected or contested at the level of the typical or the "real"—surely "working-class" people "aren't really like this?" Aside from the bid to locate the "ordinary" in the working-class, a key difference from the American serial was that Paul Watson pursued elements of a "live" temporality: The later editions were being filmed whilst the initial episodes were being aired. This meant that we saw the family *become* famous, responding to the press, TV and radio, and the wider barrage of media interest on screen. This created considerable debate and speculation about the effect of *The Family* on the Wilkinses' presentation of the self—although unlike Reality TV today, this was primarily played out at the level of reception, rather than explicitly encoded in the program itself.

There were also, of course, further marked differences from the culture of celebrity today. With respect to *An American Family,* Jeffrey Ruoff outlines how some critics saw the Louds' willingness to share their private lives "as representative of a therapeutic society thriving on a 'compulsion to confess,' an indication of the weakening of America's moral fiber."[61] But the idea of a confessional or therapy culture seems absent in the text/intertexts of *The Family* (and Furedi notably positions the 1980s as the decade in which therapy culture—as a mode of subjectivity—moves into the mainstream in Britain).[62] In a culture with more conservative boundaries of what is public/private, the Wilkinses' fame was also often positioned as a worrying burden or trial as much as a privilege or pleasure. As *The Sun*'s Alix Palmer wrote in her article "How our TV Family Pay the Price of Fame,"

> Three weeks of stardom. Three weeks of being dogged around the house . . . by a four or five man film crew. How has it left the famous . . . television family? Jaded, but bearing up. The Wilkinses of Reading are a tough lot, capable of giving as good as they get.[63]

Yet while this suggests a distance from the idea of fame as a means of self-validation the sense that both economic and symbolic capital might be "up for grabs" here, at the time, seemed to irk many middle-class critics. Celebrity, for some time, has been seen as in part replacing the entrenchment of older hierarchies based on lineage or class. In this respect, it often dramatizes discourses surrounding social mobility. As James Thomas commented in *The Daily Express* in 1974:

> Mrs. Wilkins, the power behind it all, clearly saw this experience . . . as a stepping stone to get out of the kitchen and the greengrocer's shop where she works. Already the people who make commercials are knocking on her shabby back door . . . Brewers are after them, so are paint manufacturers . . . We can only guess how long it will be before she is selling paint, complete with an Equity card . . .. Why did she allow it? . . . Mum said "I've got my chance now," and that seemed to me to say everything.[64]

Although the possibility of Mrs. Wilkins selling paint is hardly akin to the resurgence of organized working class militancy, the chafing against the constraints of class deference happening at the time, is worth acknowledging as the political and cultural backdrop to 1970s' Britain.[65] In terms of the undercurrent of resentment, it is perhaps revealing that James Thomas misquotes from the final episode: "Mum" says no such thing as "I've got my chance now," and it would take a truly resistant reading of this closing edition to discern an entrepreneurial pursuit of fame.

Furthermore, in episode 12, Watson's voice-over tells us that "the Wilkinses are still an *ordinary* family, despite contending with the pressures of fame and notoriety" (emphasis in original), and the footage of the Wilkinses seems to illustrate this fact. Mr. Wilkins (clearly responding to an interview question) explains how:

> I'm not going back to being a bus driver as I've always been a bus driver while the series has been on. So there's no difference in that. The only difference will be that I won't walk in and see a camera staring me in the eyes as soon as I

walk through the door . . . It won't make no difference to me. Life will still
carry on—regardless of the cameras.

Mrs. Wilkins' final comments in the serial also leave us with her hope that none
of them should "get anything out of this" as fame could be "disastrous," it "takes
you away from your family . . ."

Some of the family still appear on TV today (largely in documentaries
about documentary or Reality TV), which suggests that their fame was both
fleeting and remarkably enduring. Yet, although back in 1974 the Wilkins family participated in TV and radio interviews, public engagements and, in the case
of Mrs. Wilkins, a newspaper column and a book, there were no wider or more
concerted efforts to exploit their visibility (either by the Wilkinses themselves,
or the media industries). But despite the clear cultural differences between "ordinary" people and fame which might be seen to emerge from the case study of
The Family, it is not difficult to observe the discursive continuity when it comes
to "approved" and validated models of subjectivity for the famous "ordinary"
person. While Reality TV fame has often been discussed—in popular commentary at least—as representing an unprecedented democratization of fame, certain
British scholars have drawn attention to the deeply class-bound nature of this
celebrity, both with respect to the aspirants themselves, and the cultural reception they receive.[66] Gareth Palmer's article "The Un-dead: Life on the D-List,"
emphasizes how the media construction of Reality fame can actually often be
seen as providing "cautionary tales" about knowing "one's place":

> As the D-List is composed of people who have emerged from the audience it
> may be the closest representation of the ordinary as celebrity. An analysis of
> how such people are treated [by the media] is therefore revealing about what
> the media suggest is the correct way for us to behave, both as enterprising indi-
> viduals and as "ordinary" people.[67]

Palmer draws attention to the treatment of those who are seen to be aiming to
"prolong their fame," and the media punishment that is meted out to those who
fail to understand the "limited value of their celebrity." Save for the few who are
seen as "really making it," it is understood that "the respectable thing to do is to
return 'quietly' to . . . [one's] roots", "managing an inevitable decline with 'dignity'"[68]—the very same behavior expected of the Wilkinses back in 1974.

The reception afforded to the Wilkins family, and thus the middle-class distaste for their lifestyle, language, morals and bodies, might well be seen now as
an interesting precursor to contemporary mobilization of the figure of the
"chav"—what Imogen Tyler calls the latest figurative type in the British process
of "'class-making" which attempts to distinguish the "white upper and middle
classes from the white poor."[69] As Tyler[70] argues, celebrity culture, especially in
terms of its intersection with images of "ordinary" people, is a prime cultural

site through which these discourses are made and circulated. In this regard, and in terms of the historical and conceptual trajectory of this article, it is illuminating to consider the final case study of Jade Goody—especially with respect to the oft-cited claims about the democratization of modern fame.

Jade Goody: From "Hero" to Zero

Jade Goody shot to fame when she appeared as a contestant in the 2002 (U.K.) series of *Big Brother*. Loud, brash, "dim," "vulgar," and bitchy, the then twenty-one-year-old dental nurse from South London received variable media coverage, and was the subject of tabloid attacks on her weight, physical appearance and lack of education. The press took delight in reprinting "Jade-isms," or comments that appeared to reveal her extraordinary lack of intelligence. Yet toward the end of the series popular support for Goody emerged. The tabloids battled for exclusive rights to her "story," and while her fame remained controversial (did she "deserve" it?), she was reclaimed by popular magazines as a "national treasure."[71] Jade went on to become Britain's first reality TV millionaire (she was estimated to be worth £2 million by 2007), with a best-selling perfume, biography and two fitness DVDs.

Jade has often been invoked in the British context as epitomizing the changing face of modern fame, and it is for this reason that I wrote about her in 2004 in a chapter for *Understanding Reality TV*.[72] Yet Jade's role in narrating or mapping out the ideological circulation and cultural meanings of Reality TV fame now looks rather different. In 2007 Jade entered the *Celebrity Big Brother* house, and found herself at the center of a "race row" when, along with Jo O'Meara and Danielle Lloyd, she was accused of the racist bullying of Bollywood film star and fellow housemate, Shilpa Shetty. In generating both national and international debate, the "race row" incident is in many ways unparalleled in terms of the relationship between British Reality TV and media controversy.

Prior to her entry into the *Celebrity Big Brother* house, and despite her popular invocation as a totemic example of fabricated fame, Jade's image was not solely associated with discourses of manufacture. This is contradictorily suggested, for example, by PR guru Max Clifford when he explains how "Jade has that *magic formula* that proves you don't have to be talented to be a star" (emphasis added),[73] and by Executive Producer Phil Edgar-Jones, recalling Jade's first audition for *Big Brother*, describing that "she sort of had something—a little bit of an x-factor."[74] While many may have decried her brand of apparently "talentless" fame, Goody's image also capitalized on discourses of classed "authenticity" and "ordinariness," and one journalist commented how "her guilelessness is her fortune: in a world of spin, her seeming innocence is a unique selling point . . ."[75] Furthermore, in playing out the possibilities of self-transformation through social mobility, Jade is and was deeply *useful* to the celebrity system, and to constructions of individualism and opportunity in democratic capitalism more widely. As Jade's fellow housemate PJ Ellis from *Big Brother* 3 later confirmed: "It's the perfect story. She got herself a celebrity boyfriend [then Jeff Brazier] and a baby. She's left us Z-listers behind"[76]—a trajectory expressed here through images of escape and velocity. By the time she entered the *Celebrity Big Brother* house in 2007, Jade could effectively be celebrated for emerging as a reflexive individual, a veritable entrepreneur of the self who has created a successful self project,[77] even while she was of course required to balance this with a continuity of the self which retained her apparently "core" characteristics. (For example, Jade's perfume "Shhhhhh!" might be emblematic of "Brand Goody,"[78] but it sells because, like Jade, it is "accessible and down to earth").[79] When she was initially in the Big Brother house in 2002, *The Sun* famously christened Jade "the pig" ("YOU have the power to roast her . . ."[80]) As Biressi and Nunn observe, in bringing together misogyny and class prejudice, Jade was "'marked' negatively as working-class by her body [and] her voice . . ."[81] She was also seen as "bibulous, excessive, overweight and getting fatter as the series progressed,"[82] and as Beverley Skeggs[83] argues, there is a long history of working-class women being associated with discourses of corporeal excess. Thus, part of Jade's "re-education" post-*Big Brother* involved a physical and corporeal change and we might note that, in terms of a connection with Chantelle, it is again the figure of the white-working-class woman who is imagined as having a "raw" identity source that can be worked upon to produce the celebrity-commodity. Jade changed her hair from blonde to brunette (which in itself is class-coded) and had it cut into a sleek bob. She also lost three stone—a shift also exploited by, and linked to, her association with two best-selling fitness DVDs. Depositing a *Big Brother* "creation" in the *Celebrity Big Brother* house was very much in keeping with *Celebrity Big Brother's* highly self-reflexive play with discourses of fame, as previously dramatized by the use of Chantelle. But once the accusations of racism emerged (Jade and company were ignorant of the row while they remained in the house), there appeared to be a recontextualization of the signs which had made up Jade's persona. Signs which had previously signified one thing were now re-framed as representing something totally "other." For example, Jade had transformed her apparently poor command of English, and the media's reaction to it, into a "highly bankable asset."[84] Yet language was re-framed in relation to the racism incident: Jade, Jo and Danielle were all positioned as inflictors of mockery and, as Gies observes, "one of the defining moments of the race incident was . . . [the mocking of] Shilpa's English."[85] Furthermore, the perfume which had signaled Jade's "accessible" and "down to earth nature," a site upon which her elevated individualism and consumer capital could be reconciled with discourses of "authenticity," was rapidly re-framed as a potent symbol of Western imperialism. Press discourse quickly pounced on the fact that Jade's perfume was made in India.

Shilpa's sister, Shamita, proclaimed that this made Jade a hypocrite, while *The People* reported how "Dimwit Jade raked in £250,000 from her 14 days on [*CBB*] . . . This amounts to £744 an hour—5,314 times more than the workers at Pragati Glassworks in the industrial Gujarat region earn."[86]

The divesting of Jade's celebrity image was also dramatized at the level of corporeal presence. Not only did the word "pig" make an immediate reappearance in press headlines and articles (and interviews on Youtube.com were overlaid with pig noises), but the number of times that she was referred to as "fat" is astonishing given the reality of her new "svelte shape." This change was later made a corporeal reality in so far as popular magazines focused on reports that Jade was comfort-eating in the face of her declining career.[87] In the earliest post-eviction interviews, whether on TV or in popular magazines, Jade appears in dark colors (usually black and grey), head hung low, and her tear-stained face is devoid of the usual lip-gloss glamour. In these contexts, Jade is effectively required to relinquish the privileges of a celebrity identity. In disavowing the discourse of commercialism which underpins any celebrity identity, it became conventional to hear that Jade was not being paid for the interviews (discourses of promotion are rejected in order to foreground the authenticity of the confessional mode), and that "this wasn't about getting [her] . . . perfume back on the shelves."[88]

But with the mystifying myths of fame evacuated from the language of her image, Jade struggles to activate a convincing claim to authenticity. It would be an understatement to suggest that Jade's bid to apologize for her behavior was viewed with a cynical eye, and her initial post-eviction interview with Davina McCall is even listed as "scripted jade goody contrite interview" on Youtube.com.[89] The representational tropes of celebrity are here seen as so transparent (or hypertropic)[90] that they obliterate (consume) the individual they purport to represent. This creates a series of rather paradoxical images of Jade: She needs to utilize the language of "the media" in order to get her "message" (apology) across, but this very language also becomes a prison house of representation. This is well captured by *heat* magazine's interview with her. The magazine reports how "Jade tells us in a sombre tone . . . [that] she's worried about the picture for our shoot, she doesn't want people to think she is posing, or that she's asked to have her photograph taken."[91] The concept of celebrity cannot, of course, exist outside media representation, and the actions described by *heat* would normally be an expected part of any celebrity identity.

Perhaps most damaging of all to Jade's image as a Reality star was the fact that this heightened surveillance of her celebrity persona, the scrutiny of performance cues and image construction, led to the charge of a multi-faceted self, a narcissistic (postmodern) identity which is fashioned to suit the demands of the context at hand. Given the extent to which Reality TV stars are required to maintain a close semiotic relationship with their original on-screen personas, and the extent to which the idea of a consistent and unified identity is central to Reality TV's therapeutics of the self,[92] it may seem logical to suggest that the reaction to Jade in part pivoted on the fact that the race row had exposed an undesirable *disjuncture* between these spheres. This was very much the argument of PR guru Max Clifford when he insisted that "the person we thought we knew was a sham—[Jade] was not that person at all."[93] There may be some truth to Clifford's observation, but the logic of this argument does not entirely work. Indeed, a more revealing comment is offered by *heat* (the text "Jade's Future" is positioned next to an image of the star being sucked down a plughole), when it comments how *Celebrity Big Brother*:

> [S]ounded the death knell for Jade Goody's career. As someone who built her reputation on being a loveable, ditzy "if I can make it, anyone can" character, her constant bullying of Shilpa showed an ugly side we didn't know was there (or maybe we had just forgotten) . . . [94]

heat's comment "or maybe we had just forgotten," nods toward the fact that the specter of bullying had been attached to Jade's persona during her first appearance in *Big Brother*. (She was accused of being the ring-leader in the bullying of the slim, model-like, Sophie Pritchard who entered *Big Brother* as a new housemate once the show had begun. Furthermore, the invocation of Jade's pre-fame persona in the popular press had explicitly emphasized her role as a bully at school.)[95] The implication in *heat*'s description is that this behavior (which was associated with her class upbringing, but which had not previously included charges of racism), was meant to have been contained or eradicated as part of Jade's "re-education." Jade's re-education had apparently not been comprehensive enough. Furthermore, it needed to continue. Although her subsequent trip to India was constructed as an educative experience arising specifically from the racism scandal, the program *You Can't Fire Me . . . I'm Famous* ends with Jade acknowledging that she doesn't "regret going into the [*CBB*] . . . house" as it has taught her about unacceptable behavior ("I need help").[96] While "people like" Jade have been repeatedly held up by the media as examples of intrinsically democratized fame, not only is such economic and cultural success rare but, as the events of *CBB* remind us, "celebrity remains a hierarchical and exclusive phenomenon—no matter how much it proliferates."[97]

Ordinary/Celebrity

Writing in the context of star studies, Dyer[98] originally argued that stars and stardom offer a cultural site in which questions of cultural identity and personhood are worked through at any one time. This is also applicable to the relationship between "ordinary" people and Reality TV fame—perhaps even more so given the supposed proximity between the media/ordinary world engendered by the bid to recruit the participants from "the audience." In this respect, my aims and intentions in this chapter are multifaceted.

On one level, the article engages with the wider cultural view that there is now a greater blurring of the roles of viewer/performer. In conjunction with the growth of interactivity, it may seem that, for some, "the viewers have . . . taken over the airwaves"[99]—especially given that participation has been conceived as engendering "the disappearance of the audience"[100] in so far as its blurs the boundaries between production/consumption, or user/viewer. Yet if this heralds the possibilities of the "trans-audience" in increasingly democratic terms, I have suggested that we need to pay attention to the specificities of how the "ordinary" and the "celebrity" are constructed in Reality TV.

In particular, this article has interrogated debates about change and development in modern fame—not least because the emphasis on a radical break with "the past" has made a very successful bid for cultural legitimacy and acceptance. Indeed, with regard to contemporary celebrity culture, it is rare to find an acknowledgement of how, as Jessica Evans observes, "[change] often happens in a small-scale, piecemeal fashion, so that elements of the 'old' are reformulated and combined with new developments."[101] One of the challenges here, then, is to keep this balance in play. While it certainly remains important to respect the specificity of particular formats when it comes to mediations of the "ordinary" (what *The X-Factor* requires is different from what *Big Brother* requires, which in turn is different from *Wife Swap* or *The Apprentice*), this chapter has examined this potential dialectic of old and new. This underlines the importance of further research into the historical "ordinary" when it comes to ascertaining the political possibilities and implications in the relationship between "ordinary" people, visibility and fame.

If such constructions can be seen as dramatizing and working through models of selfhood it would seem that while Reality TV is often associated with reflexive models of identity, the case studies here may demonstrate some of the major criticisms which have been leveled at such models—namely that they ignore the social structures in which such fashioning takes place, including the socially differentiated restraints on agency (ethnicity, class, gender).[102] In fact, it is still (a more Foucauldian)[103] conception of the *regulated* self that seems most pertinent when it comes to analysis of how such fame can function. If celebrity is as much a form of "disciplinary regime" (especially where discourses of class and gender are concerned), as a force of social mobility, it is clear that the study of power *within* TV's "democratization" of the "ordinary" will keep us on our toes.

Notes

1. Bell, Geraldine, "Fiction: Very Ordinary People," the *Observer,* March 28, 2004, 15.
2. Quoted in Piper, 274.
3. Couldry, 2003, 45.
4. Ibid.
5. Corner, 1999, 126.
6. Wheatley, 4.
7. Teurlings, 249.
8. Evans, 13.
9. Rahman, 134.
10. Turner.
11. Turner, 155.
12. Mole, "Hypertrophic Celebrity," *Media-Culture*.org, October 2007. journal .media-culture.org.au/0411/08-mole.php (accessed October 10, 2007) (emphasis in original).
13. Mole, "Hypertrophic Celebrity," *Media-Culture*.org, October 2007. journal .media-culture.org.au/0411/08-mole.php (accessed October 10, 2007).
14. Couldry, 2000.
15. Biressi and Nunn, 99.
16. See Ellis; Langer.
17. Langer, 355 (emphasis in original).
18. See Bennett.
19. Holmes, 2004a; Turner.
20. Holmes, 2004b, 115.
21. Gamson.
22. Gamson, 144.
23. Su Holmes, 2004b.
24. MacDonald, 65.
25. Dyer.
26. MacDonald, 65.
27. Gamson, 1994.
28. *Big Brother* (Channel 4, August 6, 2007).
29. *Big Brother's Little Brother* (Channel 4, August 8, 2007).
30. Couldry, 2000, 44.
31. Couldry, 10.
32. See Kellner.
33. Root.
34. Lury.
35. Lury, 126.
36. See Boddy.
37. Teurlings, 259.
38. Teurlings, 256 (emphasis in original).
39. Teurlings, 253.
40. Teurlings, 253.

41. Root, 97.
42. Rahman, 135.
43. Giddens.
44. Giddens' concept of reflexivity should not be collapsed with the concept of self-reflexivity—as attributed to the construction of celebrities and Reality shows earlier in the article. Although both dwell self-consciously on the discursive construction of the self, I use reflexivity here to refer to specific identity structures in modern society, and self-reflexivity to indicate a self-referential form or representational process.
45. Rahman, 136.
46. Rahman, 136.
47. Ouellette and Hay.
48. Biressi and Nunn, 2005.
49. Palmer, 306.
50. Ouellette and Hay, 103.
51. Ouellette, 119.
52. Dyer, 19.
53. Dubrofsky.
54. Furedi.
55. Dubrofsky, 268.
56. Dubrofsky, 268.
57. Dubrofsky, 268 (emphasis in original).
58. *I'd Do Anything to Get on TV* (Channel 4, April 10, 2005).
59. Corner, 2004, xviii.
60. Clive Gammon, "The Family Way," *The Spectator,* April 27, 1974: 11.
61. Ruoff, 106.
62. Furedi, 19.
63. Palmer, "How our TV family pay the price of fame," the *Sun,* April 26, 1974 (BFI microfiche on *The Family*).
64. James Thomas, "This family life will never be the same again," the *Daily Express,* June 27, 1974.
65. See Moore-Gilbert.
66. Biressi and Nunn; Palmer.
67. Palmer, 38.
68. Ibid: 35.
69. Tyler, 18.
70. Imogen Tyler, "Celebrity Chav: Fame, Femininity and Social Class" (paper delivered at "Going Cheap?: Female Celebrity in the Tabloid, Reality and Scandal Genres," University of East Anglia [U.K.], June 25, 2008).
71. Biressi and Nunn, 150.
72. Holmes, 2004.
73. Quoted in Jeffries, "I know I'm famous for nothing," the *Guardian,* May 24, 2007. www.guardian.co.uk/Columnists/Column/0,,1781697,00.html (accessed October 2, 2007).
74. *You Can't Fire Me . . . I'm Famous* (BBC1, July 31, 2007).
75. Jeffries, "'I know I'm famous for nothing."
76. Cited in Braachi, "How Jade Made the Grade," the *Daily Mail,* January 4, 2007.

www.dailymail.co.uk/pages/live/femail/article.html?in_article_id=426409&in_page_id=
1879 (accessed October 10, 2007).

77. Giddens.

78. *You Can't Fire Me . . . I'm Famous* (BBC1, July 31, 2007).

79. Braachi, "How Jade Made the Grade," the *Daily Mail*, January 4, 2007.
www.dailymail.co.uk/pages/live/femail/article.html?in_article_id=426409&in_page_id=
1879 (accessed 10 October, 2007).

80. Victoria Newton, "Vote out the Pig," the *Sun*, July 3, 2002. www.thesun.co.uk
/sol/homepage/showbiz/bizarre/article185055.ece (accessed October 10, 2005).

81. Biressi and Nunn, 149.

82. Biressi and Nunn, 149.

83. Skeggs.

84. Gies, 458.

85. Gies, 458.

86. Austin and Whittingham, "Jade's a Shhypocrite," *The People*, January 21, 2007.
www.people.co.uk/news/tm_headline=jade-s-a-shhypocrite-&method=full&objectid
=18509473&siteid=93463-name_page.html (accessed October 10, 2007).

87. This appeared in several magazines, but see *Reveal*, September 9-15, 2007: 10.

88. *The Wright Stuff* (January 23, 2007), uk.youtube.com/watch?v=oknOd84f89o.

89. www.youtube.com/watch?v=lPToztoDOCU.

90. Mole.

91. "Jade—the interview," *heat*, February 3-9, 2007: 12.

92. Dubrofsky.

93. *You Can't Fire Me . . .*

94. "Everyone's Talking About . . . ," *heat*, January 27-February 2, 2007: 2.

95. See *heat*, July 27-August 2, 2002.

96. It should be emphasized that Jade always refuted the allegations of racism. She refers here to the idea of getting help to manage to her anger.

97. Turner, 84.

98. Dyer, 1986.

99. Andrejevic, 7.

100. Marshall, 12.

101. Evans, 16.

102. See Skeggs.

103. Foucault.

References

Andrejevic, Mark. *Reality TV: The Work of Being Watched*. Lanham, Md.: Rowman and
    Littlefield, 2004.
Bennett, James. "The Television Personality System: Televisual Stardom Revisited After
    Film Theory." *Screen* 49, no. 1 (2008): 32-50.
Biressi, Anita and Heather Nunn. *Reality TV: Realism and Revelation*. London: Wall-
    flower, 2005.
Boddy, William. *Fifties Television: The Industry and Its Critics*. Urbana, Ill.: University
    of Illinois Press, 1990.

Corner, John. *Critical Ideas in Television Studies.* Oxford: Oxford University Press, 1999.

———. "Afterword." In *Big Brother International: Formats, Critics and Publics,* edited by Ernest Mathijs and Janet Jones, xii-xvii. London: Wallflower, 2004.

Couldry, Nick. *Media Rituals.* London: Routledge, 2003.

———. *The Place of Media Power: Pilgrims and Witnesses of the Media Age.* London: Routledge, 2000.

Dubrofsky, Rachel E. "Therapeutics of the Self: Surveillance in the Service of the Therapeutic." *Television & New Media* 8, no. 4 (2007): 263-284.

Dyer, Richard. *Heavenly Bodies: Film Stars and Society.* London: Routledge, 1986.

Ellis, John. *Visible Fictions: Cinema, Television, Video,* 2nd ed. London: Routledge, 1992.

Evans, Jessica. "Celebrity, Media and History." In *Inside Media: Understanding Celebrity,* edited by Jessica Evans and David Hesmondhalgh, 12-55. Berkshire, U.K.: Open University Press, 2005.

Furedi, Frank. *Therapy Culture: Cultivating Uncertainty in an Uncertain Age.* London, Routledge: 2004.

Foucault, Michel. *Discipline and Punish: The Birth of the Prison.* Paris: Gallimard, 1975.

Gamson, Joshua. *Claims to Fame: Celebrity in Contemporary America.* Berkeley: University of California Press, 1994.

Giddens, Anthony. *Modernity and Self-Identity.* Cambridge, U.K.: Polity, 1991.

Gies, Lieve. "Pigs, Dogs, Cows and Commerce in *Celebrity Big Brother* 2007." *Feminist Media Studies* 7, no. 4 (2007): 456-459.

Holmes, Su. "'All You've Got to Worry About is the Task, Having a Cup of Tea, and What You're Going to Eat for Dinner': Approaching Celebrity in *Big Brother.*" In *Understanding Reality Television,* edited by Su Holmes and Deborah Jermyn, 111-135. London: Routledge, 2004a.

———. "'Reality Goes Pop!': Reality TV, Popular Music and Narratives of Stardom in *Pop Idol* (U.K.)." *Television & New Media* 5, no. 2 (2004b): 147-172.

Kellner, Douglas. "Popular Culture and the Construction of Postmodern Identities." In *Modernity and Identity,* edited by Scott Lash and Jonathan Friedman, 19-32. Malden, Mass.: Blackwell, 1992.

Langer, John. "Television's Personality System." *Media, Culture & Society,* no. 4 (1981): 351-365.

Lury, Karen. "Television Performance: Being, Acting and 'Corpsing.'" *New Formations* 26 (1994): 114-127.

MacDonald, Paul. "I'm Winning on a Star: The Extraordinary Ordinary World of Stars in Their Eyes." *Critical Survey* 7, no.1 (1995): 44-65.

Marshall, P. David. *New Media Cultures.* Oxford: Oxford University Press, 2005.

Mole, Tom. "Hypertrophic Celebrity." *Media-Culture.*org, October 2007. journal.media-culture.org.au/0411/08-mole.php (accessed October 10, 2007).

Moore-Gilbert, Bart (ed.). *The Arts in the 1970s: Cultural Closure?* London: Routledge, 1994.

Ouellette, Laurie. *Viewers Like You? How Public TV Failed the People.* New York: Columbia University Press, 2002.

Ouellette, Laurie and James Hay. *Better Living Through Reality TV: Television and Post-*

Welfare Citizenship. Malden, Mass.: Blackwell, 2008.

Palmer, Gareth. "Big Brother: An Experiment in Governance." *Television & New Media* 3, no. 3 (2002): 295-310.

———. "The Un-dead: Life on the D-List." *Westminster Papers in Communication and Culture* (WPCC) 2, no. 2 (September 2005): 37-53.

Piper, Helen. "Reality TV, *Wife Swap* and the Drama of Banality." *Screen* 45, no. 4 (2004, Winter): 273-286.

Rahman, Momin. "Jade's Confession: racism and the dialectics of celebrity." *Social Semiotics* 18, no. 2 (2008): 133-148.

Root, Jane. *Open the Box: About Television.* London: Comedia, 1986.

Ruoff, Jeffrey. *An American Family: A Televised Life.* Minneapolis: University of Minnesota Press, 2002.

Skeggs, Beverley. *Class, Self, Culture.* London: Routledge, 2003.

Teurlings, Jan. "Producing the Ordinary: institutions, discourses and practices in love game shows." *Continuum: Journal of Media & Cultural Studies* 15, no. 2 (2001): 249-263.

Turner, Graeme. *Understanding Celebrity.* London: Sage, 2004.

Tyler, Imogen. "'Chav Mum, Chav Scum': Class Disgust in Contemporary Britain." *Feminist Media Studies* 8, no. 1 (March 2008): 17-34.

Wheatley, Helen. "Introduction." In *Re-viewing Television History*, edited by Helen Wheatley, 1-16. London: I. B. Tauris, 2008.

Chapter 18
Lifestyle TV: Critical Attitudes toward "Banal" Programming
Tanja Thomas

The Conduct of Life, Lifestyle TV, and the Everyday: Contextual Dimensions

The everyday cannot be understood ex negativo, as different from other parts of life (i.e., the everyday as a non-holiday, a non-workday, as a sphere beyond thought and experience). It is not a special and autonomous structure. On the contrary, the everyday is an integral part of the life of the members of a social class and—since it cannot be examined separately—has to be recognized as part of the social power system.[1]

This chapter looks at the (sub)genre of lifestyle Reality TV, a genre that offers us a specific framing and dramatization of the everyday. But in order to look at this everyday, we need a social-theoretical contextualization of the everyday: That is why I want to refer to Elias' article "Zum Begriff des Alltags," which was published in the late 1970s, right at the beginning of this chapter.

Referring to Elias' work Dewe and Ferchow[2] argue that the increased sociological interest in the phenomena of the everyday is connected to a social-cultural and social-economic crisis. This claim led me to investigate the link between (mediatized) framings of the everyday and current moments of social crises in the following.

In addition, media support the social organization and structuring of the everyday in Western contemporary industrial societies. It has been emphasized repeatedly that the media synchronize individual lives with the "everyday" of society and help to solve conflicts or regulate the relations between family members and sexes. Audiovisual media, in particular, approximate the everyday of people in many ways. They facilitate relationships, offer contexts, overrule

275

old conventions, provide new concepts for the everyday and refer more and more everyday practices to the media or media operations.[3] Some scholars even posit that televized entertainment replaces individual experience in postmodern societies; Bublitz claims[4] that in times of globalization and media culture, society is not produced through a social synthesis, but a mass cultural one.

This is doubtful however. Nevertheless, the question of how these media texts contribute to the reproduction of the social, remains socially and politically explosive, but this explicitly does not imply that people are reduced to audiences. In contrast their contextual embeddedness may render them trans-audiences—to introduce a term to indicate that there is still a relationship between these (trans-)audiences and the media content, but without supporting the media-centric thesis.[5]

Clearly, Reality TV formats are considered particularly relevant for the everyday of their recipients, as they are explicitly described as forms of an increased framing and dramatization of everyday life. Wood and Skeggs[6] highlight that formats of Reality TV are characterized by close-ups, which generate a "realism" of "nowness" and "hereness," rather than a realism of "truth." On the other hand, they describe the use of melodramatic scenes and agree with Moseley's claim that lifestyle TV leads to "an excess of the ordinary."[7] The work of Ang,[8] Radway,[9] Geraghty,[10] and Brown[11] is also interesting in this regard. They show that media plays a role in reproducing and legitimizing social conditions—especially when these texts connect with people's everyday practices and experiences. Possible connections with everyday experiences and actions can be found on several levels: In her famous reception study of the series *Dallas*, Ang[12] emphasizes that the relation between soaps and audiences is linked to emotional processes ("emotional realism"). In addition, recipients are looking for equivalents on a cognitive-rational level; several studies[13] show that the relevance and enjoyment of media entertainment are associated with how they tie in with personal life experiences. Furthermore, performative processes also play a role: Body practices are elementary in our experiences, since they can enforce or change these experiences.[14]

Starting from the connection of Reality TV with the everyday, in combination with the connection of the everyday with the reproduction of social structures, I focus on a specific form of Reality TV, which is frequently described as lifestyle TV.[15] This term encompasses formats that deal with the design of personal appearances (makeover shows) and living spaces (DIY shows), with choosing a partner (dating shows) or ways to professional success (casting shows). The connection between lifestyle TV and the everyday seems obvious: Almost everybody cooks and eats, dresses, creates their appearance, buys furniture, looks for a partner, has relationships, and raises children. Still, there is a need to specify my understanding of the everyday, which I do in the next part of this chapter. I explain my concept of "the conduct of life," which is important for a social-theoretical analysis of lifestyle TV. Also, I illustrate how the analysis of media lifestyle techniques in lifestyle TV goes beyond analyzing representations of style, design, taste, and etiquette and how it can be expanded to include the structural analysis of governmental practices that are encoded in the televisual text. The theoretical basis of my analysis is provided in part by Foucault's later work on governmentality and the technologies of the self, which allows thinking about the ways the body becomes implicated in the television texts, which, in turn, are offered to a diversity of audiences.

In this chapter, the focus is on media texts as models for lifestyle techniques. Since these techniques are communicated to subjects not only from an outside perspective, but are also considered to be internalized and performed, I choose shows that focus on bodies, body performances and formations. Thus, I am more interested in the motto "You just have to want it, baby" of *Germany's Next Top Model* (a version of a globally aired format), than in the actual presentation of the thin bodies, or the potential effects of these shows on their recipients' physical confidence and eating disorders. In analyzing the surgery show *The Swan*, I am more concerned with the ideologies of beautification (symbolized by the slogan "from ugly duckling to beautiful swan") than with how realistic cosmetic surgery is portrayed, or with the media's influence on public attitudes toward cosmetic surgery. Finally, I discuss *Das Model und der Freak* (*The Model and the Freak*) as an example of a lifestyle TV format in which two young men are "made over" in each week's episode. Again, my interest lies in the ways their bodies are governed.

Using a gender perspective, it is interesting to see how these media offers play a part in the reproduction of specific concepts of the self and the social, including innate social inequalities. My thesis is that these programs disconnect the processes of individualization from their political context, and partake in a (re)production of an individualistic ideology. Therefore, my main question is: How relevant are media programs such as lifestyle TV, to the reproduction of social concepts and intrinsic inequalities? And what is the significance of popular culture as a mode of socialization?

Everyday Conduct of Life from a Social-Theoretical Perspective

While so far, I have emphasized the connection of the everyday with an initial social-cultural and social-economic crisis, I now focus on the social contextualization of the everyday. However, I do not interpret the mediated actions that occur within media shows as everyday practices nor do I equate them with everyday practices. My interpretation of media programs that approximate the everyday refers to the relationship between media content and the everyday, everyday experiences and everyday practices. This relationship refers in part to the discursive and material context in which lifestyle TV participants are placed, but also to the contextualized position of the trans-audiences who watch lifestyle TV programs that resonate with their everyday lives.

Moreover, I understand the everyday as a specific, immediate mode of social action, which does not refer to one coherent area of life. As it spans the social, it also relates to various practical problems. This mode of the everyday is so natural and immediate that (perhaps for that very reason) most people are not aware of it.[16] This understanding of the "everyday" has several consequences: Firstly, it looks at social practices. Secondly, it tries to identify practical problems in the everyday conduct of life, which can only be understood in the context of mediated social concepts. And, finally, it is important as it connects everyday practices and the processes of mediation.

The concept of the conduct of life functions as a hinge between lifestyle TV as a text and the everyday practices and experiences of recipients, providing theoretical ground for thinking about the trans-audience based on the concept of contextualized everyday life. The conduct of life encompasses principles, rules and procedures as well as practices, which have been institutionalized by an internalization of behavioral patterns. These practices are based on life plans and expectations, competencies and resources, interpretations and experiences on the one hand, and options and commitments, risks and restraints, norms and cultural standards on the other.[17] Access to and availability of material, cultural and social resources do not affect the immediate patterns of the conduct of life, but do impact on the produced activities, acquired objects and corresponding values. As an individual activity, the conduct of life has to be adjusted not only to resources, but also to the activities of others. Therefore, it comprises forms of delegation, cooperation, task sharing, etc.; it is the background against which people act.

When the concept of the conduct of life was developed in the early 1990s, it was connected to a shifting work/life-balance as well as to tendencies to individualization and pluralization. By this means, individualization remained fixed to the ideal of the autonomy of the conduct of life, and was addressed to the upper and middle classes. Meanwhile, however, the demise of collective security systems has become a motor for radicalizing individualism. Hartmann and Honneth[18] claim that people learn to see themselves, their abilities, behaviors and bodies as incorporated sites that they have to develop, nurture and offer independently.

Bodies are important dimensions of these so-called "incorporated sites." When the Shell youth-survey[19] asked young people aged twelve to fifteen what was "in," 92 percent of them answered "looking good," which made it the first ranked answer. Apparently, the body is "in." This refers to a myriad of body-sociological studies, which assume a relationship between the social structures of a society, and its perception and treatment of the body.[20] In approaches often referred to as globalization, individualization, mediation and commercialization, the body is articulated as the last retreat for the self, as a haven for authenticity and identity on the one hand, and as a reflexive identity project on the other.[21] In my opinion, all these conclusions have one common denominator: The body has become a project.

So how does the body become represented in lifestyle TV? What are the strategies that are developed to handle the body? How is the participants' conduct of their lives adjusted to the aforementioned social processes? How are they mediated and performed? And how are they offered to their (trans-)audiences? These questions bring me to the third part of this chapter, where I want to illustrate how media programs can be analyzed through the lens of the conduct of life concept. I especially want to show how the relationship between media programs and everyday experiences functions. Methodically my approach is based on qualitative social science analysis as a research tool to investigate social and "ideological" (in an Alterhusserian sense) meanings; in practice, this implies that the research rests on discourse analysis. Inspired by a Foucauldian perspective, lifestyle TV can be considered as an arena for knowledge articulation that makes important contributions to social realities. To some extent lifestyle TV has an impact on knowledge production and circulation. To treat lifestyle TV as an element of a regime of knowledge in media cultures requires going beyond a discourse analysis that is mainly interested in the relevance of institutions and the constitution of knowledge. It needs to integrate the production of knowledge by people and their practices, in other words, there needs to be a reference to Reiner Keller and his "sociology of knowledge approach to discourse."[22]

I argue in this chapter for a grounding of discourse theory and empirical discourse research in the sociology of knowledge, especially in the German-based *Hermeneutische Wissenssoziologie*, which follows the Peter L. Berger and Thomas Luckmann approach to knowledge. This way the analysis of social relations and politics of knowledge is recognized as well as the importance of socially constituted actors in the social production and circulation of knowledge. This also implies that the concept of "discourse" becomes connected to the methodical toolbox of qualitative social research. For empirical research on discourse, the approach thus proposes the use of analytical concepts from the sociology of knowledge tradition, such as interpretative schemes or frames, and it is open to integrate insights, i.e., from performative theory and analysis.

From External Disciplining to Self-Disciplining: "You Have to Want It, Baby" in *Germany's Next Top Model*

When the first season of *Germany's Next Top Model* was aired on TV, the host Heidi Klum faced severe criticism from the press and politicians. After the number of candidates was reduced from thirty-two to twelve, the online version of the weekly magazine, *Der Spiegel*, called them "the skinny dozen" ("das magere Dutzend"), aligning themselves with press criticism of the "skinny show." These accusations correspond with a myriad of studies that analyze the connection between media use, satisfaction with the body and (even) eating disorders. Without attempting to list all these publications, I want to give a few examples: For instance, there are early content analyses of the body ideal represented in magazines. Garner et al.[23] show how the *Playboy* centerfold models became progressively thinner between 1959 and 1978; in 1999 Spitzer, Henderson and Zivian[24] demonstrated that almost all *Playboy* centerfold models were underweight, a third of them even anorexic according to World Health Organization standards. Therefore, media content analyses show that the female beauty ideal has become increasingly thin, and that girls who see these ideal bodies in fashion and teenage magazines, or on TV, are more likely to suffer from body image dysfunctions.[25]

Harrison and Cantor[26] focused their research on TV and magazines. They found a correlation between watching series with thin (*Melrose Place, Beverly Hills 90210*), medium-weight (*Seinfeld, Northern Exposure*) and heavyset (*Roseanne, Designing Women*) actors and actresses on the one hand, and the extent to which research participants were satisfied with their own bodies on the other. Participants who preferred series with thin actors and actresses were more likely to have a disposition toward eating disorders. However, Harrison[27] argues that "thin" is an inaccurate description of U.S. body ideals. She had participants assemble a body book, which allowed them to combine any hip, waist and breast size to an image they perceived as attractive. Many participants chose a very narrow waist, extremely narrow hips and big breasts as a desirable image. People who watched *Baywatch* were more likely to choose big breasts than those who watched *Ally McBeal* or *Beverly Hills 90210*.[28] Irving[29] in an experimental study shows that patients with eating disorders are less satisfied with their own bodies after seeing very thin models, and more satisfied after seeing plus size models. The findings of Myers and Biocca[30] also show that young women are less satisfied with their own bodies after being presented with "ideal bodies" in TV shows and commercials. And a similar study conducted in Australia by Hargreaves and Tiggemann[31] investigated the effects of "thin ideal" commercials on youths. In a longitudinal study by Stice, Spangler and Agras[32] (see also Petersen[33] for a similar study), particularly young people who entered the experiment unsatisfied with their bodies, showed clear effects after viewing model bodies in fashion magazines.[34] One of the problems of the approaches in these studies is that most of them neglect civilization, rationalization, and individualization processes, which are considered, by Gugutzer[35] and others for instance, to be equally important socio-cultural causes of eating disorders. Gugutzer[36] emphasizes that eating disorders symbolize the psychological price that has to be paid by a society that is morbidly focused on performance, discipline, will power, self-control and responsibility. Thus, a media analysis of formats such as *Ger-*

many's Next Top Model, should focus not only on the staging of thin bodies, but also on the processes of self-control and disciplining. In fact, "smile, smile, smile" is the host's motto, even when the candidates are photographed on the roof of a high-rise in the freezing cold or are asked to pose in the snow. When one candidate constantly shivers, she is criticized for a lack of "body control." All the candidates in all the series are put into bikinis and weighed on the first show. But the measuring and dating of body parts as the starting point for (self)control is not limited to models: women's and fitness magazines regularly provide their readers with information about the *body mass index*. Borrowing from Foucault, this practice of comparing body data can be described as "politics of restraints that work on the body and calculate and manipulate its elements, gestures and behaviours."[37] On the show, if the jury's measurements do not match the models' application forms, the host becomes irritated—but not about possible cheating. Rather it is the candidates' incompetence to "sell" these mistakes with a smile that triggers his reaction.

Thus, this is not just about *playing* a role, it is also about *embodying* it, as Koppetsch[38] shows in her work on status and attractiveness. It seems to be required to inscribe formerly external behavioral codes on the body. During the show, the contestants are asked to embody for a photo shoot, spontaneous feelings, such as fury or joy, or to control the physical expression of their feelings when tarantulas or snakes are put on their naked skin. Prior to the jury critiquing the photos (in the presence of the contestants), each subject is asked to critique her performance. The body is part of improving the self; emotional work[39] is always body work. Identifying with the role is a central (but not the only) strategy to overcome the body. It leads to an authentic experience of conforming behavior. In this sense "You have to want it, baby" is the first rule for success in Heidi Klum's book *Heidi Klum's Body of Knowledge—8 Rules of Model Behaviour*. The models are supposed to make two traverses of a catwalk in front of an audience of miners. When one of the girls suddenly flees from this surrender to the male gaze, and hides backstage in tears, trainer Bruce challenges her with the authoritarian command: "What is that? What did I tell you?" Shortly after, the viewers are shown this girl pleading that: "I will do better" and "Give me a second chance." "Who endures it?," "Who struggles and passes?" are the key questions asked by the host. The scene in the mine is explained by a voice-over: "They throw the girls into cold water to see who learns to swim the quickest."

Analysis of such shows, in which candidates are submitted to self-disciplining processes, benefits from the perspective of governmentality studies. These studies emerged from the discussion of ideas voiced by Foucault just before his death.[40] In his last lectures, Foucault's "gouvernement" (government) spans far more than just political government or transformation of the administration to forms of self-government (self-technologies). For Foucault, "government" is a term that focuses on the interrelated constitution of power techniques, knowledge forms and subjectifying techniques. This approach is productive for the analysis of modern entertainment formats. In other words, Foucault's works can be made a reference point for performative theory. In this context, I refer to the makeover shows *The Swan* and *Das Model und der Freak* and demonstrate that the model show *Germany's Next Top Model* belongs to a number of formats that specifically address subjects that are able to sell themselves self-confidently, assertively, but nonetheless flexibly, free, and responsibly: They are entrepreneurs of the self.[41]

Working on the Body-Self: "From Ugly Duckling to Beautiful Swan" in *The Swan*

In 2004, the surgery show *The Swan—Endlich Schön (Finally Beautiful)* was aired on German TV (Pro7). Sixteen candidates underwent various surgical procedures to compete for the title *The Swan*. Two years before, RTL2 had aired the Reality soap *Beauty Klinik*. Moreover, MTV showed young men surgically transforming themselves into Brad Pitt, and trans-sexuals becoming Jennifer Lopez look-alikes in *I Want A Famous Face* (2004). Birgit Schrowange hosted a four part miniseries called *Beauty Queen* on RTL, and the documentary *Alles ist Möglich (Everything is Possible)* showed twelve people who "gained new confidence through cosmetic surgery."[42] RTL2 countered with *Schönheit um jeden Preis—Letzte Hoffnung Skalpell (Beauty at All Costs—Last Hope the Scalpel)* while Pro7 showed the U.S. series *Nip/Tuck*. The rise of these formats, and the increased reporting and proliferation of cosmetic surgery[43] in Germany[44] inspired several studies that ask whether increased media attention changes viewers' perceptions and attitudes toward plastic surgery. Some of these studies[45] examine how realistic the presentation of plastic surgery is, how the operation method influences the perception of "real" surgery, and the influence of the media on people's willingness to undergo plastic surgery. Again, the social-theoretical embedding and social-critical reflection of makeover shows in general (and specific formats in particular) have been neglected, as have detailed descriptions of represented body practices. This is peculiar, since the body helps to create social order, and social order is documented on the body.[46] Moreover, Meuser[47] shows the importance of the body, bodily self-presentation and an adequate body image for the formation of identity.

Since attractiveness helps to sustain power, to create relationships and to attract attention,[48] a social-theoretical analysis of programs like *The Swan* is impossible without considering the status of attractiveness. Koppetsch shows that "beauty," "authenticity," and "charisma" are central dimensions for framing attractiveness. His work also argues that, firstly, the visibility and demonstrative use of beautifying measures are assessed differently depending on social milieu and gender and secondly, that attractiveness does not include only the features of the (thin) body and face, but also incorporates clothing, degree of naturalness and other aspects of a habitual realization of belonging to a specific social class.[49]

Even if physical beauty (in a Bourdieuan sense) is recognized and employed by the candidates, the surgical reworking of the body in surgery shows might deliver the desired results—more self-confidence, acceptance, professional success and luck in love—but only in a specific milieu. However, against the backdrop of more and more celebrities confessing to plastic surgery, empirical evidence is still needed about whether beautifying measures remain a risk to the credibility of attractiveness in an "individualized milieu," and the risk brought by confessing a "deficit in inwardness."

The Swan also engages in measuring, photographing and visual disassembly of the body; body parts that need work—teeth, breasts, thighs—are enlarged and shown in full body shots. The women submit completely to the control of the production company. While the show is being taped, they live together, separated from their families, friends and the outside world, in a house without a single mirror. Their daily routines are determined by doctors and trainers who are responsible for fitness and psychological therapy. The camera is omnipresent, for instance when they are anesthetized or lifted from the operating table after the procedure. The scene at the end of each show when a curtain is drawn back to reveal a mirror which allows the women to see themselves in evening wear after weeks of surgeries, fitness and mental training, can be interpreted as a key scene. The bodies that these women originally considered themselves estranged from—many words expressing disgust and hatred for their bodies or body parts are uttered at the beginning of the show—have been reworked and are "ready" for the future.

Davis[50] and Borkenhagen[51] regard plastic surgery as a strategy to overcome the effects of objectifying the body by controlling the objectifying process.[52] They emphasize the ambivalence that lies behind plastic surgery, as a dialectics of empowering and disempowering. The mirror scene reunites the women with their bodies. This is reminiscent of Lacan's concept of the mirror stadium, in which the emergence of the self is explicitly tied to recognizing and identifying with the image of the self in the mirror; the child recognizes not only its own body in the mirror stadium, but also *itself* in the form of *its* body.[53] The double sense of being a body and having a body,[54] of feeling and being watched, of empowerment and disempowerment, are visualized in *The Swan*.

Self-Transformation and Norming: "Freaks" Turned into "Cool Young Men" in *Das Model und der Freak*

From an ugly "duckling" to a beautiful swan: Models Monica Ivancan and Jana Ina Zarrella "coach shy outsiders and turn the geeks into cool young men." With these words, in June 2007, Pro7 announced the new show *Das Model und der Freak* in the category "Lifestyle."[55] The wording is reminiscent of *The Swan*, which was aired on Pro7 in 2004 and focused on female candidates who were "unhappy with themselves or their bodies," but in *Das Model und der Freak* only one candidate was explicitly said to be "very unhappy with himself and his body." But these men generally share much the same problem: they "can't get it on with the girls," or are "to shy to approach women," "feel inadequate for a girlfriend" or even "have real men in their circle of friends" who "always get the girls." Or have a "big dream" which is to "finally pick up a woman in a bar."[56]

Underpinned by this mediated "problem definition," the station summarizes the show concept on its website:

> Twenty candidates in ten episodes do not only get flirting and styling tips, they mainly load up on self-confidence. For instance, the freaks take body language training and learn how to improve their demeanour. They have to overcome inner barriers and show courage—by being a nude model or having the first kiss of their lives.

According to Pro7, the goal is "fulfilling a personal dream." In an episode overview, the website details how the models proceed: They "magically turn" two "freaks" into "real guys" in each episode, "get them on the right track," "show them a completely new world," "let them sniff a new life," "make new guys out of boys," and "get them a new look." This illustrates how a new hairstyle, a new T-shirt, studying bra sizes (which makes them "ladies men") or a tandem parachute (which makes them "real men") are supposed to accomplish the "mission of a better life."[57]

Analysis of a selection of sequences shows how an individualism of self-interest, self-actualization, responsibility, and self-determination is (re)produced and staged along with this "mission": Each show begins by introducing the two candidates as so called "freaks." In most cases they are unemployed and characterized as medieval, gothic or fantasy fans, or as solitary computer geeks. The hobbies of these lonely men are often infantile activities such as playing in a sandbox or playing with legos. These presentations categorize them as "freaks" and assign them a position outside social normality. This is followed by a scene in which the models sit down on a sofa and concentrate on watching short introductory video sequences. They demonstrate astonishment, giggle or bury their faces in their hands to emphasize how much help they need. At the same time, they assure the audience how excited they are to be "working" with the "freaks."

After a face-to-face introduction, the models present their diagnoses and start the "therapy program": Shyness and inexperience are the most frequently diagnosed deficits, the "failure" to find a partner is seen as caused by personal immaturity. The men candidly admit to these "weaknesses" and explicitly express their desire for the experts' help and advice.

The show is characterized by a paradox between the individual wanting to be himself and—temporary—submission to regulation and to acknowledgement by and from the female models. The models' so-called "therapy program" consists of certain tasks and an instrumental way of handling the self, which symbolizes a reification of personal subjectivity. In one episode, Basti and Benni are asked to present themselves in a commercial.[58] Only after the video is taped they learn that it will be projected on the walls of a subway station and (sometimes with Basti and Benni present) passers-by will be asked for their opinions. Paradigmatically, this scene symbolizes a "runway economy,"[59] in which magic can also be used to explain the success of casting shows, such as *Popstars* or *Deutschland sucht den Superstar* (*German Idol*). On the one hand, it demonstrates hope for and the ideal of a quick, effortless way to wealth and good fortune; on the other hand it reveals the presence of a "marketing person" (in the sense of Erich Fromm), who experiences him- or herself through the gaze of the other, his or her personality as a commodity and the self as a salesperson. The instrumental relation to the self is expressed in an episode where the candidates practice kissing with some drama students.[60] This is supposed to increase their "luck" with Internet flirt, Wiebke. After the kissing training, "coach" Jana Ina is satisfied: "I think he believes a little more in himself now, and then, when he finally meets Wiebke, who knows, maybe he thrusts his tongue down her throat and everything will be fine."[61]

But the models are there not only to support the candidates in these kinds of "cases": Self-confidence and reassurance are actively produced via bodily experiences, for example in football training, where "one meets real guys for a change" or through a "drill instructor." After everyone is dressed in military camouflage outfit, they learn by getting yelled at: "Come on, be a man!" Afterwards, the candidates find out what it feels like to be a man: They are allowed to drill and yell at a group of young men and women. Candidate Manfred is "changed" by the experience, considering that he used to be the "type of freak everyone pities. A notorious outsider in the valley of the clueless! Visually not presentable and a hurt soul, blotched with the scars of his '*whipping boy childhood*'! . . . One against all, all against Manfred!"[62] After the drill exercise Manfred explains in interview how much he liked standing "on the other side," yelling at people, and that it was "very funny." The almost parody-like practicing of male dominant behavior is clearly associated with the military through the camouflage uniform. This institution still serves as a masculine-military identity former, where the exclusion of women has long been essential. Besides disciplinary and de-individualization practices, the military uses submission and fear tactics, which involve a negative exclusion and devaluation of the "female." *Das Model und der Freak* prepares for that as well.

A recurring element in the show is the initiation ritual: Tight-rope walking between two high rise buildings, some sixty meters above the ground, and a tandem parachute jump, symbolize the transition to a "new life." Here, the work on the self is symbolically staged, since it is the candidates themselves who have to make the decision to leave their old lives behind. Benni describes his bungee jump thus: "when I was at the end of the rope and it pulled me back up, it felt as if my old body was ripped out of me, it shattered on the ground." And the "coach" confirms: "He jumped and jettisoned all the dead weight and came up as a new Benjamin."[63] Bette[64] calls these experiences of risk a "cultural technique of affirming life": the promise and sensation of individualization lies in the visibility of demonstrative risk taking, the revitalization of bodily perception and experience, which enables the feeling of reality, assurance and presence that cannot be evoked by communication. He emphasizes that the "kick" of experiencing risk and overcoming fear serves the self-empowerment of the modern subject. At the same time it refers to the experiences of voidness if people are forced to endure as a result of the processes of social modernization—and which are, of course, not mentioned in lifestyle formats. Instead, participants work not only with, but also on the body. The last step in *Das Model und der Freak* is always the makeover, when the candidates get new clothes and a new hairstyle, and a before/after comparison is staged at the end of the show. This show element illustrates Volker Rittner's insight that the thin and vital body delivers expressive visual evidence that the power and autonomy of an individual come as tools from the body.[65]

Recent sociological studies,[66] which, like Rittner, assume a correlation between the social structures of a society and the perception, handling and behaviors of and with the body, also analyze the body as the last retreat for the self, as a haven for authenticity and identity on the one hand, and as a reflexive identity project on the other. Initially, the work on the male self is the models' task: They blindfold the candidates before the hairdresser begins cutting with no prior consultation. This exemplifies what Nina Degele[67] deals with in her empirical study about beautifying actions: Achieving beauty requires competence and the show presents competence as the ability to fulfill certain requirements and to stage them successfully for acknowledgment by others.

Again, the idea of an instrumental selfhood becomes obvious, and needs to be used to gain and maintain social acceptance. After the show, the candidates are expected to take care of themselves. In the context of individualization, a good appearance, good physical demeanor and good health seem to suffice to achieve social power.

Lifestyle TV: Popular Culture as a Mode of Socialization?

The formats *Germany's Next Top Model*, *The Swan* and *Das Model und der Freak* stage "work on the self" as a way to a "new life." The media format lifestyle TV operates with a subjectifying regime, which bundles forms of knowledge (in which individuals learn the truth about themselves), with the control and regulation mechanisms exerted by the specialists whose advice and guidance they obey.[68] Bröckling (in referring to Michel Foucault and supported by an analysis of the staging machine of *Das Model und der Freak*) highlights that the subjects and actors in the show as well as the viewers are invited to practice techniques of the social and the self. These techniques enable these individuals, on their own or with the help of operations to their bodies, their souls, their thoughts, or their behaviors, to change in a way that will help them to achieve a certain degree of happiness, purity, wisdom, perfection and immortality.[69]

Lifestyle TV then is critically involved in the processes of the (re)production of these forms of knowledge and social technologies: The possession or non-possession of economic resources as well as social and cultural capital (as action-empowering or action-discouraging potentials), is deframed, "individuality" is evoked in the mode of self-disciplining while de-individualization is enforced by normalization processes and pressures to conform. The willingness to change and for "self-actualization" (within the framework of these norms) is thus acknowledged. Lifestyle TV builds on these interlocking forces of knowledge and social technologies, and simultaneously becomes part of it. Similarly, its audiences are no longer mere audiences, but could be termed as trans-audiences emphasizing that they are permanently exposed to these forces, through the screen but also at a vast number of other social sites.

However, it is not enough to see these shows as encouraging hegemonic masculinity practices, sexist ideals and processes of objectifying the self. It is without question that viewers come up with their own readings of these shows—whether these readings are pleasurable or cynical.[70] For this reason, these popular programs should be discussed with reference to their relationship with everyday experiences of differently positioned viewers as a mode of socialization: Why is it that these programs are so popular?[71] One reason is apparently that they show the myth of a self-actualizing self—of a choice-based conduct of life in an age of inequality and uncertain acknowledgements.

Notes

1. Elias, 24.
2. Dewe and Ferchow.
3. Krotz, 2001, 29.

4. Bublitz.
5. For a critique on mediacentrism, see Couldry, 13ss.
6. Wood and Skeggs, 182.
7. Moseley.
8. Ang.
9. Radway.
10. Geraghty.
11. Brown.
12. Ang.
13. Livingstone; Cornelißen; Mikos.
14. Schroer; Davis.
15. Lewis.
16. Voß, 36.
17. Kudera, 8ss.
18. Hartmann and Honneth, 10.
19. The Shell youth survey is a study on attitudes, values, habits and social behaviour of German youngsters, which has been published every four years since 1952 by the mineral oil company Shell. At the beginning of 2006, more that 2,500 youngsters between the age of twelve and fifteen were surveyed.
20. Gugutzer, 1998; 2004; Rittner.
21. Gugutzer, 1998.
22. Keller, 2006.
23. Garner et al.
24. Spitzer et al.
25. Thompson et al.
26. Harrison and Cantor.
27. Harrison.
28. Harrison, 261.
29. Irving.
30. Myers and Biocca.
31. Hargreaves and Tiggemann.
32. Stice, Spangler and Agras, 2001.
33. Petersen.
34. For a meta-analysis of these experimental studies, see Groesz, Levine and Murnen. For a summary, see Eggermont, Beullens and van den Bulck.
35. Gugutzer, 2005.
36. Gugutzer, 1998, 351.
37. Foucault, 1994 (1975).
38. Koppetsch.
39. Hochschild.
40. For an introduction, see Lemke.
41. Duttweiler, 31.
42. See URL: www.rtl.de/ratgeber/gesundheit_alles_ist_moeglich.php (October 22, 2008).
43. For a brief history of cosmetic surgery, see Rohr.
44. Since plastic surgery is privately practiced, there is insufficient data on the num-

ber of cosmetic surgeries performed in Germany. Presumably, the number of unreported cases is high. Estimations suggest 350,000 to 400,000 surgeries. Moreover, Prof. Dr Christian J. Gabka, president of a German Association of Plastic Surgeons (Vereinigung der Deutschen Ästhetisch-Plastischen Chirurgen, VDÄPC), reports an increasing demand from patients. Members of another plastic surgery association (Gesellschaft für Ästhetische Chirurgie Deutschland e.V, GÄCD) conducted over 130,000 surgeries in 2008 and about 105,000 wrinkle treatments. (www.gacd.de/presse/pressemitteilungen/2008/2008-09-04-neue-statistik-der-schoenheitsoperationen.html [September 23, 2008]). The American Society for Aesthetic Plastic Surgery reported 11.7 million cosmetic surgeries in 2007, worth $13.2 billion (www.vdaepc.de/index.php?id=442 [September 23, 2008]).

45. Rossmann and Brosius, 507.

46. Hahn and Meuser, 8.

47. Meuser.

48. Koppetsch, 101.

49. Koppetsch, 106.

50. Davis.

51. Borkenhagen.

52. Borkenhagen, 64.

53. Borkenhagen, 65.

54. Plessner.

55. See URL: www.prosieben.de/lifestyle_magazine/das_model_und_der_freak/artikel /39983/ (June 17, 2007). Meanwhile, the show is in its second season. The first season averaged 1.32 million viewers per show, which is 13.7 percent of the targeted audience. Some episodes even achieved a market share of 15.6 percent. See URL: www.quotenmeter.de/index.php?newsid=21883 (August 30, 2007).

56. All show-related quotes are translations of the original German quotes from the show's website.

57. The hosts use this phrase repeatedly to describe their project (transcript of the show August 8, 2007).

58. See URL: www.prosieben.de/lifestyle_magazine/das_model_und_der_freak/episoden /artikel/42845/ (October 22, 2008).

59. Neckel.

60. Watch the scene at URL: www.prosieben.de/lifestyle_magazine/das_model_und _der_freak/videoplayer/41474/ (October 22, 2008).

61. All statements are verbatim translations of the statements used on the show, see URL: www.prosieben.de/lifestyle_magazine/das_model_und_der_freak/videoplayer/41474/ (July 6, 2007).

62. URL: www.prosieben.de/lifestyle_magazine/das_model_und_der_freak/episoden /artikel/42362/ (July 6, 2007).

63. Transcript of the show of September 4, 2007.

64. Bette, 21ss.

65. Rittner, 374.

66. Gugutzer; Hahn and Meuser.

67. Degele.

68. Bröckling, 39.

69. Foucault, 1993, 26.

70. Thomas and Langemeyer.
71. Fiske, 53.

References

Ang, Ien. *Watching Dallas. Soap Opera and the Melodramatic Imagination.* London: Routledge, 1986.

Bette, Karl-Heinrich. "X-treme. Soziologische Betrachtungen zum Modernen Abenteuer- und Risikosport." In *Auf's Spiel gesetzte Körper. Aufführungen des Sozialen in Sport und Populärer Kultur,* edited by Thomas Alkemeyer et al., 19-36. Konstanz, Germany: UVK, 2003.

Borkenhagen, Ada. "Gemachte Körper. Die Inszenierung des Modernen Selbst mit dem Skalpell." *Aspekte zur Schönheitschirurgie* (2001): 55-67. medpsy.uniklinikum-leipzig.de/pdf/ab_gemachte_koerper_2.pdf (accessed September 14, 2008).

Bröckling, Ulrich, Susanne Krasmann and Thomas Lemke (eds.). *Gouvernementalität der Gegenwart. Studien zur Ökonomisierung des Sozialen.* Frankfurt am Main, Germany: Suhrkamp, 2000.

Bröckling, Ulrich. *Das Unternehmerische Selbst: Soziologie einer Subjektivierungsform.* Frankfurt am Main, Germany: Suhrkamp, 2007.

Brown, Mary Ellen. *Soap Operas and Women's Talk. The Pleasure of Resistance.* Thousand Oaks, Calif.: Sage, 1994.

Brunsdon, Charlotte. "Lifestyling Britain. The 8-9 slot on British Television." *International Journal of Cultural Studies* 6, no. 1 (2003): 5-23.

Bublitz, Hannelore. *In der Zerstreuung organisiert. Paradoxien und Phantasmen der Massenkultur.* Bielefeld, Germany: Transcript, 2005.

Cornelißen, Waltraud. *Fernsehgebrauch und Geschlecht. Zur Rolle des Fernsehens im Alltag von Frauen und Männern.* Opladen, Germany: Westdeutscher Verlag, 1998.

Couldry, Nick. *Listening Beyond the Echoes. Media, Ethics, and Agency in an Uncertain World.* Boulder, Colo.: Paradigm, 2006.

Davis, Kathy (ed.). *Embodied Practices. Feminist Perspectives on the Body.* London: Sage, 1997.

Degele, Nina. *Sich Schön Machen. Zur Soziologie von Geschlecht und Schönheitshandeln.* Wiesbaden, Germany: VS, 2004.

Dewe, Bernd and Wilfried Ferchow. "Alltag." In *Handbuch Soziologie. Zur Theorie und Praxis sozialer Beziehungen,* edited by Harald Kerber and Arnold Schmieder, 16-24. Reinbek bei Hamburg, Germany: Rowohlt, 1984.

Duttweiler, Stefanie. *Sein Glück machen. Arbeit am Glück als Neoliberale Regierungstechnologie.* Konstanz, Germany: UVK, 2007.

Eggermont, Steven, Kathleen Beullens and Jan van den Bulck. "Television Viewing and Adolescent Females' Body Dissatisfaction: The Mediating Role of Opposite Sex Expectations." *Communications* 30, no. 3 (2005): 343-357.

Elias, Norbert. "Zum Begriff des Alltags. Materialien zur Soziologie des Alltags." In *Sonderheft 20/1978 der Kölner Zeitschrift für Soziologie und Sozialpsychologie,* edited by Kurt Hammerich and Michael Klein, 22-29. Opladen, Germany: Westdeutscher Verlag, 1978.

Fiske, John. "Populäre Texte, Sprache und Alltagskultur." In *Kultur—Medien—Macht.*

Cultural Studies und Medienanalyse (3. Auflage), edited by Andreas Hepp and Rainer Winter, 41-60. Wiesbaden, Germany: VS, 2006.

Foucault, Michel. "Technologien des Selbst." In *Technologien des Selbst*, edited by Luther H. Martin et al., 24-62. Frankfurt am Main, Germany: Fischer, 1993.

———. *Überwachen und Strafen*. Frankfurt am Main, Germany: Suhrkamp, 1994 (1975).

Garner, David et al. "Cultural Expectations of Thinness in Women." *Psychological Reports* 47, no. 2 (1980): 483-491.

Geraghty, Christine. *Women and Soap Opera: A Study of Prime Time Soaps*. Cambridge, U.K.: Polity Press, 1991.

Groesz, Lisa M., Michael P. Levine and Sarah K. Murnen. "The Effect of Experimental Presentation of Thin Media Images on Body Satisfaction: A Meta-Analytic Review." *International Journal of Eating Disorders* 31, no. 1 (2001): 1-16.

Gugutzer, Robert. "Zur Körperthematisierung in einer Individualisierten Gesellschaft." *Kultursoziologie* 7, no. 2 (1998): 33-54.

———. *Soziologie des Körpers*. Bielefeld, Germany: Transcript, 2004.

———. "Der Körper als Identitätsmedium: Essstörungen." In *Soziologie des Körpers*, edited by Markus Schroer, 323-355. Frankfurt am Main, Germany: Suhrkamp, 2005.

Hahn, Kornelia and Michael Meuser. "Zur Einführung: Soziale Repräsentation des Körpers—Körperliche Repräsentation des Sozialen." In *Körperrepräsentationen. Die Ordnung des Sozialen und der Körper*, edited by Kornelia Hahn and Michael Meuser, 7-16. Konstanz, Germany: UVK, 2002.

Hargreaves, Duane A. and Marika Tiggemann. "The Effect of 'Thin Ideal' Television Commercials on Body Dissatisfaction and Schema Activation During Early Adolescence." *Journal of Youth and Adolescence* 32, no. 5 (2003): 367-373.

Harrison, Kristen. "Television Viewers' Ideal Body Proportions: The Case of Curvaceously Thin Woman." *Sex Roles* 48, no. 5/6 (2003): 255-264.

Harrison, Kristen and Joanne Cantor. "The Relationship Between Media Consumptions and Eating Disorders." *Journal of Communication* 47, no. 1 (1997): 40-67.

Hartmann, Martin and Axel Honneth. "Paradoxien des Kapitalismus. Ein Untersuchungsprogramm." *Berliner Debatte Initial* 15, no. 1 (2004): 1-17.

Hochschild, Arlie R. *Das gekaufte Herz. Zur Kommerzialisierung der Gefühle*. Frankfurt am Main, Germany: Campus, 1990.

Irving, Lori M. "Mirror images: Effects of the standard of beauty on the self- and body-esteem of woman exhibiting varying levels of bulimic symptoms." *Journal of Social and Clinical Psychology* 9, no. 3 (1990): 230-242.

Keller, Reiner. "Analysing Discourse: An Approach from the Sociology of Knowledge." 2006. www.britannica.com/bps/additionalcontent/18/21647711/Analysing-Discourse-An-Approach-From-the-Sociology-of-Knowledge (accessed November 10, 2009).

Koppetsch, Cornelia. "Die Verkörperung des Schönen Selbst. Zur Statusrelevanz von Attraktivität." In *Körper und Status: Zur Soziologie der Attraktivität*, edited by Cornelia Koppetsch, 99-124. Konstanz, Germany: UVK, 2000.

Krotz, Friedrich. "Zivilisationsprozess und Mediatisierung. Zum Zusammenhang von Medien- und Gesellschaftswandel." In *Medienentwicklung und Gesellschaftlicher Wandel. Beiträge zu einer Theoretischen und Empirischen Herausforderung*, edited by Markus Behmer et al., 15-38. Wiesbaden, Germany: Westdeutscher Verlag,

2003.

———. *Die Mediatisierung Kommunikativen Handelns. Der Wandel von Alltag und Sozialen Beziehungen, Kultur und Gesellschaft durch die Medien.* Opladen, Germany: Westdeutscher Verlag, 2001.

Kudera, Werner. "Einleitung." In *Alltägliche Lebensführung. Arrangements zwischen Traditionalität und Modernisierung,* edited by Projektgruppe "Alltägliche Lebensführung," 7-14. Opladen, Germany: Leske+Budrich, 1995.

Lemke, Thomas. "Neoliberalismus, Staat und Selbsttechnologien. Ein kritischer Überblick über die Governmentality Studies." *Politische Vierteljahresschrift* 41, no. 1 (2000): 31-47.

Lewis, Tania. *Smart Living. Lifestyle Media and Popular Expertise.* New York: Peter Lang, 2008.

Livingstone, Sonia. *Making Sense of Television: The Psychology of Audience Interpretation.* Oxford, U.K.: Pergamon Press, 1990.

Meuser, Michael. "Ganze Kerle, Anti-Helden und andere Typen. Zum Männlichkeitsdiskurs in neuen Männerzeitschriften." In *Männlichkeit und soziale Ordnung. Neuere Beiträge zur Geschlechterforschung,* edited by Peter Döge and Michael Meuser, 219-236. Opladen, Germany: Leske + Budrich, 2001.

Mikos, Lothar. *Es wird dein Leben! Familienserien im Fernsehen und Alltag der Zuschauer.* Münster, Germany: Lit, 1994.

Moseley, Rachel. "Makeover Takeover on British Television." *Screen* 41, no. 3 (2000): 299-314.

———. "Real Lads do Cook . . . but Some Things Are Still Hard to Talk About." *European Journal of Cultural Studies* 4, no. 1 (2000): 32-39.

Myers, Philip N. and Frank A. Biocca. "The Elastic Body-Image: The Effect of Body Advertising and Programming on Body Image Distortions in Young Women." *Journal of Communication* 42, no. 3 (1992): 108-133.

Neckel, Sighard. *Die Tragödie des Erfolgs.* 2004. www.04.diskursfestival.de/pdf /vortragneckel.pdf (accessed April 4, 2007).

Petersen, Lars-Eric. "Der Einfluss von Models in der Werbung auf das Körperselbstbild der Betrachter/innen." *Zeitschrift für Medienpsychologie* 17, no. 5 (2005): 54-63.

Plessner, Helmuth. *Die Stufen des Organischen und der Mensch.* Frankfurt am Main, Germany: Suhrkamp, 1981.

Radway, Janice A. *Reading the Romance: Women, Patriarchy and Popular Literature.* London: Verso, 1987.

Rittner, Volker. "Körperbezug, Sport und Ästhetik. Zum Funktionswandel der Sportästhetik in komplexen Gesellschaften." *Sportwissenschaft* 19, no. 4 (1989): 359-377.

Rohr, Elisabeth (ed.). *Körper und Identität. Gesellschaft auf den Leib geschrieben.* Königstein/Taunus, Germany: Ulrike Helmer Verlag, 2004.

Rossmann, Constanze and Hans-Bernd Brosius. "Vom hässlichen Entlein zum Schönen Schwan? Zur Darstellung und Wirkung von Schönheitsoperationen im Fernsehen." *Medien- und Kommunikationswissenschaft* 53, no. 4 (2005): 507-532.

Schroer, Markus. "Selbstthematisierung. Von der (Er-)Findung des Selbst und der Suche nach Aufmerksamkeit." In *Die Ausweitung der Bekenntniskultur. Neue Formen der Selbstthematisierung,* edited by Günter Burkart, 41-72. Wiesbaden, Germany: VS,

2006.

Spitzer, Brenda L., Katherine A. Henderson and Marilyn T. Zivian, "'Gender Differences in Population Versus Media Body Sizes': A Comparison over Four Decades." *Sex Roles* 40, no. 7/8 (1999): 519-565.

Stice, Eric, Diane Spangler and Stewart W. Agras. "Exposure to Media Portrayed Thin-ideal Images Adversely Affects Vulnerable Girls. A Longitudinal Experiment." *Journal of Social and Clinical Psychology* 20, no. 3 (2001): 207-288.

Thomas, Tanja and Ines Langemeyer. "Mediale Unterhaltungsangebote aus Gesellschaftskritischer Perspektive: Von der Kritik an der Kulturindustrie zur Analyse der Gegenwärtigen Gouvernementalität." In *Kritische Theorie Heute*, edited by Rainer Winter and Peter V. Zima, 259-282. Bielefeld, Germany: transcript, 2007.

Thompson, Kevin J. et al. *Exacting Beauty. Theory, Assessment and Treatment of Body Image Disturbance.* Washington: American Psychological Association, 1998.

Voß, Günther G. *Lebensführung als Arbeit. Über die Autonomie der Person im Alltag der Gesellschaft.* Stuttgart, Germany: Enke, 1991.

Wood, Helen and Bev Skeggs. "Spectacular Morality: Reality Television and the Remaking of the Working Class." In *The Media and Social Theory*, edited by David Hesmondhalgh and Jason Toynbee, 177-194. London: Routledge, 2008.

Conclusion

Chapter 19
The Politics of the Prefix: From "Post" to "Trans" (and Back)?
Nico Carpentier and Sofie Van Bauwel

Capturing Change and Critique

The development of concepts is a human activity which is obviously situated at the core of humanity but also finds itself at the heart of the academic enterprise. Concepts structure and capture the ever-fluid knowledge and realities and offer tools for reflection and analysis. They grant access to think about and comprehend the multitude of practices and events, situations and processes, inner and outer worlds. But at the same time, they are always doomed to fail, partially because the knowledge producing systems are less self-evident. To use John Hartley's[1] words in relation to the study of media: "we, modernist intellectuals working in barely post-medieval institutions, are no longer self-evidently the source, the 'provider' of knowledge. One complication of the emergence of the new economy, creativity, and consumption is that now 'we' have serious competition. We've dissolved into our other, but so has our value." But there is more, as these concepts' implicit assumption of universal access to reality is also permanently frustrated by the sliding of the signifiers, at both the temporal and spatial level. Derrida's notion of *différance*[2] is one of the intellectual projects that allow capturing the inherent problems of the concept, as it theorizes the permanent deferral of meaning, which has to face an endless chain of signifiers. Also Ernesto Laclau's[3] use of the notion of the floating signifier, in combination with his universalism/particularism discussion, is helpful to exemplify the structural contingency of concepts. The floating signifier, a signifier that is "overflowed with meaning,"[4] assumes different meanings in different contexts/discourses. In other words, the floating signifier shows us that concepts can take on different meanings, depending on their positions in distinct discourses.

By meaning something very different in different contextualized discourses, they bear witness of the ability of concepts to cross discursive frontiers. As Laclau[5] puts it, the concept of the floating signifier allows us to "apprehend the logic of displacements of that frontier." Similarly, Laclau's discussion of the universal and the particular illustrates the impossibility to ultimately fix meanings and concepts, as the universal is an empty signifier which always requires a particular, so that this particular can be universalized in order to (attempt to) saturate the universal. The universal cannot exist without the particular. To use Laclau's words: "Now, this universality needs—for its expression—to be incarnated in something essentially incommensurable with it: a particularity."[6]

However relevant these critiques on the stability and fixation of the concept are, we should not forget that concepts can refer to their own fluidity (and temporality), showing an intertextual awareness of their own significatory particularities. Concepts can thus become self-reflexive and self-critical, and expressions of their own restrictions. This process of conceptual self-relexivity is partially embedded within the academic system itself, where debates about definitions of specific concepts are manifold and seen as common academic practice. One illustration here is the often-used introductory remark that the concept being scrutinized should be regarded as a "contested notion" or map. But sometimes, the fluidity of the concept is emphasized even more explicitly. In some cases, the concept is altered only slightly, by for instance adding or changing one of its letters. One example here is Robertson's concept of glocalization[7], a conflation of globalization and localization. But also Derrida's "quasi-transcendental"[8] concept of *différance* is an example of this strategy. In other cases, a prefix (like "post" or "trans"), with or without a hyphen, is added to a concept. Again, this addition allows authors to either critique the "original" concept, and/or to symbolize changed realities which require a conceptual reconfiguration.

These prefixed concepts are more than a "group of 'post' [or 'trans'] philosophies reflecting the uncertainties of our age" (as Sakwa claims, talking about post-communism[9]); these modifications become expressions of the fluidity and self-reflexive nature of the concept.

Early Generations of the Politics of the Prefix: Postmodernism and Post-Structuralism

Two crucial examples of the politics of the prefix are postmodernism and post-structuralism, which obviously contain a break with their predecessors (modernism and structuralism). Despite the wide variation that is covered by the concepts of postmodernism and post-structuralism, and the reluctance of some of its key practitioners to see themselves explicitly grouped under these labels,[10] we can still see both concepts as a clear critical reaction against an intellectual (and ideological) order that was seen as outdated and sometimes even as naïve.

In the case of postmodernism, we can revert to Lyotard's[11] brief description of the modern and the postmodern in his *Postmodern condition*.

> I will use the term modern to designate any science that legitimates itself with reference to a metadiscourse of this kind making an explicit appeal to some grand narrative, such as the dialectics of Spirit, the hermeneutics of meaning, the emancipation of the rational or working subject, or the creation of wealth . . . Simplifying to the extreme, I define postmodern as incredulity toward metanarratives.

More generally, the postmodern is seen as either a moment of rupture with the past, or the introduction of new ways of thinking that emphasize the rise of uncertainty, diversity, locality, changeability and indeterminacy. If we for instance take Ihab Hassan's[12] overview on the differences between modern and postmodern literature, we can see that modernism is associated with (amongst others) form, purpose, design, origin/cause, linear narration and determinacy, whilst postmodernism is linked to anti-form, play, chance, difference and indeterminacy. In other words, the "post" prefix is often used to signify a change in artistic, intellectual and societal configuration which opens up a wide variety of novel practices. Especially in the case of the less nuanced variations of postmodern theory, the "post" prefix indicates a clear and clean rupture with the past of modernism and the start of a different age where modernist logics have ceased to exist.

The idea of a clear-cut rupture or turn with the modernist past or practices has been fiercely criticized. A very brief formulation of this critique has been elaborated by Lethen: "The concept [of modernism] was constructed so as to form a dark background for the brilliant claims of Postmodernism."[13] But to do postmodern theory some justice: even Lyotard has pointed to the interwovenness of the modern and the postmodern, as illustrated by this (rather famous) quote: "A work can become modern only if it is first postmodern. Postmodernism thus understood is not modernism at its end but in the nascent state, and this state is constant."[14] This nuanced position does of course not ignore the specificity of the postmodern, as captured in Lyotard's calls to arms: "Let us wage a war on totality; Let us be witness to the unpresentable; Let us activate the differences, and save the honor of the name."[15]

A similar logic of rupture applies for post-structuralist theory, as the "post" prefix indicates a break with and critique launched against structuralism. More than is the case with postmodernism, post-structuralism engaged in a critique on its intellectual predecessor, which partially had to do with the structuralist emphasis on method and methodology and the implications of this emphasis for the paradigm's knowledge construction. As Eagleton puts it: "With the advent of post-structuralism, what seemed reactionary about structuralism was not this refusal of history, but nothing less than the very concept of structure itself"[16] Structuralism was problematized through the notion of essentialism and its refusal to see the "structurality of structure."[17] Post-structuralism relentlessly attacked and shattered the assumptions of stability that grounded the structuralist project, or in Young's words: "In brief, it may be said that post-structuralism fractures the serene unity of the stable sign and the unified subject."[18] Instead, post-structuralism emphasized how structures were inherently contradictory and unavoidably failed. This has consequences for the use of the "post" prefix, as its use implies a clear rupture with some of the core assumptions of structuralism, whilst at the same time still sharing some of its main focal points. Easthope has summarized this position as follows: "The prefix 'post-' is serious not casual for post-structuralism gets its intellectual force by being both *after* structuralism and *because* of it, because of the limitations discovered in structuralism's project."[19]

The Proliferation of the "Post" Prefix

The use of the "post" prefix has not been limited to the debates on postmodernism and post-structuralism, and a wide variety of "other" concepts have been developed, although some of these "other" concepts remain related to the debates on postmodernism and post-structuralism. For instance Bell's[20] concept of the post-industrial, which theoretizes the shift from an industrial society to a service- and science-based and information-led society, can be seen as one of the characteristics of the postmodern society. And Said's *Orientalism*[21], which played a crucial role in the development of post-colonial theory[22] with its focus on the articulation of (cultural) identities in once-colonized states, is very much indebted to Foucauldian post-structuralism.

In both cases, the post-industrial and the post-colonial, we can again witness the occurrence of a shift and/or rupture. In the post-industrial, there is a shift from the industrial to the service economy, whilst in the post-colonial condition; the shift (from being colonized to being independent) is situated in the recent past. And yet again, these shifts are not considered total and complete, as the industrial and the colonial continue to impact on (and in some cases to haunt) these "new" societies, resulting in many cases in hybrid mixtures of the industrial, the colonial and what came afterwards.

The territorial emphasis in post-colonial theory generates a strong similarity with another example of the use of the "post" prefix, namely the concepts of post-socialism or post-communism. Here, the events of 1989-1991 provide an anchoring point for the study of the political transformations that affected a large number of nations in Eurasia and caused the collapse of party states and administered economies and the entry into wild capitalist economies. As Sharad and Verdery[23] argue, post-socialism "began as simply a temporal designation: societies once referred to as constituting 'actually existing socialism' had ceased to exist as such, replaced by one or another form of putatively democratizing state," but later a more critical angle to post-socialism was added, converging to the agenda of post-colonialism. Nevertheless, when comparing post-colonialism and post-socialism, Sharad and Verdery emphasize the rupture between what had been before, and what came after: "both 'posts' followed and continue to reflect on periods of heightened political change . . . and both labels signify the complex results of the abrupt changes forced on those who underwent them: that is, becoming something other than socialist or other than colonized."

Intrinsically connected to the post-socialist (intellectual) agenda is the issue of Marxist theory, and the rise of post-Marxism. Without reverting to the discrediting discourse that—when the Wall came down—proclaimed not just the end of history but also the demise of the Marxist intellectual project, post-Marxism tried to deal with the class determinism and structuralism that characterized traditional Marxism. Especially the privileged role of the notion of class became one of the main objects of these reworkings, resulting in what Wood[24] called "the declassing of the socialist project," but what could be better termed as its de-essentialization. Post-Marxists like Laclau and Mouffe[25] continued to situate themselves within the "classic ideal of socialism" and plead for a "polyphony of voices" in which the different (radically) democratic political struggles—such as anti-racism, anti-sexism and anti-capitalism—are all allotted an equally important role. At the same time they did propagate the need to break with Marxist orthodoxy, keeping part of the intellectual inheritance intact, but at the same time structurally modifying it.[26] Interestingly, Mouffe also introduced another prefixed concept in her more recent work, namely the post-political. The starting point of her argument is the broad definition of the political, which avoids restricting the ontological dimension of conflict to institutionalized politics. In contrast to Beck's prefixed concept of sub-politics (which he distinguishes from politics insofar that "agents *outside* the political or corporatist system are allowed to appear on the stage"[27]), the political is defined as an all-encompassing concept that touches upon all human relations:

> By "the political," I refer to the dimension of antagonism that is inherent in human relations, antagonism that can take many forms and emerge in different types of social relations. "Politics" on the other side, indicates the ensemble of practices, discourses and institutions which seek to establish a certain order and organize human coexistence in conditions that are always potentially conflictual because they are affected by the dimension of "the political."[28]

The post-political then becomes an ideological hegemonic strategy that denies the inherently conflictive nature of the political, and that claims an ultimate consensus. Even the possibility of contesting these forms of identification and moral values becomes non-existent. Similar to Rancière's concept of the post-democratic,[29] the post-political represents a negation of the political, whilst still remaining firmly based within the political.[30]

The last example of a prefixed concept, which uses "post," is post-human theory. This cluster of theories looks at "how a historically specific construction called the human is giving way to a different construction called the post-human."[31] According to Hayes, the post-human is characterized by the privileging of "informational pattern over material instantiation," by defining consciousness as "an evolutionary upstart trying to claim that it is the whole show when in actually it is only a minor sideshow" and by seeing the human body as "the original prosthesis we all learn to manipulate," which allows the body to become "seamlessly articulated with intelligent machines."[32]

Reminiscent of the "ironic political myth" of the cyborg,[33] the post-human is seen as the end stage of trans-humanism, where the human as we know it becomes transformed into an entity that is structurally different from its origins. But again this transformation is not to be considered total: "the 'post' of post-humanism need not imply the absence of humanity or moving beyond it in some biological or evolutionary manner." This latter example of the use of the "post" prefix is also interesting because in this case the concepts of trans-humanity and post-humanity are both used, where the post-human signifies the final stage and outcome, while the trans-human refers to the process that will (eventually) lead to the final stage of the post-human. In short, the trans-human is still linked to the bodily flesh, whilst post-humanism has left the materiality of the body behind and articulates a transcendent space where the limits of being human are transgressed. Both concepts can for instance be found in Bostrom's article *In Defense of Posthuman Dignity.*

> Transhumanists promote the view that human enhancement technologies should be made widely available . . . Ultimately, it is possible that such enhancements may make us, or our descendants, "posthuman," beings who may have indefinite health-spans, much greater intellectual faculties than any current human being—and perhaps entirely new sensibilities or modalities—as well as the ability to control their own emotions.[34]

(Re)Signifying Fluidity: The "Trans" Prefix

As the trans-humanity/post-humanity example already indicates, the border between the "post" and "trans" prefixes is often blurred. But at the same time, the overview of the series of "post" prefixed concepts does indicate the presence of a rupture with a past situation or a set of practices or with an intellectual history, belief or reality. However present these discontinuities are, they are always accompanied with a series of continuities that bridge the past and the present. In the case of the "trans" prefix, we also see this oscillation of continuity and discontinuity, but there is a stronger emphasis on the process of change, on a simultaneous co-existence of what was and what has been transgressed, and on their fluid mergers.

Here, we would like to mention three examples, not accidentally all related to more culturalist approaches. First, the concept of the trans-national is seen (by Hannerz) as a more "humble" version of globalization to describe "any process or relationship that somehow crosses state boundaries."[35] Hannerz immediately juxtaposes the trans-national to the international, as the actors of trans-national processes are not confined to state actors, but "may now be individuals, groups, movements, business enterprises, and in no small part it is this diversity that we need to consider."[36] But there is more, as trans-nationalism is not merely linked to acts of (state) boundary-crossing. Vertovec[37] unpacks the different layers that characterize the trans-national, which can be seen as a social morphology (with ethnic diasporas as a prime example), a type of consciousness marked by dual or multitude of identifications, a mode of cultural reproduction that is characterized by a "fluidity of constructed styles, social institutions, and everyday practices,"[38] an avenue of capital (with trans-national corporations as example), a site of political engagement (represented by international nongovernmental organizations) and a (re)construction of "place" or locality (resulting in an awareness of multilocality). This brings us to an understanding of the trans-national as a process that transgresses borders, but that also leads to co-existence and simultaneity, where multilocality and multiple identities are generated.

Very much related to the trans-national is the trans-local. In his 1995 book chapter *The Production of Locality*, Appadurai deals with the complex interplay between locality—more specifically neighborhoods—and context. He argues that context provides the constitutive outside of locality, but that locality simultaneously provides us with a context. To use his words: "The central dilemma is that neighborhoods both are contexts and at the same time *require and produce* contexts."[39] At the same time, the capacity of localities to produce their "own" context and subjectivities is affected by the "locality producing capabilities of larger-scale formations (nation-states, kingdoms, missionary empires and trading cartels)."[40] As argued elsewhere,[41] the trans-local becomes the moment when the local is stretched beyond its borders, while still remaining situated in the local. The trans-local is more than "maintaining only limited, intermittent, episodic, financially uneven ties."[42] As Broeckmann[43] puts it, it is the moment where "different worlds and their local agents—individuals, organizations, machines—co-operate with global and nomadic agents within networked environments." Or in other words: "It is the moment where the local merges with a part of its outside context, without transforming itself into this context. It is the moment where the local simultaneously incorporates its context and transgresses into it. It is the moment where the local reaches out to a familiar unknown."[44] Similar to the trans-national, the "trans" prefix of trans-local refers to the transgression of the local, combined with its expansion. In Appadurai's argument, locality is merging with its context, resulting in a fluid mixture in the local and what goes beyond the local.

Finally, the concept of the trans-cultural also offers an insight in the meaning of the "trans" prefix in cultural theory. In this case, it is well worth going back to the origins of the concept, to Fernando Ortiz who defined trans-culturalism as a synthesis of two phases: the combination of "a deculturalization of the past with a métissage with the present."[45] Just like the trans-national, the concept of trans-cultural is juxtaposed to the intercultural,[46] where the latter is seen as too closely connected to what Streeck has called the "territorial view of culture"[47] and linked to essentialist approaches. Thurlow expresses his preference as follows:

> I still prefer the sense transcultural creates of moving through and across cultural systems, in whatever way they may be constituted or conceived. It allows better, I think, for the fluidity of these systems, their porous boundaries and constantly reorienting expressions, as well as the conceptual spaces that open up between traditionally defined cultural systems . . . that emerge between shifting patterns of sociocultural organisation and practice.[48]

Thurlow continues by emphasizing the connotation of trans-cultural as "beyond," which could be "signifying a transcending of essentialist or universalist ideas about culture as something unified, reified and possessed."[49] This approach implies that the trans-cultural can still be seen as a meeting between different cultures, but this meeting can become (seen as) a fluid encounter of cultural positions that are in themselves already hybrid assemblages. This again results in a perspective that emphasizes the process of merging still diverse identities, whilst denying any original position.

"Trans"/"Post" in Media Studies

This reader aims to contribute to the prefix debate (and to the politics of the prefix) by deploying a number of "trans" concepts in the field of media and communication studies, with trans-reality as the most prominent one. In order to do so, we (as editors) developed a slightly unusual procedure to elaborate these "trans" concepts, starting from a short position paper (on which the introduction of this book is based) on trans-reality, trans-genre, trans-politics and trans-audience. This position paper was then communicated to the chapter's authors, and their abstracts and first drafts of their chapters formed the basis of a negotiation between editors and authors, aimed at fleshing out the "trans" concepts as much as possible. This structural openness led to a very fruitful intellectual cross-fertilization, of which the outcomes are discussed in this concluding chapter.

Trans-Reality

The notion of trans-reality is at the core of this book project and primarily refers to the multitude of overlapping realities that structure our present-day worlds. The old notion of one objective and stable reality can hardly be considered a sophisticated tool to access our contingent contemporary realities, but at the same time we still desperately need our sense of (constructed) reality. From this perspective, the notion of post-reality would introduce the nihilist approach, to which we do not subscribe. In contrast, the notion of trans-reality allows us to capture the complex configuration of a diversity of interacting representational machineries that contribute to the construction of our worlds. The concept also allows highlighting that the different constitutive fragments of the real are fluid and contingent, and have become co-determining and co-existent.

Obviously, media organizations play a role in this process, which not necessarily implies that they have full control over the representations that are being generated. For instance Couldry[50] has already convincingly argued that "the myth of the mediated center" does not hold however hard the media industry tries to uphold this (truth) claim. This firstly implies (as Fiske already posited in *Understanding Popular Culture*[51]) that texts generated by the media industry will contain traces and slippages that give us access to other realities, for instance to "the elaborate trappings of a contemporary TV show, as well as the hardships suffered by the subjectivity of those who agree to undergo the ordeals of the self."[52] Secondly, audiences have interpretative and productive capacities, which in turn generates new (interpretations of) realities/y as Van Bauwel stresses in her case study of trauma Reality TV. Here the respondents are clearly media savvy and articulate the real as a constructed, fluid but still authentic reality.

This lack of ultimate control does of course not imply that media organizations do not intervene in the representation of reality, and that their interventions will not circulate and become intertwined with the representations generated by other (non-media) representational machineries. Moreover, we should also keep in mind that many of the present-day media organizations operate in a context of converged ownership which affects (and mainstreams) their content and production process. But also the existence of a professional production culture affects both content and process. For instance the media practices legitimized through a hegemonized identity of media professionals[53] will result (in the case of Reality TV) in "a reality that is 'staged,' with specific characteristics and procedures that can be easily controlled and guided."[54] At the same time, this staging is also as real as it can get, which again leads to the different realities offered through mediation processes, captured by the concept of trans-reality.[55] To push the argument even further, the use of fictional storylines that transcend "the boundaries of the real and the fictional"[56] (although Andacht claims that there is "no abolition of the structural border between fact and fiction"[57]) are part of the reality of fiction, which might not be factual reality, but is still real.

Another specificity of the Reality TV genre (together with many other media genres) is that is it part of a trans-national economy, which triggers a wide variety of dynamics.[58] The trans-national in itself is already a transgression of the frontiers of our imaginary communities,[59] which allows for the flows of people, meanings and money, resulting in hybrid and multiple identities (being offered and read). In the case of Reality TV, we see that the global formats[60] are often localized (at least up to a certain extent—"localization may not always be possible without undermining the features that drove the success of the format in its original market"[61]), but that in some cases the programs simply travel from one country to another.[62] In the first case, we can find the production of a mixture of different "national" (combined with "global") realities in the programs themselves, offered to audiences which in turn will produce localized readings, whilst in the latter case (with a "foreign" text) these localized readings will still remain possible.

Trans-Genre

This brings us to the notion of the trans-genre, which refers to the fluidity of genre conventions. Genre is a way to organize narration, or in an audiovisual context it can be considered "a class of programs."[63] This clustering becomes fluid, not only through the workings of (media) industries, but also through its audience receptions:

> The most important recent development in thinking about familiar entertainment genres was to put them into the context of audiences' understanding and activities. Genres are no longer seen as sets of fixed elements, but as working with repertoires of elements or fluid systems of convention and expectation.[64]

Boddin makes a similar point in this book, when he refers to the Reality TV genre as a genre that "continuously being creatively re-invented and discursively re-articulated within diverse rationalities."[65] Interestingly, he (and a number of other authors of this book) also make use of Corner's[66] concept of post-documentary television, for instance in the following quote: "its method, over time, being continuously re-invented throughout various hybrid reality TV formats, and (re-)articulated within diverse discourses and rationalities in a PDTV [Post-Documentary TV] context." Looking at the concept of post-documentary television through the lenses of the politics of the prefix, one can wonder if the "post" prefix, signifying rupture (albeit without total discontinuity with what came before), is reconcilable with the notion of the trans-genre, which emphasizes the fluid mixture of genres and their simultaneous co-existence.

Trans-Politics

Obviously, representational issues extend beyond the "mere" representation of (trans-)reality, as ideology enters into these representations, rendering them political. Here, the above-mentioned distinction Mouffe[67] makes between politics and the political can be helpful, as the broad definition of the political also allows for the inclusion of the ideological nature of media representations (together with many other societal fields) as part of the political. If we take Mouffe's definition of the political as the "dimension of antagonism that is inherent in human relations"[68] as a starting point, we can first of all argue that the sphere of (institutionalized) politics is part of the political. This perspective articulates the political as an overarching principle that is being played out in politics, but also in spheres like the media. Moreover, this conceptual articulation also allows theorizing (more than Beck's concept of sub-politics does) the sometimes interlocking co-existence of political projects in different societal spheres, without prioritizing or hierarchizing them. The political allows even for an emphasis on its potential presence in other social or cultural spheres. In this sense the political can also be seen as trans-politics, as the expansion of institutionalized politics, without ignoring the existence and importance of institutionalized politics.

As Mouffe has argued (partially in collaboration with Laclau[69]), political projects can have hegemonic ambitions, aiming to become a social imaginary, or "a horizon: it is not one among other objects but an absolute limit which structures a field of intelligibility and is thus the condition of possibility of the emergence of any object."[70] One of the strategies used to achieve this objective is to push the (truth) claims of the hegemonic discourse beyond the realm of contestation, rendering them post-political. To quote Žižek: the post-political "claims to leave behind old ideological struggles and instead focus on expert management and administration."[71] As the post-political again uses a broad view on the political (otherwise it would be termed post-politics), we can see this strategy at work in a multitude of societal spheres, including the media. Two of the chapters in this volume deal with the way the post-political enters into media representations: Police Videos Reality TV are seen to contribute to the normalization and hegemonization of the neoliberal discourse on citizenship (as responsible individuals) and Punitive TV engages in the normalization and hegemonization "of law and order by proxy,"[72] by publicly punishing the criminal. As Pinseler[73] argues, these disciplining acts work on different levels: "On the first level, viewers are taught about hegemonic conceptions of normality and deviance through normality being exemplified by depictions of deviance, and what happens to those who dare to deviate. On the second level, people are shown being punished on TV."

But the post-political not only infests media representations. As Carpentier argues in this volume, also the identity of Reality TV media professionals and more specifically their power position (symbolized by the concept of the *primum movens immobile*) has become normalized and hegemonized. The management of the media professionals and the apparent impossibility to structurally contest the unequal power relations that legitimize this management, can be seen as one of the most problematic components of Reality TV, and as a prime example of the post-political at work outside the sphere of politics. Of course, the post-political (and the hegemonic) is not total, and it can (and will) still be contested. As Salamon puts it: "There is a fine line between exploitation, empowerment and subversion. Somehow, Reality TV participants manage to dip their foot into all three camps."[74]

Trans-Audience and the Trans-Professional

Finally, the "trans" prefix can also be used in relation to the audience. Arguably, the concept of the audience has witnessed two structural shifts, which have transformed it beyond recognition. The first shift, which took place in the 1970s and 1980s of the twenteeth century, has transformed the audience from a passive and atomized individual into an active and contextualized member of society (as a consumer or citizen). Crucial to this shift was the recognition that audiences played an active role in the processes of signification and interpretation, but also that audiences were always more than "just" audiences. Their interpretative capacities and "their contextual embeddedness" may already render them trans-audiences, a concept that according to Thomas indicates "that there is still a relationship between these (trans-)audiences and the media content, but without supporting the media-centric thesis."[75] The second shift is based on the evolution of one-to-many to many-to-many communication, which was theorized at the end of the twentieth century and the first decade of the twenty-first century. An example of this type of argument can be found in Jay Rosen's essay *The People Formerly Known as the Audience*. Rosen argues that the (commercial) media system has lost control over its audiences, as it has been (re)transformed into "the public made realer, less fictional, more able, and less predictable."[76] He describes this change as follows:

> The people formerly known as the audience are those who were on the receiving end of a media system that ran one way, in a broadcasting pattern, with high entry fees and a few firms competing to speak very loudly while the rest of the population listened in isolation from one another—and who today are not in a situation like that at all.[77]

Especially the combination of two shifts can be captured by the concept of the trans-audience, where the "frontiers between audience and media professionals"[78] and the frontiers between media consumption and everyday life[79] are transgressed, resulting in what Hautakangas[80] calls a multi-positional engagement. As he puts it in relation to *Big Brother*: "Producers, fans and participants all seem to experience some control over the production and formation of the show; they all participate as audiences; and they all see themselves in the text/object position."[81]

Unavoidably, this process has also affected the media professional, to which we could then in turn refer to as the trans-professional. Hibberd formulates the optimistic scenario as follows: "The distinction between producers and publics or participants becomes more fluid, and emphatic relationships and partnerships are constructed."[82] Later, he clarifies this as follows: "Producers here are articulated as trans-professional, their professional identity being affected by the participatory process. But their mediating role does not imply the end of this professional identity, only its extension."[83]

But at the same time, this extension of the role of the media professional, captured by the "trans" prefix, is not the only option. The media professional's identity has been part of a struggle for redefinition for a considerable time. For instance the alternative/community media movement has argued incessantly that non-professionals are also capable of performing tasks that have been safeguarded for media professionals. More recently, the advent of Web 2.0 has also put considerable pressure on the position (and identity) of the media professional. Apart from turning into trans-professionals, the second option then becomes the (continued) redrawal into and post-political defense of the "traditional" definition of the media professional, which implies the articulation of the professional identity as managers of resources, in full control of the production process. Hibberd's (but also Carpentier's) chapter in this volume touches upon yet another option, which is the further abandonment of the professional norms and values through the pressures of continued commercialization, which he terms post-professional. This concept then allows problematizing the instrumentalization of audience members by media professionals, but can be expanded as a rupture with the old ethical discourses that protected and legitimitized the power positions held by media professionals.

The Politics and Analytics of Prefixing

When looking back at this book project one can wonder about the value and necessity of introducing prefixes into media studies concepts, and pushing their use to its limits. In conclusion, we believe that there are three points to be made. First, there is the obvious point that the editors and authors of this volume hold no monopoly on the use of prefixes in academic language. This concluding chapter has listed quite a substantial number of concepts that have been attributed a prefix, and many more (like for instance post-feminism and trans-gender) were omitted. Whether we like it or not, the prefixes have entered our academic language, and should be dealt with accordingly. One way of doing this is the need for an awareness of the politics of the prefix, which does show (or hide) strong conceptual, normative and/or ontological claims, situated within both the intellectual/academic debates and the (related) models used to describe our present-day (and past and future) societies. For instance the choice for either "trans" or "post" holds more weight than the four or five letters might indicate, especially because of the dynamics between the "original" and the prefixed concepts, because of the relationships of (dis-)continuity, fluidity and simultaneity covered by the prefix, and because of the normative load attached to the prefix.

Secondly, the temporariness and contextuality of prefixing should be emphasized. Conceptual re-articulations are important, because they counter conceptual (and general) conservatism and essentialism, but at the same time prefixes are naive attempts to stop the sliding of the signifier. Moreover, they are artificial and limited in their long-term applicability: Prefixing prefixed concepts is for instance not an elegant conceptual solution. Eventually, the struggle to signify should (especially when describing social realities) result in the resignification of the "original" concept or the development of new concepts. From this perspective, prefixing can be seen as part of these processes, but can only play a limited role.

Finally, during this book project, the dynamics between the two prefixes turned out to be intellectually challenging. Combining either the "trans" or "post" prefix with media studies concepts was enriching, but the real strength of these prefixes resided in analytically combining the "trans" or "post" prefix. The tensions between trans-politics and the post-political, between trans-professionalism and post-professionalism, between trans-genre and post-documentary, and (potentially) between trans-reality and post-reality have proven to be most helpful in analyzing our mediated realities.

Notes

1. Hartley, 35.
2. Derrida, 1998.
3. Laclau, 2005.
4. Torfing, 301.
5. Laclau, 2005: 133.
6. Laclau, 1996, 57.
7. Robertson.
8. Derrida, 1986. It is, as Derrida has remarked in his book *Glas*, a "quasi-transcendental" concept, insofar as the difference between words both engender meaning and forever defer meaning, différance serves as both the condition of possibility and the impossibility of meaning.

9. Sakwa, 125.

10. Illustrative is Foucault's resistance against him being labeled a structuralist: "In France, certain half-witted 'commentators' persist in labelling me a 'structuralist.' I have been unable to get it into their tiny minds that I have used none of the methods, concepts or key terms that characterize structural analysis. I should be grateful if a more serious public would free me from a connection that certainly does me honour, but that I have not deserved. There may well be certain similarities between the works of the structuralists and my own work. It would hardly behove me, of all people, to claim that my discourse is independent of conditions and rules of which I am very largely unaware, and which determine other work that is being done today. But it is only too easy to avoid the trouble of analysing such work by giving it an admittedly impressive-sounding, but inaccurate, label." Foucault, 1970, xiv.

11. Lyotard, 1984, 8.

12. Hassan, 267-268.

13. Lethen, 233.

14. Lyotard 1984, 78.

15. Lyotard, 1983, 82.

16. Eagleton, 141.

17. Derrida, 1988, 151.

18. Young, 8.

19. Easthope, 23. (Emphasis in original)

20. Bell.

21. Said.

22. This is not to ignore the important antecendents of postcolonial theory, like the work of Franz Fanon, 1963.

23. Sharad and Verdery, 10.

24. Wood, 4.

25. Laclau and Mouffe, 190.

26. In contrast, neo-Marxism is used to explicitly articulate the embrace of the theoretical and conceptual inheritance of Marxism.

27. Beck, 22. (Emphasis in original)

28. Mouffe, 101.

29. Rancière, 88.

30. See also Carpentier, in this volume.

31. Hayles, 2.

32. Hayles, 2-3.

33. Haraway, 1991. At the same time it should be noted that Haraway is uncomfortable with the appropriation of her work by posthuman theory, as she is more interested in posthumanism than in the posthuman. See Haraway in Gane and Haraway, 2006, 140.

34. Bostrom, 202.

35. Hannerz, 6.

36. Ibidem.

37. Vertovec.

38. Vertovec, 452.

39. Appadurai, 209. (Emphasis in original)

40. Appadurai, 211.

41. Carpentier.
42. Barkan, 15.
43. Broeckmann.
44. Carpentier, 246.
45. Cuccioletta, 8.
46. Thurlow.
47. Streeck.
48. Thurlow.
49. Thurlow.
50. Couldry.
51. Fiske.
52. Andacht, 41, in this volume.
53. Carpentier, in this volume.
54. Deligiaouri and Popovic, 67, in this volume.
55. Van Bauwel, 27, in this volume.
56. Pinseler, 134, in this volume.
57. Andacht, 59, in this volume.
58. Enli and McNair, in this volume.
59. Anderson.
60. Moran and Malbon.
61. Enli and McNair, 203, in this volume.
62. Hautakangas, in this volume. See also Lash and Lury.
63. Berger, 4.
64. Branston and Stafford, 77.
65. Boddin, 200, in this volume.
66. Corner.
67. Mouffe.
68. Mouffe, 101.
69. Laclau and Mouffe.
70. Laclau, 1990, 64.
71. Žižek, 40.
72. Pinseler, 142, in this volume.
73. Pinseler, in this volume.
74. Salamon, 178, in this volume.
75. Thomas, 278, in this volume.
76. Rosen, 165.
77. Rosen, 163.
78. Holmes, 254, in this volume.
79. Thomas, in this volume.
80. Hautakangas, in this volume.
81. Hautakangas, 246, in this volume.
82. Hibberd, 91, in this volume.
83. Hibberd, in this volume.

References

Anderson, Benedict. *Imagined Communities. Reflections on the Origin and Spread of Nationalism.* London: Verso, 1991.

Appadurai, Arjun. "The Production of Locality." In *Counterworks: Managing the Diversity of Knowledge*, edited by Richard Fardon, 204-225. London: Routledge, 1995.

Barkan, Elliott R. "Introduction: Immigration, Incorporation, Assimilation, and the Limits of Transnationalism." *Journal of American Ethnic History* 25, no. 2-3 (2006): 1-32.

Beck, Ulrich. "The Reinvention of Politics." In *Reflexive Modernization: Politics, Tradition and Aesthetics in the Modern Social Order*, edited by Ulrich Beck, Anthony Giddens and Scott Lash, 1-55. Cambridge, U.K.: Polity Press, 1994.

Bell, Daniel. *The Coming of Post-industrial Society: A Venture in Social Forecasting.* New York: Basic Books, 1973.

Berger, Arthur Asa. *Popular Culture Genres. Theories and Texts.* Thousand Oaks, Calif.: Sage, 1992.

Bostrom, Nick. "In Defense of Posthuman Dignity." *Bioethics* 19, no. 3 (2005): 202-214. See also www.nickbostrom.com/ethics/dignity.html.

Branston, Gill and Roy Stafford. *The Media Student's Book* (third edition). London: Routledge, 2000.

Broeckmann, Andreas. "Connective Agency in Translocal Environments: Considerations about Experimental Interfaces for the Urban Machine," 1998. www.khm.de/people/krcf/IO_tok/documents/andreas.html (accessed 22 January, 2007).

Carpentier, Nico. "The Belly of the City. Alternative Communicative City Networks." *The International Communication Gazette* 70, no. 3-4 (2008): 237-255.

Chari, Sharad and Katherine Verdery. "Thinking Between the Posts: Postcolonialism, Postsocialism, and Ethnography after the Cold War." *Comparative Studies in Society and History* 51, no. 1 (2009): 6-34.

Corner, John. "Performing the Real. Documentary Diversions." *Television & New Media* 3, no. 3 (2002): 255-269.

Couldry, Nick. *Media Rituals. A Critical Approach.* London: Routledge, 2003.

Cuccioletta, Donald. "Multiculturalism or Transculturalism. Towards a Cosmopolitan Citizenship." *London Journal of Canadian Studies* 17 (2001/2): 1-11.

Derrida, Jacques. "Structure, Sign and Play in the Discourse of the Human Sciences." In *Twentieth-Century Literary Theory*, edited by Ken M. Newton, 149-154. London: Palgrave Macmillan, 1988.

———. *Glas*, translated by John P. Leavey, Jr. and Richard Rand. Lincoln and London: University of Nebraska Press, 1986.

———. *Of Grammatology.* Baltimore, Md.: Johns Hopkins University Press, 1998.

Eagleton, Terry. *Literary Theory: An Introduction.* Oxford, U.K.: Blackwell, 1983.

Easthope, Antony. *British Post-structuralism since 1968.* London: Routledge, 1988.

Fanon, Franz. *The Wretched of the Earth*, translated by Constance Farrington. New York: Grove Weidenfeld, 1963.

Fiske, John. *Understanding Popular Culture.* London: Routledge, 1989.

Foucault, Michel. *The Order of Things: An Archaeology of the Human Sciences.* London: Tavistock, 1970.

Gane, Nicholas and Donna Haraway. "When We have Never Been Human. What is to be Done: Interview with Donna Haraway." *Theory, Culture and Society* 23, no. 7-8 (2006): 135-158.

Hannerz, Ulf. *Transnational Connections: Culture, People, Places.* London: Routledge, 1996.

Haraway, Donna. "A Cyborg Manifesto: Science, Technology, and Socialist-Feminism in the Late Twentieth Century." In *Simians, Cyborgs and Women: The Reinvention of Nature*, 149-181. New York: Routledge, 1991.

Hartley, John. *Television Truths.* Oxford, U.K.: Blackwell, 2008.

Hassan, Ihab Habib. *Dismemberment of Orpheus. Toward a Postmodern Literature.* New York: Oxford University Press, 1982.

Hayles, Katherine. *How We Became Posthuman: Virtual Bodies in Cybernetics, Literature, and Informatics.* Chicago: University of Chicago Press, 1999.

Laclau, Ernesto and Chantal Mouffe. *Hegemony and Socialist Strategy. Towards a Radical Democratic Politics.* London: Verso, 1985.

Laclau, Ernesto. *Emancipation(s).* London: Verso, 1996.

———. *New Reflections on the Revolution of our Time.* London: Verso, 1990.

———. *On Populist Reason.* London: Verso, 2005.

Lash, Scott and Celia Lury. *Global Culture Industry: The Mediation of Things.* Cambridge, U.K.: Polity Press, 2007.

Lethen, Helmut. "Modernism Cut in Half: The Exclusion of the Avant-Garde and the Debate on Postmodernism." In *Approaching Postmodernism*, edited by Douwe Fokkema and Hans Bertens, 233-238. Amsterdam: John Benjamins, 1986.

Lyotard, Jean-François. "Answering the Question: What is Postmodernism?" In *The Anti-Aesthetic: Essays on Postmodern Culture*, edited by Hal Foster, 3-16. Seattle, Wash.: Bay Press, 1983.

———. *The Postmodern Condition. A Report on Knowledge.* Manchester: Manchester University Press, 1984.

Miah, Andy. "Posthumanism: A Critical History." In *Medical Enhancements and Posthumanity*, edited by Bert Gordijn and Ruth Chadwick, 71-94. London: Springer, 2009.

Moran, Albert and Justin Malbon. *Understanding the Global TV Format.* Bristol, U.K.: Intellect, 2006.

Mouffe, Chantal. *The Democratic Paradox.* London and New York: Verso, 2000.

Ortiz, Fernando. *Cuban Counterpoint. Tobacco and Sugar.* Durham, N. C.: Duke University Press, 1995.

Rancière, Jacques. *On the Shores of Politics.* London: Verso, 2007.

Robertson, Roland. "Glocalisation: Time-space and Homogeneity-Heterogeneity." In *Global Modernities*, edited by Mike Featherstone, Scott Lash and Roland Robertson, 25-44. London: Sage, 1995.

Rosen, Jay. "Afterword: The People Formerly Known as the Audience." In *Participation and Media Production. Critical Reflections on Content Creation*, edited by Nico Carpentier and Benjamin De Cleen, 163-165. Cambridge, U.K.: Cambridge Scholars Publishing, 2008.

Said, Edward. *Orientalism.* New York: Vintage, 1978.

Sakwa, Richard. *Postcommunism.* Oxford: Oxford University Press, 1999.

Streeck, Jürgen. "Culture, Meaning and Interpersonal Communication." In *Handbook of Interpersonal Communication*, edited by Mark L. Knapp and Gerald R. Miller, 286-319. Thousand Oaks, Calif.: Sage, 1994.

Thurlow, Crispin. Transcultural Communication: A Treatise on Trans. Accessed on December 26, 2008. faculty.washington.edu/thurlow/research/transculturalcommunication.html.

Torfing, Jakob. *New Theories of Discourse: Laclau, Mouffe and Žižek*. Oxford, U.K.: Blackwell, 1999.

Vertovec, Steven "Conceiving and Researching Transnationalism." *Ethnic and Racial Studies* 22 (1999): 447-462.

Wood, Ellen Meiksins. *The Retreat from Class: A New "True" Socialism*. London: Verso, 1998.

Young, Robert J. C. *Untying the Text. A Post-Structuralist Reader*. Routledge: London, 1981.

Žižek, Slavoj. *Violence: Six Sideways Reflections*. New York: Picador, 2008.

Index

About the Authors

Fernando Andacht is a professor in the Department of Communication, University of Ottawa, and a visiting professor in communication and languages in the Universidade Tuiuti do Paraná, Curitiba. Since 1983, he has been doing research in media, culture, and society from a Peircean semiotic perspective. Lately he has worked on the representation of reality in the media (Centro Nacional de Pesquisa Research Grant 2005-2007), both on the format Big Brother, in its Latin American version, and on the Reality TV/documentary relationship. He is the author of *Uruguayan Songs of Melancholy Displacement in Latin Marica* (2009); On *Two Invisible Peoples of Americas* (2008); *On the Use of Self-disclosure as a Mode of Audiovisual Reflexivity* (2007).

Frank Boddin is a researcher working in the communication studies department of the Vrije Universiteit Brussel (VUB—Free University of Brussels) and the VUB research center CeMeSo (Center for Studies on Media and Culture). His research concentrates on the production context of documentary television genres on public service broadcasting. His main research interests are situated in cultural studies, and media sociology, more specifically the relationship between organizational culture and discourse, professional identity, and governmental power within media institutions.

Nico Carpentier is an assistant professor working in the communication studies department of the Vrije Universiteit Brussel (VUB—Free University of Brussels). He is codirector of the VUB research center CeMeSo and vice-president of the European Communication Research and Education Association (ECREA). His theoretical focus is on discourse theory, his research interests are situated in the relationship between media, journalism, politics, and culture, especially towards (mediations of) social domains as war and conflict, ideology, participation, democracy, within a variety of fictional and non-fictional media formats.

Anastasia Deligiaouri has a BA (Hons) in law, an MA (Hons) in public law and political science, and a PhD in political science. At Aristotle University of Thessaloniki (Greece), she was awarded her PhD with specialization in policial communication with distinction in 2007. During her PhD studies she was awarded a scholarship for her research from the State Scholarship Foundation of

Greece (IKY). The past five years she has been a part time lecturer in classes on media, political sciende, and law in the U.K.-affiliated colleges in Greece and private institutions, both at undergraduate and postgraduate level. She is a lawyer with a private office. She has participated in many international conferences and workshops and she has published on political communication issues, media sociology, and political discourse. Her research interests concern the interaction between media and politics, media effects, European public sphere, and discourse studies. Currently she is an adjunct lecturer in the State Higher Technological Institution of Western Macedonia in Kastoria, Greece.

Gunn Sara Enli is assistant professor in media studies in the Department of Media and Communication, University of Oslo. Her research interests include audience participation, reality-TV and popular journalism. Enli completed her PhD thesis, "The Participatory Turn in Broadcast Television," in 2007. She has published in *Media, Culture & Society, Television & New Media, Javnost—The Public,* and *Convergence,* edited two books in Norwegian, and contributed to several international anthologies.

Mikko Hautakangas (BA) is a doctoral student at the University of Tampere, Finland. His PhD thesis work deals with the audience experience in participatory television formats and the appeal of reality television; his example case is the Finnish version of *Big Brother.* Hautakangas uses the concept "peer melodrama" to discuss reality television in its social and cultural contexts, dealing with the questions of changing conventions of television programming as well as the articulations between media participation and experiencing social power. Hautakangas is also a member of the board of TACS (Tampere Center for Cultural Studies).

Matthew Hibberd is deputy head and director of the MSc in Public Relations by Online Learning in the Department of Film, Media and Journalism, University of Stirling. He is professor of communication theory at the *Libera Università Internazionale per gli Studi Sociali* (LUISS), Rome, and is visiting professor of journalism at the Interdisciplinary Center for Social Communications (CICS), Pontifical Gregorian University, also in Rome. Hibberd is a fellow of the College of Teachers in London (FCollT) and is the Scottish board member of the Voice of the Listener and Viewer (VLV).

Su Holmes (PhD) is reader in television studies at the University of East Anglia, U.K. She is the author of *British TV and Film Culture in the 1950s* (Intellect, 2005), *Entertaining TV: The BBC and Popular Television Culture in the 1950s* (Manchester U. P., 2008), and *The Quiz Show* (Edinburgh U. P., 2008), and she is currently working on a monograph on the seminal 1974 documentary serial,

The Family (*After Reality TV: Revisiting The Family*) (forthcoming, Manchester U. P.). She is also the co-editor of *Understanding Reality TV* (Routledge, 2004), *Framing Celebrity* (Routledge, 2006) and *Stardom and Celebrity: A Reader* (Sage, 2007). Her key research interests are in British TV history, popular TV genres and celebrity.

Brain McNair is professor of journalism and communication at the University of Strathclyde. He has researched and written extensively on factual media, including reality TV. His books include *Striptease Culture* (2002), *Mediated Access* (with Philip Schlesinger and Matthew Hibberd, 2003) and *Cultural Chaos* (2006). He is a regular contributor to print and broadcast media in the U.K.

Jan Pinseler (PhD) studied media and sociology in Dresden and Leicester. Currently, he is a lecturer at the University of Lueneburg (Germany). His research interests include media depictions of crime and deviance, alternative media and queer theory. He recently published a book on crime investigation programs on German television.

Mirkica Popovic is a graduate in mass media and communications and holds a Master of Science in international marketing from the University of Huddersfield, U.K. Her master's thesis was an exploratory research into the influence of advergaming as a marketing technique on the consumption habits of evolving children consumers. Popovic's research interests evolve around the social relations in online communities, media culture, political marketing, as well as around the close bond between media and marketing through examining in-game advertising, ethical consumerism, social marketing, and quality of children's media programming.

Winnie Salamon is a novelist, former journalist and lecturer in media and communications at the University of Melbourne, Australia. She is currently completing a PhD about life after reality television.

Jan Teurlings graduated from the Vrije Universiteit Brussel with a PhD on dating shows, in which he combined a Foucauldian analysis of power relationships together with actor-network theory. In 2004 he moved to the University of Amsterdam, lecturing in the Department of Media Studies. His recent work integrates Marxist and Foucauldian approaches to media.

Tanja Thomas is an assistant professor of communication studies and media culture at the University of Lueneburg, Germany. She studied arts and German media studies and gender. Her research in media studies focuses on critical media theory, cultural studies, gender studies, governmentality studies. She has published widely on media and cultural studies, on media and racism, national-ism, war, and popular culture as a mode of socialization in neo-liberal societies. Her most recent publications include anthologies on media culture and social acting (*Medienkultur und soziales Handeln*, VS, 2008) and on media and social inequalities (*Medien—Diversität—Ungleichheit*, VS, 2008). She is also co-editor of *War Isn't Hell, It's Entertainment: War in Modern Culture and Visual Media* (McFarland, 2008) and of *Keyworks in Cultural Studies* (*Schlüsselwerke der Cultural Studies*, VS, 2009).

Sofie Van Bauwel is an assistant professor at the Department of Communica-tion Studies at the University of Ghent (Belgium). She teaches audiovisual me-dia, media and gender, and cultural media studies and is a member of the Work-ing Group Film and Television Studies, where she is the co-editor of the *Working Papers on Film and Television Studies*, which is published by Acade-mia Press. She is also the vice-chair of the gender and communication section of ECREA (the European Communication Research and Education Association). Her research focuses on cultural media studies, film and television studies and gender and media. She has published on popular culture, on feminist film the-ory, and on gender and media.

Breinigsville, PA USA
21 July 2010
242158BV00001B/2/P